THE SEMANTICS OF רַע (BAD) IN ANCIENT AND MISHNAIC
HEBREW

CONTRIBUTIONS TO BIBLICAL EXEGESIS AND THEOLOGY

SERIES EDITORS

K. De Troyer (Salzburg)
G. Van Oyen (Louvain-la-Neuve)

ADVISORY BOARD

Reimund Bieringer (Leuven)
Lutz Doering (Münster)
Mark Goodacre (Duke)
Bas ter Haar Romeny (Amsterdam)
Annette Merz (Groningen)
Madhavi Nevader (St Andrews)
Thomas Römer (Lausanne)
Jack Sasson (Nashville)
Tammi Schneider (Claremont)

Philip David FOSTER

THE SEMANTICS OF רַע (BAD) IN ANCIENT AND MISHNAIC HEBREW

PEETERS
LEUVEN – PARIS – BRISTOL, CT
2022

A catalogue record for this book is available from the Library of Congress.

© 2022 — Peeters, Bondgenotenlaan 153, B-3000 Leuven

ISBN 978-90-429-4666-8
eISBN 978-90-429-4667-5
D/2022/0602/11

All rights reserved. No part of this publication may be reproduced, stored in a retrieval system, or transmitted, in any form or by any means, electronic, mechanical, photocopying, recording or otherwise, without the prior permission of the publisher.

PREFACE

This work is a lightly edited and revised version of my doctoral thesis, which I completed in 2020 at the University of Edinburgh. The main changes involve the simplification (and occasional correction) of heading structures and reference to a work on Evil in Genesis by Ingrid Faro which was published not long after my thesis was completed. I apologise to those who are colour-blind for the use of colours in this work. By the time the issue was pointed out to me it was too late to make significant changes.

A number of people greatly impacted my interest and direction of research. The person who had, perhaps the most significant early influence on me, was the late Francis I. Andersen. He took me on as a research assistant while I was completing a Master of Divinity and I am indebted to him for the great store of knowledge he sought to pass on to me. After moving to Edinburgh, my doctoral supervisors, Dr David Reimer (who moved on during my study), Prof Timothy Lim, Prof Nikolas Gisborne, and Prof John Sawyer all impacted my work in positive and unique ways for which I am most grateful. In particular, Prof Lim's direction in extra-biblical Hebrew was of great help. Towards the second half of my study, I also had the great fortune of meeting and becoming friends with Marilyn Burton. Her work on the semantics of Glory in Classical Hebrew has been an inspiration to my own, her willingness to act as a sounding-board for my ideas has sharpened my work considerably, and her friendship has been a blessing from God.

Philip D. Foster
Edinburgh, Scotland
May 2021

CONTENTS

DEDICATION. XI

ABBREVIATIONS. XIII

CHAPTER 1

INTRODUCTION. 1

1.1 The Adoption of Linguistic Theory in Biblical Studies 2
1.2 The Semantics of רֵע in Biblical Hebrew. 4
1.3 Ancient Hebrew: Corpus and Confounds 7
    1.3.1 The Corpus of Ancient Hebrew 7
    1.3.2 Confounding Factors in the Semantic Analysis of Ancient
        Hebrew. 13
1.4 Linguistic Analysis of Ancient Hebrew 18
    1.4.1 Three Cognitive Linguistic Concepts 20
    1.4.2 Lexical and Contextual Semantic Domains and Frame
        Theory 22
    1.4.3 Adjectives and a Further Look at Attributes 25
    1.4.4 Lexical Semantic Change 27
1.5 Procedure of Analysis. 29
    1.5.1 רֵע and Schema. 30
    1.5.2 Mapping the Lexical Semantic Domains of רֵע 31
    1.5.3 Semantic Domain Analysis 32

CHAPTER 2

רֵע AND SCHEMA 35

2.1 Preliminary Matters. 35
    2.1.1 Identifying and Selecting Words. 35
    2.1.2 Modification of Discourse Elements in Elided Reference 37
    2.1.3 Attribution, Predication, and Construct Chains 39
2.2 Scope Limitations and Sampling. 41
    2.2.1 Limiting the Analysis 41
    2.2.2 Sampling Method 42

VIII

CONTENTS

2.3 Analysis: How רַע Modifies Discourse Elements 45
   2.3.1 עָשָׂה רַע (to do bad) 45
   2.3.2 HUMAN 50
   2.3.3 COMMODITY 58
   2.3.4 BODY PART 62
   2.3.5 דֶּרֶךְ (way) 66
   2.3.6 דָּבָר (thing) 69
   2.3.7 שֵׁם (name) 73
   2.3.8 בִּעֵר רַע (to purge bad) 76
   2.3.9 COGNITION 80
   2.3.10 AFFLICTION 87
   2.3.11 חַיָּה (animal) 88
2.4 Conclusion 89

CHAPTER 3

MAPPING THE LEXICAL SEMANTIC DOMAINS OF רַע . . . 93

3.1 Semantic Associations of רַע 93
   3.1.1 Preliminary Matters 93
   3.1.2 Analysis of רַע (bad) 102
3.2 Association Analysis (Similarity): Round 1 112
   3.2.1 רָשָׁע (wicked) 112
   3.2.2 חֶרֶב (sword) 117
   3.2.3 רֹעַ (badness) 122
   3.2.4 רָעָה (evil) 124
   3.2.5 דֶּבֶר (plague) 128
   3.2.6 אָוֶן (villainy) 131
   3.2.7 מָוֶת (death) 134
   3.2.8 עָוֹן (iniquity) 137
   3.2.9 רָעָב (famine) 142
   3.2.10 חָמָס (violence) 144
   3.2.11 תּוֹעֵבָה (abomination) 147
   3.2.12 בְּלִיַּעַל (worthlessness) 151
   3.2.13 דָּם (blood) 153
   3.2.14 חֹשֶׁךְ (darkness) 156
   3.2.15 מִרְמָה (deceit) 160
   3.2.16 שָׂטָן (accuser/Satan) 163
   3.2.17 Discussion: First Round 164
3.3 Association Analysis: Round 2 165
   3.3.1 שֶׁקֶר (lie) 165
   3.3.2 אֹיֵב (enemy) 169

CONTENTS IX

3.3.3 חַטָּאת (sin). 173
3.3.4 מֵרַע (evildoer). 178
3.3.5 עָמָל (trouble) 180
3.3.6 עַוְלָה (injustice) 182
3.3.7 פֶּשַׁע (transgression) 184
3.3.8 צָרָה (distress) 187
3.3.9 שָׁוְא (worthlessness). 190
3.3.10 אַשְׁמָה (guilt). 193
3.3.11 זִמָּה (wickedness) 196
3.3.12 חֵטְא (sin) 197
3.3.13 כָּזָב (falsehood) 199
3.3.14 עָרִיץ (ruthless). 201
3.3.15 צָמָא (thirst) 203
3.3.16 שֶׁבֶר (destruction) 204
3.3.17 שֹׁד (destruction). 207
3.3.18 Discussion: Second Round. 208
3.4 Association Analysis: Round 3. 209
3.4.1 לֵץ (scoffer) 209
3.4.2 חָנֵף (impious) 211
3.4.3 Discussion: Third Round. 211
3.5 Semantic Association Findings 212
3.5.1 What Was Found 212
3.5.2 Conclusions 214

CHAPTER 4

SEMANTIC DOMAIN ANALYSIS 215

4.1 Scope of Domain Analysis 215
4.2 Usage of רַע Within Chapter 3 Domains 224
4.3 Major Domain 1: רָשָׁע Subdomain 226
4.3.1 Analysis of רָשָׁע (with a focus on רָשָׁע) 226
4.3.2 Preliminary Conclusion. 229
4.3.3 רַע as Part of רָשָׁע. 230
4.4 Major Domain 1: אָוֶן Subdomain. 233
4.4.1 Analysis of אָוֶן (with a focus on אָוֶן) 233
4.4.2 Preliminary Conclusion. 245
4.4.3 רַע as Part of אָוֶן. 246
4.5 Major Domain 2: עָוֹן 250
4.5.1 Analysis of עָוֹן (with a focus on עָוֹן) 250
4.5.2 Preliminary Conclusions 255
4.5.3 רַע as Part of עָוֹן. 256

X CONTENTS

4.6 Major Domain 3: רָעָה 259
    4.6.1 רָעָה as Part of רָעָה 259
    4.6.2 רַע as Part of רָעָה 260
    4.6.3 Preliminary Conclusions 262
4.7 Some Derivational Relationships of the רעע word family: רַע,
    רֹעַ and רָעָה 262
    4.7.1 רַע and רֹעַ 263
    4.7.2 רַע and רָעָה 264
    4.7.3 Preliminary Conclusions 267
4.8 Conclusion 268

CHAPTER 5

CONCLUSION 270

5.1 Main Findings. 272
5.2 Comparison with Previous Research on רַע 275
    5.2.1 A Brief Comparison with the Lexica. 277
    5.2.2 The Semantic Dictionary of Biblical Hebrew 278
5.3 Towards a New Entry for רַע. 280
5.4 Areas for Future Research 281

APPENDICES 283

A. רַע and Schema: Additional Analysis 283
    A.1 רוּחַ (spirit) 283
    A.2 DEED 284
    A.3 מַיִם (water) 286
    A.4 TIME. 287
    A.5 יֵצֶר (inclination) 290
    A.6 כֹּחַ (strength) 293
B. Mapping the Lexical Semantic Domains of רַע 294
    B.1 Words Occurring 10 Times or Less 294
    B.2 Selection and Analysis of Associations of Opposition . 300
C. Textual Matters 306
    C.1 Ben Sira 307
    C.2 Judean Desert. 310
    C.3 Other 317

BIBLIOGRAPHY 319

LIST OF NAMES 329

LIST OF EXAMPLES 333

For our God: Father, Son, and Holy Spirit.
This work is our sacrifice to you.

Mo bhean agus mo chridhe, Jess.
This work is as much yours as it is mine.

ABBREVIATIONS

This work follows the common abbreviations found in the SBL Handbook of Style, 2nd edition. However, the following abbreviations are also used.

EHLL   Encyclopedia of Hebrew Language and Linguistics
SAHD   Semantics of Ancient Hebrew Database
SDBH   Semantic Dictionary of Biblical Hebrew

CHAPTER 1

INTRODUCTION

> And very often a translator, to whom the meaning is not well known, is deceived by an ambiguity in the original language, and puts upon the passage a construction that is wholly alien to the sense of the writer... because the Greek word μοσχος means a calf, some have not understood that μοσχευματα are shoots of trees, and have translated the word "calves;" and this error has crept into so many texts, that you can hardly find it written in any other way. And yet the meaning is very clear; for it is made evident by the words that follow. For "the plantings of an adulterer will not take deep root," is a more suitable form of expression than the "calves;" because these walk upon the ground with their feet, and are not fixed in the earth by roots. In this passage, indeed, the rest of the context also justifies this translation.
>
> Now translations such as this are not obscure, but false; and there is a wide difference between the two things. For we must learn not to interpret, but to correct texts of this sort.[1]

Biblical studies has at different times and to varying degrees recognised the need for understanding the words of the biblical texts. Long before biblical studies was considered a discipline, Augustine of Hippo highlighted the issue. In his work *De Doctrina Christiana* (quoted above), he argued that we must correct errors of translation introduced through misunderstanding the possible meanings of a particular word form. More than this, he argued that discourse context can help us determine the correct sense.[2]

Today, 1,600 years later, we are still progressing our understanding of the words in the biblical text. As linguistic theory develops, so does our ability to understand how languages, both modern and ancient, work. Since the 1960s there has been a considerable amount of work into lexical semantics by linguists. This work has revised and refined ways of exploring word meaning. Some of that work is in the tradition of cognitive grammar; some comes from the theoretical developments associated with

---

[1] Augustine, *On Christian Doctrine* 2.12.18 (*NPNF* 2:540–41).

[2] Josephus also argued against false translations of the Septuagint in Against Apion 2.26–27. Flavius Josephus, *The Works of Josephus: Complete and Unabridged*, trans. William Whiston (Peabody, MA: Hendrickson, 1987), 795.

2   CHAPTER 1

computerised corpora; and some comes from research projects such as
FrameNet and WordNet. There is also theoretical work into polysemy and
into the relationship between word meaning and context. This literature
offers the biblical scholar a range of tools for exploring word meaning
with a view to refining biblical translation and interpretation.[3]

1.1 THE ADOPTION OF LINGUISTIC THEORY IN BIBLICAL STUDIES

The watershed moment for the adoption of linguistic theory in biblical
studies came in 1961 with James Barr's *The Semantics of Biblical Language*.[4] In 1972 John Sawyer described it as a "wind of change" which he
sent "through modern biblical criticism."[5] Barr begins his book with words
which remind us of the concerns of Augustine – a need for a correct understanding of language use.

> Only a little need be said about the occasion and purpose of this book.
> It is a main concern of both scholarship and theology that the Bible
> should be soundly and adequately interpreted. In recent years I have
> come to believe that one of the greatest dangers to such sound and
> adequate interpretation comes from the prevailing use of procedures
> which, ..., constantly mishandle and distort the linguistic evidence of
> the Hebrew and Greek languages as they are used in the Bible.[6]

In 1972, Sawyer published his work on terms for "salvation," *Semantics
in Biblical Research*. This work represents one of the earliest applications
of semantic field (later: domain) theory to Biblical Studies.[7] Seventeen

---

[3] Ingrid Faro has recently done some work on Evil in Genesis, working from lexical study, to exegesis, and to theology. While the lexical sample was impoverished by sample size, her work demonstrates how lexical study can add value to theological work. Ingrid Faro, *Evil in Genesis: A Contextual Analysis of Hebrew Lexemes for Evil in the Book of Genesis*, Studies in Scripture & Biblical Theology (Bellingham, WA: Lexham, 2021). Marilyn Burton has also been applying lexical work to Biblical Theology. For example, see Marilyn E. Burton, "Robed in Majesty: Clothing as a Metaphor for the Classical Hebrew Semantic Domain of כבוד," in *Clothing and Nudity in the Hebrew Bible*, ed. Christoph Berner et al. (London: T&T Clark, 2019), 289–300.

[4] First published in 1961 by Oxford University Press. James Barr, *The Semantics of Biblical Language* (Eugene, OR: Wipf & Stock, 2004).

[5] John F. A. Sawyer, *Semantics in Biblical Research: New Methods of Defining Hebrew Words for Salvation*, SBT 2.24 (Naperville, IL: A. R. Allenson, 1972), 1.

[6] Barr, *The Semantics of Biblical Language*, iii.

[7] Prior to Sawyer publishing his book there were at least two articles which applied concepts of semantic fields to Biblical Hebrew. One was authored by Barr, the other by Sawyer. Sawyer, *Semantics in Biblical Research*; James Barr, "The Image of God in the Book of Genesis: A Study of Terminology," *BJRL* 51 (1968): 11–26; John F. A. Sawyer, "Root-Meanings in Hebrew," *JSS* 12 (1967): 37–50.

INTRODUCTION

years later, the method of componential analysis[8] was popularised in Biblical Studies by Louw and Nida in their 1989 *Greek – English Lexicon of the New Testament Based on Semantic Domains*.[9] Shortly before their dictionary was published, scholars of Ancient Hebrew began discussing the need for a database containing scholarly discussion about Ancient Hebrew lexemes.[10] This led to the development of the Semantics of Ancient Hebrew Database (SAHD) project. The SAHD project aims to be a tool for stimulating further semantic research and also to make clear "not only what work has already been done, but also which workable way of approach has not been used for the study of the lexeme in question."[11] The structure of the project means that its focus is directed to the semantic (or lexical) field (or domain): "Each of these centres [universities that participate in the project] will have responsibility for a lexical field or a number of lexical fields... This approach is preferable because the subdividing of the lexical material in this way lends coherence to the description and study of the individual lexemes."[12] A number of analyses have come out of this project,[13] for example, James Aitken's *The Semantics of Blessing and Cursing in Ancient Hebrew*.[14]

At the turn of the twenty-first century, cognitive linguistic developments combined with the desire to produce a Biblical Hebrew dictionary based on semantic domains led de Blois, in cooperation with the UBS, to commence work on the *Semantic Dictionary of Biblical Hebrew* (SDBH).[15] Many entries are now available, but the dictionary is still in development.[16]

It is now clear that the use of linguistic theory in the study of biblical languages has come of age. It is increasingly common to hear discussion

---

[8] Developed out of semantic field theory and linguistic anthropology during the 1950s and 60s in Europe and the USA. Dirk Geeraerts, *Theories of Lexical Semantics* (Oxford: Oxford University Press, 2010), 70.

[9] J. P. Louw and Eugene A. Nida, *Greek-English Lexicon of the New Testament: Based on Semantic Domains* (New York: UBS, 1989).

[10] J. Hoftijzer, "The History of the Data-Base Project," in *Studies in Ancient Hebrew Semantics*, ed. T. Muraoka, AbrNSup 4 (Louvain: Peeters, 1995), 65.

[11] J. Hoftijzer and Graham I. Davies, "Semantics of Ancient Hebrew Database," [SAHD] http://www.sahd.div.ed.ac.uk/info:description.

[12] Semantics of Ancient Hebrew Database, "Lexeme Index," http://www.sahd.div.ed.ac.uk/info:lexeme_index.

[13] Many of which are available through links on the website. Hoftijzer and Davies, "SAHD."

[14] James K. Aitken, *The Semantics of Blessing and Cursing in Ancient Hebrew*, ANESSup 23 (Louvain: Peeters, 2007). Some of the SAHD studies to date are available free through the SAHD website.

[15] Reinier de Blois and UBS, *Towards a New Dictionary of Biblical Hebrew Based on Semantic Domains* (Woerden, Netherlands: UBS, 2000).

[16] UBS, "SDBH," 2021, http://semanticdictionary.org/.

4   CHAPTER 1

of the languages in the framework of one linguistic theory or another.
Monographs applying linguistics to the study of the biblical languages,
once few and far between, are now becoming common-place.[17] With the
application of linguistic developments to the production of dictionaries and
reference grammars,[18] it is next to impossible to engage with the study of
biblical languages without engaging (even unknowingly) with ideas drawn
from linguistic theory. It is in this tradition, and with the goal of illuminating the Biblical text that this study into the meaning of the word רַע (bad)[19]
stands.

1.2 THE SEMANTICS OF רַע IN BIBLICAL HEBREW

Although רַע is inevitably dealt with in the standard dictionaries, these
do not provide us with a thorough understanding of the word. They tend
towards "mere translation glosses (in the case of BDB and KB), or glosses
supplemented with lists of systematic syntagmatic distribution of lexical

---

[17] For example, the following monographs on Ancient Hebrew semantics have been pub-
lished from 2010: Marilyn E. Burton, *The Semantics of Glory: A Cognitive, Corpus-
Based Approach to Hebrew Word Meaning*, SSN 68 (Leiden: Brill, 2017); Aaron
J. Koller, *The Semantic Field of Cutting Tools in Biblical Hebrew: The Interface of
Philological, Semantic, and Archaeological Evidence*, CBQMS 49 (Washington, DC:
The Catholic Biblical Association of America, 2012); Daniel Leavins, *Verbs of Leading
in the Hebrew Bible* (Piscataway, NJ: Gorgias, 2011); Michael D. Rasmussen, *Con-
ceptualizing Distress in the Psalms: A Form-Critical and Cognitive Semantic Study of
the* צרר *[1] Word Group*, Gorgias Biblical Studies 66 (Piscataway, NJ: Gorgias, 2018);
Stephen L. Shead, *Radical Frame Semantics and Biblical Hebrew: Exploring Lexical
Semantics*, BibInt 108 (Leiden: Brill, 2011); Wendy L. Widder, *"To Teach" in Ancient
Israel: A Cognitive Linguistic Study of a Biblical Hebrew Lexical Set*, BZAW 456 (Boston:
De Gruyter, 2014); Francesco Zanella, *The Lexical Field of the Substantives of "Gift"
in Ancient Hebrew*, SSN 54 (Leiden: Brill, 2010).
[18] For example, Christo H. J. van der Merwe, Jacobus A. Naudé, and Jan H. Kroeze, *A
Biblical Hebrew Reference Grammar*, 2nd ed. (London: Bloomsbury, 2017).
[19] This word has been divided into adjective and noun uses (e.g. David J. A. Clines ed.,
"רע I, II," *DCH* 7:505–9). However, Miller-Naudé and Naudé argue that these are in
fact one word, arguing that רַע always behaves, syntactically, like a Hebrew Adjective,
not a Hebrew Noun. From a semantic point of view the distinction is likely to make
little difference, as can be seen from de Blois's work. Cynthia L. Miller-Naudé and
Jacobus A. Naudé, "Is the Adjective Distinct from the Noun as a Grammatical Category in Biblical Hebrew?," *IDS* 50 (2016): 1–9; Cynthia L. Miller-Naudé and Jacobus A. Naudé, "A Re-Examination of Grammatical Categorization in Biblical Hebrew,"
in *From Ancient Manuscripts to Modern Dictionaries: Select Studies in Aramaic, Hebrew
and Greek*, ed. Tarsee Li and Keith D. Dyer, Perspectives on Linguistics and Ancient
Languages 9 (Piscataway, NJ: Gorgias, 2017), 273–308; Reinier de Blois, *Towards
a New Dictionary of Biblical Hebrew Based on Semantic Domains* (New York: UBS,
2001), 105.

INTRODUCTION

items (in the case of Clines)."[20] These glosses provide a limited understanding of the words, attempting to convey in the target language (e.g. English), what the word means. Although the SDBH makes use of glosses, it also makes use of definitions and more detailed explanations of meaning, improving on the standard dictionaries. While this work was being carried out, רַע was not yet covered in the SDBH or by a study of a substantial corpus using similar techniques. Although it is now covered in the SDBH, the current work highlights some issues with the representation of רַע there. These will be addressed in the conclusion (§5.2.2).

The theological dictionaries tend to include fuller descriptions of רַע, with the Theological Dictionary of the Old Testament being the most thorough:

> [T]he semantic spectrum of r^{rr} [רעע] and its derivatives is well defined
> by its usage…. Each of these terms covers the most varied aspects of
> everything not good or negative; they do not make a distinction between
> "bad" and "evil," and so the exact meaning of r^{rr} in each instance can
> be determined only from contextual clues. Semantic foci come to light
> only in specific types of usage.[21]

This definition from Dohmen highlights a common issue with the search for word meaning in Biblical Hebrew: the idea of root meaning. Dohmen appears to commit what James Barr called the "root fallacy"[22] by suggesting the root conveys meaning to the terms. Words which share a root (a word family) share idiosyncratic, not systematic relationships with each other.[23] Therefore, they should be analysed as semi-independent units. Despite this, studies which attempt to analyse the root can still shed light on רַע itself. Dohmen's definition is instructive in that it suggests that רַע is general in meaning, covering everything negative.[24]

---

[20] Christo H. J. van der Merwe, "Lexical Meaning in Biblical Hebrew and Cognitive Semantics: A Case Study," *Bib* 87 (2006): 85.

[21] C. Dohmen and D. Rick, "רעע," *TDOT* 13:562.

[22] Barr, *The Semantics of Biblical Language*, 100; James Barr, "Did Isaiah Know about Hebrew 'Root Meanings'?," *ExpTim* 75 (1964): 242. But see Sawyer who argues that the root may have some, more nuanced, role in meaning. Sawyer, "Root-Meanings in Hebrew."

[23] Although Cruse illustrates this with the example of "cook" in English, the essential insight concerning derivational relations can be seen in Hebrew too (such as in Sawyer's analysis and Verheij's analysis of the binyanim in general). Alan Cruse, *Meaning in Language: An Introduction to Semantics and Pragmatics*, 3rd ed., Oxford Textbooks in Linguistics (Oxford: Oxford University Press, 2013), 133–34; Sawyer, "Root-Meanings in Hebrew"; Arian J. C. Verheij, *Bits, Bytes, and Binyanim: A Quantitative Study of Verbal Lexeme Formations in the Hebrew Bible*, OLA 93 (Leuven: Peeters, 2000).

[24] Dohmen's definition is similar to that of Faro in her work on Genesis. She also treats the רעע root together. She argues that "the Hebrew root word רע (evil) is a hypernym,

6 CHAPTER 1

Myhill studied רַע from a "semantic primitive" point of view. He argues that רַע forms a subjective, negative judgement of something, concluding that: "Something is ra' if it causes a negative subjective reaction on the part of some being, and it involves seeing this ra' thing from the point of view of that being."[25] Like Dohmen's work, Myhill's study suggests that רַע may be general in meaning. However, it goes beyond Dohmen's work by arguing that it is a subjective judgement; that is, something seen from a particular perspective, rather than being seen as "an inherent, objective quality of the thing."[26]

Van Steenbergen completed a worldview and semantic domain analysis of the domain of NEGATIVE MORAL BEHAVIOUR in Isaiah. Although limited in extent, and therefore limited in the generalisability of its findings, this work included the analysis of the root רעע, and therefore, also the adjective רַע. Van Steenbergen highlighted some aspects that warrant more careful attention. He separates the domain of NEGATIVE MORAL BEHAVIOUR into two subdomains: subdomain A, חטא (sin), עָוֹן (iniquity), and פֶּשַׁע (transgression); and subdomain B, אָוֶן (villainy), רעע (bad), and רֶשַׁע (wicked).[27] These are linked more strongly to different worldview variables that van Steenbergen identifies. Subdomain A is more closely linked to *Causality* (relationship to the divine), but subdomain B is more closely linked to *Self-Other* (relationship between humans).[28] He also attempts definitions of the various terms/roots with that for רעע being: "A deliberate form of negative moral behaviour of various degrees of specificity, regularly associated with active involvement in specific kinds of unacceptable behaviour."[29]

Van Steenbergen's findings are of great interest. Although the study is limited in scope and relies on analysis of roots, his findings challenge the descriptions of Dohmen and Myhill. His analysis from the perspective of semantic domains and worldview is particularly valuable. Unfortunately his analysis is limited to the book of Isaiah and so may be less reliable.[30]

---

a major category word with a broad range of meaning referring to anything perceived as bad: from unpleasant, ugly, displeasing, deficient, to harmful, sinful or wicked (not simply morally sinister as commonly depicted), with the chief antonym being טוב (good)." Faro, *Evil in Genesis*, 195–96.

[25] John Myhill, "Subjective Hebrew Ra' and Objective English Evil: A Semantic Analysis," *Humanities: Christianity and Culture* 28 (1997): 5.

[26] Myhill, "Subjective Hebrew Ra'," 1–2.

[27] The glosses used here were chosen for the current work.

[28] Gerrit Jan van Steenbergen, *Semantics, World View and Bible Translation: An Integrated Analysis of a Selection of Hebrew Lexical Items Referring to Negative Moral Behaviour in the Book of Isaiah* (Stellenbosch: Sun, 2006), 157.

[29] Van Steenbergen, *Semantics, World View and Bible Translation*, 186.

[30] Due to the low sample size there is an increased likelihood of artefacts of analysis.

INTRODUCTION

In my Master's thesis from 2016, I sought to delimit the semantic domain of רעע. This work relied, like Dohmen and van Steenbergen, on analysis of roots. It was also limited to the Latter Prophets. However, it did highlight a number of links between the רעע word family and the terms חֶרֶב (sword) and רָעָב (famine) which deserve further investigation.[31]

The current work on רַע will draw on lexical and cognitive semantic theory to analyse רַע. An initial question arises from the findings of Dohmen and Myhill: to what extent may רַע be considered a general term? The analysis will seek to draw attention to the domains of operation of רַע as well as how it functions in some of these domains. While a complete study of רַע and its domains is beyond the scope of this work, it will present a more accurate picture of the meaning and use of רַע.

1.3 ANCIENT HEBREW: CORPUS AND CONFOUNDS[32]

The reader will notice that I have moved from discussing Biblical Hebrew to Ancient Hebrew. In moving towards a thorough linguistic analysis of the words of interest, we must consider what the appropriate corpus of investigation will be. Biblical Hebrew is not a language in itself, but a portion of Ancient Hebrew more generally. As such, regardless of whether our object is to understand the ancient language or the canonical language, an analysis of Ancient Hebrew in general is appropriate.[33]

There are a number of factors which can confound the semantic analysis of Ancient Hebrew. Before I discuss confounding factors, I will discuss the texts that are included in the Ancient Hebrew corpus (§1.3.1). I will then discuss the confounding factors and argue that although uncertainty is introduced into linguistic analysis through the sources of variation this does not eliminate the possibility of meaningful analysis (§1.3.2).

1.3.1 The Corpus of Ancient Hebrew

The earliest attestations of the Hebrew language occur with the abecedaries found at ʿIzbet Sartah (1200–1000 BCE) and Tel Zayit (1000–900 BCE),

---

[31] Philip D. Foster, "A Delimitation of the Semantic Field of רעע in the Latter Prophets" (MDiv diss., Melbourne School of Theology, 2016), 60.

[32] "Confound" is a term from statistics referring to a factor in analysis which confounds.

[33] Especially due to the relatively small corpus size. To exclude any part of Ancient Hebrew "would be to limit the linguistic evidence in a field where the material is already and inevitably highly delimited." Aitken, *Semantics of Blessing and Cursing*, 23.

8   CHAPTER 1

and the Gezer Calendar (1000–900 BCE).[34] There is a significant, although
small amount, of extra-biblical Hebrew attested from such sources prior to
250 BCE.[35] Although the biblical text was written much earlier, the earliest extant writings come from 250 BCE, from the Qumran texts. The main
biblical manuscript used is the Leningrad Codex (1000 CE) which is considered to be a more or less faithful representation of the textual tradition
designated "Masoretic" (MT). The Qumran and Judean Desert texts contain writings from 250 BCE to the Bar Kochba period (132–135 CE).[36]
However, as with the biblical texts, this does not necessarily represent
when the extant Hebrew was composed as many manuscripts show signs
of being copies of even earlier manuscripts. Mishnaic Hebrew is generally
considered to be later Hebrew; however, more on that below.

The corpus of Ancient Hebrew has been described in varying ways.
Clines defines the corpus as "all kinds of Hebrew from the period prior
to about 200 CE, that is, earlier than the Hebrew of the Mishnah."[37] This
definition is generally accepted.[38] Thus under this definition, the various corpora of texts included in the Ancient Hebrew corpus are: Biblical
Hebrew; Ancient Hebrew Inscriptions; Qumran manuscripts (biblical
texts, and sectarian and non-sectarian texts);[39] and other manuscripts from
the Judean Desert up to and including the Bar Kochba period.[40]

As hinted at above, the corpus of Biblical texts requires further clarifica-
tion. This selection is not limited to a single canonical version of the text.
The practice of textual criticism has uncovered the existence of variant
literary editions of biblical texts, all of which need to be considered

---

[34] Ian Young, Robert Rezetko, and Martin Ehrensvärd, *Linguistic Dating of Biblical Texts*
(London: Equinox Pub, 2008), 1:6–7.

[35] Graham I. Davies, *Ancient Hebrew Inscriptions: Corpus and Concordance*, 2 vols.
(Cambridge: Cambridge University Press, 1991–2004).

[36] Emanuel Tov, *Textual Criticism of the Hebrew Bible*, 3rd ed. (Minneapolis, MN:
Fortress, 2012), 99; Uri Mor, "Bar Kokhba Documents," *Encyclopedia of Hebrew
Language and Linguistics.*

[37] Clines, *DCH* 1:14.

[38] For example Aitken, *Semantics of Blessing and Cursing*, 23; but see Young, Rezetko,
and Ehrensvärd who present a table that excludes post-Biblical, pre-mishnaic texts from
Ancient Hebrew while noting that terminology is flexible, Young, Rezetko, and Ehrensvärd,
Linguistic Dating of Biblical Texts, 1:7–8.

[39] See Dimant for divisions within Qumran texts. Devorah Dimant, "The Qumran Manuscripts: Contents and Significance," in *Time to Prepare the Way in the Wilderness:
Papers on the Qumran Scrolls by Fellows of the Institute for Advanced Studies of the
Hebrew University, Jerusalem, 1989–1990*, ed. Devorah Dimant and Lawrence H. Schiffman, STDJ 16 (Leiden: Brill, 1995), 23–58; Devorah Dimant, "Sectarian and Non-
Sectarian Texts from Qumran: The Pertinence and Usage of a Taxonomy," *RevQ* 24
(2009): 7–18.

[40] Aitken, *Semantics of Blessing and Cursing*, 23–24.

INTRODUCTION 9

as valid forms of Ancient Hebrew. In addition to this, the definition of Ancient Hebrew is problematic with regards to Mishnaic Hebrew. Mishnaic Hebrew existed prior to 200 CE, and could be considered a distinct dialect of Ancient Hebrew.

Alternative Versions of Biblical Manuscripts as Examples of Ancient Hebrew

With the discovery of many ancient manuscripts of the Hebrew Scriptures in the Judean desert, it has become apparent that there are more textual traditions than those found in the Masoretic Text (MT), Old Greek (OG), and Samaritan Pentateuch (SP). In response to the analysis of discovered texts, Emmanuel Tov has formulated a theory of textual plurality in Ancient Israel where many textual traditions abounded.

> The discovery of the Leviticus scroll was coincidental, just as the preservation of ⅏ [OG] and ⅏ [SP] alongside 𝔐 [MT] was a matter of textual coincidence. Therefore, it would not be logical to assume that only four early texts existed for the book of Leviticus. Rather, one has to think in terms of a large number of such texts that related to each other in the same manner as the four that are known. In other books, one also discerns more than just two or three texts.... Therefore, 𝔐, ⅏, ⅏, which were often described as the three central witnesses of the biblical text, actually reflect only three of a much larger number of ancient texts. This assumed textual plurality is illustrated by the different groups of texts found at Qumran.[41]

The implication of this for the analysis of Ancient Hebrew is that we cannot rely on text critical judgements to reach a text for analysis. Rather, textual plurality implies many similar but different variants of the text which may or may not have linguistic corruptions. Textual variation does not imply linguistic corruption and so all instances of the text need to be examined on their own merits. In practice there is likely to be only a small number of syntactic/semantic linguistic variations which need separate analysis because the similarities between texts are greater than the differences and only a very small proportion of the total text includes the words under investigation.

Isaiah 45:7b (examples 1.1 and 1.2 below)[42] is a prime example of a text that requires a dual analysis. It also illustrates an additional issue: Text group

---

[41] Tov, *Textual Criticism*, 160.
[42] Due to the large number of examples in this work, examples are numbered sequentially by chapter. Thus, the first example in chapter 1 is example 1.1. Similarly, the first example in chapter 4 is example 4.1.

10 CHAPTER 1

variation is not the only source of textual variation. 1QIsa^a XXXVIII, 13a (Isa. 45:7b) is clearly well-formed Ancient Hebrew text, and 1QIsa^a is generally regarded as proto-Masoretic,[43] but the context contains a difference from the MT that is semantically important[44]: It is constructed using the antonym טוֹב (good) rather than שָׁלוֹם (peace).

1.1. 1QIsa^a XXXVIII, 13a

עושה טוב ובורה רע

[I] make [what is] good and create [what is] bad...

1.2. Isaiah 45:7b

עֹשֶׂה שָׁלוֹם וּבוֹרֵא רָע

[I] make peace and create [what is] bad...

This contextual variation has the potential to determine the nuance of the adjective רָע such that it takes on a different meaning.[45]

Textual variants may also exist which lead to the analysis of a portion of text that would not be analysed otherwise. 4Q27 20–22, 29b contains a fragmentary variant reading of Numbers 22:32b. Here we find a use of the feminine form of the adjective רָע that does not appear in the standard MT.[46] The difference can be seen in examples 1.4 and 1.5.

---

[43] The scribe is considered somewhat careless, most differences from the Masoretic text are of orthography and morphology. However, there are a number of other changes present that may be the result of conscious changes to the text. Tov, *Textual Criticism*, 105, 137, 256.

[44] Note that there are a number of orthographic differences; however, these are purely orthographic differences and unimportant for a semantic analysis. Most of these differences are due to the introduction of a vowel letter. However, one is due to the loss of the aleph because of the preceding vowel "a III-*aleph* verb is rarely found marked with a final *heh*, as in וירה 'he feared' (4Q381 50, 4) for 'וירא.'" Eric D. Reymond, *Qumran Hebrew: An Overview of Orthography, Phonology, and Morphology*, RBS 76 (Atlanta: SBL, 2013), 86.

[45] For example, Moshavi presents the case of בָּקַשׁ in Biblical Hebrew which shows some variation of meaning depending on the antonyms in use. Adina Moshavi, "How to Distinguish between General Words and Polysemous Words in the Hebrew of the Bible: A Study in the Verb ביקש" [Hebrew], *Leshonenu* 66 (2004): 36, 46. See Borochovsky for an example of contextual variation of meaning in Modern Hebrew. Esther Borochovsky Bar Aba, "Variety in the Meaning of the Verb: General Meaning, Contextual Meaning and Polysemy" [Hebrew], *Leshonenu* 68 (2006): 113–14.

[46] It also does not appear in any other source. 4Q27 appears closest in textual character to the Samaritan Pentateuch, but has a number of unique variants. Eugene C. Ulrich et al., eds., *Qumran Cave 4: Genesis to Numbers*, DJD 12 (Oxford: Clarendon, 1994), 213–15. Using the same letters as 4Q27 (but in a different order) the Samaritan Pentateuch appears to record the verb הֵרַע (to do/make bad) at this point.

INTRODUCTION   11

1.3. 4Q27 20–22, 29b

כיא רעה הדרך לנגדי

because [your] way is bad before me.

1.4. Numbers 22:32b

כִּי־יָרַט הַדֶּרֶךְ לְנֶגְדִּי

because [your] way is slippery[47] before me.

The fragmentary nature of 4Q27 20–22 does not necessitate eliminating this occurrence from the analysis. One very good reason for analysing it is that the clause within which it sits is entirely complete. However, because parts of the context are fragmentary it is difficult to see how the term functions within the wider discourse of 4Q27. To some degree we can rely on the readings of other versions of Numbers 22 for the wider context as it is unlikely the discourse context would vary much even if individual words do. This allows some measure of contextual judgement to be made.

It should be noted here that alternate versions of the biblical text may be found in writings that are not designated "biblical." The "biblical" designation of Qumran texts simply refers to those which are copies of now canonical texts. The commentaries of Qumran (e.g. the Habakkuk Pesher) reproduce large portions of biblical text, but are considered non-biblical texts themselves.[48] In my analysis, any reproduction of biblical text (whether as a quote or as a whole or partial manuscript) is treated as biblical text (although where it is a quote, features from outside the quote may be relevant to the linguistic analysis).[49]

Mishnaic Hebrew

Although Mishnaic Hebrew is not considered part of the Ancient Hebrew corpus, it is considered to have coexisted as a dialect of spoken

---

[47] This word has translation difficulties. I accept the suggestion in HALOT. See Ludwig Köhler and Walter Baumgartner, "טרט," *HALOT* 1:438.

[48] John Starr has a helpful discussion concerning the classification of Qumran texts. John M. Starr, *Classifying the Aramaic Texts from Qumran: A Statistical Analysis of Linguistic Features*, (London: T&T Clark, 2017), 3–9.

[49] This same procedure applies in the case of any manuscripts identified as probable copies of a common source. For example, 1Q28 (1QS) has a number of recensions. 4Q258 I, 1 contains a variant recension of 1Q28 V, 1 which contains significant syntactic/semantic differences and so both are analysed. In contrast, 4Q260 IV, 4–5 has a clause containing רע which appears to be an identical reading of 1Q28 X, 17–18. This is analysed once.

12   CHAPTER 1

Hebrew during the Second Temple period and possibly before.[50] There are
a number of clear cases of Mishnaic Hebrew forms appearing in Biblical
Hebrew:

> Cases ... may be found in the biblical texts from the end of the First
> Temple period onwards, but especially in the post-exilic period. They
> attest the existence of a Hebrew dialect which was gaining currency
> towards the end of the biblical period but was to become a written
> language only after several centuries had passed.[51]

Written Mishnaic Hebrew can be divided into two main portions: the
Tannaim, and the Amoraim. The Amoraim was formed from "the end of
the third century down to about 500 CE" during a period when the spoken
language was most likely Aramaic.[52] The Tannaitic literature (the Mishnah,
the *Tosefta*, the halachic *midrashim* and *Seder 'Olam Rabba*, 70–200 CE[53])
was earlier and represents "living speech current in various regions of
Palestine"[54] prior to 200 CE. Furthermore, although not Mishnaic Hebrew,
some Qumran documents (the Copper Scroll and 4QMMT) and the Bar
Kochba letters demonstrate numerous Mishnaic Hebrew forms.[55]

Gad Sarfatti has demonstrated that the Tannaitic literature can provide
valuable information for studying the semantics of "Ancient Hebrew."[56]
This is really unsurprising. If comparative Semitics can be useful for illuminating Ancient Hebrew then surely a Hebrew dialect which overlaps in
time with "Ancient Hebrew" is all the more so. As such, Mishnaic Hebrew,
often representative of speech prior to 200 CE, can be included in the
corpus of investigation for the current study.[57]

---

[50] Moshe Bar-Asher, "Mishnaic Hebrew: An Introductory Survey," *HS* 40 (1999): 118;
Miguel Pérez Fernández, *An Introductory Grammar of Rabbinic Hebrew*, trans. John
F. Elwolde (Leiden: Brill, 1997), 8–9.
[51] Bar-Asher, "Mishnaic Hebrew," 119; see also Pérez Fernández, *An Introductory Grammar*, 9–10.
[52] Bar-Asher, "Mishnaic Hebrew," 116.
[53] Young, Rezetko, and Ehrensvärd, *Linguistic Dating of Biblical Texts*, 1:7.
[54] Bar-Asher, "Mishnaic Hebrew," 116.
[55] Dimant states that 4QMMT is Mishnaic Hebrew, whereas Young, Rezetko, and Ehrensvärd are more cautious. Settling the case, Qimron has shown that Dead Sea Scrolls
Hebrew forms at least one distinct dialect of Hebrew which does not represent a linear
development from Biblical to Mishnaic Hebrew. Furthermore, 4QMMT is distinctly this
form of Hebrew. Dimant, "Sectarian and Non-Sectarian Texts," 12; Young, Rezetko, and
Ehrensvärd, *Linguistic Dating of Biblical Texts*, 1:237; Elisha Qimron, *A Grammar of
the Hebrew of the Dead Sea Scrolls* (Jerusalem: Yad Yizhak Ben-Zvi, 2018), 42.
[56] Young, Rezetko and Ehrensvärd also argue this. See Gad B. Sarfatti, "Mishnaic Vocabulary and Mishnaic Literature as Tools for the Study of Biblical Semantics," in *Studies
in Ancient Hebrew Semantics*, ed. T. Muraoka, AbrNSup 4 (Louvain: Peeters, 1995),
33–48; Young, Rezetko, and Ehrensvärd, *Linguistic Dating of Biblical Texts*, 1:248.
[57] Although the Amoraic literature may also be very valuable for the study of Ancient
Hebrew and may not vary greatly from the Tannaitic literature, it does come from a later

INTRODUCTION

Summary of Corpora

In summary, the biblical portion of the Ancient Hebrew corpus may at times contain multiple versions which require separate semantic analyses. Furthermore, previous designations of Ancient Hebrew have made what seems a somewhat artificial and problematic dividing line for the Ancient Hebrew corpus which eliminates Mishnaic Hebrew. Because Mishnaic Hebrew is represented in the period in question, and because there are cases of the biblical and Qumran texts using Mishnaic Hebrew forms such that there is some overlap between the represented dialects, pre-200 CE Mishnaic Hebrew could be included in the diverse corpus of Ancient Hebrew (although the standard vocabulary of Ancient and Mishnaic Hebrew is maintained).

Despite the study being, in theory, extended to all Tannaitic literature, a pragmatic factor not mentioned above is the availability of texts as morphologically tagged electronic corpora. Due to time limitations the current study is limited to those texts which are available as morphologically tagged electronic documents in Accordance bible software.[58] Only one portion of the Tannaitic literature is currently available in this form: the Mishnah. As such, from the Tannaitic literature, only the Mishnah is included.[59]

1.3.2 Confounding Factors in the Semantic Analysis of Ancient Hebrew

There are a number of factors which can confound semantic analysis of Ancient Hebrew. These include linguistic factors such as diachrony, genre, poetry/prose, dialects, sources, discourse/narrative.[60] Human error in text transmission and analysis of texts should also be acknowledged.

Additionally, there may be limits to the applicability of studies due to the limited corpus size from which to analyse Ancient Hebrew.[61] A small

---

stage of the language when Mishnaic Hebrew was not "living speech." Inclusion would mean the need to take account of confounds related to this. For this reason, the Amoraic literature is not considered.

[58] Oaktree Software, "Accordance – Bible Software for Mac, Windows, iPad and iPhone," https://www.accordancebible.com/.

[59] The tagged manuscript is the Kaufmann manuscript. This is compared at times to the untagged Eshkol manuscript.

[60] T. Muraoka, "A New Dictionary of Classical Hebrew," in *Studies in Ancient Hebrew Semantics*, ed. T. Muraoka, AbrNSup 4 (Louvain: Peeters, 1995), 98.

[61] Clines estimates a corpus size of around 353,396 words (this estimate excludes Tannaitic literature as seen in his definition of the corpus presented in §1.3.1). Clines, *DCH* 1:28. Of particular note is that some very common Hebrew words never feature in Biblical Hebrew, or they only feature very rarely. James Barr, *Biblical Words for Time*, 2nd ed. (London: SCM, 1969), 107.

14   CHAPTER 1

corpus means that certain types of analysis have limited applicability.[62] That is, we cannot be sure if conclusions based on the data represent the semantic structure of Ancient Hebrew or are simply the result of an inadequate sample.

I will first discuss the factors of diachrony and dialects (§1.3.2.1), and then move on to what can be known from the corpus we have, taking into account the limitations of corpus size (§1.3.2.2).

1.3.2.1 *Diachrony and Dialects*

There has been much recent discussion of diachronic and dialectic variation in specifically Biblical Hebrew. Therefore, much of this section will be a discussion on variation present in Biblical Hebrew.

Biblical Hebrew

It is generally accepted that both diachronic and dialectic variation are present in Biblical Hebrew. However, how much weight to place on each source of variation is debated. The standard view of diachrony in Biblical Hebrew has been that there is clear development from Early Biblical Hebrew (EBH) to Late Biblical Hebrew (LBH), the exile marking the transition period.[63] One of the most prominent voices arguing for a clear division is Avi Hurvitz:

> Yet, despite its seemingly uniform façade, beneath the surface BH exhibits a remarkable diversity of styles and plurality of linguistic traditions extending over some one thousand years.... Most significant are the differences observable between Classical BH (= CBH [SBH]), which reflects pre-Exilic times, and Late BH (= LBH), which displays numerous post-Classical neologisms unattested in the early sources.[64]

---

[62] For example, verb valency analysis. (Verb valency refers to the number and type of phrases that are required by a particular verb for a well-formed construction.) In his paper on valency analysis, Forbes refers to an article on studying valency in English corpora which says "the BNC [British National Corpus] contains only 100 million words". In comparison, Biblical Hebrew has around 300,000 words. See Francis I. Andersen and A. Dean Forbes, *Biblical Hebrew Grammar Visualized*, LSAWS 6 (Winona Lake, IN: Eisenbrauns, 2012), 167–68; A. Dean Forbes, "The Proper Role of Valency in Biblical Hebrew Studies," in *Contemporary Examinations of Classical Languages (Hebrew, Aramaic, Syriac, and Greek): Valency, Lexicography, Grammar, and Manuscripts*, ed. Timothy Martin Lewis, Alison Salvesen and Beryl Turner, Perspectives on Linguistics and Ancient Languages 8 (Piscataway, NJ: Gorgias, 2016), 105; Steven T. Piantadosi, Harry Tily, and Edward Gibson, "Word Lengths Are Optimized for Efficient Communication," *Proceedings of the National Academy of Sciencesa* 108 (2011): 3528.

[63] Young, Rezetko, and Ehrensvärd, *Linguistic Dating of Biblical Texts*, 1:10.

[64] Avi Hurvitz, *A Concise Lexicon of Late Biblical Hebrew: Linguistic Innovations in the Writings of the Second Temple Period*, VTSup 160 (Boston: Brill, 2014), 1.

INTRODUCTION   15

Young, Rezetko, and Ehrensvärd have argued against this clear distinction between EBH (Hurvitz's CBH) and LBH. After an extensive study they conclude that "These two general language types, EBH and LBH, are best taken as representing two tendencies among scribes of the biblical period: conservative and non-conservative."[65] Their theory is that Biblical Hebrew represents multiple dialects each undergoing diachronic developments: "If anything, then, we are 'multichronic' or 'polychronic' with regard to our views on the Bible."[66]

In response, Dean Forbes has demonstrated that the analysis of Young, Rezetko, and Ehrensvärd was statistically unsound.[67] However, Forbes does argue that the EBH–LBH distinction needs to have a greater evidential basis: "Assertions in the literature regarding the increased or decreased attestation of features in Late Biblical Hebrew as opposed to Early Biblical Hebrew are too often based on impressions rather than hard evidence."[68]

In order to provide an approach using hard evidence, Forbes examines other possible sources of variation: "In focusing on text dating, one must also take into account other possibly active variables such as authorship, dialect, source, style, and text type."[69] In addition to these sources of variation are additional factors which Forbes draws out. These factors are described as *noise effects* and include: text transmission noise, feature noise, and class noise.[70]

Text-transmission noise refers to how the text has been altered (inadvertently or intentionally) during transmission. Feature noise refers to inconsistency introduced through human analysis. The feature refers to any linguistic feature that is being analysed, such as a syntactic or semantic feature, phrase or clause type.[71] "Differing feature tallies may result from feature noise produced by inconsistent mark-up."[72] Class noise refers to how texts are selected for comparison. If certain texts are selected as

---

[65] Young, Rezetko, and Ehrensvärd, *Linguistic Dating of Biblical Texts*, 1:361; but see both volumes for their entire argument.

[66] Robert Rezetko and Ian Young, *Historical Linguistics and Biblical Hebrew: Steps toward an Integrated Approach* (Atlanta: SBL, 2014), 595.

[67] Forbes examines their work from a statistical point of view. A. Dean Forbes, "The Diachrony Debate: Perspectives from Pattern Recognition and Meta-Analysis," *HS* 53 (2012): 7–42; for other responses to their work see Cynthia L. Miller and Ziony Zevit, eds., *Diachrony in Biblical Hebrew*, LSAWS 8 (Winona Lake, IN: Eisenbrauns, 2012).

[68] Forbes, "The Diachrony Debate," 41.

[69] Forbes, "The Diachrony Debate," 40.

[70] Forbes, "The Diachrony Debate," 11–12.

[71] An example of feature noise may be seen at the time of writing in Genesis 2:9, where the noun דַּעַת (knowledge) is incorrectly marked Accordance as being in construct form when it is actually a verbal noun which governs the following words. GKC, §115d.

[72] Forbes, "The Diachrony Debate," 12.

16   CHAPTER 1

examples of Late Biblical Hebrew, but some are actually not, then the data is contaminated: "This contamination can lead to faulty inferences."[73]

In addition to these factors, an analysis of diachrony in Biblical Hebrew needs to take into account dialects, oral versus written sources, as well as other sociolinguistic factors.[74] Concluding his 2017 work on diachrony, Forbes writes:

> Sensitive to the sources of uncertainty discussed earlier and aware of the many options presented, definition of research protocols remains to be done, as does the assessment of each protocol's relative likelihood of success. Protocols having the greatest promise should be implemented. I hope to cover these topics in future work.[75]

From this conclusion we can see that there is still much work to be done before any firm grasp on diachronic variation can be reached.[76]

Ancient Hebrew

The state of the research on Biblical Hebrew is indicative of the lack of certainty surrounding a diachronic and dialectic description of Ancient Hebrew more generally. Moshe Bar-Asher, in discussing the position of the Hebrew of Ben Sira and Qumran in relation to Biblical and Mishnaic Hebrew, writes: "it is not possible to draw a line that runs through the strata of BH, through the Hebrew of Ben Sira and Qumran, and into MH;

---

[73] Forbes, "The Diachrony Debate," 12.
[74] A. Dean Forbes, "On Dating Biblical Hebrew Texts: Sources of Uncertainty / Analytic Options," in *From Ancient Manuscripts to Modern Dictionaries: Select Studies in Aramaic, Hebrew and Greek*, ed. Tarsee Li and Keith D. Dyer, Perspectives on Linguistics and Ancient Languages 9 (Piscataway, NJ: Gorgias, 2017), 266–67. Forbes refers to the works of Polak, Rendsburg, and Kim in reference to these factors. See Frank Polak, "Sociolinguistics: A Key to the Typology and the Social Background of Biblical Hebrew," *HS* 47 (2006): 115–62; Gary Rendsburg, "A Comprehensive Guide to Israelian Hebrew: Grammar and Lexicon," *Orient* 38 (2003): 5–35; Dong-Hyuk Kim, *Early Biblical Hebrew, Late Biblical Hebrew, and Linguistic Variability: A Sociolinguistic Evaluation of the Linguistic Dating of Biblical Texts*, VTSup 156 (Leiden: Brill, 2013).
[75] Forbes, "On Dating Biblical Hebrew Texts," 269.
[76] Ronald Hendel and Jan Joosten published a substantial work during the writing of this current work. They accept the existence of dialects and literary styles as confounds, but find evidence for three main phases or "chronolects" of the language. Their three phases are: CBH, TBH [transitional Biblical Hebrew]; and LBH. "CBH is at home in the monarchical period… TBH is at home in the Neo-Babylonian and early Persian periods. LBH is at home in the mid-Persian period through the Greek age." Despite their findings they write, "We emphasize that there are many gaps in our knowledge in each of these areas. The extant data are piecemeal and incomplete." Ronald S. Hendel and Jan Joosten, *How Old Is the Hebrew Bible? A Linguistic, Textual, and Historical Study*, AYBRL (New Haven: Yale University Press, 2018), 98, 121–22.

INTRODUCTION   17

there are cases in which instead we must reconstruct parallel lines dividing between different dialects of one language, each going in its own direction."[77]

1.3.2.2 *Analysis Under Sub-Optimal Conditions: Corpus Size and Linguistic Variation*

Given the size of the corpus and the sources of variation, how can one hope to know anything about Ancient Hebrew? Zatelli and others have sought to address the issues of variation in semantic analysis through the use of functional language distinctions.[78] A functional language is a portion language which is "unitary from the chronological, geographic, social and stylistic point of view"; it is "synchronic, synoptic, synstratic, synphasic."[79]

Zanella divides the Ancient Hebrew corpus into twelve functional languages.[80] He uses these twelve classes to analyse the nouns for "gift" in Ancient Hebrew. However, in creating so many sub-corpora within the data he multiplies the problem of insufficient data.[81] In his divisions he also increases the effects of noise by having a system that relies on debated divisions. Disregarding the issue of corpus size, the state of the research simply does not yet seem to warrant any clear diachronic or dialectic boundary placement between Biblical texts.

Ruling out such approaches that divide the text further means an analysis which must be cognizant of the presence of confounding factors. It also means the need for methods which do not require rigid diachronic and dialectic divisions, but are attentive to the presence of such features. It means any analysis is tentative in nature and aware of its limitations. It means opening the analysis to every possible example of Ancient Hebrew and allowing the possibility of gleaning meaningful information from a separate dialect of the Hebrew language (Mishnaic Hebrew). We must affirm with Burton that while it would be preferable to be able to analyse

---

[77] Moshe Bar-Asher, *Studies in Classical Hebrew*, ed. Aaron J. Koller, SJ 71 (Berlin: De Gruyter, 2014), 150.

[78] Ida Zatelli, "Functional Languages and Their Importance," in *Studies in Ancient Hebrew Semantics*, ed. T. Muraoka, AbrNSup 4 (Louvain: Peeters, 1995), 55–64.

[79] Ida Zatelli, "The Study of the Ancient Hebrew Lexicon: Application of the Concepts of Lexical Field and Functional Language," *Kleine Untersuchungen Zur Sprache Des Alten Testaments Und Seiner Umwelt* 5 (2004): 134.

[80] Zanella, *The Lexical Field*, 34.

[81] That is, his corpora have such small sample sizes that there are often very few (i.e. less than 5) occurrences of particular words in each corpus. Conclusions from such small usage samples are suspect.

18 CHAPTER 1

each language type on its own, in practice "the boundaries of such corpora are impossible to identify with confidence, and even were they identifiable the corpora so defined would be too limited and fragmentary to provide us with meaningful data."[82]

1.4 LINGUISTIC ANALYSIS OF ANCIENT HEBREW

> For purposes of studying language as part of cognition, an expression's meaning is first and foremost its meaning for a single (representative) speaker... An individual's notion of what an expression means develops through communicative interaction and includes an assessment of its degree of conventionality in the speech community.[83]

Methods of analysis appropriate to the corpus of Ancient and Mishnaic Hebrew can be found in the field of Cognitive Semantics. Such a field does not require clear boundaries to be set between parts of a language. In a cognitive description of language, language is always changing and developing. Inevitably this means that in synchronic snapshots of language, word meanings and linguistic structures display fuzzy boundaries (or prototypicality features)[84] which would be expected from a system in flux.

In the field of Cognitive Semantics the linguistic system is considered part of a larger cognitive system that involves culture and worldview as well as basic perception.[85] It is in this vein that van Wolde writes near the beginning of her 2009 work *Reframing Biblical Studies*:

> I intend to prove that it is possible for biblical scholarship to study meaning as "emergent reality," which on the one hand arises from linguistic, logical, and literary structures, from experience and perception-based cognitions, and from cultural- and context-bound routines; and on the other hand constitutes a new reality of its own.[86]

Reinier de Blois's SDBH works from a cognitive semantic viewpoint. His framework contains a number of useful features for describing the Ancient and Mishnaic Hebrew corpus. The most attractive of these features is his distinction between *lexical semantic domains* and *contextual*

---

[82] Burton, *The Semantics of Glory*, 39.

[83] Ronald W. Langacker, *Cognitive Grammar: A Basic Introduction* (New York: Oxford University Press, 2008), 30.

[84] Geeraerts, *Theories of Lexical Semantics*, 187.

[85] Although this feature may not necessarily be emphasised clearly in every analysis.

[86] Ellen J. van Wolde, *Reframing Biblical Studies: When Language and Text Meet Culture, Cognition, and Context* (Winona Lake, IN: Eisenbrauns, 2009), 20–21.

INTRODUCTION   19

semantic domains. These domains are integrally related to *cognitive catego-ries* and *cognitive context* respectively (see §1.4.1 and §1.4.2).[87] Another useful feature is his use of frame theory in describing the lexical seman-tic domains. However, while his framework is helpful, aspects of it have been found wanting. Bosman, in her study of lexemes of AFFECTION, found the framework unwieldy at times. She found a simpler framework to be more helpful in her study of AFFECTION.[88]

An additional critique concerns the diachronic nature of the Biblical Hebrew corpus. I argued for the need to study Ancient and Mishnaic Hebrew as a whole with an eye to its diachronic nature. The SDBH is unfor-tunately limited to the biblical texts. It also takes a synchronic approach: "A dictionary based on semantic domains, however, is structured in such a way that there is not much room for such a diachronic approach."[89] At times a word's meaning may be disambiguated through attention to diachronic semantic change. While arriving at a sure timeline of devel-opment of Biblical Hebrew within the Hebrew language may be impos-sible with the extant texts, allowing space for diachronic (not to mention dialectic) analysis could add weight to a particular interpretation over another.[90]

Therefore, while presenting certain aspects of de Blois' theory here, my analysis will does not strictly adhere to his framework. Instead, his descrip-tion of cognitive semantic theory is used to provide the reader with an understanding of the base on which this work builds. In application of methodology, I will maintain some fluidity, holding to general principles of cognitive semantic theories rather than conforming rigidly to a particular framework. In doing so I draw insights from a variety of linguistic theo-ries[91] as well as disciplines offering insights into world-knowledge (such as anthropology).

I will first briefly cover three concepts from Cognitive Linguistics high-lighted by de Blois (cognitive categories, cognitive context, and metaphor/metonymy; §1.4.1). This is followed by elements of Frame Semantics

---

[87] De Blois, *Towards a New Dictionary*, 26.

[88] She also listed a number of other shortcomings where she felt de Blois' framework did not adequately emphasise certain features. See Tiana Bosman, "Biblical Hebrew Lexicol-ogy and Cognitive Semantics: A Study of Lexemes of Affection" (PhD diss., University of Stellenbosch, 2011), 116–19.

[89] De Blois, *Towards a New Dictionary*, 10.

[90] For example, see my treatment of יָפֶה (beautiful) in Ecclesiastes. Philip D. Foster, "Is Everything 'Beautiful' or 'Appropriate' in Its Time? יָפֶה and Semantic Change," *JNSL* 45 (2019): 41–55.

[91] So the reader will see that, at various points throughout this work, reference is made to a variety of linguistic theories.

20 CHAPTER 1

drawn from both de Blois and FrameNet (§1.4.2). I also draw on some cognitive semantic discussion of adjectives and their modification of attributes (§1.4.3). Finally, pathways of lexical semantic change identified in linguistic literature are highlighted (§1.4.4).[92]

1.4.1 Three Cognitive Linguistic Concepts

De Blois builds on cognitive linguistic research on cognitive categories, cognitive context, and metaphor, metonymy, and mappings. These contain many variations in the linguistic literature. However, the general concepts are of importance in a cognitive semantic analysis of language.

Cognitive Categories

Cognitive categories refer to the categorical groupings within which humans think. This does not lead to a universal categorisation. Rather, classifications are intricately related to the "system of experiences, beliefs, and practices of a particular social or ethnic group."[93]

In addition to their dependency on worldview, cognitive categories contain prototype structures. This is such that there are typical and atypical members of a category.[94] Categories contain sets of *attributes* which the speakers of a language consider important to the category. For a bird, attributes may include: "(1) it has two wings, (2) it has two legs, (3) it can fly, (4) it has a beak, (5) feathers, and (6) it lays eggs."[95] Members of a category need not share all attributes. Atypical members are expected to share less attributes than typical ones.[96]

Lastly, the cognitive categories have fuzzy boundaries. Objects may be members of multiple categories and be a typical member of one category, but an atypical member of another.[97]

---

[92] Although semantic change in רע is ultimately not detected, it was considered as a possible factor in each stage of analysis.

[93] De Blois demonstrates this with an example of categorisation by the Osage Indians. See de Blois, *Towards a New Dictionary*, 22; de Blois' example is drawn from Lévi-Strauss who draws from La Flesche on the Osage, see Claude Lévi-Strauss, *The Savage Mind*, trans. George Weidenfeld (Hertfordshire, UK: The Garden City, 1966), 59.

[94] In the modern category of birds, a well-trodden example of an a-typical bird is the penguin.

[95] De Blois, *Towards a New Dictionary*, 23.

[96] Such description may derive from Wittgenstein's description of GAME. Cruse, *Meaning in Language*, 58; see also Ludwig Wittgenstein, *Philosophical Investigations*, trans. G. E. M. Anscombe (Oxford: Basil Blackwell, 1958), §66–§68.

[97] De Blois, *Towards a New Dictionary*, 23.

INTRODUCTION   21

Cognitive Context

The cognitive context is, from a discourse perspective, the "situation in which an utterance is embedded" and, from a cognitive perspective, a "mental phenomenon."[98]

> The boy was building a sandcastle with his bucket and his spade.
>
> In this example, four objects are interacting with each other: a boy, a sandcastle, etc. This interaction is often referred to as a *situation*. In certain cultures this is a common sight.... An utterance like this conjures up a mental image in the mind of the hearer: a cognitive representation of *building a sandcastle*. Ungerer and Schmid (1996:47) call this *context*.[99]

In addition to this, certain contexts are cognitively related to others, such that these also come to mind. The set of contexts are referred to as a cognitive model.[100]

Metaphor, Metonymy, and Mappings

In essence, certain concepts are borrowed from one domain of language to help explain another concept. Lakoff and Johnson provide the following example:

> theories (and arguments) are buildings
>
> Is that the *foundation* for your theory? The theory needs more *support*. The argument is *shaky*. We need some more facts or the argument will *fall apart*. We need to *construct* a *strong* argument for that...[101]

In this example, terms appropriate to the domain of buildings are said to be mapped to the target domain of theories. More recently this phenomenon

---

[98] De Blois, *Towards a New Dictionary*, 23.

[99] De Blois, *Towards a New Dictionary*, 23.

[100] An example of a set of contexts given by de Blois are: sunbathing, swimming, and windsurfing. See de Blois, *Towards a New Dictionary*, 23. The idea of the cognitive model is seen in the work of Lakoff (Idealized Cognitive Model) as well as Fillmore (Frame). Fillmore and Lakoff both discuss the noun *bachelor* which assumes a certain model of the world concerning marriage and marriageable age. Lakoff writes "The idealized model says nothing about the existence of priests, "long-term unmarried couplings," homosexuality... With respect to the idealized cognitive model, a *bachelor* is simply an unmarried adult man." George Lakoff, *Women, Fire, and Dangerous Things: What Categories Reveal about the Mind* (Chicago: The University of Chicago Press, 1987), 70; see also Charles J. Fillmore, "Towards a Descriptive Framework for Spatial Deixis," in *Speech, Place, and Action: Studies of Deixis and Related Topics*, ed. R. J. Jarvella and Wolfgang Klein (Chichester: Wiley, 1982), 34.

[101] George Lakoff and Mark Johnson, *Metaphors We Live By* (Chicago: University of Chicago Press, 2003), 46.

22 CHAPTER 1

has been described in terms of blending. In blending theory features are drawn from both the source and target domains leading to a "blend space" which does not fit perfectly in either source or target domain, but is essentially a new concept.[102] Through use these metaphors can become conventional and lexicalised such that a metaphoric use becomes a conventional meaning of a word (see §1.4.4).[103]

De Blois gives חֶרֶב (sword) as an example. In Biblical Hebrew it is often "used in a metaphorical sense, with focus on the activity that a sword is most commonly used for: 'violence, aggression, war.'"[104] However, some uses cannot be neatly categorised, but appear to share both physical and metaphorical senses simultaneously.[105] This category confusion between physical and metaphoric sense can be understood in terms of blending theory in that the use shares features of both, but cannot be solely categorised as either.

1.4.2 Lexical and Contextual Semantic Domains and Frame Theory

De Blois integrates the concepts of cognitive categories and cognitive contexts into his dictionary in the form of lexical and contextual domains. The *lexical* meaning of a word is considered to be "the meaning of a word within its minimal context."[106] The minimal context refers to the minimal amount of context needed for the mind to categorise the word. Different types of words have different amounts of minimal context: "*Objects* usually do not require too much context in order for human beings to be able to identify them. In the case of *Events* this is somewhat different. The latter often require a number of semantic arguments, such as: *Agent, Experiencer, Goal,* etc."[107]

In contrast to the lexical meaning, the contextual meaning supplies the wider context for the utterance. This context allows us to "get a much

---

[102] Geeraerts, *Theories of Lexical Semantics*, 211.

[103] De Blois writes "Certain metaphors and other figures of speech are so common in Biblical Hebrew that it becomes hard to see them as highly marked specialized expressions. They seem to have been lexicalized and have become a structural part of the language." De Blois, *Towards a New Dictionary*, 28.

[104] De Blois, *Towards a New Dictionary*, 28.

[105] De Blois uses the example of Jeremiah 47:6–7 for this point. See de Blois, *Towards a New Dictionary*, 28. Koller argues for homonymy based on comparative linguistic evidence and diachronic development. However, the description is in terms of metaphoric development which led to lexical polysemy. See Koller, *The Semantic Field of Cutting Tools*, 164–65.

[106] De Blois, *Towards a New Dictionary*, 26.

[107] De Blois, *Towards a New Dictionary*, 26.

INTRODUCTION
23

more complete meaning of that concept within that particular context."[108]
De Blois' example of soldier and carpenter is useful for understanding the
interplay between the two:

> Lexical entries like **soldier** and **carpenter**, for example, could be cov-
> ered by one single *lexical* semantic domain: *People*. From a *contextual*
> perspective, however, the former would need to be assigned to a *con-
> textual* domain like *Warfare*, whereas the latter would fit well under the
> *contextual* domain *Crafts*.[109]

There is a significant amount of interplay between the two domains.
De Blois writes "the boundaries between *lexical* and *contextual* meaning
can be vague and fuzzy at times, and in certain cases there may be some
overlap between both levels of classification."[110]

The combination of classifications are what leads to a contextualised
meaning. This is important for looking at the senses a word can take.
De Blois gives the example of חֶבֶל (rope). He notes that lexically this
can be classified as something like *Artefact*. However, it can be used in
a number of different contexts such as: measuring; hunting; construction;
maritime activities; and submission.[111] Words can also take multiple lexical meanings.[112]

De Blois incorporates frame theory into his lexical semantic domains. He
describes four conceptual frames (objects, events, referents, and markers).[113]
Each conceptual frame contains its own *slots* which help "to identify all
relevant semantic features for each lexical unit and lead to a uniform set
of definitions for each *lexical* semantic domain."[114] For example, his frame
for *Objects>People* contains four slots described as follows:

1. *Description*: All relevant information concerning the nature of this
   person.
2. *Source*: Information concerning the geographical location and social
   status of this type of person.
3. *Function*: Information concerning the function of this person in relation to other people.
4. *Connotation*: Stereotypical qualities of this type of person.[115]

---

[108] De Blois, *Towards a New Dictionary*, 26.
[109] De Blois, *Towards a New Dictionary*, 26.
[110] De Blois, *Towards a New Dictionary*, 32.
[111] De Blois, *Towards a New Dictionary*, 26–27.
[112] See de Blois' example: de Blois, *Towards a New Dictionary*, 27–28.
[113] Descriptions can be found on the website UBS, "SDBH."
[114] De Blois, *Towards a New Dictionary*, 29–30.
[115] De Blois, *Towards a New Dictionary*, 39–40.

24 CHAPTER 1

These slots are helpful for understanding how a word is used as they construct a definition out of the cognitive background of the concept. In this sense it is tied closely to the cognitive model.

In Frame Semantics attention is given to both the cognitive model and to a more immediate frame. The more immediate frame contains information relevant to the situation (or event) being described. For example, in the [COMMERCIAL TRANSACTION] frame "the BUYER gives the SELLER some MONEY, and the SELLER gives the BUYER the GOODS."[116] This description of a commercial transaction event describes what is necessary for the situation to occur. The items in small caps are considered frame elements. Core frame elements are elements which are necessary for the event to occur,[117] but need not necessarily be used in every sentence that evokes the frame.[118]

Certain words (used in certain ways) are considered to be based on a frame such that they *evoke* that frame. In this way "the word *hot* is capable of evoking a temperature scale frame in some contexts and a particular taste sensation in others."[119] Any interpretation of such a word requires a judgement about which frame is relevant in the context.[120] Here we see a tie to contextual information which can be of vital importance in judging which frame is in play. In terms of de Blois' lexical and contextual domains, the relevant context for determining which frame is evoked could come from either level.[121]

Summary

In summary, lexical and contextual semantic domains are useful concepts for considering the interaction of multiple levels of influence on the meaning of a word. In addition to these concepts, Frame Semantics is a useful tool as it gives a more complete picture for a word's use within its lexical domain.

---

[116] Charles J. Fillmore, Christopher R. Johnson and Miriam R. L. Petruck, "Background to FrameNet," *International Journal of Lexicography* 16 (2003): 239.

[117] Josef Ruppenhofer et al., *FrameNet II: Extended Theory and Practice* (Berkeley: International Computer Science Institute, 2016), 23.

[118] Elements may be omitted in various ways. See Sue Atkins, Charles J. Fillmore and Christopher R. Johnson, "Lexicographic Relevance: Selecting Information From Corpus Evidence," *International Journal of Lexicography* 16 (2003): 269–70.

[119] We could also add that it can evoke a physical appearance frame in still other contexts. Fillmore, Johnson, and Petruck, "Background to FrameNet," 236.

[120] Fillmore, Johnson, and Petruck, "Background to FrameNet," 236.

[121] See also the theory of Lexical Priming in which both immediate and higher level factors (such as discourse) influence contextual interpretation. Michael Hoey, *Lexical Priming: A New Theory of Words and Language* (London: Routledge, 2005).

INTRODUCTION   25

1.4.3 Adjectives and a Further Look at Attributes

From a cognitive linguistic perspective, "Adjectives are relational terms that profile a schematic semantic content as well as the quality of a noun."[122] As such, for any particular use of an adjective, when describing its meaning, one must take into account the noun it qualifies. Van Wolde presents the example of בָּרִיא (fat), arguing that in relation to cows it refers to those which are of a healthy size (Gen 41).[123] However, in relation to food it simply refers to good food (Hab 1:16) rather than the physical quality of "fatness."[124] Examples 1.5–1.7 demonstrate some of the uses of בָּרִיא.

1.5. Judges 3:17b, 22a

וְעֶגְלֹון אִישׁ בָּרִיא מְאֹד { ...}
וַיָּבֹא גַם־הַנִּצָּב אַחַר הַלַּהַב וַיִּסְגֹּר הַחֵלֶב בְּעַד הַלָּהַב

Now Eglon was a very fat man {...}
And the handle also went in after the blade, and the fat closed over the blade.

1.6. Habakkuk 1:16

עַל־כֵּן יְזַבֵּחַ לְחֶרְמֹו וִיקַטֵּר לְמִכְמַרְתֹּו כִּי בָהֵמָּה שָׁמֵן חֶלְקֹו וּמַאֲכָלֹו בְּרִאָה

Therefore he sacrifices to his net and makes offerings to his fishing net, because by them his portion is fat and his food is fat.

1.7. m. Miqwa'ot 8:4b

ר׳ יֹוסֵה אֹומ׳ בָּחֹולֶה וּבַזָּקֵן טָמֵא בַּיֶּלֶד וּבַבָּרִיא טָהֹור

Rabbi Yose says, "The sick and the old are unclean, the boy and the healthy are clean."

In example 1.5, physical appearance of a human is on view. It clearly refers to physical size, as can be seen in the following incident of the fat closing over Ehud's blade when he stabbed Eglon. However, in example 1.6 it qualifies food rather than appearance – this is a natural derivation from the uses in Genesis 41: healthy animals and crops are good for food.[125] Finally, in a mishnaic example, example 1.7 contrasts with example 1.5,

---

[122] Van Wolde, *Reframing Biblical Studies*, 147.
[123] Their understanding of "fat" would also be different from a modern perspective, but might be reconstructed through knowledge of cattle in ancient Egypt. Van Wolde, *Reframing Biblical Studies*, 147.
[124] Van Wolde, *Reframing Biblical Studies*, 147–48.
[125] Van Wolde, *Reframing Biblical Studies*, 148. See also UBS, "SDBH," בָּרִיא. This derivation may also be seen in English *healthy* which can refer to food which is expected to make one healthy.

26   CHAPTER 1

showing that בְּרִיא (at least by the time of the Mishnah) could act as an
antonym of חוֹלֶה (sick), thus demonstrating a link with health that appears
to have little to do with size.

In terms of *Cognitive Categories* (§1.4.1), we might say that בְּרִיא
can modify different *attributes* when modifying a person or food. The
attributes which are modified can be derived from the *Cognitive Context*
(§1.4.1),[126] which in these cases appear to be retrievable as the noun referent of בְּרִיא.[127] However, we must note that while both examples 1.5 and
1.7 modify a person, the attribute differs. The first refers to the physical
attribute of size, whereas the last refers to the attribute of vitality: both
being valid attributes of the category "person."[128] These features can be
clearly seen from the cognitive context (specifically, the discourse): the
use in example 1.5 sets up an incident concerning physical size, but the
use in example 1.7 contrasts with חוֹלֶה (sick). From a Frame Semantic
perspective, we may also see the frame that is evoked by בְּרִיא differs from
description of physical appearance (example 1.5), to effect (food that leads
to health, example 1.6), to vitality (example 1.7).

Van Wolde suggests that the quality of a noun is profiled by an adjective. However, this example suggests the relationship may be between adjective schema and modified attribute (the modified element of the discourse).[129]
Any particular noun may be capable of having the same adjective modify

---

[126] This being a cognitive, mental phenomenon, it necessarily includes not only linguistic,
but extra-linguistic context. We must remember that non-linguistic information which
would be assumed by the expected audience of a text is liable to being left out of the
text. This means care is needed to try to attend to aspects of meaning which may be
foreign to modern readers of an ancient text, but commonplace to the original audience. The idea for the following explanation is inspired by the work of Vyvyan Evans
who is particularly notable for highlighting the need to differentiate between the lexical and conceptual. Vyvyan Evans, *How Words Mean: Lexical Concepts, Cognitive
Models, and Meaning Construction* (Oxford; New York: Oxford University Press,
2009); Vyvyan Evans, "A Unified Account of Polysemy within LCCM Theory,"
Lingua 157, Supplement C (2015): 100–123; Patrick J. Duffley, "How Words Mean:
Lexical Concepts, Cognitive Models, and Meaning Construction (Review)," *Cognitive
Linguistics* 23 (2012): 217–21; Gregory L. Murphy, "How Words Mean: Lexical Concepts, Cognitive Models, and Meaning Construction (Review)," *Language* 87 (2011):
393–96.
[127] The referent is not present in example 1.7. However, m. Miqwa'ot 8:4 has בַּעַל קֶרִי
(a person who has a nocturnal emission) earlier which forms the referent here. There
are cases where a noun referent is not present with רע. This case is discussed in §2.1.2.
[128] This bears similarities to James Pustejovsky's qualia theory. Pustejovsky argues that
adjectives can subselect a feature of the words they modify through what he calls "selec-
tive binding." James Pustejovsky, *The Generative Lexicon* (Cambridge, MA: MIT Press,
1995), 89, 127.
[129] Pre-empting discussion of cases where *attribute* cannot properly be used to describe
the modified element (see §2.1.2).

INTRODUCTION   27

different attributes (for examples of this see chapter 2) given different
cognitive contexts. In addition, the selection of attribute may control which
frame is evoked by the adjective, leading to different possible expressions
of the more abstract schematic content that makes up a word (בָּרִיא in this
case).[130]

1.4.4 Lexical Semantic Change

Diachrony, change in meaning over time, is seen as an undoubtable
influence in the Ancient and Mishnaic Hebrew corpus (§1.3.2.1). Therefore, it needs to be taken into account. Because the present study is on
the adjective עַר, the type of language change that is of interest is lexical
semantic change. This change is likely present in the examples of בָּרִיא
above, with example 1.7 appearing to have little connection to physical
fat.

While the development of grammatical meaning in languages is "almost
exclusively unidirectional,"[131] the picture has seemed less stable when
it comes to changes in lexical meaning. Despite this, there is a general
tendency to move from: the external to the internal; the external or internal to the metalinguistic; and the more objective to the more subjective.[132] Traugott lists the different types of lexical change that have been
identified:

> 1. Metaphorization: conceptualizing one thing in terms of another, as
>   in terms of similarity, for example, the use of Latin *ad* "to" + *mit*
>   "send" for locution (*admit*), or of *tissue* "woven cloth" for "aggre-
>   gation of cells in animals or plants."

---

[130] We might say that בָּרִיא prototypically refers to physical size. However, it connotes
health. When used of food, the health aspect comes to the fore implying food that makes
one healthy. In addition the mishnaic use relies on this development to simply refer
to a healthy person without reference to size. Note that other mishnaic uses indicate
a much broader use of בָּרִיא (likely indicating lexical development), so although this
description illustrates the point, it may not perfectly fit the data.

[131] Elizabeth Closs Traugott, "Semantic Change," in *Oxford Research Encyclopedia of
Linguistics* (Oxford: Oxford University Press, 2017), §4, http://dx.doi.org/10.1093/
acrefore/9780199384655.013.323; see Traugott and Dasher for a more extensive analysis of regularity in semantic change. Elizabeth Closs Traugott and Richard B Dasher,
Regularity in Semantic Change (Cambridge: Cambridge University Press, 2001).

[132] Hollmann just refers to subjectification. Bybee summarises findings from Traugott
which apply to both grammaticalization and lexical change. Willem B. Hollmann,
"Semantic Change," in *English Language: Description, Variation and Context*, ed.
Jonathan Culpeper et al., 2nd ed. (London: Palgrave, 2018), 246; Joan L. Bybee, *Lan-
guage Change*, Cambridge Textbooks in Linguistics (Cambridge: Cambridge University
Press, 2015), 203–4.

28   CHAPTER 1

2. Metonymization: association, usually in terms of contiguity, for instance, *board* "table" > "people sitting around a table, governing body." Many traditional examples of metonymic shift involve part for whole (often called "synecdoche"), as in *keel* for *ship*.
3. Pejoration: association of a term with negative meaning, such as, Old English *stincan*, "smell (sweet or bad)" > *stink*, *cnafa* "boy" > *knave*, *conceit* "idea, opinion" > "overestimation of one's qualities."
4. Amelioration: association of a term with positive meaning, such as Middle English *nice*, "foolish, innocent" > "pleasant," and examples of pre-emption of meaning as a symbol of pride (e.g. *queer*).
5. Narrowing: restriction of meaning, as in Old English *deor* "animal" > *deer* (a specific kind of animal).
6. Generalization: extension of meaning, as in Latin *armare* "cover one's shoulders" > *arm*.[133]

Certain pairs such as 3 and 4, and 5 and 6 generate opposite changes which makes change appear to some degree arbitrary. However, the changes are motivated by various factors such as "shifts in socio-cultural attitudes and conceptual structures."[134] It is certain that facets of a language will change over time, but this does not guarantee that a certain word will change. When change does occur it affects the lexical domain. For example, when generalisation occurs, if this means a word takes on functions which another word usually has then the words are in competition. One word may become obsolete, but still be used in idiomatic phrases. "For example, *tide* used to mean 'time' but many of its uses were overtaken by the word *time*, and *tide* has been left to designate the rise and fall of the sea, except in words such as *even-tide* or *Yule-tide* where it still means 'time.'"[135]

Words and senses may coexist for a short or long time during the process of change and may or may not drop out entirely over time. In Bybee's example of *tide*, the usual sense of *time* has almost entirely dropped out, but the sense relating to the sea is prominent.

In the Ancient and Mishnaic Hebrew corpus it can be expected that lexical change will be present.[136] However, which particular form(s) of

---

[133] Traugott, "Semantic Change," §3.1.
[134] Traugott, "Semantic Change," §3.1. See also Sarfatti who lists a number of words that went from concrete to abstract concepts between Biblical and Mishnaic Hebrew as well as another series of words that became restricted to concrete meanings. Sarfatti, "Mishnaic Vocabulary and Mishnaic Literature," 37–39.
[135] Bybee, *Language Change*, 207.
[136] For example see Koller's study on the verb בּוֹא (come), Landman's study on words for "lips" and "tongues" in Ancient Hebrew, and my recent study on יָפֶה (beautiful). Aaron Koller, "To Come and to Enter: Synchronous and Diachronic Aspects in the Semantics of the Verb 'לבוא' in Ancient Hebrew" [Hebrew], *Leshonenu* 78 (2013):

INTRODUCTION 29

change, and which direction they take cannot be known prior to examination. Possible changes may be found to occur in רַע through examination of its use and the uses of words related to it. This second part is important because a reduced scope of use may not be easily detected; however, if (for example) another word is seen to be used for some functions that רַע was used for in earlier texts this may indicate a diachronic change of limitation of meaning.[137] As mentioned in §1.4, these factors were attended to during analysis. However, evidence for change in רַע itself was not found and so there is little discussion on change in רַע beyond this point.[138]

1.5 PROCEDURE OF ANALYSIS

In this work, I draw on lexical and cognitive semantic theory to analyse רַע in Ancient and Mishnaic Hebrew. Thus, underlying all analysis is an understanding of language as "emergent reality" where, among other things, underlying cultural contexts impact textual meaning (§1.4). The analysis will progress from an analysis of the contribution of רַע to the discourse element it modifies (§1.5.1), to mapping the lexical semantic domains of רַע in its combinative use (§1.5.2), to the analysis of the combinative use of רַע in some domains (§1.5.3).

In my analysis I must necessarily make use of English glosses for words. As a rule, for terms considered core to the analysis, I maintain the same gloss across all uses of each word. The use of English glosses should not be seen as representing a one-to-one link with the English word, but as a way of maintaining a link to particular Hebrew words. Therefore, the meaning of the gloss is not always relevant. This also led to the unusual selection of "villainy" as a gloss for אָוֶן.[139]

149–164; Yael Landman, "On Lips and Tongues in Ancient Hebrew," *VT* 66 (2016): 66–77; Foster, "Is Everything 'Beautiful' or 'Appropriate' in Its Time?"

[137] A caveat needs to be added here: neat chronological divisions in texts is often not possible (especially with biblical texts). However, texts can often be broadly categorised into periods. See §§1.3.2.1–1.3.2.2.

[138] This is not to say that attention to this detail was unfruitful. It was only through attention to potential semantic change in רַע that I identified semantic change in טוֹב and יָפֶה. That paper was an offshoot of work deemed irrelevant to the current research question. See Foster, "Is Everything 'Beautiful' or 'Appropriate' in Its Time?"

[139] The choice for this is twofold. First, it allows glosses of אָוֶן and עָוֹן (iniquity/sin) to be distinguished while still distinguishing עָוֹן from terms such as חַטָּאת (sin). Second, "iniquity," through its use to translate terms such as עָוֹן, has acquired senses proper to those terms. The use of villainy was considered a relatively good way to avoid such links.

30   CHAPTER 1

The analysis makes use of SMALL CAPITALS. This style is used to identify concepts. For example, it is used to identify discourse elements that רַע modifies (such as ACT or HUMAN). However, it is also used more generally to identify semantic concepts relevant to particular domains (such as DECEIT). Colour is systematically used in examples to highlight important features. Blue is reserved for words from the רעע word family. Similarly, green, teal, yellow, and red are reserved for domain-specific highlighting in Chapter 4. Due to the large number of examples used in this work, examples are numbered sequentially by chapter, with the first example in chapters 1 through 4 being numbered 1.1, 2.1, 3.1, and 4.1.

1.5.1 רַע and Schema

The analysis of Chapter 2 builds on §1.4.3. That is, רַע, as an adjective, is treated as a relational term that profiles a schematic semantic content as well as the quality of a discourse element (see §2.1.2).[140] In this chapter I examine the schematic meaning of רַע (the specific contribution of רַע to the discourse element it modifies).[141] This involves applications from frame semantics within ancient categories and context (see §1.4.2 and application to the COMMERCIAL TRANSACTION frame in §2.1.2). In order to make the analysis manageable, the scope is reduced with just over two thirds (67.6%) of occurrences of רַע receiving full analysis (§2.2).

The starting point is from the findings of prior research, which suggest רַע forms a general negative qualification, and may be appropriate in all areas that may be considered negative. This, then, is the null hypothesis[142] for the schema of רַע and assumed accurate unless conflicting evidence is found. The elements רַע modifies are identified first before analysing how רַע modifies the elements. The procedure for determining elements and how רַע modifies the elements involves examining features of the immediate discourse (the immediate cognitive context, see §1.4.1), which indicate what element is on view, while attending to relevant details from other sources, which have a bearing on the world knowledge of the speaking community (e.g. related texts, see explanation of בְּעֵר רַע in §2.3.8; archaeological finds, and anthropological research, see footnotes

---

[140] Using a modified form of van Wolde's definition given in §1.4.3.

[141] I use discourse element (or element) instead of attribute to allow for reference to a wider group of features that are not necessarily attributes. This is necessitated by features discussed in §2.1.2.

[142] The null hypothesis comes from statistics and refers to the hypothesis that there is no distinction between groups. It is the hypothesis for which one seeks to find disconfirming evidence.

INTRODUCTION   31

to the COMMERCIAL TRANSACTION example in §2.1.2). The chapter examines the findings of both Dohmen and Myhill, which both relate to this level. Some attention is also paid to the objective–subjective distinction in Myhill.

1.5.2 Mapping the Lexical Semantic Domains of רַע

In Chapter 3, I use linguistic analysis to map some[143] of the lexical semantic domains (§1.4.2) of רַע. These domains will represent some of the words sharing specific cognitive categories within ancient Israelite thought (§1.4.1). One main way lexical semantic domains have been mapped in Ancient Hebrew is through parallelism analysis. In Ancient Hebrew parallelism is pervasive.[144] One of the forms of parallelism is semantic, an example of which is found in the text from example 1.2.

> 1.7. Isaiah 45:7a

> יוֹצֵר אוֹר וּבוֹרֵא חֹשֶׁךְ עֹשֶׂה שָׁלוֹם וּבוֹרֵא רָע

> [I] form light and create darkness,
> [I] make peace and create bad...

In this verse there are multiple levels of semantic parallelism. The verbs for forming are in semantic parallel with each other, and the nouns (and adjective) of things formed are in semantic parallel with each other. The first pair of nouns are semantic opposites, and the second pair (one noun and one adjective) are presented as semantic opposites. The parallelism structure invokes a metaphoric comparison of light and dark with peace and רָע.

This example demonstrates how parallelism can be used to highlight paradigmatic relationships of similarity and opposition (orange and purple with respect to רַע).[145] However, the example also highlights a potential problem: Darkness is in a relation of similarity to רַע but surely would not be considered part of the same lexical domain. The question then

---

[143] This pre-empts limitations of the method of mapping the domains.

[144] It is especially prevalent in poetry, but also present in prose to varying degrees. Berlin describes the difference in terms of the "constructive principle" of the literature. Adele Berlin, *The Dynamics of Biblical Parallelism*, rev. ed., The Biblical Resource Series (Grand Rapids, MI: Eerdmans, 2008), 5–6. However, this description overplays the role of parallelism in poetry. It is better to speak in terms of appositive style in ancient Hebrew poetry. Robert D. Holmstedt, "Hebrew Poetry and the Appositive Style: Parallelism, *Requiescat in pace*," *VT* 69 (2019): 617–48.

[145] See my previous work where I discuss the use of parallelism to highlight relationships in more detail. Foster, "A Delimitation," 23–31.

32   CHAPTER 1

becomes how one is able to avoid ascribing them to the same domain using parallelism analysis. This should be able to be done through examining frequency of parallelism and cross-checking those items found in parallel against each other. Burton has employed a rigorous method of analysis involving cross-checking of words in her study on כָּבוֹד (glory) which I will replicate in the current work:

> Our method, then, will be as follows:
>
> 1) to identify the words associated with רַע as pairings and parallel terms;
> 2) to identify the word associations of each of these, paying particular attention to overlaps between the lists produced;
> 3) to eliminate words from these lists based on the following criteria:
>   i) they have no association with any other word associated with רַע;
>   ii) while they have some association with limited other words associated with רַע, they have significant, obvious associations with a separate set of words not associated with רַע.[146]

This procedure will be applied to map some of the lexical domain(s) appropriate to רַע. However, in addition to considering parallel terms, the analysis will be broadened to a wider group of semantic associations, allowing phrasal parallels.[147]

1.5.3 Semantic Domain Analysis

In Chapter 4, the (lexical) semantic domains which are mapped in Chapter 3 are partially (in order to make the scope manageable) analysed to determine how רַע functions as a part of those domains. The analysis is done with particular reference to words which are expected to provide the greatest interpretive power for understanding the use of רַע in relation to these domains (§4.1). This selection also leads to a brief comparison between the use of רַע and two other terms in the רעע word family: רֹע and רָעָה. Findings from the domain analyses are applied to understanding the use of רַע.

As with Chapter 2, this analysis involves close examination of, primarily, the immediate discourse making up occurrences of words in each domain (the immediate cognitive context, see §1.4.1). Frequently occurring

---

[146] The word כבוד has been replaced with רַע. Burton, *The Semantics of Glory*, 50.

[147] The procedure for this is dealt with in §3.1.1. It also has implications for how relationships are viewed. Instead of talking in terms of paradigmatic relationships of similarity and opposition, semantic associations are viewed in terms of relative prosody (i.e. whether they have similar or different prosody to רַע, see §3.1.1.3).

INTRODUCTION   33

contextual features unique to each domain are identified. For example, with the אָוֶן (DECEIT) subdomain, the features of SPEECH, and PLANNING are frequently detected with particular syntactic and semantic relations to אָוֶן words (see §4.4.1). Furthermore, to the extent that רַע participates within this semantic domain it is seen to take on features of the domain. This is perhaps seen more clearly with the עָוֹן domain where רַע, used within the cognitive context (§1.4.1) of that domain, takes features of the cognitive categories (§1.4.1) of the עָוֹן domain, and so we see רַע used to refer to GUILT and PUNISHMENT for רַע ACTS (see §2.3.8 and §4.5).

CHAPTER 2

רַע AND SCHEMA

As stated in §1.5.1, the null hypothesis[1] for the schematic use of רַע is that רַע provides a general negative modification to the discourse element it modifies. Another feature to be tested in this Chapter is the objective–subjective distinction Myhill makes.

2.1 PRELIMINARY MATTERS

In order to test the null hypothesis, discourse elements must first be identified. However, prior to that we need to identify and select occurrences of רַע for analysis. How this is done is discussed in §2.1.1. There are also various matters to discuss in relation to the identification and modification of elements (§§2.1.2–2.1.3).

2.1.1 Identifying and Selecting Words

The first step in the process of analysis is the identification of words. With all the tools available it is easy to overlook this crucial step. Concerning the biblical and mishnaic texts, the question of how to treat pointing (both) and accentuation (biblical only) becomes important. Both of these features were added later to the texts. If pointing is ignored, there are a number of words which become visually indistinguishable. In particular, we can note that the words רַע and רֹעַ (evil) are both spelt the same.[2]

---

[1] The null hypothesis comes from statistics. It is the hypothesis for which one seeks to find disconfirming evidence.

[2] In addition to this example taken from within the semantic domains of רַע, there are a number of ambiguities found with רַע. The following non-exhaustive list also takes into account the additional ambiguities as a result of the feminine form of the adjective (רָעָה):
  1. The Qal stem of the verb from the same word family has ambiguities in the: 3MS qatal conjugation; 3FS qatal conjugation; and the participles.
  2. The noun רָעָה (evil).
  3. The noun רֵעַ (neighbour).
  4. The noun רֹעֶה (shepherd) and verb of the same word family.

36   CHAPTER 2

It would be easy to become entangled in the process of identifying words from the consonantal text. However, the aim of this analysis is not to determine how to best distinguish between homographs. It is also not to distinguish between homonyms. While this is valuable work, it is not within the scope of the current analysis. For the purpose of the current analysis a certain amount of statistical error was deemed acceptable: it was decided to begin from a position of trust in the Masoretic pointing and the work found in certain concordances.[3] These sources are cross-checked against the Accordance software tagged texts and critical judgements are made where discrepancies arise.

Following on from this, an issue that was not dealt with in Chapter 1 (§1.3.1) is the issue of how to handle parallel texts, and refrains. Should repeated text be counted as one occurrence or as multiple occurrences? That is, should they be dealt with in the same manner as *quoted text* (i.e. only semantically significant variations being considered)?

In the biblical corpus there are substantial sections of parallel texts between Samuel–Kings and Chronicles (e.g. 1 Kgs 21:2 and 2 Chr 33:2 are identical) in addition to some other areas. However, there is evidence that these uses form parts of edited works. The Chronicler demonstrates no qualms with modifying his source and producing significant variations (e.g. 2 Sam 24:13 and 1 Chr 21:11–12).[4] In the Judean Desert corpus there are works that contain extensive rewriting of parts of the biblical corpus. For example, the Temple Scroll (11Q19) contains rewriting of much of the laws in Deuteronomy. In addressing this issue Burton writes: "the conscious repetition of a text by more than one author is suggestive that the word associations within it are acceptable, rather than idiosyncratic;

---

[3] There is likely to be a higher degree of error for the mishnaic portion of the corpus due to the lack of access to a complete concordance of the Mishnah. This meant a greater reliance on the Accordance tagging which was clearly deficient in some cases, (e.g. between the feminine form of the adjective רַע and the feminine noun רָעָה). There are often minor discrepancies between the references listed in the concordance for the Dead Sea Scrolls and Accordance for 1QH[a]. The current work follows the references in Accordance which uses the reconstruction by Stegemann and Schuller and found in Eileen M. Schuller and Carol A. Newsom, *The Hodayot (Thanksgiving Psalms): a study edition of 1QH[a]*, EJL 36 (Atlanta: SBL, 2012). The primary concordances used for the other corpuses were Abraham Even-Shoshan, *A new concordance of the Bible: for the Torah, the Prophets, and the Writings*, rev. ed. (Jerusalem: Kiryat Sefer, 1992); Dominique Barthélemy and O. Rickenbacher, *Konkordanz zum Hebräischen Sirach: mit Syrisch-Hebräischem Index* (Göttingen: Vandenhoeck und Ruprecht, 1973); Martin G. Abegg, James E. Bowley and Edward M. Cook, *The Dead Sea Scrolls Concordance*, 3 vols (Leiden: Brill, 2003–2015); Davies, *Ancient Hebrew Inscriptions*.

[4] On the assumption that the Chronicler had Samuel–Kings as their source. It is possible that both texts updated a common source.

רַע AND SCHEMA 37

it also indicates that the earlier text is present to the consciousness at least of the author, and almost certainly to the wider community."[5]

This leads Burton to include parallel texts as separate instances of use. She follows the same procedure for refrains. The fact that these texts are not straight reproductions of the original, but show extensive modifications, weighs the argument in favour of inclusion of these texts as multiple occurrences. Therefore, explicitly interpretive works such as the Habbakuk pesher (1QpHab) are treated as containing lemmata of the biblical text, and parallel/reworked material is treated as separate usage. The biblical references in the Mishnah show evidence of being treated as quotes that need to be explained and are, therefore, also treated as lemmata of the biblical text. Judean Desert manuscripts that look like direct copies of other Judean Desert manuscripts are treated in the same manner as copies of biblical texts; that is, only semantically significant variations are counted.

Once occurrences of words are identified, the issue of fragmentary texts must be dealt with. There are many occurrences (primarily in the Judean Desert corpus) that contain incomplete sentences or a single word, or in which רַע is partially damaged. Where texts were judged too damaged for productive semantic analysis they were immediately eliminated from the analysis (e.g. where only part of a sentence remains).[6] However, some occurrences with damaged text were included when the context could be reconstructed with relative certainty. These occurrences are addressed in Appendix C.

2.1.2 Modification of Discourse Elements in Elided Reference

An additional question concerns uses of רַע where it does not syntactically modify another word in its clause. In these cases, we might ask whether the word should be considered itself to refer (i.e. רַע to be considered a noun), or whether there is an elided word which should be considered to provide the relevant reference. However, I suggest that this approach would miss the point. In §1.4.1 and §1.4.3, I discussed adjectives and attributes. Attributes refer to the features within a cognitive category which speakers of a language consider important (e.g. one attribute of a bird is that it has two wings).[7] It was argued in §1.4.3, that it is not adequate to

---

[5] Burton, *The Semantics of Glory*, 55.
[6] Exceptions were made to this rule where an obvious semantic association occurred, such as with a clear antonym. While these exceptions may be unproductive for this stage of analysis, they were left in for the purpose of giving a more complete picture in (§3.1.1.1).
[7] De Blois, *Towards a New Dictionary*, 23.

38   CHAPTER 2

say that adjectives "profile a schematic semantic content as well as the
quality of a noun."[8] Instead it was suggested that the relationship is between
schema and modified attribute (the modified element of the discourse).
However, when we reach the case of elided reference, it appears that this
definition is not broad enough. I suggest that the adjective schema may also
modify an element that arises, not from the presence of a noun in particular,
but from a particular cognitive context. This element is primarily identified
through discourse and so will be referred to from here on as the *discourse
element* or *element*.[9]

An example of this can be found in example 2.1 below.

2.1. Proverbs 20:14

רַע רַע יֹאמַר הַקּוֹנֶה וְאֹזֵל לֹו אָז יִתְהַלָּל

"Bad! Bad!" says the buyer, and going away he boasts.

In example 2.1, רַע appears to be used predicatively. However, the thing
that is declared רַע must be retrieved from both the surrounding text and
world knowledge. The scene of the text is a price negotiation: הַקּוֹנֶה (the
buyer) is trying to get the lowest price for his purchase by protesting that
the seller's asking price (whether barter or money)[10] is bad. This scene
is made clear through the following features:

1. Mention of the buyer: The scene is one of a transaction involving a
   buyer and seller, goods and a commodity (barter or money).[11]
2. He goes away: This implies leaving the marketplace[12] or other relevant
   location in which the initial scene – the buying – took place.

---

[8] Van Wolde, *Reframing Biblical Studies*, 147.

[9] This group includes attributes where attributes are the element modified. Again, this bears
similarity to qualia theory. Pustejovsky argues that different adjectives bind with different
substructures. Pustejovsky, *The Generative Lexicon*, 127–131. However, we are dealing
with cases where the substructure is a product of cognitive context, or a particular cultural
frame indicated by discourse.

[10] "Money, simply understood, is a mechanism for indirect exchange." As such, this could
include commodities such as grain, lead, copper, and silver. Silver was one of the most
common and widely accepted forms. Joshua T. Walton, "Trade in the Late Bronze and
Iron Age Levant," in *Behind the Scenes of the Old Testament: Cultural, Social, and
Historical Contexts*, ed. Jonathan S. Greer, John W. Hilber and John H. Walton (Grand
Rapids, MI: Baker, 2018), 417.

[11] In Frame Semantics terms, we might think of this in terms of an Ancient Israelite COM-
MERCIAL TRANSACTION frame. For the FrameNet commercial transaction frame in English
see International Computer Science Institute, "Commercial_transaction," Frame Index,
https://framenet2.icsi.berkeley.edu/fnReports/data/frameIndex.xml?frame=Commercial_
transaction.

[12] King and Stager suggest the marketplace would have been immediately adjacent to the
city gate. These bazaars would likely have contained various types of shops as in the

רַע AND SCHEMA

39

3. The buyer boasts [of his purchase]: This implies that although the buyer protested the asking price, he feels he won out in the transaction.

These features make it clear that the phrase "רַע רַע" is presented as a false claim expected to form part of a price negotiation. The buyer knows the price is not רַע, but he makes the claim to achieve the most personal gain possible. The whole scene is constructed by the entire cognitive context: words and world knowledge.[13] This context makes it relatively clear what element רַע modifies.

The modified discourse element on view is available from the scene of the text. It would be clear to the text's original audience what the buyer is talking about because it is a common scene in their market. The element is the ASKING PRICE.[14] It does not need to be lexically specified in the text. The element is not properly a feature of the word רַע, nor of any other word in the text, but a feature arising out of the cognitive context.[15]

2.1.3 Attribution, Predication, and Construct Chains

We must also consider the relationships between attribution, predication, and construct chains as it relates to the use of רַע. It would be a mistake to assume that every time רַע modifies אִישׁ it modifies the same element. When רַע forms part of a construct chain which predicatively or attributively modifies אִישׁ, the word with which רַע is in construct is primary for determining the element in view.

2.2. 1 Samuel 25:3b

וְהָאִישׁ קָשֶׁה וְרַע מַעֲלָלִים

...and the man was severe and bad of deeds.

---

one excavated in Ashkelon. Philip J. King and Lawrence E. Stager, *Life in Biblical Israel*, LAI (Louisville, KY: Westminster John Knox, 2001), 191.

[13] World knowledge is important to understand the concept of price haggling. Being a rather unusual thing in Western societies, it is not difficult to imagine a person who has no concept of haggling and so misses the point of the proverb. Without knowing about haggling a person may see this as saying that buyers simply complain, rather than that they attempt to manipulate the seller as part of a culturally accepted practice of price negotiation.

[14] Someone might question whether the element is the product or the price for the product. However, whichever is the case makes little difference. Ultimately, it is a dispute over price: the buyer disputes whether the goods deserve the price.

[15] This understanding of adjective modification allows us to easily include cases which have been considered, at times, as noun uses of רַע (e.g. §2.3.1). See n.19 §1.1 for a brief discussion on noun and adjective categories.

40 CHAPTER 2

2.3. Ben Sira 14:3b

ולאיש רע עין לא נאוה חרוץ

...and for the man who is bad of eye, gold is not seemly.

In example 2.2 the severe and bad deeds of the man, Nabal, become clear in the following discourse. He behaves in a harsh and inhospitable manner to David and his men, who had protected his shepherds and sheep (1 Sam 25:10–11, 15–16). However, in example 2.3, the focus of the phrase רע עַיִן is on the attitude of the person. The following discourse makes this clear: the person with such an attitude harms themselves by not allowing themselves to enjoy what they have (cf. Prov 29:6; m. 'Abot 5:13).[16]

2.4. Ben Sira 14:4–5

מונע נפשו יקבץ לאחר ובטובתו יתבעבע זר
רע לנפשו למי ייטיב ולא יקרה בטובתו

The one who withholds from himself gathers for another, and a stranger will revel in his goods. [He is] bad to himself: to whom does he do good? He does not meet[17] with his goods.

Although we might make the judgement that Nabal in 1 Samuel 25 was רע עַיִן based on his actions, the phrase invites comparison with Nehemiah 9:35 where רע directly modifies מַעֲלָל. In Nehemiah 9, the Levites confess the sins of their forefathers (e.g. Neh 9:18, 26, 28). When we get to 9:35, the Levites are recounting the response (or lack of response) of their forefathers to God's faithful dealing with them (9:33–34).

2.5. Nehemiah 9:35b

וְלֹא־שָׁבוּ מִמַּעַלְלֵיהֶם הָרָעִים

...but they did not turn from their bad deeds.

These examples demonstrate the relationship between attribution and predication, and construct chains when it comes to the element רע modifies.

---

[16] Patrick William Skehan and Alexander A. Di Lella, *The Wisdom of Ben Sira: A New Translation with Notes*, AB 39 (New York, NY: Doubleday, 1987), 259. Although it does not use the phrase רע עַיִן and so was not chosen for the example above, the mishnah in m. 'Abot 5:13 is particularly instructive about the concept of the *bad eye* referring to the attitude of a person. אַרְבַּע מִידוֹת בְּנוֹתְנֵי צְדָקָה רוֹצֶה שֶׁיִּתֵּן וְאַל יִתְּנוּ אֲחֵרִים עֵינוֹ רָעָה בְּשֶׁלְאֲחֵרִים [שֶׁ]יִּתְּנוּ אֲחֵרִים וְהוּא לֹא יִתֵּן עֵינוֹ רָעָה בְּשֶׁלּוֹ (There are four types of almsgivers: he that is minded to give but not that others should give – he begrudges what belongs to others; he that is minded that others should give but not that he should give – he begrudges what belongs to himself... [Translation from Danby])

[17] Old Greek has εὐφρανθήσεται (enjoy). Whether or not קרה is correct, it seems likely that it implies enjoyment of goods.

רַע AND SCHEMA   41

In example 2.2, רַע modifies מַעֲלָלִים (deeds), but specifically those done by an אִישׁ (man).[18] In example 2.3, רַע modifies עַיִן (eye), but specifically that of an אִישׁ.[19] Syntactically speaking, in these examples, רַע primarily modifies the word with which it forms a construct chain. As a unit, these construct chains form adjectival phrases[20] that modify אִישׁ either predicatively (example 2.2) or attributively (example 2.3).

2.2 Scope Limitations and Sampling

The word רַע occurs a total of 540 times in the analysed text.[21] This figure is made up of 354[22] uses in the Hebrew Bible, 55 in Ben Sira, 43 in the Judean Desert texts, 1 in the Ancient Hebrew inscriptions, and 87 in the Mishnah (reported henceforth in the form: [354; 55; 43; 1; 87]). In 216 of the occurrences of רַע [128; 17; 21; 0; 49], it syntactically modifies another word, either attributively or predicatively. Conversely, 324 of the occurrences of רַע [226; 38; 22; 1; 38], occur in other uses without syntactically modifying another word through attributive or predicative relations.

A much smaller proportion of uses of רַע occur as part of a construct phrase. רַע occurs as part of a construct phrase 80 times [47; 7; 17; 0; 9]. In 18 of these occurrences, רַע syntactically modifies another word, either attributively or predicatively [10; 0; 5; 0; 3]. The greater portion of רַע's uses in a construct phrase occur without syntactically modifying another word through attributive or predicative relations [37; 7; 12; 0; 6].

2.2.1 Limiting the Analysis

For completeness it would be ideal to analyse all 540 occurrences of רַע. However, in order to extend the scope to an analysis of the domains

---

[18] In example 2.5 the human aspect is specified by the pronominal suffix and the verbal subject which is provided by the discourse (Neh 9:34).

[19] It may be valid to discuss whether either רַע מַעֲלָלִים or רַע עַיִן can properly be considered concepts to apply to non-human entities. However, the point here is that caution needs to be taken in coming to conclusions about the element רַע modifies: the word it is attributed to does not necessarily provide all the information required.

[20] Or appositional phrases depending on the terminology one desires to use. "Syntactically speaking an appositional element is always an adjectival modification." Van der Merwe, Naudé and Kroeze, *A Biblical Hebrew Reference Grammar*, §29.2.

[21] This figure excludes the occurrences of רַע which fit the criteria for exclusion in §2.1.1.

[22] Five occurrences which contain semantically significant variants were added: Genesis 41:3, 4 (SP); 4Q27 20–22, 29 [Num 22:32]; 1QIsaᵃ XXXVIII, 13 [Isa 45:7]; and XLVIII, 19 [Isa 59:7].

42   CHAPTER 2

of use of רַע (Chapters 3 and 4), the analysis must be reduced in size. This means selecting a sample of extant uses of רַע to be analysed in detail for this stage of the analysis.[23]

There are various ways a sample could be selected. The desire is for the sample to be representative of the use of רַע in the speaking community. Random sampling methods may be attractive for achieving a representative sample. However, these would open up the risk of drawing unwarranted conclusions from unusual uses of רַע based on a lack of knowledge about conventional use. In order to address this issue, groups of uses which share important similarities and demonstrate higher frequencies are valuable. Examining such uses of רַע will lower the risk of misinterpreting the unusual while helping to evaluate what the conventional use of רַע is. This should allow for both stable patterns and novel usage to be detected more easily within the categories analysed.

2.2.2 Sampling Method

In selecting usage groups for analysis, we must first determine what kinds of groups should be permitted. The sampling method aims to select groups for analysis which are of sufficient size and share important similarities. In addition to this, a large sample of the total uses of רַע (around 2/3 uses) analysed in their various groupings should allow for representativeness to be achieved.

This method of group selection means that groups may be defined by different features. The single largest group of uses of רַע is in the phrase עָשָׂה רַע (to do bad). The use of רַע as the object of the verb עָשָׂה is expected to have a relatively stable meaning, so this can be selected as one group. This is an example of a group defined based on the relationship of רַע to a verb.

Groups may also be defined based on the relationship of רַע to a noun, or a group of words connoting a concept.[24] For example, uses which modify מַעֲשֶׂה, מֵעָלִיל, or מַעֲלָל attributively, predicatively, or in construct, can be analysed together as they all convey a similar sense: DEED. Similarly, uses of רַע which modify body terms (פָּנִים, לֵב, עַיִן etc.) can be analysed together. In the first group – words conveying DEED – we may expect a

---

[23] While all instances of רַע were analysed in the process of this work, the scope limitation means not all instances receive the same level of attention at various parts of the work.

[24] The group COGNITION (§2.3.9) includes uses where רַע is governed by a verb, and other uses where it is governed by a noun. Nevertheless, these uses appeared to demonstrate suitable cohesion in preliminary analysis to be included as its own group.

רַע AND SCHEMA

similar element to be modified across the group due to the words being similar in meaning. In the second group – BODY PART – we may expect to see a similar pattern of modification occurring, with similar kinds of elements being prototypically selected.[25] By considering such occurrences together we are able to examine the behaviour of רַע in areas which we may expect to be logically connected. These hypotheses are tested in the analysis.[26]

An important decision needs to be made concerning how to treat uses which do not syntactically modify another word through attributive, predicative, or construct relations. For many of these uses, some important detail concerning the element(s) רַע modifies is clear. In such cases they can be analysed with cases where רַע modifies words sharing those elements. Two examples demonstrate this.

2.6. Exodus 21:7a, 8a

וְכִי־יִמְכֹּר אִישׁ אֶת־בִּתּוֹ לְאָמָה {...}
אִם־רָעָה בְּעֵינֵי אֲדֹנֶיהָ

If a man sells his daughter as a *female slave* {...} if [she is] *bad* in the eyes of her lord...

2.7. Proverbs 24:19–20

אַל־תִּתְחַר בַּמְּרֵעִים אַל־תְּקַנֵּא בָּרְשָׁעִים
כִּי | לֹא־תִהְיֶה אַחֲרִית לָרָע נֵר רְשָׁעִים יִדְעָךְ

Do not fret over *evildoers*, do not be jealous of the *wicked*,
For the *bad* has no future, the lamp of the *wicked* will be extinguished.

In the first, example 2.6, אָמָה (female slave) is present in the discourse and provides enough to know רַע modifies a HUMAN discourse element. In the second, example 2.7, the structure of the verse places רַע in semantic parallelism with מְרֵעִים (evildoers) and רְשָׁעִים (wicked). This parallelism means we expect רַע to refer to a category of HUMAN. The parallelism is made clear by the structure, in the first line there are two versets with identical morphological and syntactic structure. This line forms the instruction to not fret over or be jealous of two groups of humans placed in parallel (מְרֵעִים and רְשָׁעִים). The second line also contains two sections which provide the reason for the instructions in the first line. The parallels are not as tightly structured; however, it describes the end of the groups mentioned in the first line. While we may expect different elements to be modified

---

[25] Hebrew body terms are often used to describe emotions and character qualities (see §2.3.4).
[26] Some of these groupings will group in terms that rarely occur: מַעֲלִיל only occurs once.

44 CHAPTER 2

by רַע in examples 2.6 and 2.7, both refer to categories of HUMAN and may be treated together for the same reason modification of BODY PARTS can be treated together: we may expect to see a similar pattern of modification occur across the terms.

The selection of groupings for analysis relies in large part on the intuition of the researcher following an examination of all uses of רַע across the analysed texts. This was considered acceptable as the groupings themselves are not chosen to represent actual conceptual groups in Ancient Israelite thought, but are chosen as a way of splitting the analysis into manageable subsections which are likely to contain some internal cohesion. The selection process provides a way to analyse a sample of how רַע modifies elements while keeping occurrence numbers high enough to be relatively sure that usual uses of רַע will be taken into account and some unusual occurrences will be encountered. Table 2.1 below presents an ordered list of the groups that will be analysed in detail at this stage.

All groupings selected contribute to 1% or more of the occurrence of רַע.[27] This led to an analysis of how רַע modifies elements for just over two thirds (67.6%) of the uses of רַע. However, not all groups are presented in §2.3. Analysis of groups with less than ten occurrences (none of which added any significant contribution to the findings) are presented in Appendix A. The one exception to this was the חַיָּה (animal) group. This group was included due to the significance of the phrase חַיָּה רָעָה in later chapters.

Table 2.1. Groups for Analysis.

Group	Total Occurrence	Percentage of Occurrences	Cumulative Occurrence	Cumulative Percentage
עָשָׂה רַע (to do bad)	88	16.3%	88	16.3%
HUMAN	57	10.6%	145	26.9%
COMMODITY	43	8.0%	198	36.7%
BODY PART	28	5.2%	226	41.9%
דֶּרֶךְ (way)	23	4.3%	249	46.1%

---

[27] It was noted above that the sample has a degree of arbitrariness to it. Another researcher may find additional useful groupings which contribute to greater than 1% of the occurrences of רַע, or may argue for the inclusion of more or less items into some groupings. However, the current grouping was deemed adequate for the purposes of understanding the conventional way(s) that רַע modifies elements.

Group	Total Occurrence	Percentage of Occurrences	Cumulative Occurrence	Cumulative Percentage
דָּבָר (thing)	17	3.1%	261[28]	48.3%
שֵׁם (name)	16	3.0%	277	51.3%
בִּעֵר רַע (to purge bad)	14	2.6%	291	53.9%
COGNITION	12	2.2%	303	56.1%
AFFLICTION	11	2.0%	314	58.1%
חַיָּה (animal)	9	1.7%	323	59.8%
רוּחַ (spirit)	9	1.7%	332	61.5%
DEED	8	1.5%	340	63.0%
מַיִם (water)	7	1.3%	347	64.3%
TIME	6	1.1%	353	65.4%
יֵצֶר (inclination)	6	1.1%	359	66.5%
כֹּחַ (strength)	6	1.1%	365	67.6%

2.3 ANALYSIS: HOW רַע MODIFIES DISCOURSE ELEMENTS

Due to the usual nature of adjectives as modifying a discourse element with a schematic semantic content (schema), the following analysis attempts to identify the elements modified by רַע in each of the selected groups. This allows for some attention to be paid to the schema of רַע – how it modifies elements and what it evokes – and to test the definitions of both Dohmen and Myhill (who appear to focus on what could be considered the schematic meaning of רַע).

2.3.1 עָשָׂה רַע (to do bad)

The most common use of רַע in the analysed texts is (הָ)עָשָׂה רַע – to do (the) bad [thing]. It occurs 88 times in the analysed texts [80; 1; 7; 0; 0]. This use accounts for 16.3% of the uses of רַע. In 83% (73) of its uses, it appears with the article. In just six instances it occurs with רַע attributively modifying another word – either דָּבָר (thing/word) or מְאוּמָה (anything). In three occurrences it occurs in a construct phrase with כֹּל (every). Example 2.8 (below) demonstrates the way the phrase generally appears.

---

[28] Five uses of דָּבָר occur in the phrase עָשָׂה דָּבָר רַע and so overlap with עָשָׂה רַע. This means דָּבָר only contributes 12 occurrences to the cumulative occurrence and percentage.

46 CHAPTER 2

2.8. 1 Kings 11:6a

וַיַּעַשׂ שְׁלֹמֹה הָרַע בְּעֵינֵי יְהוָה

Solomon did the bad in the eyes of the LORD.[29]

Due to the nature of its occurrence as a relatively fixed phrase, it is expected these uses will present a relatively uniform use of רַע.

Occurrences: Gen 31:29; Num 32:13; Deut 4:25; 9:18; 13:12; 17:2, 5; 19:20; 31:29; Judg 2:11; 3:7, 12 (×2); 4:1; 6:1; 10:6; 13:1; 1 Sam 15:19; 29:7; 2 Sam 12:9; 1 Kgs 11:6; 14:22; 15:26, 34; 16:19, 25, 30; 21:20, 25; 22:53; 2 Kgs 3:2; 8:18, 27; 13:2, 11; 14:24; 15:9, 18, 24, 28; 17:2, 11, 17; 21:2, 6, 9, 15, 16, 20; 23:32, 37; 24:9, 19; Isa 56:2; 65:12; 66:4; Jer 7:30; 32:30; 39:12; 52:2; Mal 2:17; Ps 34:17; 51:6; Prov 2:14; Eccl 4:17; 8:11, 12; Neh 9:28; 13:17; 2 Chr 12:14; 21:6; 22:4; 29:6; 33:2, 6, 9, 22; 36:5, 9, 12; Sir 7:1 (C 3r8); 1QS I, 7; 1QH[a] VI, 29; 4Q370 1 I, 2; 4Q390 1, 4; 1, 9; 2 I, 8; 11Q19 LV, 16.

Modified Element(s)

The basic element modified by רַע in these uses is relatively straight-forward to determine. רַע functions in 82 of these occurrences as the grammatical object of the verb עָשָׂה, as in example 2.8 above. In this relationship, the element it modifies, by virtue of being the object of the verb עָשָׂה, is clearly construed as something done: an ACT. Example 2.9 demonstrates this clearly.

2.9. Deuteronomy 17:2b–3a

אִישׁ אוֹ־אִשָּׁה אֲשֶׁר יַעֲשֶׂה אֶת־הָרַע בְּעֵינֵי יְהוָה־אֱלֹהֶיךָ לַעֲבֹר בְּרִיתוֹ
וַיֵּלֶךְ וַיַּעֲבֹד אֱלֹהִים אֲחֵרִים וַיִּשְׁתַּחוּ לָהֶם

> …a man or a woman who does the bad [thing] in the eyes of the Lord your God, transgressing his covenant, who went and served other gods and bowed down to them…

The explanatory clauses in the following discourse elaborate on exactly which רַע thing is in view here. They make it clear that it is the ACT of serving other gods that is in view.

While it might be feasible that in an עָשָׂה רַע clause the element could be construed as something made (based on the semantics of עָשָׂה), this relationship never appears directly in the analysed texts. The closest use to this may be in Isaiah 45:7 (example 2.10). In this passage רַע is not the

---

[29] These examples have been considered uses of abstract nouns. However, these can be considered syntactically valid uses of the Hebrew Adjective. See n.19 §1.1.

רַע AND SCHEMA   47

grammatical object of עָשָׂה, but of בָּרָא (create). However, it is included with the rest of the list in the demonstrative pronominal object of עָשָׂה in the following clause (כָל־אֵלֶּה, all *these*).

2.10. Isaiah 45:7

יוֹצֵר אוֹר וּבוֹרֵא חֹשֶׁךְ עֹשֶׂה שָׁלוֹם וּבוֹרֵא רָע אֲנִי יְהוָה עֹשֶׂה כָל־אֵלֶּה

[I] form light and create darkness, make peace and create bad, I am the LORD who makes all these.

Thus, while it may have occurred, there are no examples in the analysed texts of רַע as the grammatical object of עָשָׂה modifying the element MADE.

In six occurrences רַע attributively modifies another word and forms part of the grammatical object of עָשָׂה. As is demonstrated in examples 2.11–2.13, the inclusion of the noun דָּבָר (thing) or מְאוּמָה (anything) does not appear to change the element in view: רַע still modifies an ACT.

2.11. Deuteronomy 17:5a

וְהוֹצֵאתָ אֶת־הָאִישׁ הַהוּא אוֹ אֶת־הָאִשָּׁה הַהִוא אֲשֶׁר עָשׂוּ אֶת־הַדָּבָר הָרָע הַזֶּה

You shall bring forth that man or that woman who did this bad thing...

2.12. Nehemiah 13:17b

וָאֹמְרָה לָהֶם מָה־הַדָּבָר הָרָע הַזֶּה אֲשֶׁר אַתֶּם עֹשִׂים וּמְחַלְּלִים אֶת־יוֹם הַשַּׁבָּת

...and I said to them, "What is this bad thing which you are doing, profaning the Sabbath day?"

2.13. Jeremiah 39:12

קָחֶנּוּ וְעֵינֶיךָ שִׂים עָלָיו וְאַל־תַּעַשׂ לוֹ מְאוּמָה רָע כִּי אִם כַּאֲשֶׁר יְדַבֵּר אֵלֶיךָ כֵּן עֲשֵׂה עִמּוֹ

Take him and set your eyes on him. Do not do anything bad to him, but as he says to you, do with him.

In examples 2.11–2.13, neither דָּבָר nor מְאוּמָה contributes anything substantial to the element רַע is modifying. As with example 2.9 above, the element on view is still an ACT. This can be seen even clearer when we consider that example 2.9 in the discourse refers to the same ACT as example 2.11, but without the presence of דָּבָר.

One clausal variation which may introduce an important variation in the element is the presence of the beneficiary in example 2.13. However, this also occurs in other examples, such as example 2.14 below.

2.14. Genesis 31:29a

יֶשׁ־לְאֵל יָדִי לַעֲשׂוֹת עִמָּכֶם רָע

It is within my power to do bad to you.

48 CHAPTER 2

The presence of the beneficiary narrows the type of acts that may be on view. These are specifically acts directed towards another person. This may be seen as a subset of the ACT category rather than a different element. For example, in example 2.15, the context refers to one who is found to be a false witness (עֵד־שֶׁקֶר) who planned to harm his אָח (brother/kinsman).

> 2.15. Deuteronomy 19:19a, 20b
>
> וַעֲשִׂיתֶם לוֹ כַּאֲשֶׁר זָמַם לַעֲשׂוֹת לְאָחִיו {...}
> וְלֹא־יֹסִפוּ לַעֲשׂוֹת עוֹד כַּדָּבָר הָרָע הַזֶּה בְּקִרְבֶּךָ
>
> You will do to him as he planned to do to his brother {…} and they will no longer do such a bad thing as this within you.

The "bad thing" on view here is acting with the intent to harm another, specifically through being a false witness. In verse 19 it is made clear that the ACT is one which has a beneficiary. Therefore, עָשָׂה רַע can refer to an ACT which has a beneficiary without the beneficiary being stated within the עָשָׂה רַע clause.

Modifying the Element(s)

Now that we have established what the modified element is, we may ask how the element is modified by רַע. What schematic content does רַע contribute to its clause? In some uses, רַע appears to indicate a negative evaluation of an ACT. We can see this use appearing in example 2.16.

> 2.16. Isaiah 65:12b
>
> יַעַן קָרָאתִי וְלֹא עֲנִיתֶם דִּבַּרְתִּי וְלֹא שְׁמַעְתֶּם וַתַּעֲשׂוּ הָרַע בְּעֵינַי וּבַאֲשֶׁר לֹא־חָפַצְתִּי בְּחַרְתֶּם
>
> …because I called and you did not answer, I spoke and you did not hear, you did the bad in my eyes and what I did not delight in, you chose.

The clausal parallel between the עָשָׂה (to do) clause and חָפֵץ (to delight) clause strengthens a reading in which רַע forms a negative evaluation – something which one does not like. This reading can also be seen in example 2.17.

> 2.17. 1 Samuel 29:6b–7
>
> חַי־יְהֹוָה כִּי־יָשָׁר אַתָּה וְטוֹב בְּעֵינַי צֵאתְךָ וּבֹאֲךָ אִתִּי בַּמַּחֲנֶה כִּי לֹא־מָצָאתִי בְךָ רָעָה מִיּוֹם בֹּאֲךָ אֵלַי עַד־הַיּוֹם הַזֶּה וּבְעֵינֵי הַסְּרָנִים לֹא־טוֹב אָתָּה
> וְעַתָּה שׁוּב וְלֵךְ בְּשָׁלוֹם וְלֹא־תַעֲשֶׂה רָע בְּעֵינֵי סַרְנֵי פְלִשְׁתִּים

רַע AND SCHEMA

"As the LORD lives, you are upright, so it is good in my eyes that you come and go with me in the army,[30] because I have not found wrong in you from the day you came to me until this day. However, in the eyes of the princes you are not good. Now, turn and go in peace. Do not do a bad [thing] in the eyes of the princes of the Philistines.

In this example, the Philistine king Achish provides an evaluation of David (and the reason for it) as the reason for his declaring a certain course of action to be "good in his eyes." However, the Philistine princes have given a different evaluation for a different reason (1 Sam 29:4–5). They reason that David, a renowned Israelite warrior, will turn on them in battle to gain Saul's favour. This leads to their evaluation of him as "not good" and consequently his fighting in the battle is "bad in their eyes."

We may question whether רַע profiles a negative evaluation, or simply the negative quality, with the evaluation aspect being driven by the phrase בְּעֵינֵי (in the eyes of). Indeed, some uses appear to make a clear case for רַע being something that can go beyond individual evaluations, to what is more generally recognised. We see this in example 2.18.

2.18. Malachi 2:17b

בֶּאֱמָרְכֶם כָּל־עֹשֵׂה רָע טוֹב | בְּעֵינֵי יְהוָה וּבָהֶם הוּא חָפֵץ

…when you say, "All doers of bad are good in the eyes of the LORD, and in them he delights."

The implication in example 2.18 is that there is a certain verifiable or objective standard against which certain acts can be recognised as רַע. Without such a standard it would not be outrageous to suggest that the Lord considers such people to be טוֹב (good). This example appears to provide counter evidence to Myhill's subjective רַע.

Example 2.19 provides more in support of this, suggesting an ACT, objectively evaluated as רַע, which the Lord opposes.

2.19. Psalm 34:17

פְּנֵי יְהוָה בְּעֹשֵׂי רָע לְהַכְרִית מֵאֶרֶץ זִכְרָם

The face of the LORD is against doers of bad, to cut their remembrance off from the land.

רַע may also be used to evoke a scale. Whereas in example 2.18, what is evoked is the distinct, objective line between רַע and טוֹב, in example 2.20, a scale of רַע is evoked.

---

[30] See Clines, "מַחֲנֶה 3b," *DCH* 5:223.

50   CHAPTER 2

2.20. 2 Kings 21:9

וְלֹא שָׁמֵעוּ וַיַּתְעֵם מְנַשֶּׁה לַעֲשׂוֹת אֶת־הָרָע מִן־הַגּוֹיִם אֲשֶׁר הִשְׁמִיד יְהוָה מִפְּנֵי
בְּנֵי יִשְׂרָאֵל

They did not listen, and Manasseh led them astray to do worse than
the nations whom the LORD had destroyed before the children of
Israel.

The scale is clear in example 2.20 through use of the comparative מִן
construction. In this scale one group may be said to ACT in a way that is
to a greater degree רַע (i.e. worse) than another.

All uses of the עָשָׂה רַע clause in the analysed texts appear to fit in
with this general description of רַע: a simple negative modification of the
element ACT. Furthermore, there was some evidence to suggest that רַע
is used in an objective fashion. It appears to be used in both objective and
subjective ways.[31] Additionally, the evidence points to רַע having the flexibility to evoke a scale of severity (example 2.20) or simply a category
(e.g. example 2.18).

2.3.2 HUMAN

The next most common use of רַע in the selected groupings is when it
modifies a HUMAN discourse element. This accounts for 57 (10.6%) occurrences of רַע in the analysed texts [37; 14; 0; 0; 6]. In 33 of these occurrences, רַע appears without syntactically modifying another word either
attributively or predicatively. In the remaining 26 occurrences רַע modifies a range of words including: אָב (father), אִישׁ (man), אָדָם (human),
אִשָּׁה (woman), בַּת (daughter), דּוֹר (generation), הָמָן (Haman), חָבֵר (com-
panion), חֵלֶק (lot), מִשְׁפָּחָה (family), עֶבֶד (slave), עֵדָה (congregation), עֵר
(Er), עַם (people), שָׁכֵן (neighbour). This variation in this group immediately alerts us to the likelihood that we will find multiple HUMAN discourse elements.

Occurrences: Gen 13:13; 28:8; 38:7; Exod 21:8; Num 11:1, 10;
14:27, 35; Deut 1:35; 1 Sam 30:22; Jer 2:33; 6:29; 8:3; 12:14; 13:10;
15:21; Ezek 7:24; 30:12; Ps 10:15; 140:2; Job 21:30; 35:12; Prov 2:12;
4:14; 6:24; 11:21; 12:12, 13; 14:19; 15:3; 17:11; 24:20; 28:5; 29:6;

---

[31] Given that words always (or almost always) move from objective to subjective meanings
(subjectification), but not the other way around, finding evidence for objectivity discon-
firms Myhill's arguments. Hollmann demonstrates subjectification with the example of
very in Middle English which referred to truth (i.e. very knight), but now is a subjective
assertion "a very interesting area." Hollmann, "Semantic Change," 246.

רַע AND SCHEMA 51

Esth 7:6; Neh 2:1; 1 Chr 2:3; Sir 6:1 (A 2r6); 11:33 (A 4v25); 12:4 (A 5r5); 12:6 (A 5r5); 14:6 (A 5v25); 31:24 (B 4v6); 33:27 (E 1v16); 37:3 (B 7r11), 11 (B 7v3); 39:25 (B 9r13)*, 27 (B 9r16)*; 41:5 (B 10v14); 42:5 (Mas1h 4:11), 6 (B 11v8); m. Ned. 9:3; m. Soṭah 1:4; m. 'Abot 1:7; 2:9 (×2); 5:12.

Modified Element(s)

A common element that רַע modifies in this group is HUMAN(BEHAVIOUR). That is, רַע qualifies a human with respect to their behaviour. This can be shown in a number of configurations. In example 2.21, רַע modifies HUMAN(BEHAVIOUR) and does not syntactically modify another word through attributive, predicative, or construct relations.

2.21. Job 21:30–31

כִּי לְיוֹם אֵיד יֵחָשֶׂךְ רָע לְיוֹם עֲבָרוֹת יוּבָלוּ
מִי־יַגִּיד עַל־פָּנָיו דַּרְכּוֹ וְהוּא־עָשָׂה מִי יְשַׁלֶּם־לוֹ

That the bad one is spared on the day of calamity, they are carried [i.e. rescued] on the day of wrath? Who will declare his way to his face, and who will repay him [for] what he has done?

רַע here clearly modifies a human. Furthermore, from verse 31, we can see that it is his way or pattern of behaviour (דַּרְכּוֹ) and what he has done (עָשָׂה) which is in view. In this case, the element in view is the BEHAVIOUR of the human.[32] That is, the combinative use of רַע here refers to people who act in ways that are considered bad.

HUMAN(BEHAVIOUR) is also commonly in view when אִישׁ is modified.

2.22. Genesis 13:13 (cf. Gen 18.20, 23–32)

וְאַנְשֵׁי סְדֹם רָעִים וְחַטָּאִים לַיהוָה מְאֹד

The men of Sodom were bad and great sinners to the LORD.

2.23. Ben Sira 37:10–11 (Sir D 1r14, 17b)

אל תועץ {...}
עם אִישׁ רַע על גמילות חסד

Do not consult {...} with a bad man concerning repayment for loyalty.

---

[32] It is, at times, difficult to differentiate between ACT and BEHAVIOUR as they commonly sit together (see §2.3.5 and §A.2). However, in the context here, what is important is the pattern of behaviour rather than an isolated ACT: the comment concerns those who gain power through oppression as in verse 28 אַיֵּה בֵית־נָדִיב וְאַיֵּה אֹהֶל | מִשְׁכְּנוֹת רְשָׁעִים (Where is the house of the prince, and where is the tent of the dwellings of the wicked ones?).

52 CHAPTER 2

In these examples, the discourse indicates that the BEHAVIOUR of the person(s) is in view. In example 2.22, this is indicated by חַטָּאִים, and clarified for the modern reader by the discussion between the Lord and Abraham in Genesis 18:20, 23–32. In example 2.23, the instruction implies an אִישׁ רַע will not give good advice concerning repayment for loyalty because of bias.[33]

We also see this element in the following mishnaic use where רַע modifies אָב (father).

> 2.24. m. Nedarim 9:3b
>
> אָמ' קוֹנָס שֶׁאֵנִי נוֹשֵׂא לִפְלוֹנִית שֶׁאָבִיהָ רַע אָמְרוּ לוֹ מֵת [אוֹ] שֶׁעָשָׂה תְשׁוּבָה
>
> [If] he said, "Qonas[34] if I marry a certain one because her father is bad." They said to him, "He died." or that "He repented."

In example 2.24, the HUMAN(BEHAVIOUR) element can be deduced by the reference to תְּשׁוּבָה (repentance) – turning from behaviour – which negates the vow made on the basis of the father being רַע.

While what constitutes רַע HUMAN(BEHAVIOUR) may differ, when רַע modifies a human female, it appears that behaviour is often in view.

> 2.25. Jeremiah 2:33
>
> מַה־תֵּיטִבִי דַּרְכֵּךְ לְבַקֵּשׁ אַהֲבָה לָכֵן גַּם אֶת־הָרָעוֹת לִמַּדְתִּי אֶת־דְּרָכָיִךְ
>
> How well you direct[35] your way to seek love that you[36] have even taught the bad women your ways.

It is somewhat enigmatic as to who the bad women are. However, from the context it seems that they are understood here as women who seek illicit relationships. In this passage Israel is personified as a bride (Jer 2:2) who has turned away from her husband to seek illicit relationships – representing the people's turning to other gods. It is presented as remarkable that they are even able to teach the רָעוֹת (bad women) their ways – suggesting that they know the business of the רָעוֹת better than the רָעוֹת do.

---

[33] The series of people Ben Sira says not to consult with contrast with the one who always fears God in 37:12. For context, two other items in the list demonstrating bias are: עם אשה אל צרתה (with a woman concerning her rival); ומלוכד על מלחמה (and from a captured person concerning war).

[34] Vocalic substitute for "Qorban," "used for a vow of abstinence." See Jastrow, קוֹנָס and קוֹנָם.

[35] See Clines, "יטב 5," *DCH* 4:205.

[36] This translation follows the Qere which, syntactically speaking, makes sense of the passage. The Ketiv and Qere forms may represent differences between the written and oral traditions of the text as transmitted since the texts were composed. Yosef Ofer, *The Masora on Scripture and Its Methods* (Berlin: De Gruyter, 2018), 85–107.

רַע AND SCHEMA   53

This use, then, appears to favour the element of HUMAN(BEHAVIOUR) – specifically sexual behaviour. This can also be seen in example 2.26.

> 2.26. Proverbs 6:24–25a

לִשְׁמָרְךָ מֵאֵשֶׁת רָע מֵחֶלְקַת לָשׁוֹן נָכְרִיָּה
אַל־תַּחְמֹד יָפְיָהּ בִּלְבָבֶךָ

> ...to keep you from the bad woman, from the smooth foreign tongue. Do not desire her beauty in your heart...

In this example, the bad woman (lit. woman of bad)[37] refers to a woman who pursues illicit relationships, implying the element HUMAN(BEHAVIOUR). This is made clear by (among other things) the command not to desire her beauty, and later (Prov 6:29) the reference to one who comes (הַבָּא) to the wife of his neighbour (אֵשֶׁת רֵעֵהוּ).

In example 2.27, the modified element is still HUMAN(BEHAVIOUR), but the focus may be wider than in examples 2.24–2.25 where sexually illicit behaviour was on view.

> 2.27. Ben Sira 42:1b, 6a (Sir B 11v3b, 8a)

אך על אלה אל תבוש {...}
על אשה רעה חותם חכם

> Only concerning these [things] you should not be ashamed {...} of putting a wise seal on a bad wife.

This example from Ben Sira refers to using a seal to prevent a bad wife from leaving home.[38] In this sense the element being modified is most likely HUMAN(BEHAVIOUR) with the behaviour being anything which an אִשָּׁה (wife) may be considered (by the ancient Israelite) likely to do if she is רַע and permitted to leave home.[39]

Uses of people groups also appear to modify the element BEHAVIOUR.

> 2.28. Deuteronomy 1:35[40]

אִם־יִרְאֶה אִישׁ בָּאֲנָשִׁים הָאֵלֶּה הַדּוֹר הָרָע הַזֶּה אֵת הָאָרֶץ הַטּוֹבָה אֲשֶׁר נִשְׁבַּעְתִּי
לָתֵת לַאֲבֹתֵיכֶם

---

[37] This is an unusual way for the relationship between noun and adjective to be expressed. One might interpret it as the wife of a bad man. However, it is the more natural reading to see רָע as qualifying אִשָּׁה and there is a comparable use: in Proverbs 28:5, אַנְשֵׁי־רָע (bad men) occurs.

[38] Skehan and Di Lella, *The Wisdom of Ben Sira*, 482.

[39] It is possible that in addition to sexual misconduct, misconduct of speech (and possibly other areas) are in view. Misconduct of speech is viewed as a negative quality for a wife in Proverbs 21:9 // 25:24 (אֵשֶׁת מִדְיָנִים, wife of quarrelling) and Ben Sira 25:20 (Sir C 5r12–5v2 = אשת לשון, wife of tongue).

[40] Cf. Numbers 14:27, 35 and the use modifying עֵדָה.

54   CHAPTER 2

Not one of these men, this bad generation will see the good land which
I swore to give to your fathers...

2.29. Jeremiah 13:10a, c

הָעָם הַזֶּה הָרָע הַמֵּאֲנִים | לִשְׁמוֹעַ אֶת־דְּבָרַי {...} וַיֵּלְכוּ אַחֲרֵי אֱלֹהִים אֲחֵרִים לְעָבְדָם

This bad people, who refuse to hear my words {...} and went after
other gods to serve them...

In examples 2.28 and 2.29, HUMAN(BEHAVIOUR) is clearly in view. In
example 2.28, the event being described which justifies the label רַע is
the behaviour of the Israelites in refusing to trust the Lord by fighting the
Amorites (Deut 1:27–33). In example 2.29, the people are labelled as
those who served other gods – their behaviour being on view.

In contrast, consider example 2.30 where evidence of BEHAVIOUR is not
found in the discourse.

2.30. Genesis 28:8–9

וַיַּרְא עֵשָׂו כִּי רָעוֹת בְּנוֹת כְּנָעַן בְּעֵינֵי יִצְחָק אָבִיו
וַיֵּלֶךְ עֵשָׂו אֶל־יִשְׁמָעֵאל וַיִּקַּח אֶת־מָחֲלַת | בַּת־יִשְׁמָעֵאל בֶּן־אַבְרָהָם אֲחוֹת נְבָיוֹת
עַל־נָשָׁיו לוֹ לְאִשָּׁה

Esau saw that the daughters of Canaan [i.e. Esau's Canaanite wives] were
bad in the eyes of Isaac his father. [So] Esau went to Ishmael and he
took Mahalat, daughter of Ishmael, son of Abraham, sister of Nebaiot,
as his wife in addition to his [other] wives.

In this example it seems more likely that the reason for the women
being considered רַע is related to kinship (Gen 27:46–28:2). Endogamous
marriages (within the kinship group) were generally preferred over exogamous marriages among the ancient Israelite people group:[41] Isaac's father,
Abraham, instructed his servant to find a wife for Isaac from among his
family, specifically saying that he should not find a wife from בְּנוֹת כְּנַעֲנִי
(the daughters of the Canaanites; Gen 24:3–4). Here then, the element is
HUMAN(KINSHIP), this is made explicit by the use of כְּנָעַן (of Canaan) not
to mention Esau's solution to the problem: an endogamous marriage
within Abraham's wider descendants.[42]

---

[41] Exogamous marriages build relationships with other people groups (Gen 34:9–10, 16).
Conversely, endogamous marriages strengthen existing relationships. Victor Harold
Matthews and Don C. Benjamin, *Social World of Ancient Israel, 1250–587 BCE* (Peabody, MA: Hendrickson, 1993), 13–17. Howell and Paris suggest that Jacob and Rachel
were defending the patrilineage by taking the birth right and blessing. Brian M. Howell
and Jenell Paris, *Introducing Cultural Anthropology: A Christian Perspective*, 2nd ed.
(Grand Rapids, MI: Baker, 2019), 173–74.

[42] This concept is recognised by commentators, but not explained explicitly in terms of
KINSHIP. For example see Bruce K Waltke, *Genesis: A Commentary* (Grand Rapids, MI:

רַע AND SCHEMA — 55

There is one use which appears to modify the element of APPEARANCE.

2.31. Nehemiah 2:1b–2

וָאֶשָּׂא אֶת־הַיַּיִן וָאֶתְּנָה לַמֶּלֶךְ וְלֹא־הָיִיתִי רַע לְפָנָיו
וַיֹּאמֶר לִי הַמֶּלֶךְ מַדּוּעַ | פָּנֶיךָ רָעִים וְאַתָּה אֵינְךָ חוֹלֶה אֵין זֶה כִּי־אִם רֹעַ לֵב וָאִירָא
הַרְבֵּה מְאֹד

> I took the wine and gave it to the king. I had not been bad in his presence
> [before].[43] The king said to me, "Why is your face bad? You are not
> sick, this can be nothing but badness of heart." I was very afraid.

In example 2.31, it is clear that the initial use of רַע, which modifies the
speaker (Nehemiah), is describing the state of having a bad face, badness
of heart, or both. This can be profitably compared with Ben Sira 13:25
(example 2.32).

2.32. Ben Sira 13:25 (Sir A 5v19)

לֵב אנוש ישנא פניו אם לטוב ואם לרע

> The heart of a person will change his face, whether for good or for bad.

From this statement in Ben Sira and from a similar one in Proverbs (15:13),
it seems that there was considered to be a direct link between appearance
and internal state. Thus, it seems reasonable that in example 2.31, the first
use of רַע – which modifies a HUMAN rather than BODY PART – is referring
to appearance.[44] Because of his רַע APPEARANCE, the king presumes his
internal state is also bad (רֹעַ לֵב).[45]

Example 2.33 displays another use in which the modified element does
not appear to be limited to BEHAVIOUR.

2.33. Exodus 21:7a, 8a, c

וְכִי־יִמְכֹּר אִישׁ אֶת־בִּתּוֹ לְאָמָה {...}
אִם־רָעָה בְּעֵינֵי אֲדֹנֶיהָ אֲשֶׁר־לֹא[46] יְעָדָהּ וְהֶפְדָּהּ {...} בְּבִגְדוֹ־בָהּ

> If a man sells his daughter as a female slave {...} if [she is] bad in the
> eyes of her lord so that[47] he has not designated her, then he shall let
> her be redeemed {...} because he has behaved treacherously with her.

Zondervan, 2001), 383; Gordon J. Wenham, *Genesis 16–50*, WBC 2 (Waco, TX: Word,
1994), 214.

[43] [before] is included to make the temporal sense of the clause – which is apparent from
the discourse – clear.

[44] Cf. Nehemiah 2:3 which further strengthens the case for this use referring to APPEARANCE.

[45] See §2.3.4 for more on BODY PART usage.

[46] Qere reads לוֹ (who has designated her to himself). לֹא appears to make more sense of
the description "behaved treacherously" because in that case he would be expected to
"designate" her, but he has not.

[47] The result use of אֲשֶׁר as a subordinating conjunction is considered rare. However, it
makes the most sense of this clause as it explains the actions of the lord (אָדוֹן) which

56 CHAPTER 2

Here the element appears to be some aspect concerning which a person who is an אָמָה might be evaluated. The discourse lacks information that might help us evaluate the element more specifically than this. It appears that the sale is expected to end in marriage or concubinage, either to her master (אָדוֹן) or his son (Exod 21:9).[48] If her master does not designate her it is a breach of the contract so "he has behaved treacherously." In this case, it seems that רַע refers to anything negative which may lead to the master neglecting to designate the אָמָה. This points to a general view of רַע as modifying any element applicable by the ancient Israelite culture to the אָמָה: that is, something which makes their master consider them unsuitable.[49]

The evidence has shown that when רַע directly modifies a HUMAN, the specific elements it modifies vary. Identified elements include: BEHAVIOUR, KINSHIP, and APPEARANCE. In addition, example 2.33 provides an example where the element might simply be anything applicable to a human with the role in question (אָמָה). Therefore, this range of elements likely indicates that רַע may modify any element applicable to a human or the role in which that human is described. The element is not specified by the use of רַע, but by the cognitive context of the use.

While the elements of BEHAVIOUR, KINSHIP, and APPEARANCE are described as single elements, this does not imply uniformity. Variation is seen in the elements described as HUMAN(BEHAVIOUR). In the examples specific behaviours were sometimes clear from the surrounding discourse (e.g. sexual behaviour, examples 2.25–2.26), whereas at other times it seemed more general (e.g. example 2.27). Where behaviours are not specified, it is expected that cognitive context more widely may provide the context required (i.e. through cultural categories). That is to say, some things considered by the ancient Israelite to be רַע for an אָב (father) to do would not overlap with things considered רַע for an אִשָּׁה (woman/wife) to do. This is due to the expected duties/roles of different groups within society.

Modifying the Element(s)

As with many of the cases of עָשָׂה רַע use, in some of the cases where רַע modifies HUMAN discourse elements it is clearly a negative judgement.

could be considered treacherous (בָּגַד). Van der Merwe, Naudé and Kroeze, *A Biblical Hebrew Reference Grammar*, §36.3.1.1.5.b.

[48] Scholarly opinion is divided on whether the אָמָה should be considered a wife or concubine. T. Desmond Alexander, *Exodus*, ApOTC 2 (London: Apollos, 2017), 475.

[49] Propp suggests that this may include unattractiveness. This seems plausible. William H. C. Propp, *Exodus 19–40: A New Translation with Introduction and Commentary*, AB 2A (New York: Doubleday, 2006), 197.

רַע AND SCHEMA

In Genesis 28:8 (example 2.30) which modifies KINSHIP, the women are said to be bad בְּעֵינֵי יִצְחָק (in the eyes of Isaac). This refers to a negative judgement of their KINSHIP status by Isaac. Similarly, in Exodus 21:8 (example 2.33) the אָמָה (female slave) is said to be evaluated בְּעֵינֵי אֲדֹנֶיהָ (in the eyes of her lord). In example 2.33, it seems that the evidence is in favour of seeing this as any negative judgement of the אָמָה which would make her lord want to get rid of her.[50]

While רַע appears to have more specific use in other cases, this can usually be attributed to the discourse. For example, in Jeremiah 2:33 (example 2.25), although רָעוֹת does not directly modify any term, the discourse makes clear that illicit sexual behaviour is in view. It is natural then, that this use should be interpreted in light of what bad things are being discussed in the discourse: that is, the women are evaluated negatively with respect to sexual behaviour (the element determined from discourse).[51]

In many cases, an objective moral meaning may be implied. It might be argued that the term means something akin to "evil." However, in such cases the objective sense may be adequately derived from the text. Where the discourse lacks reference to subjectivity, appearing to present an evaluation which has no indication that the reader may disagree, we may reasonably take רַע to be objective in use. Ben Sira 12:2–4 is a good example of this:

2.34. Ben Sira 12:2–4

היטב לצדיק ומצא תשלומת אם לא ממנו מייי
אין טובה למנוח רשע וגם צדקה לא עשה
תן לטוב ומנע מרע

Do good to the righteous and find a reward, if not from him, from the LORD. There is nothing good for the one who gives rest[52] to the wicked, he does not even do an act of charity. Give to the good, and withhold from the bad.

---

[50] This last bit can be seen from Exodus 21:8 specifying that under such conditions the אָמָה should be able to be redeemed, or, if he treats her poorly, set free for nothing (Exod 21:11). That is, her master must want to be rid of her without a chance of financial gain.

[51] It may be that רָעוֹת refers to a specific category of people in ancient Israelite thought. This is attractive because the text appears to refer to a known group. However, this cannot be established or discredited from the available evidence. Regardless, it is clear from the discourse that the רָעוֹת in example 2.24 are women evaluated negatively with respect to illicit sexual activity.

[52] This translation treats מנוח verbally. This makes the most sense of the passage, and is supported by Skehan, and Parker and Abegg. Skehan and Di Lella, *The Wisdom of Ben Sira*, 242; Oaktree Software, "Ben Sira English," ed. Benjamin H. Parker and Martin G. Jr. Abegg, 2008, https://www.accordancebible.com/store/details/?pid=BENSIRA-E.

58 CHAPTER 2

In example 2.34, the *righteous*, the *wicked*, the *good*, and the *bad* are all groups which the reader is expected to be able to identify. The writer assumes that the reader will identify the same people as them and in the preceding discourse presents objective outcomes which the negative groups bring about.[53]

From the evidence, there is no clear reason to believe that רַע modifies HUMAN discourse elements beyond the simple negative modification which was seen in §2.3.1. The combinative meaning appears to be governed by the elements (and what is considered by the ancient Israelite to be a negative qualification of the element), with רַע contributing a negative judgement of that element.

2.3.3 COMMODITY

A more difficult grouping to determine concerns elements that relate to common commodities.[54] These uses account for around 43 (8.0%) occurrences of רַע in the analysed texts [20; 1; 2; 0; 20]. In 21 of these occurrences, 13 of which are in the Mishnah, רַע appears without syntactically modifying another word attributively, predicatively, or through a construct relation. In the remaining 23 occurrences, it modified the following words: אֶרֶץ (land), בָּצָל (onion), יַיִן (wine), מַאֲכָל (food), מַרְאֶה (appearance), מָעָה (a coin), מָקוֹם (place), נָוֶה (dwelling), נֶטַע (plant), פָּרָה (cow), צֶמַח (plant), תְּאֵנָה (fig).

Occurrences: Gen 41:3 (×2),[55] 4 (×2),[56] 19, 20, 21, 27; Lev 27:10 (×2), 12, 14, 33; Num 13:19, 20:5; Jer 24:2, 3 (×2), 8; Prov 20:14; Sir 3:28 (Sir A 1r18); 4Q365 32, 7; HazGab 22*; m. Ter. 2:6 (×4); 6:6; m. Ketub. 13:10 (×3); m. Ned. 9:8 (×2); m. B. Meṣ. 4:1 (×2); m. B. Bat. 5:6 (×4); m. ʿArak. 9:2; m. Meʿil. 6:4 (×2); m. Zabim 2:2.

---

[53] For example, Ben Sira 11:34a reads לא תדבק לרשע ויסלף דרכך ויהפכך מבריתיך (Do not cling to a wicked [person], he will subvert your way and turn you from your covenant).

[54] It was difficult to determine how to treat land. King and Stager point out that "Land was inalienable (at least in principle) and was not a commodity but patrimony, subject to the customary rules of inheritance." King and Stager, *Life in Biblical Israel*, 193. However, technically land could still be sold, it just could not be sold irrevocably (Lev 25:23–28). Therefore, land was included with the commodities. Technically, human categories such as slaves might also be included in this group. These will not be considered here because they are considered in the group where רַע modifies a HUMAN discourse element.

[55] MT and Samaritan Pentateuch.

[56] MT and Samaritan Pentateuch.

רע AND SCHEMA

59

Modified Element(s)

It is obvious at a glance that multiple elements are being modified in this group. It is logical that the relevant element(s) for אֶרֶץ (land) will be different from מַאֲכָל (food), or מָעָה (coin). A small selection of examples from this group is provided below (examples 2.35–2.37). This will be followed by an examination of some less straightforward cases.

2.35. Leviticus 27:32–33b

וְכָל־מַעְשַׂר בָּקָר וָצֹאן כֹּל אֲשֶׁר־יַעֲבֹר תַּחַת הַשָּׁבֶט הָעֲשִׂירִי יִהְיֶה־קֹּדֶשׁ לַיהוָה
לֹא יְבַקֵּר בֵּין־טוֹב לָרַע וְלֹא יְמִירֶנּוּ

For every tithe of the herd and flock, every tenth which passes under the staff will be holy to the Lord. One shall not seek [to distinguish] between good and bad, nor substitute for it.

In this example the syntactic referent is הָעֲשִׂירִי (the tenth). It includes both בָּקָר (herd) animals and צֹאן (flock) animals. Therefore, the element is LIVESTOCK and is general with respect to class of livestock.

2.36. Numbers 20:5

וְלָמָה הֶעֱלִיתֻנוּ מִמִּצְרַיִם לְהָבִיא אֹתָנוּ אֶל־הַמָּקוֹם הָרַע הַזֶּה לֹא | מְקוֹם זֶרַע
וּתְאֵנָה וְגֶפֶן וְרִמּוֹן וּמַיִם אַיִן לִשְׁתּוֹת

Why have you made us come up from Egypt, to bring us to this bad place? It is not a place of fig and vine and pomegranate, and there is no water to drink!

In this example the element is clearly LAND, specifically viewed with reference to its arable quality.

2.37. m. Terumot 2:6b

זֶה הַכְּלָל כָּל שֶׁהוּא כִלְאַיִם בַּחֲבֵירוֹ לֹא יִתְרוֹם מִזֶּה עַל זֶה אֲפִילוּ מִן הַיָּפֶה עַל
הָרַע

This is the general rule: if the two kinds [of produce] are Diverse Kinds,[57] he may not separate heave-offering from one in place of the other, even from the better in place of the worse.

In this example, the discourse contains a discussion about how heave offering is separated from kinds of produce. After discussing various cases, the general rule (example 2.37) is stated. The element in this example is PRODUCE.

---

[57] Following Danby's translation of כִּלְאַיִם.

60 CHAPTER 2

One example which is more complex was examined in detail in example 2.1, §2.1.2 (example 2.38 below). It was argued that the element is the ASKING PRICE of goods.

2.38. Proverbs 20:14

רַע רַע יֹאמַר הַקּוֹנֶה וְאֹזֵל לֹו אָז יִתְהַלָּל

"Bad! Bad!" says the buyer, and going away he boasts.

This example will not be repeated. However, two additional examples (2.39 and 2.40) are examined below.

2.39. Ben Sira 3:28 (Sir A 1r17–18)

אל תרוץ לרפאות מכ}{ל}{<<ת>> ליק כי אין לה רפואה כי מנטע רע נטעו

Do not hasten to heal the wound of a scoffer, because there is no remedy for it: he is a shoot from a bad plant.

Although this is used to describe a person, it does so metaphorically, and in the metaphor it is important that רַע modify the element PLANT. This refers to plants which are cultivated through plant cuttings and shoots, such as with the vine (and requires an understanding of vine cultivation known to ancient Israel).[58] The metaphor works on the fact that a shoot from a bad plant can only produce another bad plant.[59]

2.40. m. Nedarim 9:8a

קוֹנָס יַיִן שֶׁאֲנִי טוֹעֵם שֶׁהַיַּיִן רַע לַמֵּעַיִים

"Qonas[60] if I taste wine, because wine is bad for the belly."

In example 2.40, רַע modifies יַיִן (wine). However, as with the construct phrase, so with the preposition phrase לַמֵּעַיִים: it specifies the aspect with which יַיִן is considered bad. Therefore, the element modified is not WINE or BELLY, but the element modified is the interaction: EFFECT OF WINE ON THE BELLY. It is because of this interaction that the speaker binds themselves by oath not to drink wine, and it is this element that is modified. This is made clearer when considering the following line:

2.41. m. Nedarim 9:8b

אָמְרוּ לֹו וַהֲלֹא מְיוּשָּׁן יָפֶה לַמֵּעַיִים הוּתַר בִּמְיוּשָּׁן לֹא בִמְיוּשָּׁן בִּלְבָד הוּתַר אֶלָּא
בְּכָל הַיַּיִן

---

[58] King and Stager, *Life in Biblical Israel*, 98.

[59] This would be well known in such an agricultural society (cf. Matt 7:16–20; 12:33; James 3:12).

[60] Vocalic substitute for "Qorban," "used for a vow of abstinence." See Jastrow, קוֹנָס and קוֹנָם.

רַע AND SCHEMA

They said to him, "Is not old [wine] good for the belly?" He is permitted with respect to old [wine], [and] he is not permitted with old [wine] alone, but with all wine.

Example 2.41 makes clear that if some wine is not bad for the belly then the premise for calling wine (in general) bad is false and the oath is annulled. It is the preposition phrase, together with the words for wine, which indicate which element is modified.

Modifying the Element(s)

In the examples above (2.35–2.41), it appears likely that רַע modifies elements by providing a simple negative judgement – the same way it was found to operate in §2.3.1 and §2.3.2. However, as with example 2.20 (§2.3.1), some of these examples also provide evidence of a continuous scale with degrees of goodness and badness. This is evident in examples 2.35 and 2.37, where the text implies an evaluation on a continuous scale from רַע to טוֹב and רַע to יָפֶה (bad to good).[61] This scalar use is seen clearly in the valuation of a dedicated house (example 2.42).

2.42. Leviticus 27:14

וְאִישׁ כִּי־יַקְדִּשׁ אֶת־בֵּיתוֹ קֹדֶשׁ לַיהוָה וְהֶעֱרִיכוֹ הַכֹּהֵן בֵּין טוֹב וּבֵין רַע כַּאֲשֶׁר יַעֲרִיךְ אֹתוֹ הַכֹּהֵן כֵּן יָקוּם

When a man dedicates his house as holy to the LORD, the priest shall value it between good and bad, as the priest values it, so it shall stand.

The implication here is that there are not two set values, but that the priest is to discern the value of a specific house. This is unsurprising. For a term used in trade that provides a simple negative judgement with a simple positive judgement as its opposite we would be surprised if there was not a scalar dimension. Trade would be severely hampered if there were only two categories of value.

In the area of commodities, the scale can be either foregrounded (e.g. example 2.42) or not (e.g. example 2.38). While there may be degrees of רַע imagined in example 2.38, this is not relevant to the scene. However,

---

[61] The alternation between טוֹב and יָפֶה from biblical to mishnaic use is of interest from a semantic change perspective, but does not appear to convey much concerning *how* רַע modifies elements. The use of טוֹב and יָפֶה may vary depending on which elements are modified (in mishnaic use), as יָפֶה appears to take over some, but not all uses which טוֹב had earlier. For a partial analysis on the change in use of יָפֶה see Foster, "Is Everything 'Beautiful' or 'Appropriate' in Its Time?"

62   CHAPTER 2

in example 2.42, the scale is important to the scene as the quality and
therefore value of the house is set. As was seen with ACT in §2.3.1, רַע,
in certain uses, evokes a scale.

2.3.4 BODY PART

There are 28 occurrences (5.2%) in the analysed text where רַע modifies
a body part [11; 6; 2; 0; 9]. Just three of these occurrences occur without
modifying the body part through attributive, predicative, or construct relations. The remaining uses modify: לֵב (heart), לָשׁוֹן (tongue), פָּנִים (face),
and עַיִן (eye). The use of the phrases יַד רַע and כַּף רַע (hand/palm of bad)
deserve comment here too.

Occurrences: Gen 40:7; Jer 3:17; 7:24; 11:8; 16:12; 18:12; Prov 23:6;
25:20; 26:23; 28:22; Neh 2:2; Sir 13:25 (Sir A 5v19); 14:3 (Sir A 5v23);
14:10 (Sir A 5v27); 31:13 (Sir B 4r3; Sir B 4r4 ×2); 4Q393 3, 5; 4Q525
13, 2*; m. Ter. 4:3; m. Soṭah 9:15; m. 'Abot 2:9 (×2); 11; 5:13 (×2),
19; m. ʿArak. 3:5.

Modified Element(s)

As with §2.3.2 and §2.3.3, due to the nature of the grouping, a variety of
elements are on view. As was hinted at in example 2.3 (§2.1.3) and examples 2.31 and 2.32 (§2.3.2), BODY PART terms can be used to refer to more
than the physical objects themselves. Furthermore, a direct link between
internal and external states may have been understood (example 2.31,
§2.3.2). It is outside the scope of this paper to examine the exact uses of
the different BODY PART terms, which, from examining a lexicon, can be
quickly seen as quite broad. Elements modified when the different words
are used are presented below, starting with לֵב.

2.43. Proverbs 25:20

מַעֲדֶה בֶּגֶד ׀ בְּיוֹם קָרָה חֹמֶץ עַל־נָתֶר וְשָׁר בַּשִּׁרִים עַל לֶב־רָע

One who takes off clothes on a cold day, vinegar on a wound,[62] and
one who sings songs to[63] a bad heart.

---

[62] Clines "נתר II," *DCH* 5:817–18. Greek: ἕλκει. Waltke demonstrates that this is the
most likely interpretation for נָתֶר here. Bruce K. Waltke, *The Book of Proverbs: Chapters 15–31*, NICOT (Grand Rapids, MI: Eerdmans, 2005), 306. Either it refers to something irritating, or something that renders something else (a sodium mineral) ineffective.
Roland E. Murphy, *Proverbs*, WBC 22 (Nashville, TN: Nelson, 2000), 189, 193.
[63] The preposition עַל marks the addressee (cf. Job 33:27; Isa 40:2; Jer 6:10; Hos 2:16).

רַע AND SCHEMA

63

In example 2.43, we can see that the element in view is a mental state: HEART(EMOTION). The proverb makes this clear through comparison with the set of things that should not go together.[64]

2.44. Jeremiah 11:8a

וְלֹא שָׁמְעוּ וְלֹא־הִטּוּ אֶת־אָזְנָם וַיֵּלְכוּ אִישׁ בִּשְׁרִירוּת לִבָּם הָרָע

They did not listen, they did not incline their ear, and they went each in the stubbornness of their bad heart.

In example 2.44, we can see from the discourse that the element refers to the thing that a person wants to do. Thus it might be termed HEART(WILL). לָשׁוֹן (tongue) is only modified by רַע in the Mishnah.

2.45. m. ʿArakin 3:5b

הָאוֹמֵר בְּפִיו חָמוּר יָתֵר מִן הָעוֹשֶׂה מַעֲשֶׂה שֶׁכֵּן מָצִיאנוּ שֶׁלֹּא נִתְחַתַּם גְּזַר דִּין עַל אֲבוֹתֵינוּ בַּמִּדְבָּר אֶלָּא עַל לְשׁוֹן הָרַע

The one who says with his mouth suffers more than the one who does an act. Thus we find that the judgement was sealed against our fathers in the desert only by reason of a bad tongue.[65]

In this example, the element being modified is SPEECH, with לָשׁוֹן functioning as a metonym for speech.[66]

Like לָשׁוֹן, פָּנִים (face) also occurs infrequently. Two of these uses were discussed in §2.3.2 and related to APPEARANCE which could be taken to reflect an internal state. The other use also appears to modify the element APPEARANCE.

2.46. Genesis 40:6b–7a, c

וַיַּרְא אֹתָם וְהִנָּם זֹעֲפִים
וַיִּשְׁאַל אֶת־סְרִיסֵי פַרְעֹה {...} לֵאמֹר מַדּוּעַ פְּנֵיכֶם רָעִים הַיּוֹם

He saw them, that they were vexed. He asked Pharaoh's officials {...} "Why are your faces bad today?"

In example 2.46, Joseph's question concerns what can be visually discerned – appearance. Thus, it is clear that APPEARANCE is in view and that this is considered to indicate a state of mind.

---

[64] Waltke writes "Whereas the figures pertain to senselessly paining the body, the topic pertains to insensitively paining the heart." Waltke, *The Book of Proverbs: Chapters 15–31*, 329.

[65] Translation adapted from Danby.

[66] Landman has shown that this use of לָשׁוֹן occurs from biblical to mishnaic texts, with wider use in later texts. Landman, "On Lips and Tongues in Ancient Hebrew," 70–77.

64 CHAPTER 2

Uses with עַיִן (eye) are the most common in the analysed texts. As with לֵב (heart), עַיִן appears to occur with רַע when modifying something internal.

2.47. Proverbs 28:22

נִבְהָל לַהוֹן אִישׁ רַע עָיִן וְלֹא־יֵדַע כִּי־חֶסֶר יְבֹאֶנּוּ

A man bad of eye hastens after wealth, he does not know that lack will come on him.

2.48. m. ʾAbot 5:13a

אַרְבַּע מִדּוֹת בְּנוֹתְנֵי צְדָקָה רוֹצֶה שֶׁיִּתֵּן וְאַל יִתְּנוּ אֲחֵרִים עֵינוֹ רָעָה בְּשֶׁלַאֲחֵרִים
[שֶׁ]יִּתְּנוּ אֲחֵרִים וְהוּא לֹא יִתֵּן עֵינוֹ רָעָה בְּשֶׁלּוֹ

There are four types of almsgivers: he that is minded to give but not that others should give – his eye is bad concerning what belongs to others; he that is minded that others should give but not that he should give – his eye is bad concerning what belongs to himself...[67]

In these examples, the element being modified is difficult to label using English categories. The element could perhaps be labelled: EYE(MENTAL STATE). It appears to be closely tied to how a person relates to possessions. This hypothesis is strengthened in considering the use of the antonym טוֹב with עַיִן in example 2.49, and the antonym יָפֶה with עַיִן in the halakhic definition in example 2.50.[68]

2.49. Proverbs 22:9

טוֹב־עַיִן הוּא יְבֹרָךְ כִּי־נָתַן מִלַּחְמוֹ לַדָּל

He who is good of eye will be blessed, because he gives from his bread to the poor.

This demonstrates that a positive EYE(MENTAL STATE) would lead to sharing of possessions.

2.50. m. Terumot 4:3a, c

שִׁעוּר תְּרוּמָה עַיִן יָפָה מֵאַרְבָּעִים {...} וְהַבֵּינוֹנִית מֵחֲמִשִּׁים וְהָרָעָה מִשִּׁשִּׁים תָּרֵם

[This is] the measure of the heave offering: [If a man has] a beautiful eye [he separates], one-fortieth [of his produce] {...} And the [one with] average [eye], one-fiftieth. And the [one with] bad [eye], one-sixtieth.

---

[67] Translation adapted from Danby.

[68] This use of cognitive category EYE is also seen in Matthew's gospel. In Matthew 6:19–24 we see the two categories of EYE (ἁπλοῦς and πονηρὸς, generous and wicked) linked to how one acts with wealth.

רַע AND SCHEMA   65

While example 2.50 does not appear to refer to moral categories (rather stating a variety of acceptable offerings), it does display a scale representing generosity with goods.[69] However, the element may be broader than this, as demonstrated by further examples of the use of עַיִן.

> 2.51. 1 Kings 20:6b

> וְהָיָה כָּל־מַחְמַד עֵינֶיךָ יָשִׂימוּ בְיָדָם וְלָקָחוּ

> …and all [that] your eyes desire they will lay their hands on and take.

> 2.52. Ben Sira 9:8a (Sir A 3v6a)

> העלים עין מאשת חן ואל תביט אל יפי לא לך

> Conceal [your] eye from a charming woman and do not look at beauty [which] is not yours.

These examples indicate that the eye may be considered an organ of desire. Therefore, it is likely the EYE(MENTAL STATE) is much wider in meaning.[70] Regardless of the exact meaning of עַיִן, which is beyond the scope of the current work, where רַע is used with עַיִן the element may be described as EYE(MENTAL STATE). Comparison with a use of עַיִן=EYE(PHYSICAL) may be useful here.

> 2.53. 1 Samuel 16:12b

> וְהוּא אַדְמוֹנִי עִם־יְפֵה עֵינַיִם וְטוֹב רֹאִי

> He was ruddy, with beautiful eyes, and was good of appearance.

In example 2.53, the discourse clearly contrasts with that of examples 2.47–2.52. In this example the surrounding words clearly relate to physical appearance. In examples 2.47–2.52, however, the language speaks of how the quality of one's "eye" affects certain actions.

Finally, there are three occurrences which involve the construct phrase יַד רַע or כַּף רַע (hand/palm of bad). While these might be expected to be BODY PART uses, they modify a HUMAN discourse element. This can be demonstrated with example 2.54.

> 2.54. Jeremiah 15:21

> וְהִצַּלְתִּיךָ מִיַּד רָעִים וּפְדִתִיךָ מִכַּף עָרִצִים

> I will save you from the hand of bad [ones] and I will redeem you from the palm of ruthless [ones].

---

[69] Foster, "Is Everything 'Beautiful' or 'Appropriate' in Its Time?" 51–52.

[70] The word עַיִן exhibits a wide range of uses. The ones we are discussing here may be subsumed under "mental or emotional states." Allan M. Harman, "עין," *NIDOTTE*, 3:383–88.

66   CHAPTER 2

In this use, יָד and כַּף function in a standard use to refer to the power of a certain group.[71] The parallel structure in this example combined with the plural forms clearly demonstrates that the elements modified by רַע and עָרִיץ (ruthless) are HUMAN.

Modifying the Element(s)

As with the other elements, so with the set identified above. There is no evidence to suggest רַע does anything more than provide a simple negative evaluation of the discourse element. A person with a לֵב that is רַע either experiences negative emotion or has a will which is considered bad depending on which element is specified by the cognitive context. A person with a לָשׁוֹן that is רַע is one who speaks badly (where the element selected is SPEECH). A person with a פָּנִים that is רַע is someone whose facial APPEARANCE is bad, and it is thought to display an inward state. A person with an עַיִן that is רַע is someone with a certain mental state – EYE(MENTAL STATE) – which leads to greedy behaviour.

The negative qualification provided by רַע appears to be objectively verifiable (e.g. for the רַע of עַיִן it is verifiable by observing the person's actions). As with uses to modify ACT and COMMODITY elements, רַע may be used as part of a scale to modify BODY PART elements, although this use may represent uncommon use with the only occurrence being with EYE(MENTAL STATE) in a halakhic definition (example 2.50).

2.3.5 דֶּרֶךְ (way)

There are 23 occurrences in the analysed text where רַע modifies דֶּרֶךְ (way) [22; 0; 0; 0; 1].[72]

Occurrences: Num 22:32 (4Q27 20–22, 29); 22:34; 1 Kgs 13:33; 2 Kgs 17:13; Jer 18:11; 23:22; 25:5; 26:3; 35:15; 36:7; Ezek 13:22; 20:44; 33:11; 36:31; Jonah 3:8, 10; Zech 1:4; Ps 36:5; 119:101; Prov 8:13; 28:10; 2 Chr 7:14; m. 'Abot 2:9.

Modified Element(s)

The most common way this phrase appears is with the verb שׁוּב מִ- (to turn from). Example 2.55 illustrates this use.

---

[71] Clines, "יָד 4," and "כַּף 1b," *DCH* 4:82; 4:450.
[72] In one use of רַע, דֶּרֶךְ was in the immediate context, but elided from the clause.

רַע AND SCHEMA

2.55. 2 Kings 17:12–13

וַיַּעַבְדוּ הַגִּלֻּלִים אֲשֶׁר אָמַר יְהוָה לָהֶם לֹא תַעֲשׂוּ אֶת־הַדָּבָר הַזֶּה
וַיָּעַד יְהוָה בְּיִשְׂרָאֵל וּבִיהוּדָה בְּיַד כָּל־נְבִיאֵו כָל־חֹזֶה לֵאמֹר שֻׁבוּ מִדַּרְכֵיכֶם
הָרָעִים וְשִׁמְרוּ מִצְוֺתַי חֻקּוֹתַי...

They served idols which the Lord had said to them, "You shall not do
this thing." The Lord warned Israel and Judah by the hand of every
prophet of his and every seer, saying, "Turn from your bad ways, and
keep my commandments, my statutes…"

In this use, רַע modifies the element BEHAVIOUR. This is clear from the
preceding discourse (they served idols) and the remedy (keep my commandments…): both indicate ongoing patterns of behaviour rather than
individual acts. Whereas עָשָׂה רַע modifies ACT, דֶּרֶךְ רַע can modify BEHAV-
IOUR. An occurrence without מִ־ שׁוּב is presented below.

2.56. Proverbs 28:10a

מַשְׁגֶּה יְשָׁרִים ׀ בְּדֶרֶךְ רָע בִּשְׁחוּתוֹ הוּא־יִפּוֹל

One who misleads the upright in a bad way will fall in his own pit.

In this example, contextual information is lacking to easily distinguish
between ACT and BEHAVIOUR. The attempt at distinction is complicated by
uses such as example 2.57 below.

2.57. Ezekiel 20:43–44a

וּזְכַרְתֶּם־שָׁם אֶת־דַּרְכֵיכֶם וְאֵת כָּל־עֲלִילוֹתֵיכֶם אֲשֶׁר נִטְמֵאתֶם בָּם וּנְקֹטֹתֶם
בִּפְנֵיכֶם בְּכָל־רָעוֹתֵיכֶם אֲשֶׁר עֲשִׂיתֶם
וִידַעְתֶּם כִּי־אֲנִי יְהוָה בַּעֲשׂוֹתִי אִתְּכֶם לְמַעַן שְׁמִי לֹא כְדַרְכֵיכֶם הָרָעִים וְכַעֲלִילוֹתֵיכֶם
הַנִּשְׁחָתוֹת

You will remember there your ways and all your deeds with which you
defiled yourselves, and you will loathe yourselves because of all your
evils which you have done. You will know that I am the Lord when
I deal with you according to my name, not according to your bad ways
and your corrupt deeds.

This example appears to blur the boundaries between the BEHAVIOUR
– ACT distinction made above. It seems that BEHAVIOUR and ACT can be
considered in semantic parallel, constituting a single unit. By clarifying
the ways and deeds as "evils which you have done," the text further
demonstrates that דֶּרֶךְ can be considered in terms of ACTS. Thus, דֶּרֶךְ may
also be able to refer to the ACTS of a behavioural pattern. Thus the elements being modified by רַע in these uses may be some combination of
BEHAVIOUR and ACT.

68   CHAPTER 2

In addition to this, another element appears in one mishnaic use:

2.58. m. 'Abot 2:9a

אָמַ' לָהֶם צְאוּ וּרְאוּ אֵי זוֹ הִיא דֶּרֶךְ רָעָה שֶׁיִּתְרַחַק מִמֶּנָּה [הָ]אָדָם
ר' אֱלִיעֶזֶר אוֹ' עַיִן רָעָה...

> He said to them, "Come, see what is the bad way, that a man should
> take himself far from it."
> Rabbi Eliezer says, "A bad eye."...

In example 2.58, דֶּרֶךְ רָעָה (bad way) does not so much refer to a
pattern of behaviour as the thing which leads to certain behaviours;
that is, "the fundamental" of a bad life.[73] This can be demonstrated from
the first answer to the question which was established (§2.3.4) to refer
to something internal, the presence of which is seen in the actions of a
person. This suggests that the concept, by the time of this portion of the
Mishnah,[74] could be generalised to refer to the cause of a behavioural
pattern. The element in example 2.58 is, therefore, INTERNAL STATE(LEADS
TO BEHAVIOUR).

Modifying the Element(s)

As with other uses of רַע, we see what may be subjective and objective
use. In example 2.55, the negative qualification of the people's ways
is based on the judgement that disobeying the Lord's commands is רַע
behaviour. That this use is subjective may be supported by the discourse
as it relates to doing (עָשָׂה) what is רַע in the Lord's sight (2 Kings 17:2).[75]
In contrast, the use in example 2.56 presents a distinction between what
the יָשָׁר (upright) are expected to do and the דֶּרֶךְ רַע (bad way). This use
is objective: it presents a maxim with a threat of judgement declaring what

---

[73] Herford refers to the earlier question of 2:9 which asks about the דֶּרֶךְ טוֹבָה (the good
way) as meaning "what is the fundamental of a right life? or, what is the clue to the right
way of life?" The answers, he says, "imply abstract qualities." R. Travers Herford, *Pirkē
Aboth*, 3rd ed. (New York: Jewish Institute of Religion, 1945), 53.

[74] Assuming the names and sayings are correctly attributed, these are Rabbis from the
initial stages following the destruction of the temple. Isayah M. Gafni, "The Historical
Background," in *The Literature of the Sages*, ed. Shemu'el Safrai (Assen, Netherlands:
Van Gorcum, 1987), 1:14–20; Abraham Goldberg, "The Mishna – A Study Book of
Halakha," in *The Literature of the Sages*, ed. Shemu'el Safrai (Assen, Netherlands: Van
Gorcum, 1987), 1:214, 1:236.

[75] It is subjective from a linguistic point of view because the judgement is delivered in a
subjective manner (what God considers to be the case). This does not negate the possibility of it being objective from a theological point of view (e.g. God considers something
to be truth, therefore it is truth).

רַע AND SCHEMA   69

is the case. This would lose all its force if the דֶּרֶךְ רַע was subjectively determined. This is similar with m. 'Abot 2:9 which contasts the דֶּרֶךְ רָעָה (example 2.58) with the דֶּרֶךְ טוֹבָה.

Therefore, when used with דֶּרֶךְ, as in other uses, רַע appears to operate generally across subjective and objective uses. In both subjective and objective use, it forms a negative qualification of the modified element.

2.3.6 דָּבָר (thing)

There are 17 occurrences of רַע modifying דָּבָר in the analysed texts [15; 0; 2; 0; 0]. However, five of these were in the phrase עָשָׂה דָּבָר רַע and were covered in §2.3.1. They will not be discussed again here. The elements and how רַע modifies them are discussed together below.

Occurrences: Exod 33:4; Deut 13:12; 17:1; 17:5; 19:20; 23:10; Josh 23:15; 1 Sam 2:23; 2 Kgs 4:41; 17:11; Ps 64:6; 141:4; Eccl 8:3, 5; Neh 13:17; 1QM VII, 7; X, 1.

Elements and Modification

דָּבָר (thing) is a semantically general noun. Therefore we may expect it to allow many different elements. However, it is polysemous, meaning *word* in many uses, and in such use can be modified by רַע.

> 2.59. Exodus 33:3a, 4a
>
> אֶל־אֶרֶץ זָבַת חָלָב וּדְבָשׁ כִּי לֹא אֶעֱלֶה בְּקִרְבְּךָ כִּי עַם־קְשֵׁה־עֹרֶף אַתָּה פֶּן־אֲכֶלְךָ בַּדָּרֶךְ
>
> וַיִּשְׁמַע הָעָם אֶת־הַדָּבָר הָרָע הַזֶּה וַיִּתְאַבָּלוּ
>
> "Go up to a land flowing with milk and honey, but I will not go up in your midst lest I consume you on the way, because you are a stiff-necked people." The people heard this bad word and they mourned.

This begins with the Lord speaking to Moses. Thus the modified element here is DECLARATION. It is the thing that the Lord told Moses he would do. It is made clear by the discourse and the use of the verb שָׁמַע (to hear). The element here is evaluated negatively by the hearers.[76] This is clear from their response: mourning.

In example 2.60, the דָּבָר is used as "thing" to refer to a feature of an animal.

---

[76] For another example of this use see Jeremiah 42:6.

70 CHAPTER 2

2.60. Deuteronomy 17:1

לֹא־תִזְבַּח לַיהוָה אֱלֹהֶיךָ שׁוֹר וָשֶׂה אֲשֶׁר יִהְיֶה בוֹ מוּם כֹּל דָּבָר רָע כִּי תוֹעֲבַת יְהוָה אֱלֹהֶיךָ הוּא

You shall not sacrifice to the LORD your God a bull or sheep which has a defect in it, any bad thing, because it is an abomination to the LORD your God.

The phrase כֹּל דָּבָר רָע (any bad thing) is in apposition to מוּם (defect). The element could be termed ANIMAL(FEATURE) here, as any דָּבָר (thing) that could be bad in a sacrifice is necessarily any feature that could be considered less than perfect. Deuteronomy 15:21 offers two examples of animal defects: פִּסֵּחַ (lame) and עִוֵּר (blind). רָע provides a simple negative evaluation of the feature. Thus the phrase refers to part of the animal that does not serve its proper function.

דָּבָר is also used in euphemisms. "Euphemism is characterized by avoidance language and evasive expression"[77] and that is exactly what we see in the following examples.

2.61. Deuteronomy 23:10–11a

כִּי־תֵצֵא מַחֲנֶה עַל־אֹיְבֶיךָ וְנִשְׁמַרְתָּ מִכֹּל דָּבָר רָע כִּי־יִהְיֶה בְךָ אִישׁ אֲשֶׁר לֹא־יִהְיֶה טָהוֹר מִקְּרֵה־לָיְלָה

When you go out to camp against your enemies, you will keep yourself from every bad thing. If any man among you becomes not clean from the occurrence of the night…

2.62. 1QM VII, 6b–7

ורוח יהיה
בין כול מחניהמה למקום היד כאלפים באמה וכול ערות דבר רע לוא יראה סביבות כול מחניהם

There will be a space between all their camps for the place of the hand, around two thousand cubits, so no nakedness of a bad thing will be seen in the surrounds of all their camps.

These somewhat cryptic-sounding examples demonstrate the use of דָּבָר רָע in avoidance language concerning bodily excretions. In examples 2.61 and 2.62, the phrase refers to a set of possible negative events which contains the whole set of bodily excretions that may occur (Deut 23:10–15). The construction is not particularly important in itself. It is what the euphemisms allude to that is important to the discourse. רָע, in example 2.61,

---

[77] Keith Allan and Kate Burridge, *Euphemism & Dysphemism: Language Used as Shield and Weapon* (New York: Oxford University Press, 1991), 3.

רַע AND SCHEMA   71

and עֶרְוַת (nakedness) and רַע, in example 2.62,[78] qualifies דָּבָר so that the euphemism is understood. Although the construction serves a highly specific purpose, there is no reason to take the use of רַע in these examples as other than a negative qualification of דָּבָר as an EVENT. In the discourse, however, it is apparent that this particular use is euphemistic such that discourse enforces a specific meaning. In example 2.61, the euphemism becomes clear in the second verse, whereas in example 2.62, the preceding discourse leads one to expect it, as does the presence of עֶרְוַת at the start of the phrase.

דָּבָר may refer to an ACT when not directly governed by the verb עָשָׂה.

> 2.63. 1 Samuel 2:23
>
> וַיֹּאמֶר לָהֶם לָמָּה תַעֲשׂוּן כַּדְּבָרִים הָאֵלֶּה אֲשֶׁר אָנֹכִי שֹׁמֵעַ אֶת־דִּבְרֵיכֶם רָעִים מֵאֵת כָּל־הָעָם אֵלֶּה
>
> He said to them, "Why are you doing such things as these? I am hearing of your bad deeds from all these people."

The discourse, in this case, clearly links the second use of דָּבָר with the first which is governed by עָשָׂה. Thus it is clear that the element being modified is an ACT as in §2.3.1. Similarly, רַע functions as a negative evaluation of the acts being performed.

The phrase can also refer to covenant curses.

> 2.64. Joshua 23:15a
>
> וְהָיָה כַּאֲשֶׁר־בָּא עֲלֵיכֶם כָּל־הַדָּבָר הַטּוֹב אֲשֶׁר דִּבֶּר יְהוָה אֱלֹהֵיכֶם אֲלֵיכֶם כֵּן יָבִיא יְהוָה עֲלֵיכֶם אֵת כָּל־הַדָּבָר הָרָע עַד־הַשְׁמִידוֹ אוֹתְכֶם
>
> Just as every good thing has come upon you, which the Lord your God spoke to you, so the Lord will bring on you every bad thing until he has destroyed you...

In this case the use contrasts with its opposite דָּבָר טוֹב (good thing). In the discourse it is clear that these phrases refer to the covenant blessings and curses (cf. Deut 11:26–28). The element being modified may be described as EVENT. However, the element EVENT is constrained by the discourse to all the elements which are applicable to the covenant blessings and curses. The adjectives take the role of simple positive and negative evaluations which serve to foreground the blessings and curses respectively.

The phrase can also refer to something poisonous.

---

[78] עֶרְוַת appears on its own in Deuteronomy 23:15.

72   CHAPTER 2

2.65. 2 Kings 4:40b, 41b

וְהֵמָּה צָעֲקוּ וַיֹּאמְרוּ מָוֶת בַּסִּיר אִישׁ הָאֱלֹהִים וְלֹא יָכְלוּ לֶאֱכֹל { ...}
וְלֹא הָיָה דָּבָר רָע בַּסִּיר

They cried out and said, "O man of God, there's death in the pot!"
and they were not able to eat. {...} There was no bad thing in the
pot.

Prior to this example, unidentified wild fruit and gourds were put into
the pot. This leads to the scene above where דָּבָר רָע is in parallel with מָוֶת
(death). The people who were eating were able to taste something they
identified as poisonous leading to the cry "There's death in the pot!" Thus
we may identify the element being modified here as FOOD. Again רָע provides a simple negative evaluation leading to the combinative meaning
"nothing bad/inedible/dangerous" in the pot.

דָּבָר also refers to something that comes before a king.

2.66. Ecclesiastes 8:3b

אַל־תַּעֲמֹד בְּדָבָר רָע כִּי כָּל־אֲשֶׁר יַחְפֹּץ יַעֲשֶׂה

Do not stand in a bad thing, because all he [the king] desires he will
do.

This is referring to what one should or should not do in a king's presence. The phrase דָּבָר רָע could simply be referring to standing against
the wishes of the king – in a thing that is רָע according to the king.[79] We
might consider the element being modified broadly as a THING constrained by the discourse to THING(WHICH MAY COME BEFORE A KING). It
is likely that רָע modifies דָּבָר in the same manner as elsewhere, providing a simple negative evaluation. In such a use, רָע is clearly subjective,
with the merit of the matter being determined by the king. This can be
seen in the end of the example, in particular through the use of חָפֵץ (to
desire).

Summary

As expected, דָּבָר can be used as a place holder for a wide variety of
elements. Similarly to elsewhere, רָע appears to contribute a simple negative evaluation to the element it modifies.

[79] Longman and Murphy comment on the trouble of achieving specificity with this phrase.
Tremper Longman, *The Book of Ecclesiastes*, NICOT (Grand Rapids, MI: W.B. Eerdmans, 1998), 212; Roland E. Murphy, *Ecclesiastes*, WBC 23A (Waco, TX: Word Books,
1992), 83.

2.3.7 שֵׁם (name)

There are 16 occurrences of רַע modifying שֵׁם in the analysed texts [3; 1; 3; 0; 9]. The elements and how רַע modifies them are discussed together below.

Occurrences: Deut 22:14, 19; Neh 6:13; Sir 6:1 (Sir A 2r6); 4Q159 2–4, 8; 11Q19 LXV, 8; LXV, 15; m. Soṭah 3:5; m. Giṭ. 4:7; m. Sanh. 1:1, 2; m. Šebu. 10:2; m. Bek. 8:7; m. ʿArak. 3:1, 5 (×2).

Elements and Modification

All but two of the extant uses of the phrase שֵׁם רַע (bad name) occur in reference to the sexual reputation of a woman. This use may be driven by the legal usage of the phrase in Deuteronomy 22 (vv. 14 and 19) which is then taken up in the uses from the Judean Desert and the Mishnah (examples 2.68–2.69).

> 2.67. Deuteronomy 22:13–14
>
> כִּי־יִקַּח אִישׁ אִשָּׁה וּבָא אֵלֶיהָ וּשְׂנֵאָהּ
> וְשָׂם לָהּ עֲלִילֹת דְּבָרִים וְהוֹצִיא עָלֶיהָ שֵׁם רָע וְאָמַר אֶת־הָאִשָּׁה הַזֹּאת לָקַחְתִּי
> וָאֶקְרַב אֵלֶיהָ וְלֹא־מָצָאתִי לָהּ בְּתוּלִים
>
> If a man takes a wife and goes to her and hates her and sets on her deeds of things and brings on her a bad name and says, "I took this woman, and when I came to her I did not find her to have virginity.

In example 2.67, phrase עֲלִילֹת דְּבָרִים (deeds of things) is avoidance language (euphemistic). From the later use of בְּתוּלִים (virginity) we can tell it refers to an accusation of sexual immorality. Thus the accusation leads to giving the woman a bad name. The element being modified here is REPUTATION which has been damaged by accusation. Given the discourse enforcing a sexual sense, the element may be more specifically considered to be REPUTATION(SEXUAL). To this element, רַע provides a negative qualification.

> 2.68. 4Q159 2–4, 8–9a
>
> כי יוצו איש שם רע על בתולת ישראל אם ב] -- [קחתו אותה יואמר ובקרוה] -- [
> נאמנות ואם לוא כחש עליה והומתה
>
> If a man brings forth a bad name on a virgin of Israel, if at [--] he takes her he will say, then trustworthy women will examine her [--]. If he did not lie concerning her, she will be put to death.

Example 2.68 is a rewrite of the law from Deuteronomy 22:14–20.

CHAPTER 2

2.69. m. Soṭah 3:5b

וְאִם אַתָּה [אוֹמֵ'] שֶׁהַזְּכוּת תּוֹלָה בַּמַּיִם הַמְאָרְרִים מַדְהֵא אַתָּה אֶת הַמַּיִם בִּפְנֵי כָל הַנָּשִׁים הַשּׁוֹתוֹת וּמוֹצִיא אַ{וֹ}תָּה שֵׁם רַע עַל הַטְּהוֹרוֹת

...and if you say, "Merit suspends [the effects] of the curse giving water, you weaken the water for all the women who drink, and you bring forth a bad name on the pure ones.

While this use is not directly from Deuteronomy 22, it still relates to REPUTATION(SEXUAL). Example 2.69 relates to the legal case of Numbers 5:13–28 in which a woman is suspected by a jealous husband of sexual infidelity. The argument here is that merit cannot be said to suspend the curse of Numbers 5 because that would mean those who do not exhibit the symptoms of the curse may still be considered guilty of sexual infidelity, thus leading to a bad reputation for the undeserving. רַע provides the same schematic contribution as with examples 2.67 and 2.68: negative qualification.

2.70. m. Giṭṭin 4:7a

הַמּוֹצִיא אֶת אִשְׁתּוֹ מִשֵּׁם שֵׁם רַע לֹא יַחֲזִיר

The one who causes his wife to go forth [i.e. divorce] because of a bad name may not cause her to return [i.e. remarry].

In this example the discourse does not make clear what the bad reputation refers to. However, due to the other uses in the Mishnah,[80] specifically in how they appear tied to the language of Deuteronomy 22, and due to the clear reference in the Babylonian Talmud to sexual immorality in explaining this passage,[81] the element here should also be taken as REPUTATION(SEXUAL). Therefore, in the Mishnah, it appears that the phrase שֵׁם רַע may be slightly idiomatic to refer to a particular type of negative reputation: the sexual reputation of a woman. Two further examples of שֵׁם רַע demonstrate that this is not the only use of the phrase in the extant texts. Although these other uses are in reference to males, it leaves open the possibility that שֵׁם רַע could have described a woman's negative reputation more generally given the right context.

2.71. Nehemiah 6:13

לְמַעַן שָׂכוּר הוּא לְמַעַן־אִירָא וְאֶעֱשֶׂה־כֵּן וְחָטָאתִי וְהָיָה לָהֶם לְשֵׁם רָע לְמַעַן יְחָרְפוּנִי:

---

[80] M. Šebiʿit 10:2; m. Soṭah 3:5; m. Sanhedrin 1:1; m. Bekorot 8:7; m. ʾArakin 3:1, 5.

[81] b. Giṭṭin 46a reads שלא יהו בנות ישראל פרוצות בעריות – that the daughters of Israel will not break forth with genitals (i.e. be promiscuous with regard to forbidden sexual relations). Sefaria, "The William Davidson Talmud," https://www.sefaria.org/texts/Talmud.

רַע AND SCHEMA   75

> For this he was hired: so that I would be afraid and I would do this and sin, so they could give me a bad name and so they could revile me.

In example 2.71, the action which Nehemiah's enemies hoped to get him to do was to flee to the temple and hide – to behave as a coward. His enemies sought to tarnish his reputation so as to thwart the wall-building project. Thus, the modified element REPUTATION here, and רַע contributes a negative judgement on that.

> 2.72. Ben Sira 5:14a, c, e; 6:1 (Sir A 2r3–4, 6)

> אל תקרא בעל שתים {...} כי {...} חרפה רעהו בעל שתים {...}
> ותחת אוהב אל תהי שונא שם רע וקלון תוריש חרפה כן איש רע בעל שתים

> Do not be called two-tongued {…} because {…} reproach is the companion of the two-tongued. {…} In place of a friend, do not be a foe. You will take possession of a bad name, shame, and reproach. So [it is for] a bad man, the two-tongued.

This example forms part of a larger passage on "duplicity in speech" (Sir 5:9–6:1).[82] Example 2.72 makes clear that reproach comes from being called בַּעַל שְׁתַיִם (lit. master of two = two-tongued). The element being modified is thus REPUTATION and as in the above uses, רַע contributes a negative judgement on it: being two-tongued leads to a bad reputation, shame, and reproach.

Summary

שֵׁם is exclusively used of reputation in the uses where it is modified by רַע. In these cases, רַע was found to modify elements of REPUTATION(SEXUAL) in reference to women and REPUTATION in reference to men. It appears that the phrase שֵׁם רַע could refer to a woman's sexual reputation in the Mishnah with little else in the context. This suggests idiomatic use of the phrase in the legal discourse of the Mishnah, but not necessarily in normal speech.[83] As has been found elsewhere, רַע appears to provide a negative qualification to the element outside the Mishnah. In the Mishnah it exhibits some signs of having been used as an idiomatic phrase, with specific legal reference.

---

[82] Skehan and Di Lella, *The Wisdom of Ben Sira*, 183–85.

[83] Sarfatti puts it this way: "MH being a more '*halacha*-centered' language than BH (*halacha* meaning Jewish religious law), many words that had a general and rather broad sense in BH restricted their sense in MH and became specific terms relating to religious law and life." One of the examples he gives of this change is בְּרִית (covenant) which refers specifically to circumcision in the Mishnah. Sarfatti, "Mishnaic Vocabulary and Mishnaic Literature," 38.

76 CHAPTER 2

2.3.8 בְּעֵר רַע (to purge bad)

רַע occurs as the grammatical object of the verb בְּעֵר (to purge) 14 times [9; 0; 5; 0; 0]. All of these occurrences are in Deuteronomy and the rewriting of these laws in the Temple Scroll (11Q19). In this use it never modifies another word through attributive, predicative, or construct relations.

Occurrences: Deut 13:6 // 11Q19 LIV, 18; Deut 17:7; 17:12 // 11Q19 LVI, 10; Deut 19:19 // 11Q19 LXI, 19; Deut 21:21 // 11Q19 LXIV, 6; Deut 22:21, 22, 24 // 11Q19 LXVI, 4; Deut 24:7.

Elements and Modification

All occurrences follow the same clausal pattern (example 2.73), with the only variation being in Deuteronomy 17:12 // 11Q19 LVI, 10 (example 2.74).

2.73. Deuteronomy 13:6b

וּבִעַרְתָּ הָרָע מִקִּרְבֶּךָ

You shall purge the bad from your midst.

2.74. 11Q19 LVI, 10b

ובערתה הרע מישראל

You shall purge the bad from Israel.

The immediate clauses give us little information from which to determine the modified element. It appears that the element is something that can be physically purged from within the people group. However, there is more information in the wider discourse.

2.75. Deuteronomy 13:6a, c

וְהַנָּבִיא הַהוּא אוֹ חֹלֵם הַחֲלוֹם הַהוּא יוּמָת כִּי דִבֶּר־סָרָה עַל־יְהוָה אֱלֹהֵיכֶם {...}
לְהַדִּיחֲךָ מִן־הַדֶּרֶךְ אֲשֶׁר צִוְּךָ יְהוָה אֱלֹהֶיךָ לָלֶכֶת בָּהּ וּבִעַרְתָּ הָרָע מִקִּרְבֶּךָ

That prophet, or that dreamer of dreams will be put to death, because he spoke rebellion against the LORD your God {...} to lead you from the way in which the LORD your God commanded you to walk. You shall purge the bad from your midst.

In this verse the discourse element appears to be HUMAN. That is, the רַע to be purged is the person who sought to mislead the people.[84] However,

---

[84] This appears to be how the Old Greek translator and Targums interpret it. For example, Targum Onqelos has וּתְפַלֵּי עָבֵיד דְּבִישׁ מִבֵּינָךְ (You shall purge the doer of evil from among you). BHQ has a brief discussion on the phrase at 13:6. See Carmel McCarthy, ed., *Deuteronomy*, BHQ 5 (Stuttgart: German Bible Society, 2007). This is also a common

רַע AND SCHEMA

77

it is possible the element could also be an ACT.[85] In the following example this appears more likely.

2.76. Deuteronomy 22:21

וְהוֹצִ֨יאוּ אֶת־הַֽנַּעֲרָ֜ אֶל־פֶּ֣תַח בֵּית־אָבִ֗יהָ וּסְקָלוּהָ֩ אַנְשֵׁ֨י עִירָ֤הּ בָּֽאֲבָנִים֙ וָמֵ֔תָה כִּֽי־עָשְׂתָ֤ה נְבָלָה֙ בְּיִשְׂרָאֵ֔ל לִזְנ֖וֹת בֵּ֣ית אָבִ֑יהָ וּבִֽעַרְתָּ֥ הָרָ֖ע מִקִּרְבֶּֽךָ

They will bring forth the young woman to the entrance of the house of her father and the men of her city will stone her with stones and she will die, because she has done an outrageous thing in Israel by prostituting the house of her father. You shall purge the bad from your midst.

In this example the gender of רַע does not match the feminine gender of what would be the human referent if the element were HUMAN. This weighs in favour of the element being an ACT.

However, because the masculine form is the unmarked gender, if בְּעַר הָרַע is being used as a unifying phrase in the discourse, it could be used for pragmatic reasons with the unmarked gender in Deuteronomy 22:21. This repetition may have been used to reinforce the sense that *anyone* who does any רַע thing should be purged.

There is another possibility when one considers the worldview presented in the biblical texts.

2.77. Deuteronomy 19:13[86]

לֹא־תָח֥וֹס עֵֽינְךָ֖ עָלָ֑יו וּבִֽעַרְתָּ֧ דַֽם־הַנָּקִ֛י מִיִּשְׂרָאֵ֖ל וְט֥וֹב לָֽךְ

Your eye shall not pity him. You shall purge the blood of the innocent from Israel, and it will be well with you.

This example refers to how the people are commanded to deal with murder. It demonstrates a similar use in Deuteronomy in which the verb בְּעַר takes an object that refers to the guilt incurred from an action. In the Israelite worldview, such guilt impacts the land, not just the murderer themselves. This can be seen in a similar legal case in Numbers 35:30–34.[87]

---

way for commentators to interpret the use in 13:6. For example, see Duane L. Christensen, *Deuteronomy 1:1–21:9*, 2nd ed., WBC 6A (Nashville, TN: Thomas Nelson, 2001), 271; Eugene H. Merrill, *Deuteronomy*, NAC 4 (Nashville, TN: Broadman & Holman, 1994), 231.

[85] This appears to be the way Thompson has taken it. J. A. Thompson, *Deuteronomy: An Introduction and Commentary*, TOTC 5 (Downers Grove, IL: IVP, 1974), 193.

[86] Cf. Deut 21:9.

[87] Van Wolde also makes this point in her work on מלא. However, her interest is more in how the defilement or pollution of the land occurs than the legal requirements for purifying the land. Van Wolde, *Reframing Biblical Studies*, 234–36.

78 CHAPTER 2

2.78. Numbers 35:33–34

וְלֹא־תַחֲנִיפוּ אֶת־הָאָרֶץ אֲשֶׁר אַתֶּם בָּהּ כִּי הַדָּם הוּא יַחֲנִיף אֶת־הָאָרֶץ וְלָאָרֶץ
לֹא־יְכֻפַּר לַדָּם אֲשֶׁר שֻׁפַּךְ־בָּהּ כִּי־אִם בְּדַם שֹׁפְכוֹ
וְלֹא תְטַמֵּא אֶת־הָאָרֶץ אֲשֶׁר אַתֶּם יֹשְׁבִים בָּהּ אֲשֶׁר אֲנִי שֹׁכֵן בְּתוֹכָהּ כִּי אֲנִי יְהֹוָה
שֹׁכֵן בְּתוֹךְ בְּנֵי יִשְׂרָאֵל

You must not pollute the land in which you are, because blood pollutes the land and atonement cannot be made for the land for the blood which is shed in it except by the blood of the shedder. You shall not defile the land in which you are dwelling, within which I am dwelling because I the LORD am dwelling in the midst of the children of Israel.

In this case, the legal requirements are tied into cultic observance. The only way given to maintain the presence of the Lord among the people in this case is to follow the law. In Deuteronomy this comes through in that the law must similarly be followed to experience the covenant blessings of the Lord rather than curses (cf. Deut 11:26–28). There is also a very similar usage in Judges.

2.79. Judges 20:12b–13a

לֵאמֹר מָה הָרָעָה הַזֹּאת אֲשֶׁר נִהְיְתָה בָּכֶם
וְעַתָּה תְּנוּ אֶת־הָאֲנָשִׁים בְּנֵי־בְלִיַּעַל אֲשֶׁר בַּגִּבְעָה וּנְמִיתֵם וּנְבַעֲרָה רָעָה מִיִּשְׂרָאֵל

What is this evil which was among you? Now, give [up] the men, sons of wickedness who are in Gibeah and we will put them to death. Let us purge evil from Israel.

The major difference between example 2.79 and the uses of בֵּעֵר רַע is that the object is the cognate noun רָעָה.[88] The case is one of gang rape resulting in death. Whether or not this would be considered in terms of דָּם (blood) is difficult to know. However, the use of the singular noun here rather than the plural adjective (with a human referent) suggests something to do with the act itself is to be purged rather than the perpetrators. Therefore, it is likely that the word is being used metonymically to refer to the stain on the land (or perhaps society)[89] which comes from the act

---

[88] This could be the case of a misplaced ה as suggested in the apparatus to the BHS (but not BHQ). However, we will consider this on the assumption that רָעָה is correct.

[89] Given that the רַע is to be purged from among them as opposed to from the land. Woods appears to interpret 13:6 as referring to a stain on society, "Finally, Israel is exhorted to *purge*... the *evil* (that which contaminates society and damages relationship with Yahweh) from among you." Edward J. Woods, *Deuteronomy: An Introduction and Commentary*, TOTC 5 (Downers Grove, IL: IVP, 2011), 196. However, the evidence is in favour of considering it in terms of a stain on the land as that is a category commonly invoked in defilement contexts. See van Wolde, *Reframing Biblical Studies*, 256. Faro

רַע AND SCHEMA

79

for which atonement (through observing legal requirements) must be made. This is in line with the metonymic use of other words such as עָוֹן which refer to iniquitous actions (example 2.80).[90]

2.80. Leviticus 10:17

מַדּוּעַ לֹא־אֲכַלְתֶּם אֶת־הַחַטָּאת בִּמְקוֹם הַקֹּדֶשׁ כִּי קֹדֶשׁ קָדָשִׁים הִוא וְאֹתָהּ | נָתַן לָכֶם לָשֵׂאת אֶת־עֲוֹן הָעֵדָה לְכַפֵּר עֲלֵיהֶם לִפְנֵי יְהוָה

"Why have you not eaten the sin offering in the holy place, since it is most holy and given to you to bear the iniquity [i.e. guilt incurred by iniquity] of the congregation to atone for them before the LORD?"

To purge the bad would be then to perform a legally mandated act which allows for a continued relationship between Israel and the Lord.[91] This analysis anticipates the findings of chapters 3 and 4. The use of רַע in the phrase בָּעֵר רַע, then, appears to refer to guilt incurred by a רַע ACT. The semantic pattern present here is a common one for this semantic domain, in which רַע participates (see major domain עָוֹן, §4.5).

Summary

In cases where רַע is the grammatical object of בָּעֵר (to purge), the element was found to most likely be an ACT. This combination follows a semantic pattern common to the semantic domain עָוֹן (analysed in §4.5) whereby the term functions as a metonym to refer to the guilt incurred by such an act. This was demonstrated with the metonymic use of the word עָוֹן (example 2.80). This section presents an example of a use of רַע that does not conform to the standard use seen to this point. Here רַע is shown to refer not simply to a negative qualification, but to guilt, specifically guilt incurred by a רַע ACT. It is at the "רַע ACT" level that רַע functions as a negative qualification. This use will be seen in chapter 4 to be a development deriving from its use in a particular semantic domain.

also has some relevant observations to do with corrupt behaviour corrupting the land. Faro, *Evil in Genesis*, 207–9.

[90] This usage is less common, but seen in a variety of words referring to iniquitous action. For two examples, see Clines, "עָוֹן 2," and "חַטָּאת 4," *DCH* 6:310; 3:198.

[91] The incident of the מַעַל (sin) of Achan in Joshua 7 provides further support for this assessment of the cognitive context. It demonstrates how the act of one person can lead to a damaged relationship between God and his people. Furthermore, by executing Achan the people mend their relationship with God and are then able to conquer Ai with God's help (Josh 8). The work of van Wolde also supports this view. She writes, "Because the land is considered polluted by blood shed illicitly, purification procedures should be followed in order to secure YHWH's residence in the land. The land should be respected, because it is YHWH's dwelling place." Van Wolde, *Reframing Biblical Studies*, 256.

80 CHAPTER 2

2.3.9 COGNITION

There are 12 occurrences in the analysed text where רע relates to cognition [7; 0; 5; 0; 0].[92] All but four of these uses were governed by either the verb יָדַע (to know) or הֵבִין (to understand). Three were governed by the substantive דַּעַת (knowledge),[93] and one by the noun שֵׂכֶל (understanding). In three occurrences in the Judean Desert texts, manuscript damage renders any thorough analysis of the usage impossible.[94] Therefore only 9 occurrences can be analysed for this portion of analysis.

Occurrences: Gen 2:9, 17; 3:4, 22; Deut 1:39; 2 Sam 19:36; 1 Kgs 3:9; 1Q28ᵃ I, 10–11*; 4Q303 8*; 4Q416 1, 15*; 4Q417 1 I, 18*; 4Q418 2+ 2a–c, 7*.

Elements and Modification

Much has been said and speculated about the tree of knowledge of good and evil (Genesis occurrences). However, because those uses have less hints within the discourse that help us to understanding the usage of רע, they will be examined towards the end of this section.

2.81. Deuteronomy 1:34b–35, 39

וַיִּשָּׁבַע לֵאמֹר

אִם־יִרְאֶה אִישׁ בָּאֲנָשִׁים הָאֵלֶּה הַדּוֹר הָרָע הַזֶּה אֵת הָאָרֶץ הַטּוֹבָה אֲשֶׁר נִשְׁבַּעְתִּי לָתֵת לַאֲבֹתֵיכֶם {...}

וְטַפְּכֶם אֲשֶׁר אֲמַרְתֶּם לָבַז יִהְיֶה וּבְנֵיכֶם אֲשֶׁר לֹא־יָדְעוּ הַיּוֹם טוֹב וָרָע הֵמָּה יָבֹאוּ שָׁמָּה

He swore, "Not one of these men, this bad generation will see the good land which I swore to give to your fathers. {...} As for your children concerning whom you said "they will become plunder", your children who do not know today good and bad, they will go in there.

From example 2.81, it appears that the ability to "know good and bad" is not something expected of children. HUMAN(BEHAVIOUR) is the element modified by the first part of the example (see example 2.28, §2.3.2). The flow of the argument then, implies that the same element is in view in the

---

[92] This group may be larger; however, this selection was chosen based on an initial analysis of all occurrences of רע in the analysed texts.

[93] Bruce K. Waltke and Michael Patrick O'Connor, *An Introduction to Biblical Hebrew Syntax* (Winona Lake, IN: Eisenbrauns, 1990), §36.2.1.e.

[94] However, they display the antonymic relationship between טוב and רע and so have been retained for the chapter 3 analysis. 4Q303 8; 4Q416 1, 15; and 4Q418 2+2–c, 7 were excluded from this stage of analysis due to textual damage.

רַע AND SCHEMA 81

second part of the example: while the generation being addressed is described as רַע (i.e. having רַע BEHAVIOUR), the children are described as neither knowing טוֹב nor רַע BEHAVIOUR.

Another example of this use of רַע with COGNITION appears in 1Q28ᵃ.

2.82. 1Q28ᵃ I, 4–11a

בבוא{ּי}ם יקהילו אתכול הבאים מטף עד נשים וקראו בא] אֶת[

[כ]ול חוקי הברית ולהבינם בכול משפטיהמה פן ישגו במ] הֹ[

וזה ^ה^סרך לכול צבאות העדה לכול האזרח בישראל ומן נע] [

[לל]מדהו בספר ההגי וכפי יומיו ישכילוהו בחוקי הברית ול] [

[ ]סרו במשפטיהמה עשר שנים] [בוא בטֿף⁹⁵ וב]ֿן] עשרים שנ] [

[ ] הפקודים לבוא בגורל בתוך משפ[ח]תו ליחד בעד]ת] קודש ולוא יֿ] .[

אל אשה לדעתה למשכבי זכר כיאם לפי מילואת לו עש[רי]ם שנה בדעתו] טוב[

ורע

> When they come, they shall assemble all those who come (including women and children), and they shall read [?] [a]ll the statutes of the covenant, making them know all their judgements, lest they err [?]. This is the rule for all the hosts of the congregation, for every native in Israel. From [?] [to ins]truct him in the Book of Hagu. In accordance with his days, they will instruct him in the statutes of the covenant and [?] [?] in their ordinances. Ten years [?] he is to be considered a youth and [?] twenty yea[rs] [?] [?] the ranks to come into the membership within his fam[i]ly, joining with the holy congregat[ion]. He must not [?] to a woman for sexual intercourse,⁹⁶ until he is fully twe[nt]y years old, when he knows [good]⁹⁷ and bad.⁹⁸

Example 2.82 appears to indicate that instruction up to 20 years of age was expected (by the community that produced the text) to culminate in "knowing good and bad."⁹⁹ Instruction aims to avoid covenant (legal and or cultic) breaches (1Q28ᵃ I, 5) and is focused on "Scripture with an

---

⁹⁵ Accordance reads טב, but tags it as טַף (children). On viewing the image it appears that the letter may have been corrected. The final letter appears part way between the usual ב of this scribe and the ף of טף in line 4. The image can be viewed online at https://www.deadseascrolls.org.il/explore-the-archive/image/B-278249.

⁹⁶ "to know her, for the lying of a male." See Clines, "מִשְׁכָּב 10," DCH 5:527.

⁹⁷ Although טוֹב is missing from the text, the regularity of the expression and the size of the gap means we can have a high degree of confidence in the reconstruction. The gap can be viewed online in the tenth line of the image at https://www.deadseascrolls.org.il/explore-the-archive/image/B-278249.

⁹⁸ This translation is based on the translation of Wise, Abegg, and Cook. Oaktree Software, "Qumran Non-Biblical Manuscripts: A New English Translation," ed. Michael O. Wise, Martin G. Jr. Abegg and Edward M. Cook, 2009, https://www.accordancebible.com/store/details/?pid=QUMENG. Some of their reconstructions are retained in the text and translation.

⁹⁹ Wassen discusses lines 6–8 in connection with the education of children. Cecilia Wassen, "On the Education of Children in the Dead Sea Scrolls," SR 41 (2012): 350–63.

82 CHAPTER 2

emphasis on religious law."[100] It is possible that age 20 represented some form of coming-of-age with admission into the general membership and the right to marry.[101] However, not everything is open to the male aged 20 – for example, it is not until age 30 that he can serve in a variety of official capacities (1Q28ᵃ I, 13–18). The content of instruction indicates what is being taught is how to behave, hence the element in this example is, as with example 2.81, BEHAVIOUR.

Example 2.83 is slightly different.

> 2.83. 1 Kings 3:7–9
>
> וְעַתָּה יְהוָה אֱלֹהָי אַתָּה הִמְלַכְתָּ אֶת־עַבְדְּךָ תַּחַת דָּוִד אָבִי וְאָנֹכִי נַעַר קָטֹן לֹא אֵדַע צֵאת וָבֹא
>
> וְעַבְדְּךָ בְּתוֹךְ עַמְּךָ אֲשֶׁר בָּחָרְתָּ עַם־רָב אֲשֶׁר לֹא־יִמָּנֶה וְלֹא יִסָּפֵר מֵרֹב
>
> וְנָתַתָּ לְעַבְדְּךָ לֵב שֹׁמֵעַ לִשְׁפֹּט אֶת־עַמְּךָ לְהָבִין בֵּין־טוֹב לְרָע כִּי מִי יוּכַל לִשְׁפֹּט אֶת־עַמְּךָ הַכָּבֵד הַזֶּה
>
> Now, LORD my God, you have made your servant king in the place of David, my father, and I am a young man and do not know going and coming. Your servant is in the midst of your people whom you chose, a great people who cannot be numbered nor be counted because of their greatness. Give to your servant a hearing heart to judge your people, to discern between good and bad because who is able to judge this, your great people?

This example uses a different verb – a synonym[102] of יָדַע – which could mean a slightly different meaning is intended. While the verb שָׁפַט is commonly taken in the sense of legal judgement, the discourse clearly indicates a wider meaning than the English term "judge" allows ("rule" may be more appropriate).[103] Solomon claims he is too young to know "going

---

[100] Wassen, "On the Education of Children," 353. It appears, from 1QSᵃ I, 11, that women were also instructed and expected to testify against their husbands if they turned aside from the rules of the cult. If this reading is correct, it would lend support to the view that at age 20, when they get married, men are expected to know and do right behaviour (according to the definition of the cult). Tal Ilan, "Reading for Women in 1QSa (Serekh Ha-Edah)," in *The Dead Sea Scrolls in Context: Integrating the Dead Sea Scrolls in the Study of Ancient Texts, Languages, and Cultures*, ed. Armin Lange, Emanuel Tov and Matthias Weigold (Leiden: Brill, 2011), 66–69; see also Joan E. Taylor and Philip R. Davies, "On the Testimony of Women in 1QSa," *DSD* 3 (1996): 231–35.

[101] Schiffman suggests that the knowledge refers to sexual awareness. However, he does not present a convincing case to back this up. He does tie it to puberty, but then takes the knowledge itself to refer to the commands as with the knowledge comes the obligation to obey the commands. Lawrence H. Schiffman, *The Eschatological Community of the Dead Sea Scrolls: A Study of the Rule of the Congregation*, SBLMS 38 (Atlanta: Scholars, 1989), 16n33, 19.

[102] Clines, "בין," *DCH* 2:142–46. Willem A. VanGemeren, ed., *NIDOTTE* 5:114–15.

[103] This interpretation is also supported by Clines, "שפט 3a," *DCH* 8:533.

רַע AND SCHEMA 83

and coming,"[104] he gives the reason for the difficulty in "judging" to be how numerous the people are. The reason is not because of the difficulty of cases that come before him, but the size of the people he is to govern. Therefore, it is clear that he asks for the ability to discern in order to rule the people well.[105] The element then, includes the set of duties applicable to a king. This may include behaviour, but perhaps should be primarily seen with regard to the ability to discern the truth in legal judgements (for which Solomon receives praise directly afterwards demonstrating that he has received the gift from God: 1 Kgs 3:16–28).[106]

The following example may be similar to example 2.83, referring to discernment in how to govern well.

2.84. 2 Samuel 19:36

בֶּן־שְׁמֹנִים שָׁנָה אָנֹכִי הַיּוֹם הַאֵדַע ׀ בֵּין־טוֹב לְרָע אִם־יִטְעַם עַבְדְּךָ אֶת־אֲשֶׁר אֹכַל וְאֶת־אֲשֶׁר אֶשְׁתֶּה אִם־אֶשְׁמַע עוֹד בְּקוֹל שָׁרִים וְשָׁרוֹת וְלָמָּה יִהְיֶה עַבְדְּךָ עוֹד לְמַשָּׂא אֶל־אֲדֹנִי הַמֶּלֶךְ

I am eighty years old today. Can I know between good and bad? Or can your servant taste – what I eat or what I drink? Or can I still hear the sound of singing men and singing women? Why should your servant be an additional burden to my lord the king?

In example 2.84, King David has just offered to provide for the man speaking (Barzillai) as a reward for his loyalty in providing for the king (2 Sam 19:33–34, 37). This example suggests that "knowing good and bad" is an ability that can be lost with very old age. In this case it has been linked by some with discerning what is pleasurable from what is not.[107] However, this may not be the case. Barzillai presents himself as being concerned not with whether he will benefit from the king, but rather with not being a מַשָּׂא (burden) to the king.[108] In this light, the lack

---

[104] I.e. to "carry on daily business." Simon J. DeVries, *1 Kings*, WBC 12 (Waco, TX: Word, 1985), 52.

[105] Lissa M. Wray Beal, *1 & 2 Kings*, ApOTC 9 (Downers Grove, IL: IVP, 2014), 87.

[106] DeVries sees the request as asking for the ability to determine truth from falsehood in order to administer justice. However, he finds expression of this request in Solomon's ability "to suppress all outward show of rebelliousness to the end of his reign." So he interprets it more widely than just truth versus falsehood. DeVries, *1 Kings*, 52–53.

[107] For example, Anderson writes, "he would have been unable to enjoy the pleasures of court-life… He also pointed out that he was no longer able to tell the difference between good and bad. We take it as a rhetorical exaggeration, referring to what is pleasant and unpleasant rather than to ethical values." A. A. Anderson, *2 Samuel*, WBC 11 (Waco, TX: Word, 1989), 239.

[108] Baldwin sees emphasis in the concern about burdening the king (rather than his own pleasure). Joyce G. Baldwin, *1 and 2 Samuel: An Introduction and Commentary*, TOTC 8 (Downers Grove, IL: IVP, 2008), 296.

84   CHAPTER 2

of ability to distinguish between טוֹב and רָע would indicate his inability to be a counsellor. His inability to taste or hear would indicate an inability to provide input into selection of food and entertainment. By presenting himself as an unworthy burden he is able to secure a place in the court for Chimham (2 Sam 19:39).[109] The element being modified by טוֹב and רָע here is likely the same or very similar to that in example 2.83. It would refer to the things about which a king may seek counsel: to discern between positive and negative judgements/decisions.

From examples 2.81–2.84, it appears that "knowing (between) good and bad" refers to discernment. This discernment might take various nuances. In examples 2.81–2.82, it appears to be that which a person is expected to be taught and learn as they age. In examples 2.83–2.84, the discernment is in reference to the duties of a king to rule well. While the sample of phrases is small, it is notable that all uses appear to be closely linked to behaviour. As such it seems that it refers to discerning between right and wrong. With reference to the king (and his counsellors) that extends to judging the behaviour of others as טוֹב or רָע.

Having analysed these examples, we turn to the use in Genesis. They are all fairly similar, relating to עֵץ הַדַּעַת טוֹב וָרָע (the tree of the knowledge of good and bad) and its function in the story. We will look at one example here.

2.85. Genesis 3:5–6a

כִּי יֹדֵעַ אֱלֹהִים כִּי בְּיוֹם אֲכָלְכֶם מִמֶּנּוּ וְנִפְקְחוּ עֵינֵיכֶם וִהְיִיתֶם כֵּאלֹהִים יֹדְעֵי טוֹב וָרָע
וַתֵּרֶא הָאִשָּׁה כִּי טוֹב הָעֵץ לְמַאֲכָל וְכִי תַאֲוָה־הוּא לָעֵינַיִם וְנֶחְמָד הָעֵץ לְהַשְׂכִּיל

"For God knows that in the day you eat from it your eyes will be opened, and you will be like God, knowing good and bad." The woman saw that the tree was good for food, and that it was a desirable thing for the eyes and the tree was desirable to give understanding…

Example 2.85 exhibits a parallel structure, with the tree being considered with reference to food, the eyes, and knowledge. These parallels are colour coded in the example. This structure means that the phrase "knowing good and bad" is in semantic parallel with the verb הַשְׂכִּיל (to give understanding). In light of examples 2.81–2.84, such understanding is likely to concern how to live. However, the manner of knowing is to be the same as that of God and the manner of receiving it is not sanctioned by God. The implication of it being an unsanctioned activity may be that

---

[109] This would be more valuable as he would be securing a long-term position in the king's court. Victor Harold Matthews, "The Unwanted Gift: Implications of Obligatory Gift Giving in Ancient Israel," *Semeia* 87 (1999): 96.

רַע AND SCHEMA

it is knowledge of good and bad according to their own, and not God's, judgement.[110]

Consider example 2.86 below. 4Q417 contains parallels to Genesis 1–3.[111] However, a key difference between the texts that make up 4QInstruction and Genesis 2–3 is that the prohibition on eating to gain knowledge of good and bad is "inconsistent with one of the most important goals of 4QInstruction" (to attain this knowledge)[112] and so unlikely to have been part of the original text.

2.86. 4Q417 1 I, 16b–19

וינחילׄוׄׄנׄו לאנוש עם ֯עם֯ רוח כ]י[אׄ

כתבנית קדושים יצרו ועוד לוא נתן הגו֯י לרוח בשר כי לא ידע בין

[טו]בׄ לרע כמשפט [ר]וחו [ ] [ ] ואתה בן מבין הבט [ ] ברז נהיה ודע

[ ]ת כול חי והתהלכו יפקוד[113] עׄׄל מעש[יו][114]

He bequeathed it [the Vision of Hagu] to Enosh with a people of spirit, because according to the image of holy ones he formed him. But he did not again give Hagu to the spirit of flesh, because it did not know between [goo]d[115] to bad according to the judgement of his [i.e. God's] [sp]irit [ ] But you, understanding son, look on the mystery that is to be[116] and know [ ]? all life and the way one conducts himself he appoints over [his] deed[s].

[110] Wenham argues that it refers to acquisition of wisdom and that in this passage it refers to pursuit of it without reference to revelation and God which is said to be the beginning of knowledge (Prov 1:7). Gordon J. Wenham, *Genesis 1–15*, WBC 1 (Waco, TX: Word, 1987), 63.

[111] John J. Collins, "In the Likeness of the Holy Ones: The Creation of Humankind in a Wisdom Text from Qumran," in *The Provo International Conference on the Dead Sea Scrolls: Technological Innovations, New Texts, and Reformulated Issues*, ed. Donald W. Parry and Eugene Ulrich, STDJ 30 (Leiden: Brill, 1999), 609–18; John Strugnell, Daniel J. Harrington, and Torleif Elgvin, *Qumran Cave 4, Sapiential Texts, Part 2, 4Q Instruction (Mûsar Lĕ Mēvîn): 4Q415 Ff. with a Re-Edition of 1Q26*, DJD 34 (Oxford: Clarendon, 1994), 165–66; Matthew J. Goff, "The Worldly and Heavenly Wisdom of 4QInstruction" (PhD diss., University of Chicago, 2002), 110–13. It may also conflate some aspects of Genesis 1–3. Elgvin draws attention to this with particular reference to the trees of the garden which are all said to give knowledge (4Q423 1–2 I, 1–2). Strugnell, Harrington, and Elgvin, *Qumran Cave 4*, 509; see also Goff, "The Worldly and Heavenly Wisdom," 121.

[112] Goff, "The Worldly and Heavenly Wisdom," 125.

[113] Accordance reads הֺפקוד. However, from the photograph, the י should be preferred. Goff, "The Worldly and Heavenly Wisdom," 303.

[114] I follow Goff here. Goff, "The Worldly and Heavenly Wisdom," 303–4.

[115] As with example 2.82, the regularity of expression and the size of the gap (not to mention a portion of the final letter being present) means we can be sure טוב is the missing word in example 2.85. The gap can be viewed online in the eighteenth line of the image at https://www.deadseascrolls.org.il/explore-the-archive/image/B-370823.

[116] Goff's translation of רז נהיה. He also suggests "the eternal mystery." He notes that "No translation, however, fully captures the phrase's temporal sense." Matthew J. Goff, "The Mystery of Creation in 4QInstruction," *DSD* 10 (2003): 169.

86 CHAPTER 2

The presence of the preposition phrase כמשפט [ר]וחו (according to the judgement of his [sp]irit) may be a useful help for understanding the Genesis text. As noted above, the prohibition against gaining knowledge in Genesis 2–3 is missing here. The knowledge on offer in 4Q417 is viewed positively and that on offer in Genesis 2–3 is viewed negatively. Additionally, the knowledge in 4Q417 is explicitly that which is according to the judgement of God's spirit. This fits well with the suggestion that the knowledge in Genesis 2–3 is that which Adam and Eve take without reference to God's judgement.

Another feature of knowledge of טוב and רַע in 4Q417 may help us understand the extent of such knowledge. The knowledge appears tied to the acquisition of wisdom, which is gained through "contemplation upon revealed mysteries" and makes one like the angels through the attainment of heavenly wisdom.[117] The mysteries which give such knowledge appear connected to wider knowledge of creation.[118] However, in example 2.86, the contrast between the "people of spirit" and the "spirit of flesh" and their respective ties to right and wrong action[119] indicate that the knowledge has a strong relationship with such actions.

Given the analysis in examples 2.81–2.84, where such knowledge is related to discerning what right action is, it seems that this is the knowledge in view in the Genesis text. However, knowledge which allows good "moral judgement" may involve a wide array of information. Additionally, from the use with monarchs and their advisors (examples 2.83–2.84), it appears to be more than simply moral judgement, but ability to make wise decisions in general.[120]

Summary

This group of uses is unusual. However, it seems likely that the usage in reference to COGNITION is tied to wisdom to know the appropriate course of action. In such use, טוב and רַע act as opposing categories of positive and negative courses of action. This group appears to be used primarily concerning right and wrong actions according to God. However, it contains a more general sense of wisdom to make wise judgements about

---

[117] Goff, "The Worldly and Heavenly Wisdom," 113, 120.
[118] Goff, "The Mystery of Creation."
[119] Goff, "The Worldly and Heavenly Wisdom," 108–13.
[120] Thus a general knowledge may be considered a part of this as it aids good decision making. Such general knowledge wisdom was given to Solomon by God (1 Kgs 5:9–14 [Eng. 4:29–34]).

רַע AND SCHEMA

things which may not be considered moral: for example, a moral ruler may not rule well, but knowledge of good and bad appears to cover both morality and statesmanship.

2.3.10 AFFLICTION

There are 11 occurrences of רַע modifying a word which indicates a human disease or affliction in the analysed texts [6; 0; 5; 0; 0]. In such use it modifies שְׁחִין, נֶגַע, מַחֲלֶה, מַדְוֶה, חֳלִי, and תַּחֲלֻאִים.

Occurrences: Deut 7:15; 28:35, 59; Job 2:7; Eccl 6:2; 2 Chron 21:19; 1QpHab IX, 2; 4Q181 1, 1; 4Q368 10 I, 8*; 4Q504 1–2 III, 8*; 11Q5 XXIV, 12.

Example 2.87 demonstrates this use of רַע.

> 2.87. Deuteronomy 7:15a
>
> וְהֵסִיר יְהוָה מִמְּךָ כָּל־חֹלִי וְכָל־מַדְוֵי מִצְרַיִם הָרָעִים
>
> The Lord will turn from you every sickness, and all the bad diseases of Egypt...

It appears that the element being modified here is AFFLICTION. However, a disease is clearly already a negative thing in that it negatively impacts human life (and so has negative prosody)[121] and as such is not described with terms such as טוֹב. Applying a negative modification may be expected to amplify the sense of severity. This assessment is supported by three uses where רַע sits in semantic parallel with גָּדוֹל (great). Example 2.88 demonstrates this use.[122]

> 2.88. Deuteronomy 28:59
>
> וְהִפְלָא יְהוָה אֶת־מַכֹּתְךָ וְאֵת מַכּוֹת זַרְעֶךָ מַכּוֹת גְּדֹלוֹת וְנֶאֱמָנוֹת וָחֳלָיִם רָעִים וְנֶאֱמָנִים
>
> The Lord will make your wounds and the wounds of your descendants extraordinary, great and lasting wounds, and bad and lasting sicknesses.

In this example, the neutral גָּדוֹל and negative רַע function as amplifiers of severity modifying AFFLICTION. In this use, רַע may be considered to apply a negative modification. רַע can be considered as the negative pole of a טוֹב to רַע scale. While the positive end of the scale is not relevant

---

[121] Using the definition of Monika Bednarek, "Semantic Preference and Semantic Prosody Re-Examined," *Corpus Linguistics and Linguistic Theory* 4 (2008): 133.

[122] It also occurs in 4Q181 1, 1 and 4Q368 10 I, 8 although the discourse is fragmented.

88   CHAPTER 2

when considering AFFLICTION, the application of the negative term serves
to indicate severity by evoking the negative end of the scale.

2.3.11 חַיָּה (animal)

There are 9 occurrences of רַע modifying חַיָּה (animal) in the analysed
texts [7; 0; 0; 0; 2]. This use appears to exist in very specific circumstances, always in the phrase חַיָּה רָעָה.

Occurences: Gen 37:20, 33; Lev 26:6; Ezek 5:17; 14:15, 21; 34:25;
m. Taʿan. 3:5; m. ʾAbot 5:9.

From the examples 2.89–2.91 presented below, it appears that חַיָּה רָעָה
refers to a dangerous animal. It eats people (example 2.89), its removal is
considered a blessing (example 2.90), and it can be a punishment (examples 2.91). The effects of having חַיָּה רָעָה in the land is comparable to that
of famine and war (examples 2.90–2.91).

> 2.89. Genesis 37:20
>
> וְעַתָּה | לְכוּ וְנַהַרְגֵהוּ וְנַשְׁלִכֵהוּ בְּאַחַד הַבֹּרוֹת וְאָמַרְנוּ חַיָּה רָעָה אֲכָלָתְהוּ וְנִרְאֶה
> מַה־יִּהְיוּ חֲלֹמֹתָיו
>
> Come now, lets kill him and throw him in one of the cisterns. We will say
> a bad animal ate him, then we will see what will become [of] his dreams!

> 2.90. Leviticus 26:6
>
> וְנָתַתִּי שָׁלוֹם בָּאָרֶץ וּשְׁכַבְתֶּם וְאֵין מַחֲרִיד וְהִשְׁבַּתִּי חַיָּה רָעָה מִן־הָאָרֶץ וְחֶרֶב
> לֹא־תַעֲבֹר בְּאַרְצְכֶם
>
> I will give you peace in the land. You will lie down and none will
> frighten [you]. I will remove [the] bad animal from the land and [the]
> sword will not pass through your land.

> 2.91. Ezekiel 5:17
>
> וְשִׁלַּחְתִּי עֲלֵיכֶם רָעָב וְחַיָּה רָעָה וְשִׁכְּלֻךְ וְדֶבֶר וָדָם יַעֲבָר־בָּךְ וְחֶרֶב אָבִיא עָלַיִךְ
> אֲנִי יְהוָה דִּבַּרְתִּי
>
> I will send on you famine and [the] bad animal. They will bereave you
> of children. Plague and blood will pass through you and I will bring
> [the] sword on you. I the LORD have spoken.

However, חַיָּה can operate in the above contexts without רַע. In fact,
there are more examples of חַיָּה used without רַע than with it in these
contexts, and these include variation of use within texts (and thus within
idiolects and dialects).[123] Consider examples 2.92–2.93:

---

[123] These include: Ex 23:29; Lev 26:21; Deut 7:22; Isa 35:9; Jer 12:9; Ezek 29:5; 34:5,
8, 28; Hos 2:14; 13:8. Ben Sira 39:30 may also be included here, however it is modified
by a term indicating dangerous quality: שֵׁן (tooth).

רַע AND SCHEMA
89

2.92. Ezekiel 33:27b

אֲשֶׁר בֶּחֳרָבוֹת בַּחֶרֶב יִפֹּלוּ וַאֲשֶׁר עַל־פְּנֵי הַשָּׂדֶה לַחַיָּה נְתַתִּיו לְאָכְלוֹ וַאֲשֶׁר בַּמְּצָדוֹת
וּבַמְּעָרוֹת בַּדֶּבֶר יָמוּתוּ

Whoever is in the waste places will fall by the sword, whoever is in the field I will give to the animal for its food, and whoever is in the strong-holds and in the caves will die by the plague.

2.93. Job 5:22–23

לְשֹׁד וּלְכָפָן תִּשְׂחָק וּמֵחַיַּת הָאָרֶץ אַל־תִּירָא
כִּי עִם־אַבְנֵי הַשָּׂדֶה בְרִיתֶךָ וְחַיַּת הַשָּׂדֶה הָשְׁלְמָה־לָךְ

You will laugh at destruction and at famine, and from the animal of the land you will not fear. Because your covenant is with the stones of the field, and the animal of the field has made peace with you.

If, as Clines suggests,[124] חַיָּה is taken to refer to wild animals then these examples would present natural behaviour of that category. In the cognitive context, an element of the category ANIMAL(WILD) is that it is HARMFUL TO HUMANS. This is such that a sign of divine blessing is having peace with the חַיָּה (example 2.93, cf. Job 5:8, 17). רַע is not necessary to understand such animals are dangerous. However, when רַע is applied it emphasises the negative aspects of the חַיָּה. As when רַע modifies AFFLICTION, a negative חַיָּה is considered with respect to how it affects humans.

2.4 CONCLUSION

The analysis of chapter 2 (§2.3) has demonstrated that רַע can modify a wide range of differing elements. In most circumstances of use, רַע provides a negative qualification to the element. This can give the impression of a wide range of polysemes. However, such variations are due not to variations in how רַע operates, but in the elements it modifies; elements which themselves need to be understood within the cognitive context of the ancient society. That being said, there were some variations in the operation of רַע.

Firstly, the manner in which רַע modifies elements which are neutral versus those which are negative[125] needs addressing. In both examples 2.94

---

[124] Clines has argued that חַיָּה is generally used to describe wild animals. See Clines, *DCH* חַיָּה II and David J. A. Clines, "Cattle, Flocks and Other Beasts: Why Terms for Animal Groups Matter" (paper presented at the 23rd Congress of IOSOT, Aberdeen, 2019).

[125] This is similar to negative semantic prosody, although that concept is used in reference to words themselves. Bednarek, "Semantic Preference," 133; see also John McHardy Sinclair, *Trust the Text: Language, Corpus and Discourse* (London: Routledge, 2004), 144–45.

90   CHAPTER 2

and 2.95, רַע applies a negative qualification. However, in 2.94 it amplifies a negative element and in 2.95 it modifies a neutral element.

    2.94. Psalm 144:10b

הַפּוֹצֶה אֶת־דָּוִד עַבְדּוֹ מֵחֶרֶב רָעָה

The one who rescues David, his servant, from the bad sword.

In example 2.94, the element being modified by רַע is not the implement SWORD, but the element of a sword: HARMFUL TO HUMANS.

    2.95. Jeremiah 24:2

הַדּוּד אֶחָד תְּאֵנִים טֹבוֹת מְאֹד כִּתְאֵנֵי הַבַּכֻּרוֹת וְהַדּוּד אֶחָד תְּאֵנִים רָעוֹת מְאֹד
אֲשֶׁר לֹא־תֵאָכַלְנָה מֵרֹעַ

One basket had very good figs, like the first-ripe figs, and the other basket had very bad figs which could not be eaten from badness.

In example 2.95, the element modified is the quality of the figs: FRUIT(QUALITY). It is a neutral element which is considered on a scale of טוב to רַע.

These examples demonstrate that where רַע modifies an element that may be considered as negative, it serves to emphasise the negative element of the concept in view. For the examples of חֶרֶב (sword) and חַיָּה (animal), this entails foregrounding the negative element HARMFUL TO HUMANS of the concepts SWORD and ANIMAL(WILD).[126] In contrast, for תְּאֵנָה (fig), the element FRUIT(QUALITY) is modified to become FRUIT(BAD QUALITY).[127]

Secondly, contrary to Myhill,[128] רַע has both objective and subjective usage.[129] רַע may also evoke a negative category in contrast to טוב (or יָפֶה) or the negative direction of a scale.[130] These uses may be visualised as in

---

[126] This is a feature that can be seen in "overlapping antonyms." Where the element being modified is negative, it would likely be impossible for טוב to occur. This can perhaps be seen with terms of AFFLICTION (§2.3.10) although the argument is from silence. As an example of this from English, Cruse presents "?*How good is Mary's toothache?*." Cruse, *Meaning in Language*, 157.

[127] It might be argued that the element here is still HARMFUL TO HUMANS. However, in example 2.95, these bad quality figs are presented as being maximally bad in that they cannot be eaten. The qualification implies that a scale of טוב to רַע is understood, and that something רַע is not necessarily inedible. The qualification was necessary to indicate that these particular רַע figs were inedible.

[128] Myhill, "Subjective Hebrew Raʿ."

[129] The objective use was indicated a number of times across a number of areas: ACT, examples 2.18–2.19 §2.3.1; HUMAN, example 2.34 §2.3.2; EYE(MENTAL STATE), §2.3.4 (used in examples 2.47–2.52); BEHAVIOUR, example 2.55 §2.3.5. Subjective use is clearly indicated at times through use of phrases such as בְּעֵינֵי- (in the eyes of…).

[130] The scalar use was detected a number of times across a number of areas: ACT, example 2.20 §2.3.1; COMMODITY, examples 2.35, 2.37, and 2.42 §2.3.3; GENEROSITY, example 2.50 §2.3.4 (in use with עַיִן; eye).

Figure 2.1 below, with A corresponding to the categorical use and B corresponding to relative scalar use.

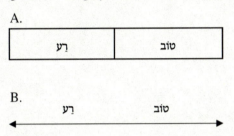

Figure 2.1. Category Versus Scalar Use of רַע

Lastly, an unexpected variation in the use of רַע was found in §2.3.8. In the phrase בִּעֵר רַע, it was shown to refer not simply to a negative qualification, but to GUILT, specifically GUILT incurred by a רַע ACT. While the explanations of some commentators tend towards this description,[131] it does not appear to have been clearly laid out as a meaning of רַע. This is examined further in Chapter 4 (§4.5) where it is demonstrated that such use is a semantic pattern common to the semantic domain עָוֹן. In such use the term functions as a metonym to refer to the GUILT incurred by an ACT. This portion of the finding is outside the definitions previously highlighted by Dohmen and Myhill. It points to the existence of polysemy in the use of רַע specifically driven by the semantic domain of use.[132] It also points to the value of the semantic domain investigations pursued in Chapters 3 and 4.

---

[131] Woods refers to the "evil" being "that which contaminates society" which appears to be this idea of guilt derived from a רַע ACT. Woods, *Deuteronomy*, 196. Merrill also appears to approach this interpretation in his explanations of 17:7 and 22:21. In particular in commenting on 22:21 he writes, "Only her death at the hands of the community could remove the disgrace brought about by her deed." Merrill, *Deuteronomy*, 261, 304.

[132] This is also goes unnoticed in DCH which lists such uses of רַע under "(ethical) evil." Clines, "רַע II 2," *DCH* 7:507–8.

CHAPTER 3

MAPPING THE LEXICAL SEMANTIC DOMAINS OF רַע

Chapter 2 identified one use of רַע which appeared to be influenced by a semantic pattern common to a specific semantic domain of use. In this chapter I begin the process of describing that semantic domain (and some additional ones) by mapping the lexical semantic domains of רַע using a semantic association analysis. Although this only leads to a partial picture of the domains of use of רַע, it does add important information to our understanding of רַע.

3.1 SEMANTIC ASSOCIATIONS OF רַע

3.1.1 Preliminary Matters

Before beginning the analysis, a few data management issues need to be discussed. These include two issues of identification (of words where textual damage is an issue, §3.1.1.1; and of semantic associations, §3.1.1.2), classification of semantic associations (§3.1.1.3), and the presentation of data (§3.1.1.4). Data presentation also includes some discussion of what can and cannot be said from statistics presented. Finally, additional details for determining which words are likely to be within the semantic domains of רַע are addressed (§3.1.1.5).

3.1.1.1 Textual Damage and Semantic Associations

In Chapter 2 (§2.1.1), I dealt with the process for identifying and selecting words for analysis. However, I did not discuss instances where textual damage impacted semantic associations. There were a number of occurrences where a semantic association was clearly present, but the text was damaged enough that the semantic associate was lost. An example of this can be found in Ketef Hinnom I, 9–10.[1]

---

[1] This text is rather damaged, but the important section presented here is in good condition but for the damage to the association.

94 CHAPTER 3

3.1. Ketef Hinnom I, 9–10

ᵒ𐤒 𐤙𐤉𐤛 𐤄[?] /𐤙𐤙 𐤙𐤉𐤅𐤁[𐤁]

[ha]b-beraka mik-kol [?]ḥ we-me-ha-ra°
… [the] blessing from every [?] and from the ᵒ𐤒 (*ra°*; bad).

While there is some conjecture over whether 𐤙𐤉𐤅𐤁 (*beraka*; blessing)
is the correct reading,[2] it is fairly clear that there is a semantic association
between the missing word and ᵒ𐤒 (*ra°*). The word has been reconstructed
in various ways, the most convincing of which may be 𐤄𐤉 (*paḥ*; snare).[3]
However, this word does not feature a common semantic association with
רַע and so it must be designated as a text where the semantic association
is too uncertain. In these cases the occurrence was counted initially, but
excluded from statistics (see §3.1.1.4).

However, on some occasions the target word or semantic associates
were included where they were partially missing or damaged but judged
as certain to be original.[4] These occurrences, along with less damaged
occurrences are marked by an asterisk (*) and reasons for inclusion are
addressed in Appendix C.

3.1.1.2 *Identifying Semantic Associations*

After occurrences (to be analysed) of a target word are identified, the
next step is to identify semantic associations of a word. Due to the likelihood of falsely imposing a foreign structure onto the language, it seems
appropriate to be liberal in the inclusion of semantic associations. As an
example of something that could be contentious, take Jonah 3:10:

3.2. Jonah 3:10

וַיַּרְא הָאֱלֹהִים אֶת־מַעֲשֵׂיהֶם כִּי־שָׁבוּ מִדַּרְכָּם הָרָעָה וַיִּנָּחֶם הָאֱלֹהִים עַל־הָרָעָה
אֲשֶׁר־דִּבֶּר לַעֲשׂוֹת־לָהֶם וְלֹא עָשָׂה

---

[2] Aḥituv writes "It is uneasy…" because "We did not encounter a blessing "from" something." He justifiably calls this reading "difficult" while presumably treating it as the most
likely from the evidence. Shmuel Aḥituv, *Echoes from the Past: Hebrew and Cognate
Inscriptions from the Biblical Period*, Carta Handbook (Jerusalem: Carta, 2008), 52–53.

[3] Although it may be tempting to resolve the difficulties by reading the lost letter as 𐤕 and thus
reading 𐤄𐤕 (*'āḥ*; brother) and ᵒ𐤒 (*rēa°*; neighbour), Barkay has also found some small
evidence of the downward stroke of the 𐤉 which would be difficult to reconcile with
the letter 𐤕. Gabriel Barkay et al., "The Amulets from Ketef Hinnom: A New Edition
and Evaluation," *BASOR*, 334 (2004): 58–59; Jeremy Daniel Smoak, *The Priestly Blessing
in Inscription and Scripture: The Early History of Numbers 6:24–26* (New York: Oxford
University Press, 2015), 26.

[4] One full reconstruction was included due to analysis and use in §2.3.9: 1Q28ᵃ I, 10–11
(see also §C.2).

MAPPING THE LEXICAL SEMANTIC DOMAINS OF רע 95

God saw their works, that they had turned from their רָעָה (ADJ.FS.bad) way and God relented concerning the רָעָה (N.FS.evil) that he said he would do to them and did not do [it].

In this example it is difficult to determine whether to count the phrase דֶּרֶךְ רָעָה as being semantically associated to the noun רָעָה (evil). We might argue that the use of the noun is clearly different in that it refers to a destructive event (Jonah 3:4). However, this argument may be applying a theological distinction on to what, linguistically, may not exist.

In cases such as these, there is great potential for imposing foreign cognitive categories and context (see §1.4.1) onto the text. For this reason, cases with a significant degree of uncertainty were considered to be semantically associated in the first instance, relying on later stages of analysis to eliminate any anomalous inclusions.

Example 3.2 pre-empts the next question: how do we deal with semantic associations involving phrases? Certain phrases may occur within certain domains where the individual words (or some of the individual words) would be absent. For example, there is a certain set of associations common to Leviticus,[5] Ezekiel, and the Mishnah:

3.3. Ezekiel 14:21a

כִּי כֹה אָמַר אֲדֹנָי יְהֹוִה אַף כִּי־אַרְבַּעַת שְׁפָטַי | הָרָעִים חֶרֶב וְרָעָב וְחַיָּה רָעָה וָדֶבֶר שִׁלַּחְתִּי

For thus says the Lord God "How much more when I send my four bad judgements, sword, and famine, and bad animals, and plague…

The words חֶרֶב (sword), רָעָב (famine), and דֶּבֶר (plague) only occur consistently with רע when it modifies חַיָּה (animal). This may be grounds for analysing the phrase חַיָּה רָעָה as a unit. However, initially phrasal units will be displayed as subsections within the analysis table. This will allow information to be visualised without hastening to a conclusion about how certain phrases function in the analysed Ancient Hebrew and Mishnaic Hebrew texts.

Including phrases like this immediately begs the question of when to include a phrase. The answer is that it depends on whether or not individual words or phrases are in semantic associations. Example 3.4 provides a good example where phrases can be properly separated.

---

[5] In Leviticus the association occurs with חֶרֶב (sword) only.

96   CHAPTER 3

3.4. Jeremiah 23:22b

וְיִשֻׁבוּם מִדַּרְכָּם הָרָע וּמֵרֹעַ מַעַלְלֵיהֶם

and if they turn from their bad way and from the badness of their
deeds.

In this example it is quite clear that the terms דֶּרֶךְ (way) and מַעֲלָל (deed)
are semantic parallels. The semantic associations in the phrases are רֹעַ‖רַע
and מַעֲלָל‖דֶּרֶךְ. Because these types of phrases are not represented in the
tables below we must be cautious in interpreting what the data means.
For example, רַע (bad) and טוֹב (good) appear in a wide range of contexts,
but the phrases they occur in and the frequency of these occurrences is
not represented in Table 3.3 (§3.1.2).

An important and closely related issue concerns when a string of text
is considered "too long" to be included as a semantic association. Clearly
clauses can be semantically associated to each other, or a word can be
semantically associated to a clause. We could argue that a dictionary definition is semantically associated to the word it defines. However, it would be
misguided to include such things in a semantic association analysis that aims
to determine semantic domains.

3.5. Ezekiel 36:31

וּזְכַרְתֶּם אֶת־דַּרְכֵיכֶם הָרָעִים וּמַעַלְלֵיכֶם אֲשֶׁר לֹא־טוֹבִים וּנְקֹטֹתֶם בִּפְנֵיכֶם עַל
עֲוֺנֹתֵיכֶם וְעַל תּוֹעֲבוֹתֵיכֶם

You shall remember your bad ways and your deeds which were not good
and you will be loathsome in your sight because of your iniquities and
your abominations.

In example 3.5, an association exists between דַּרְכֵיכֶם הָרָעִים (your רַע
ways), מַעַלְלֵיכֶם אֲשֶׁר לֹא־טוֹבִים (your deeds which were not good), עֲוֺנֹתֵיכֶם
(your iniquities), and תּוֹעֲבוֹתֵיכֶם (your abominations). The association
between רַע and טוֹב need not take into account the phrases. However, for
the associations with עָוֹן and תּוֹעֵבָה the entire phrase is important. It was
decided that phrases such as מַעַלְלֵיכֶם אֲשֶׁר לֹא־טוֹבִים (your deeds which
were not טוֹב) should be included. Furthermore, this is semantically a
negation of מַעֲלָלִים טוֹבִים (טוֹב deeds). Therefore, the schematic מַעֲלָל טוֹב
was tabulated as an association of תּוֹעֵבָה (abomination).[6] By way of contrast, 1 Kings 15:26 affords an example of what is not included.

---

[6] This is for ease of analysing tabulated data. At times this leads to schematic phrases
being tabulated that may not exist in the analysed text. Therefore, tabulated phrases
should not be assumed to be consistently what appears in text.

MAPPING THE LEXICAL SEMANTIC DOMAINS OF רַע 97

3.6. 1 Kings 15:26

וַיַּעַשׂ הָרַע בְּעֵינֵי יְהוָה וַיֵּלֶךְ בְּדֶרֶךְ אָבִיו וּבְחַטָּאתוֹ אֲשֶׁר הֶחֱטִיא אֶת־יִשְׂרָאֵל

He did the bad [thing] in the eyes of the LORD and he went in the way
of his father and in his sin with which he caused Israel to sin.

Example 3.6 is a difficult case. At face value it may appear that דֶּרֶךְ
(way) and חַטָּאת (sin) are semantic associates of רַע (bad). However, we
must note that the construction is not רַע אָבִיו (the רַע *of his father*). Therefore, we are led to the conclusion that to "do the רַע [thing]" is to "walk
in the way of *his father*" and also "in his father's sin." Thus "the רַע" is
semantically associated to the action of *walking in his father's sin* rather
than the term חַטָּאת (sin). We then might modify the analysis of the associations of that verse to the following:

3.7. 1 Kings 15:26

וַיַּעַשׂ הָרַע בְּעֵינֵי יְהוָה וַיֵּלֶךְ בְּדֶרֶךְ אָבִיו וּבְחַטָּאתוֹ אֲשֶׁר הֶחֱטִיא אֶת־יִשְׂרָאֵל

He did the bad [thing] in the eyes of the LORD and he went in the way
of his father and in his sin with which he caused Israel to sin.

This analysis of the semantic associations acknowledges the importance
of the verbs in the association. The association is between the two actions
to an extent that casts serious doubt on whether a close relationship exists
between the individual words. The discourse context supports this conclusion. The "sin" turns out to be primarily the gold calves created by Jeroboam
(1 Kgs 12:28–30; cf. "the sin of Jeroboam" 1 Kgs 15:34; 16:19, 25–26).

As a rule of thumb, verbs and verb phrases were excluded from analysis.
This is because of the issue outlined above through examples 3.5 and 3.6:
verbs are generally associated with our target words in a more complex
fashion such that they are out of the scope of the analysis. However, at
times verbs do feature, particularly as participles denoting people who
do an action. A prime example is found in the phrase פֹּעֲלֵי אָוֶן (doers of
villainy).[7] Although this phrase contains a verb, it is quite clear that it is
within the scope of the current analysis:

3.8. Psalm 28:3a

אַל־תִּמְשְׁכֵנִי עִם־רְשָׁעִים וְעִם־פֹּעֲלֵי אָוֶן

Do not drag me off with the wicked and with the doers of villainy.

---

[7] Readers may be surprised by the choice of "villainy" as a gloss for אָוֶן. The choice for this
is twofold. First, it allows glosses of אָוֶן and עָוֹן to be distinguished. Second, "iniquity,"
through its use to translate terms such as עָוֹן, has acquired senses proper to those terms.
The use of villainy was considered a relatively good way to avoid such links.

98 CHAPTER 3

Here the participle פּוֹעֲלֵי (doers) functions as a way of modifying the semantics of אָוֶן (villainy) from a thing to a person who does such a thing. In contrast to the issue in examples 3.6–3.7, the reference in example 3.8 is to a group of people (a thing) rather than an action.

Two final issues bear mention here: when two identical semantic associations occur within the same clause; and the distance of words in association.

3.9. Isaiah 5:20a

הוֹי הָאֹמְרִים לָרַע טוֹב וְלַטּוֹב רָע

Woe to those who say of what is bad "it is good" and of what is good "it is bad"…

While this case technically involves two occurrences of our target word רַע, it is counted as one occurrence for statistical purposes as it appears to comprise of a single contrast. As a consequence, while it is counted as two occurrences in our corpus it is excluded from some statistics in the same manner as occurrences where a semantic association was lost (see §3.1.1.4).

On rare occasions words are considered to be semantically associated when they occur over a number of verses. The greatest separation is perhaps seen in Ezekiel 14:13–19. These verses contain the same series of associations as seen in example 3.3. That is, the association occurs between the words: חֶרֶב (sword); רָעָב (famine); דֶּבֶר (plague), and the phrase חַיָּה רָעָה (רַע beast).

3.10. Ezekiel 14:13a, 15a, 17a, 19a

בֶּן־אָדָם אֶרֶץ כִּי תֶחֱטָא־לִי לִמְעָל־מַעַל וְנָטִיתִי יָדִי עָלֶיהָ וְשָׁבַרְתִּי לָהּ מַטֵּה־לָחֶם
וְהִשְׁלַחְתִּי־בָהּ רָעָב { ... }
לוּ־חַיָּה רָעָה אַעֲבִיר בָּאָרֶץ { ... }
אוֹ חֶרֶב אָבִיא עַל־הָאָרֶץ הַהִיא { ... }
אוֹ דֶּבֶר אֲשַׁלַּח אֶל־הָאָרֶץ הַהִיא

Son of man, when a land sins against me by acting unfaithfully and I stretch out my hand against it, and I break its staff of bread and I send famine against it {…}
If I cause bad animals to pass through the land {…}
Or I bring sword upon that land {…}
Or I send plague to that land…

In these cases the discourse structure must be such that the words or phrases are clearly construed by the author as semantically associated. In the above example this is demonstrated through the clause structures of

MAPPING THE LEXICAL SEMANTIC DOMAINS OF רע   99

the pronouncements. The conclusion is also made more certain through the verse that immediately follows (Ezek 14:21, example 3.11 below) which describes each of these in a list of אַרְבַּעַת שְׁפָטַי הָרָעִים (my four רע judgements).

3.1.1.3 *Initial Classification of Semantic Associations*

Semantic associations are initially classified by whether the similarity or contrast between two words or phrases is on view. This contains a rough judgement on the semantic prosody of the terms, which is to say the positive or negative connotation of the words or phrases.[8] For example, whereas in example 3.3 (replicated below as example 3.11), the words חֶרֶב (sword), and רָעָב (famine) may be considered in terms of their differences, in the text, their similarity as types of judgement is foregrounded. Their negative prosody as types of judgement is foregrounded. What distinguishes them from each other is relevant, but is not the focus of the text. The focus is their similar status as a רע judgements.

> 3.11. Ezekiel 14:21a
>
> כִּי כֹה אָמַר אֲדֹנָי יְהוִֹה אַף כִּי־אַרְבַּעַת שְׁפָטַי | הָרָעִים חֶרֶב וְרָעָב וְחַיָּה רָעָה וָדֶבֶר שִׁלַּחְתִּי
>
> For thus says the Lord God "How much more when I send my four bad judgements, sword, and famine, and bad animals, and plague...

Contrast this with example 3.9 above, where רע and טוב (good) are in semantic association. There, the prosody between the terms is in contrast. Rather than being concerned with what is similar, it is what is different (i.e. the contrast) between the terms that is being foregrounded. The analysis follows this basic categorisation, splitting associations by whether they have similar or contrasting prosody. This separation allows for an appropriately different treatment of words construed in similarity to those construed in opposition (see discussion in §3.1.2) and should aid the process of determining word meaning.

3.1.1.4 *Presentation of Data*

In each section of the analysis, raw occurrence data is presented first. This figure *will rarely match* what can be found in the concordances because certain occurrences are excluded at the initial stage (see §3.1.1.1

---

[8] This should not be confused with semantic preference which refers to which words a particular word collocates with. Bednarek, "Semantic Preference," 133.

100 CHAPTER 3

and §2.1.1). This is followed by the number of occurrences of the focus word with one or more semantic association and an *estimate* of the frequency of use of the focus word with semantic associations in the analysed Ancient Hebrew and Mishnaic Hebrew texts.[9]

The estimate is the percentage of uses of the focus word which contain one or more semantic association. To create this estimate, occurrences which were included in the corpus totals were excluded from the calculation: texts that were too fragmentary to determine whether or not a semantic association existed (e.g. §3.1.1.1, example 3.1); and the second occurrence when the focus word was used twice as part of the one idea (e.g. §3.1.1.2, example 3.9). This statistic is important because some words are used frequently in semantic associations whereas other words are rarely used in semantic associations. Where this second group coincides with less frequent words it can lead to a paucity of data and difficulty in determining the status of a word as within or outside the semantic domains of רע.

Following the initial statistics, data is presented in three tables. The first table contains frequencies of occurrence for each focus word in semantic associations. These are divided into semantic associations of similarity and opposition. The similarity and opposition columns *rarely add up to the total* column. This is because a particular occurrence can co-occur with one or more association of similarity *and* opposition. Additionally, the table only represents the occurrence of the focus word with *one or more* associations of similarity or opposition (depending on the column). No effort was taken at this point to describe occurrence with multiple associations.

The second and third tables present the full list of associations of similarity and opposition respectively. As mentioned in §3.1.1.2, phrases are represented in the table where the entire construction is necessary for the association. Occurrence data is split across phrase combinations; adding the occurrence figures will give a total for any given focus word. Focus words are ordered by frequency and then alphabetically. Location data (verse references) is given for the location of the main word under analysis in the section.[10]

---

[9] As an estimate it is subject to a certain degree of error. It should be treated as an estimate and not an exact figure. The general rule is. the more frequent the word, the more reliable the estimate. With words that occur rarely we may draw tentative conclusions from very high or very low figures.

[10] Semantic associates occasionally occur in a different verse, and very occasionally a different paragraph. For example, the association found in example 3.10 is recorded as Ezekiel 14:15 in Table 3.2, but as 14:17 in Table 3.11.

MAPPING THE LEXICAL SEMANTIC DOMAINS OF רַע 101

The decision was made to represent lexemes and phrases schematically. This means using the least marked forms.[11]. Where participles were used substantively, the participle is generally represented with the masculine singular form with a ו vowel letter. Predicative uses of adjectives are included together with attributive uses where the reference is the same and represented in attributive form. Finite verbs (when they appear) are represented by the third person masculine singular forms in the binyan they appear.

3.1.1.5 *Selection of Words*

The procedure for selection is according to the method in Chapter 1 (§1.5.2). It is on the basis of association to רַע, and words associated with רַע. Conversely, exclusion is on the basis of limited association with רַע and words associated with רַע. Words in associations of opposition are not as directly relevant to plotting the lexical semantic domain of רַע, therefore only associations of similarity are selected as target words for analysis in this chapter.[12]

In the process of delimiting the semantic domains of רַע we need to identify which words or phrases to select for association analysis. Using a numerical cut-off as the initial criteria is an effective method because many of the less common occurrences are expected to be outside the semantic domains of רַע. Following Burton, I will use three occurrences as the initial cut-off.[13] Despite this being the first criteria, others are used and applied

---

[11] Although in phrases construct forms are retained. Occasional exceptions were also made where least marked forms were not extant in the analysed texts.

[12] Some associations of opposition were selected for further analysis based on more stringent criteria. This did not produce any exceptional results, but did suggest some areas for future analysis. It is presented in Appendix B.2.

[13] Burton uses a chi-square test to determine her cut-off according to statistical significance. Burton, *The Semantics of Glory*, 60n42. For various reasons the assumptions that go into using that test are badly violated in the current analysis and so the test is not appropriate (see below). However, a selection of three occurrences should allow a manageable quantity of words to be analysed while relying on cross-checking in later phases of analysis to pick up any that should have been included. Ultimately, the current analytical method relies on patterns of associations. Therefore, the cross-checking of associations should provide adequate testing of domain eligibility.
The chi-square test for cooccurrence requires using a specific criteria for distance in order to calculate values for observed, and expected frequencies of association. Due to the format of the text, an easy rough estimate might use verse criteria. That is, cooccurrence within X number of verses. However, some important cases of semantic association occur across a number of verses (perhaps the most notable being in example 3.10). These cases would need to be excluded from calculation, which could skew results for certain associations and not fit the criteria for the current study. Additionally, the Mishnah is

102 CHAPTER 3

(see §3.1.2).[14] Words or phrases that occur in semantic association three or more times with any given other word or phrase will be referred to as *frequent* associates. Where words are grouped with phrases, the focus word shared in common is selected for further analysis.

Initially, words in associations of similarity are analysed further. Most frequent associates of רַע are analysed in the first round of analysis (§3.2). Most frequent associates of these words which occur at least once with רַע are analysed in the second round of analysis (§3.3). Any other words that are deemed in need of analysis are analysed in the third round of analysis (§3.4).

Using a numerical cut-off naturally runs the risk of excluding words which rarely occur in the corpus. In cases of words that occur 25 times or less and are associates, but not frequent associates of רַע or words related to רַע, they will be considered for analysis or exclusion in the third round after more frequent words that are related to רַע have been selected. Any word that occurs 10 times or less in the corpus is unlikely to contribute much to the understanding of רַע. Its extremely low frequency means no firm conclusions could be drawn. Nevertheless, such words are analysed in Appendix B.1 if they occur in association at least once with רַע.

3.1.2 Analysis of רַע (bad)

As noted in Chapter 2 (§2.2), the term רַע occurs a total of 540 times in the corpus. This figure is made up of 354[15] uses in the Hebrew Bible, 55 in Ben Sira, 43 in the Judean Desert texts, 1 in the Ancient Hebrew inscriptions, and 87 in the Mishnah [354; 55; 43; 1; 87]. Of these 540 occurrences, 253 occurrences (47%)[16] had identifiable lexical or phrasal semantic associations. These are broken down into corpus and association type in Table 3.1 below.

---

divided into *mishnayot*. Individual *mishnayot* are generally a lot longer than a Biblical Hebrew verse. The amount of work required to create a relatively stable estimate of distance for testing across corpora would be a significant project in itself. Therefore, this test could not be carried out effectively for the current data.

[14] See also §4.1. Most additional criteria are adapted from Brezina, McEnery, and Wattam's criteria for collocations. Vaclav Brezina, Tony McEnery and Stephen Wattam, "Collocations in Context: A New Perspective on Collocation Networks," *International Journal of Corpus Linguistics* 20 (2015): 140–41.

[15] Five occurrences which contain semantically significant variants were added: Genesis 41:3, 4 (SP); 4Q27 20–22, 29 [Num 22:32]; 1QIsa^a XXXVIII, 13 [Isa 45:7]; and XLVIII, 19 [Isa 59:7].

[16] Four occurrences were eliminated under the conditions specified in §3.1.1.1.

MAPPING THE LEXICAL SEMANTIC DOMAINS OF רֵעַ 103

Table 3.1. Number of Identifiable Lexical and
Phrasal Semantic Associations by Type of Association[17]

Corpus	Similarity		Opposition		Total
	n.	%	n.	%	n.
Hebrew Bible	92	62.6	75	51.0	147
Ben Sira	15	57.7	14	53.8	26
Judean Desert	12	42.9	18	66.7	27
Inscriptions[18]	0	–	0	–	0
Mishnah	8	15.1	46	86.8	53
Total	127	50.0	154	60.5	253

As we can see from Table 3.1, רֵעַ has a bias in semantic associations towards associations of opposition (60.5% vs. 50.0%).[19] However, this is driven by the Mishnah which showed a strong bias towards associations of opposition (86.8% vs. 15.1%). There is a bias towards associations of similarity in the Hebrew Bible corpus, no observable bias in Ben Sira, and slight bias towards opposition in the Judean Desert manuscripts. The list of associations of similarity can be seen in Table 3.2, and associations of opposition can be seen in Table 3.3.

Table 3.2. רֵעַ in Associations of Similarity

Lexeme	Association	No.	Location
רָשָׁע	רַע –	9	Ezek 7:24; Ps 10:15; Job 21:30; Prov 4:14; 12:12; 14:19; 24:20; Sir 11:33; 12:6
	עַיִן רָעָה –	1	’Abot 5:13
	שָׁכֵן רַע –	1	’Abot 1:7
חֶרֶב	רַע –	1	Sir 39:29*
	חַיָּה רָעָה –	6	Lev 26:6; Ezek 5:17; 14:15, 21; m. Ta‘an. 3:5; m. ’Abot 5:9
	חֳלִי רַע –	1	4Q504 1–2 III, 8
יַד חֶרֶב	רַע –	1	Job 5:19

[17] While column totals are simple addition, row totals are not. This is because a certain use of a word may exhibit both associations of similarity as well as associations of opposition.

[18] There was one (likely) non-identifiable parallel in KHinn I, 10 (see §3.1.1.1 example 3.1). The parallel requires reconstruction. The figure was excluded from the total for the purpose of statistical analysis.

[19] Statistic is for one or more association of opposition versus one or more association of similarity.

Lexeme	Association	No.	Location
רֹעַ	רַע –	7	Jer 23:22; 24:2; 24:3; 24:8; 25:5; 26:3; 1QHᵃ XV, 6
	רַע תֹּאַר –	1	Gen 41:3
רֹעַ לֵב	פָּנִים רָעִים –	1	Neh 2:2
רָעָה	רַע –	5	Deut 31:29; 1 Kgs 21:20; Jer 32:30; Ps 52:5 Eccl 8:11
	דֶּרֶךְ רַע –	2	Ezek 20:44; Jonah 3:10
	חַיָּה רָעָה –	1	Ezek 14:21
דֶּבֶר	רַע –	1	Sir 39:29*
	חַיָּה רָעָה –	4	Ezek 5:17; 14:15, 21; m. 'Abot 5:9
	חֳלִי רַע –	1	4Q504 1–2 III, 8
אָוֶן	רַע –	4	Isa 59:7; Mic 2:1; Ps 36:5; Prov 12:21
	עֲצַת רַע –	1	Ezek 11:12
גָּדוֹל	רַע –	2	Deut 6:22; Ezek 8:9
מַכָּה גְדוֹלָה	חֳלִי רַע –	1	Deut 28:59
	מַחֲלָה רַע –	1	4Q368 10 I, 8*
מִשְׁפָּט גָּדוֹל	מַחֲלָה רַע –	1	4Q181 1, 1
מָוֶת	רַע –	4	Deut 30:15; Job 5:19; Sir 11:14; 37:18
	דָּבָר רַע –	1	2 Kgs 4:41
עָוֹן	רַע –	2	Prov 16:6; Sir 7:1
	דֶּרֶךְ רַע –	1	Ezek 36:31
	מַעֲשֶׂה רַע –	2	Ezra 9:13; 4Q169 3–4 III, 3
רָעָב	חַיָּה רָעָה –	4	Ezek 5:17; 14:15, 21; m. 'Abot 5:9
	חֳלִי רַע –	1	4Q504 1–2 III, 8*
רַק	רַע –	2	Gen 41:20, 27
רַק בָּשָׂר	רַע מַרְאֶה –	2	Gen 41:3, 4
	רַע תֹּאַר –	1	Gen 41:19
חָמָס	רַע –	3	Isa 59:7; Jonah 3:8; Ps 140:2
שֶׁבֶת חָמָס	יוֹם רַע –	1	Amos 6:3²⁰
תּוֹעֵבָה	רַע –	2	2 Kgs 21:2; 2 Chr 33:2
	דָּבָר רַע –	1	Deut 17:5
	דֶּרֶךְ רַע –	1	Ezek 36:31

---

[20] The exact meaning of הַמְנַדִּים לְיוֹם רָע וַתַּגִּישׁוּן שֶׁבֶת חָמָס (Oh ones who put away the evil day and you bring near the seat of violence) is disputed (as the different interpretations in the commentaries attest). However, the verbs are in parallel and the two versets are syntactically parallel. At minimum this structure would create a forced semantic parallel. Francis I. Andersen and David Noel Freedman, eds., *Amos: A New Translation with Introduction and Commentary*, AB 24A (New York: Doubleday, 1989), 555–56; Shalom M. Paul, *Amos: A Commentary on the Book of Amos*, ed. Frank Moore Cross, Hermeneia (Minneapolis: Fortress, 1991), 204–5.

MAPPING THE LEXICAL SEMANTIC DOMAINS OF רַע 105

Lexeme	Association	No.	Location
בְּלִיַּעַל אִישׁ בְּלִיַּעַל דְּבַר בְּלִיַּעַל		1 1 1	1 Sam 30:22 Sir 11:33 Ps 101:4
דָּם	רַע – חַיָּה רָעָה –	2 1	Isa 33:15; 1QHᵃ XV, 6 Ezek 5:17
חֹשֶׁךְ		3	Isa 5:20; 45:7; Prov 2:12
יְרֵא אֱלֹהִים	סָר מֵרָע –	3	Job 1:1, 8; 2:3
יָשָׁר	סָר מֵרָע –	3	Job 1:1, 8; 2:3
מִרְמָה	רַע – דְּבַר רַע –	2 1	Ps 34:14; 52:5 Jer 5:28
קָטָן	רַע – רַע עַיִן –	2 1	m. Meʿil. 6:4 (×2) Sir 14:3
שָׂטָן	יֵצֶר רַע – פֶּגַע רַע –	1 2	11Q5 XIX, 16 1 Kgs 5:18; 4Q504 1–2 IV, 13*
תָּם	סָר מֵרָע –	3	Job 1:1, 8; 2:3
דַּק בָּשָׂר	רַע מַרְאֶה –	2	Gen 41:3, 4
הֶבֶל	חֳלִי רַע – עִנְיַן רַע –	1 1	Eccl 6:2 Eccl 4:8
זָר	רַע – רָעֵי גוֹיִם –	1 1	Ezek 30:12 Ezek 7:24
חַטָּאת	רַע – דֶּרֶךְ רַע –	1 1	11Q5 XXIV, 6 Ezek 33:11
מַר		2	Isa 5:20; Jer 2:19
מֵרַע מֵרַע אוֹהֵב		1 1	Ps 24:20 Sir 37:3
עִוֵּר	מוּם רַע –	2	Deut 15:21; 11Q19 LII, 10
עָרִיץ		2	Jer 15:21; Ezek 30:12
פִּסֵּחַ	מוּם רַע –	2	Deut 15:21; 11Q19 LII, 10
פֶּשַׁע	רַע – דֶּרֶךְ רַע –	1 1	Sir 10:6 Ezek 33:11
צָרָה	רַע – שְׁמוּעָה רָעָה –	1 1	Sir 51:12 3Q5 1, 3
שֶׁקֶר		2	Ps 52:5; 119:101
אִוֶּלֶת	מַעֲשֵׂי רַע –	1	1QHᵃ V, 20*
אוֹיֵב	הָמָן רַע –	1	Esth 7:6
אֹפֶל		1	Job 30:26

106 CHAPTER 3

Lexeme	Association	No.	Location
אַרְבֶּה	חַיָּה רָעָה –	1	m. Taʿan. 3:5
אֵשׁ		1	Sir 39:29*
אַשְׁמָה גְדוֹלָה[21]	מַעֲשֶׂה רַע –	1	Ezra 9:13
בֶּלַע		1	Ps 52:5
בַּעַל שְׁתַיִם	אִישׁ רַע –	1	Sir 6:1
בָּרָד		1	Sir 39:29*
גֵּאָה	דֶּרֶךְ רַע –	1	Prov 8:13
גָּאוֹן	דֶּרֶךְ רַע –	1	Prov 8:13
גָּלוּת	חַיָּה רָעָה –	1	ʾAbot 5:9
דַּל	רַע תֹּאַר –	1	Gen 41:19
דִּמְעָה		1	Sir 31:13
הוֹלֵלוֹת		1	Eccl 9:13
זִמָּה	כְּלִי רַע –	1	Isa 32:7
זֹעֵף	פָּנִים רָעִים –	1	Gen 40:7
הַוָּה		1	Ps 52:5
חַטָּא		1	Gen 13:13
חַיַּת שֵׁן		1	Sir 39:29*
חָסִיל	חַיָּה רָעָה –	1	m. Taʿan. 3:5
חֶרֶב רָעָה – יַד בֶּן נֵכָר		1	Ps 144:10
יֵרָקוֹן	חַיָּה רָעָה –	1	m. Taʿan. 3:5
כְּאֵב נֶאֱמָן כְּאֵב עוֹמֵד	חַיִּים רָעִים –	1[22]	Sir 30:17
כָּזָב		1	Hos 7:15
לֵבָב עִקֵּשׁ		1	Ps 101:4
מִדְיָנִים		1	Prov 6:14
מוּם	דָּבָר רַע –	1	Deut 17:1
מַכְאוֹב	יֵצֶר רַע –	1	11Q5 XIX, 16
מְעַט		1	Gen 47:9

---

[21] The decision was made to include this phrase here rather than with גָּדוֹל (great) because אַשְׁמָה (guilt) is being intensified by גְדוֹלָה (great-FS).

[22] Both כְּאֵב נֶאֱמָן (chronic pain) and כְּאֵב עוֹמֵד (continuous pain) occur in an association of similarity with the same use of חַיִּים רָעִים (bad life) and appear to be synonymous. For this reason it has been coded as one occurrence rather than two.

MAPPING THE LEXICAL SEMANTIC DOMAINS OF רע 107

Lexeme	Association	No.	Location
מִשְׁרָה		1	m. Ber. 3:5
נֶאֱמָן		1	Deut 28:59
נֶאֱצָה		1	Neh 9:28
נָדִיב		1	Job 21:30
נָחָשׁ	כֶּלֶב רַע –	1	m. Ned. 9:3
נָכְרִי	אִשָּׁה רָעָה –	1	Prov 6:24
נִשְׁחָת		1	Ezek 20:44
סִכְלוּת	הוֹלֵלוֹת רָעָה –	1	Eccl 10:13
עָוֶל		1	Sir 41:6
עַוְלָה	דָּבָר רַע –	1	Ps 64:6
עָמָל		1	Hab 1:13
עַקְרָב		1	Sir 39:29*
עֹשֵׂה סֵטִים		1	Ps 101:4
עָשׁוּק	מַעֲשֶׂה רַע –	1	Eccl 4:3
עֹשֶׁק		1	Ps 73:8
פַּחַד		1	4Q525 14 II, 12
פִּי תַהְפֻּכָה	דֶּרֶךְ רַע –	1	Prov 8:13
פִּיד		1	Job 31:29
פֶּלֶא		1	Sir 3:21
פָּרִיץ	רָעֵי גוֹיִם –	1	Ezek 7:24
פֶּתֶן		1	Sir 39:29*
צָמָא		1	4Q504 1–2 III, 8
צַר	הָמָן רַע –	1	Esth 7:6
קָטוֹן		1	m. Me'il. 6:4
קָלוֹן	שֵׁם רַע –	1	Sir 6:1
קָם עַל	הֵבִיא רַע –	1	Isa 31:2
קָשֶׁה	רַע מַעֲלָל –	1	1 Sam 25:3
רוּחַ טְמֵאָה	יֵצֶר רַע –	1	11Q5 XIX, 16
רֵישׁ		1	Sir 11:14
רְמִיָּה		1	Ps 52:5
רָע	פָּנִים רָעִים –	1	Neh 2:2
רֶשַׁע		1	Ps 5:5

108 CHAPTER 3

Lexeme	Association	No.	Location
שֶׁבֶר		1	Isa 59:7
שֹׁד		1	Isa 59:7
שִׁדָּפוֹן	חַיָּה רָעָה –	1	m. Taʿan. 3:5
שָׁוְא		1	Sir 30:17
שַׁחַד		1	Isa 33:15

Table 3.3. רַע in Associations of Opposition

Lexeme	Association	No.	Location
טוֹב	רַע –	88	Gen 2:9, 17; 3:5, 22; 24:50; 31:24, 29; 41:27; Lev 27:10, 12, 14, 33; Num 13:19; Deut 1:39; 30:15; Josh 23:15; 1 Sam 29:7; 2 Sam 13:22; 14:17; 19:36; 1 Kgs 3:9; 22:8, 18; 2 Kgs 2:19; Isa 5:20; 7:15, 16; 1QIsaᵃ XXXVIII, 13; Jer 24:2, 3, 8; 40:4; 42:6; Ezek 36:31; Amos 5:14, 15; Mic 1:12; Mal 2:17; Ps 34:15; 36:5; 37:27; 52:5; Job 2:10; 30:26; Prov 14:19, 22; 15:3; 31:12; Eccl 12:14; 2 Chr 18:17; Sir 11:14, 31; 12:4; 13:14, 15; 14:10; 31:24; 37:18, 27; 39:25 (×2)*; 39:27*, 34*; 1QS I, 4; II, 3; X, 18; 1Q28ᵃ I, 11; 4Q303 8; 4Q365 32, 7; 4Q367 3, 10; 4Q380 1 II, 5*; 4Q410 1, 6*; 4Q416 1, 15*; 4Q417 1 I, 18*; 4Q418 2+2a–c, 7; 4Q423 1–2 I, 7; 4Q423 5, 6*; 4Q525 14 II, 12; 11Q19 LV, 16; m. Ber. 9:2, 5; m. ʾAbot 2:9 (×5); 5:19
טוֹבָה הַשְּׁמוּעָה	דְּבַר רַע –	1	1 Sam 2:23
אוֹהֵב טוֹב	רַע –	1	Sir 37:3
יָפֶה		29	Gen 41:3, 4, 19; m. Ter. 2:6 (×4); 4:3; 6:6; m. ʿOr. 1:5; Šabb. 22:4; m. Ketub. 13:10 (×3); m. Ned. 9:8 (×2); m. B. Meṣ. 4:1 (×2); m. B. Bat. 5:6 (×4); m. ʿArak. 9:2; m. ʾOhal. 18:6; m. Miqw. 10:6 (×2); m. Zabim 2:2; 3:1; 4:3
הֲנָאָה/הֲנָיָיה[23]		10	m. Sanh. 8:5 (×10)

---

[23] These are listed under the same entry in Jastrow's dictionary. In all locations where associations of opposition with רַע exist, הֲנָאָה is found in the Eshkol manuscript and הֲנָיָיה is found in the Kaufmann manuscript. It is written below following the Kaufmann spelling.

MAPPING THE LEXICAL SEMANTIC DOMAINS OF רַע

Lexeme	Association	No.	Location
שָׁלוֹם	רַע –	5	Isa 45:7; 59:7; Ps 34:15; Prov 12:20; 4Q525 14 II, 12
	פֶּגַע רַע –	1	4Q504 1–2 IV, 13
צַדִּיק	רַע –	3	Prov 11:21; 12:13; 14:19
	אִישׁ רַע –	1	Prov 29:6
	עוֹשֵׂה רַע –	1	Ps 34:17
בָּרִיא	רַע –	1	Gen 41:20
	רַע מַרְאֶה –	1	Gen 41:4
בְּרִיא בָּשָׂר	רַע מַרְאֶה –	1	Gen 41:3
	רַע תֹּאַר –	1	Gen 41:19
אוֹר		3	Isa 5:20; 45:7; Job 30:26
חַיִּים		3	Deut 30:15; Sir 11:14; 37:18
מִשְׁפָּט	רַע –	2	Isa 56:2; 59:7
	דְּבַר רַע –	1	Eccl 8:5
חָפֵץ	רַע בְּעֵינ- –	2	Isa 65:12; 66:4
יָשָׁר		2	Jer 40:4; 11Q19 LV, 16
צֶדֶק		2	Ps 52:5; HazGab 20
בֵּינוֹנִי		1	m. Ter. 4:3
בְּרָכָה	פֶּגַע רַע –	1	4Q504 1–2 IV, 13
דַּרְכֵי אֱמֶת	מַעֲשֵׂי רַע –	1	1QH^a V, 20*
חָבֵר		1	Sir 37:3
חָכָם	חֵלֶק רַע –	1	ʾAbot 5:12
חָכְמָה	מַעֲשֵׂי רַע –	1	1QH^a V, 20
חָסִיד	עַיִן רָעָה –	1	ʾAbot 5:13
יֹשֶׁר		1	Prov 2:12
מְבַקְשֵׁי יהוה	אַנְשֵׁי רַע –	1	Prov 28:5
מַרְפֵּא		1	Prov 13:17
מָתוֹק		1	Isa 5:20
נְדִיבָה	כְּלֵי רַע –	1	Isa 32:7
נֹעַם		1	Prov 15:26
עֹשֶׁר		1	Sir 11:14
עֵת	דְּבַר רַע –	1	Eccl 8:5
צְדָקָה		1	Isa 56:2
תָּם לֵבָב		1	Ps 101:4

110 CHAPTER 3

Observations

Perhaps the most obvious observation is that the first three associations of opposition each occur more frequently than any of the associations of similarity. Of these, the second occurs primarily in the Mishnah, and the third exclusively within one verse (*mishnah*) of the Mishnah. As a result of this bias towards a small selection of oppositions, there were only 28 groups of words and phrases in associations of opposition. In contrast there were 101 groups of words and phrases in oppositions of similarity.

The most frequent association occurred between רַע (bad) and טוֹב (good), with a total of 89 times.[24] This is presumably indicative of their status as antonyms. The large number of associations of רַע (bad) and יָפֶה (beautiful) in the Mishnah indicates two antonym pairs in Mishnaic Hebrew.[25]

There was an unusual grouping of words and phrases listed as frequent associates of similarity: יָשָׁר (straight); יְרֵא אֱלֹהִים (one who fears God); and תָּם (perfect). These are clearly opposite concepts to someone who does רַע (bad); however, they are in an association of similarity with the phrase סָר מֵרָע (one who turns from bad).

Words Selected for Association Analysis

The initial list for association analysis in the "similarity" group is: רָשָׁע (wicked); חֶרֶב (sword); רֹע (badness); רָעָה (evil); דֶּבֶר (plague); אָוֶן (villainy); גָּדוֹל (great); מָוֶת (death); עָוֹן (iniquity); רָעָב (famine); רַק (thin); חָמָס (violence); תּוֹעֵבָה (abomination); בְּלִיַּעַל (worthlessness); דָּם (blood); חֹשֶׁךְ (darkness); מִרְמָה (deceit); קָטָן (small); and שָׂטָן (accuser/Satan). In addition to these there were two words and one phrase associated with the phrase סָר מֵרָע (one who turns from רַע): יָשָׁר (straight); יְרֵא אֱלֹהִים (one who fears God); and תָּם (perfect).

One of these inclusions has good reason to be eliminated without further analysis: גָּדוֹל (great). גָּדוֹל is used in associations of similarity with both רַע and its antonym טוֹב (for טוֹב: Isa 5:9). This is a clear indication that the word does not function as a member of the domains of רַע, but takes another role. In fact, the only time that רַע is in an association of similarity

---

[24] This figure is much greater than the 35 times Burton found them occurring *in parallelism*. This is because the current study includes the Mishnah, looks for *associations* rather than the more narrow *parallel*, and takes into account a wider textual context. Burton, *The Semantics of Glory*, 85.

[25] I have partially analysed the changing use of טוֹב and יָפֶה in my work Foster, "Is Everything 'Beautiful' or 'Appropriate' in Its Time?"

MAPPING THE LEXICAL SEMANTIC DOMAINS OF רַע   111

with גָּדוֹל is when they modify a negative element. In addition to the three uses with AFFLICTION (§2.3.10), there were two additional ones. One has a clear negative prosody (Ezek 8:6–9, both words modify תּוֹעֵבָה). The other time is in Deuteronomy 6:22 in the context of the judgements on Egypt during the Exodus.

3.12. Deuteronomy 6:22

וַיִּתֵּן יְהוָֹה אוֹתֹת וּמֹפְתִים גְּדֹלִים וְרָעִים | בְּמִצְרַיִם בְּפַרְעֹה וּבְכָל־בֵּיתוֹ לְעֵינֵינוּ

And the LORD set great and bad signs and wonders on Egypt, on Pharaoh, and on all his house before our eyes.

While the terms אוֹת (sign) and מוֹפֵת (wonder) may not have negative prosody themselves, in the context their reference is to the destructive events against Egypt which are negative. Both רַע and גָּדוֹל, then, modify a negative element. While גָּדוֹל may function like רַע under certain circumstances to emphasise a negative element, it represents a limited cooccurrence and overlap in uses. It should also be considered outside the semantic domains of רַע.[26]

Because of its status as the antonym to גָּדוֹל, קָטָן (small) can be removed from the initial analysis. If it is indicated as a potential member of the semantic domains of רַע through the analyses of other associations it will be reintroduced.

רַק (thin) only occurs five times, every time with רַע.[27] It will be tentatively considered part of the semantic domains of רַע, but such low frequency of use means no firm conclusions can be drawn.

Finally, although the current method might suggest the need to analyse frequent associates of the phrase סָר מֵרָע (one who turns from רַע), יָשָׁר (straight), יְרֵא אֱלֹהִים (one who fears God), and תָּם (perfect) will not be analysed further here. The phrase סָר מֵרָע has the opposite prosody to רַע, being something which is considered good rather than bad. Therefore, these uses should be considered along with oppositions when looking at רַע itself.

Words for inclusion in the first round of analysis can therefore be reduced to: רָשָׁע (wicked); חֶרֶב (sword); רֹעַ (badness); רָעָה (evil); דֶּבֶר (plague); אָוֶן (villainy); מָוֶת (death); עָוֹן (iniquity); רָעָב (famine); חָמָס (violence); תּוֹעֵבָה (abomination); בְּלִיַּעַל (worthlessness); דָּם (blood); חֹשֶׁךְ (darkness); מִרְמָה (deceit); and שָׂטָן (accuser/Satan).

---

[26] DCH includes both רַע and טוֹב as synonyms of גָּדוֹל due to their method for selection of synonyms (co-occurrence of two or more times). See Clines, "גָּדוֹל," DCH 2:320. They also note that words may be selected which do not qualify as synonyms or antonyms. See Clines, DCH 1:21.

[27] Two of which are Samaritan Pentateuch variants.

112 CHAPTER 3

3.2 ASSOCIATION ANALYSIS (SIMILARITY): ROUND 1

3.2.1 רָשָׁע (wicked)

רָשָׁע occurs 353 times in the analysed texts [266;[28] 18; 42; 0; 27]. In total, רָשָׁע has 235 occurrences (68%)[29] with at least one semantic association. Its occurrence with semantic associations by corpus is shown in Table 3.4 below. Tables 3.5 and 3.6 show the semantic associations of similarity and opposition respectively.

Table 3.4. Number of Identifiable Lexical and
Phrasal Semantic Associations with רָשָׁע by Type of Association

Corpus	Similarity		Opposition		Total
	n.	%	n.	%	n.
Hebrew Bible	73	40.6	127	70.6	180
Ben Sira	7	77.8	5	50.0	10
Judean Desert	10	40.0	18	72.0	25
Inscriptions	0	–	0	–	0
Mishnah	4	20.0	17	85.0	20
Total	94	40.0	167	71.1	235

Table 3.5. רָשָׁע in Associations of Similarity

Lexeme	Association	No.	Location
רַע		9	Ezek 7:21; Ps 10:15; Job 21:28; Prov 4:14; 12:12 14:19; 24:20; Sir 11:34; 12:6
עֵין רָעָה		1	'Abot 5:13
שָׁכֵן רַע		1	'Abot 1:7
אִישׁ אָוֶן		1	Isa 55:7
בַּעַל אָוֶן		1	4Q418 126 II, 7
מְתֵי אָוֶן		1	Job 22:18
פּוֹעֲלֵי אָוֶן		6	Ps 28:3; 92:8; 94:3; 101:8; 141:10; Prov 10:30
עָרִיץ		7	Isa 13:11; Ps 37:35; Job 15:20; 27:13; 1QH[a] X, 12; X, 26; 4Q434 1 I, 5*
אוֹיֵב		6	Ps 3:8; 9:6; 17:9; 37:20; 55:4; 92:8

---

[28] Three occurrences were added from the Judean Desert corpus: 4Q76 IV, 12 [Mal 3:21]; 4Q83 9 II, 7 [Ps 71:4]; CD XI, 21 [Prov 15:8].

[29] Five occurrences were eliminated under the conditions specified in §3.1.1.1.

MAPPING THE LEXICAL SEMANTIC DOMAINS OF רַע   113

Lexeme	Association	No.	Location
לֵץ		6	Ps 1:1; Prov 3:33; 9:7; 19:28; Sir 15:9; 1QHᵃ X, 12
בּוֹגֵד		4	Jer 12:1; Prov 2:22; 21:18; 1QHᵃ X, 12
בְּלִיַּעַל		2	Job 34:18; Sir 11:34
עֵד בְּלִיַּעַל		1	Prov 19:28
עֲדַת בְּלִיַּעַל		1	1QHᵃ X, 26
גּוֹי		4	Ps 9:6, 17, 18; Sir 35:23
חָנֵף		4	Job 20:5; 27:7; Prov 11:9; Sir 16:6
מֵרַע		4	Ps 26:5; 37:10; Job 8:22; Prov 24:19
שׂוֹנֵא		1	Job 8:22
שׂוֹנֵא יהוה		1	2 Chr 19:2
שׂוֹנֵא צַדִּיק		1	Ps 34:22
שׂוֹנֵא צִיּוֹן		1	Ps 129:4
אוֹהֵב חָמָס		1	Ps 11:5
אִישׁ חָמָס		2	Ps 140:5; Prov 3:33
חַטָּא		3	Ps 1:1, 5; 104:35
מְתֵי שָׁוְא		2	Ps 26:5; Sir 15:9
סוֹד שָׁוְא		1	1QHᵃ X, 26
שֶׁקֶר		1	Ps 109:2
דּוֹבֵר שֶׁקֶר		1	Ps 101:8
שִׂפְתֵי שֶׁקֶר		1	Ps 31:18
אִישׁ כָּזָב		1	Sir 15:9
דּוֹבְרֵי כָזָב		1	Ps 58:4
גֵּאֶה		2	Ps 94:3; Job 40:12
זֵד		2	Isa 13:11; 11Q5 XVIII, 13
זָדוֹן		1	Sir 35:23
אִישׁ זָדוֹן		1	Sir 15:9
חוֹטֵא		2	Prov 11:31; Eccl 8:13
חָלָל		2	Ezek 21:30; Ps 73:3
כְּסִיל		2	Prov 3:33; 19:28
מוֹאֵס		2	CD VII, 9; XIX, 6
עַוָּל		2	Job 27:7; Sir 16:11
פּוֹשֵׁעַ		2	Ps 37:38; 1QHᵃ X, 12
אִישׁ דָּם		1	Ps 139:19
אַכְזָרִי		1	Sir 35:23
אִשָּׁה פְּרוּשָׁה		1	m. Soṭah 3:4

114 CHAPTER 3

Lexeme	Association	No.	Location
בּוּז		1	Prov 18:3
גַּאֲוָה		1	Ps 36:12
גַּס רוּחַ		1	'Abot 4:7
דָּתָן		1	Ps 106:18
זָר	רִשְׁעֵי אֶרֶץ –	1	Ezek 7:21
חוֹמֵץ		1	Ps 71:4
חֶלְכָה		1	1QHᵃ XII, 35
חָמוֹץ		1	4Q83 9 II, 7
חָסִיד שׁוֹטֶה		1	m. Soṭah 3:4
חֶרְפָּה		1	Prov 18:3
חָתֵף		1	Sir 32:22
טָמֵא		1	Eccl 9:2
מוֹשֵׁל		1	Isa 14:5
מְעַוֵּל		1	Ps 71:4
מַקְשֵׁה עֹרֶף		1	Sir 16:11
מִרְמָה		1	Ps 109:2
מַת		1	Ps 17:13
נָדִיב		1	Job 21:28
נָלוֹז		1	Prov 3:33
נֶעְלָם		1	Ps 26:5
עֲדַת אֲבִירָם		1	Ps 106:18
עוֹבֵד עֲצַבִּים		1	1QpHab XIII, 4
עוֹזְבֵי תוֹרָה		1	Ps 119:53
עֲוִיל		1	Job 16:11
עָוֶל	דֶּרֶךְ רִשְׁעָה –	1	Ezek 3:19
עַוְלָה		1	4Q88 IX, 6*
עוֹשֵׂה רְמִיָּה		1	Ps 101:8
פָּרִיץ	רִשְׁעֵי אֶרֶץ –	1	Ezek 7:21
קָלוֹן		1	Prov 18:3
רֶשַׁע	דֶּרֶךְ רִשְׁעָה –	1	Ezek 3:19
שׁוֹגֶה מֵחֹק		1	Ps 119:119
שׁוֹטֶה		1	'Abot 4:7

MAPPING THE LEXICAL SEMANTIC DOMAINS OF רַע 115

Lexeme	Association	No.	Location
שָׂטָן		1	Ps 109:6
שִׂנְאָה		1	Ps 109:2
תֵּבֵל		1	Isa 13:11
תַּהְפֻּכָה		1	Prov 10:32

Table 3.6. רָשָׁע in Associations of Opposition

Lexeme	Association	No.	Location
צַדִּיק		128	Gen 18:23; 25 (×2); Exod 9:27; 23:7; Deut 25:1; 2 Sam 4:11; 1 Kgs 8:32; Isa 3:11; Isa 5:23; Ezek 3:18; 13:22; 18:20, 21, 27; 21:8, 9; 33:12, 14, 19; Hab 1:4, 13; Mal 3:18; Ps 1:6; 7:10; 11:2, 5; 32:10; 37:12, 16, 17, 21, 28, 32, 40; 55:4; 75:11; 97:10; 112:10; 146:9; Job 22:18; 36:6; Prov 2:22; 3:33; 4:19; 9:7; 10:6, 7, 11, 16, 20, 24, 25, 28, 30, 32; 11:8, 10, 23, 31; 12:5, 7, 10, 12, 21, 26; 13:5, 9, 25; 14:19, 32; 15:6; CD XI, 21; Prov 15:28, 29; 17:15; 18:5; 21:12, 18; 24:15, 16, 24; 25:26; 28:1, 12, 28; 29:2, 7, 16, 27; Eccl 3:17; 7:15; 8:14 (×2); 9:2; 2 Chr 19:2; Sir 12:3; 13:17; 16:11; CD I, 19; IV,7; XX,21; 1QHᵃ VII, 30; XII, 39; XV, 15; 1Q34bis 3 I, 2; 4Q177 9, 7; 4Q508 1, 1; 4Q511 63 III, 4; m. Sanh. 6:5; 8:5 (×5); 10:3, 5; m. 'Abot 1:8; 4:15; 5:1; m. Neg. 12:5
נֶפֶשׁ צַדִּיק		1	Prov 10:3
יָשָׁר		10	Ps 11:6; 37:38; Prov 2:22; 3:33; 11:11; 12:6; 14:11; 15:8; 21:18, 29
יְשַׁר לֵב		4	Ps 11:2; 32:10; 94:13; 97:10
יְשַׁר דֶּרֶךְ		2	Ps 37:14; 1QHᵃ X, 12
חָסִיד		7	1 Sam 2:9; Ps 37:28; 97:10; m. 'Abot 5:10, 11, 13, 14
דַּל		4	Isa 11:4; Ps 82:2, 4; 4Q418 126 II, 7
טוֹב		4	Eccl 9:2; Prov 14:19; 1QHᵃ VI, 23; 11Q5 XVIII, 13
עָנִי		4	Ps 37:14; 82:2; Job 36:6; Prov 3:33
אֶבְיוֹן		3	Ps 37:14; 82:4; 1QHᵃ XIII, 19

116 CHAPTER 3

Lexeme	Association	No.	Location
חָכָם		3	Prov 3:33; 9:7; Sir 15:9
עָנָו		3	Isa 11:4; Ps 37:10; 147:6
תָּם		3	Ps 37:38; Job 8:22; 9:22
תָּמִים		3	Ps 37:20; Prov 2:22; 11:5
זוֹרֵעַ צְדָקָה		1	Prov 11:18
מְרַדֵּף צְדָקָה		1	Prov 15:9
צֶדֶק	דֶּרֶךְ רְשָׁעָה –	1	Ezek 3:19
מוֹרֵה צֶדֶק		1	1QpHab XI, 4
אוֹהֵב יהוה		1	Ps 145:20
אִישׁ שָׁלוֹם		1	Ps 37:38
אֱמוּן		1	Prov 13:17
בּוֹטֵחַ בִּיהוה		1	Ps 32:10
בָּחִיר		1	1QpHab V, 5
בָּרֵי לֵבָב		1	Ps 73:3
זוֹבֵחַ		1	Eccl 9:2
טָהוֹר		1	Eccl 9:2
יְגִיעַ כַּף		1	Job 10:3
יְגִיעֵי כֹחַ		1	Job 3:17
יְרֵא יהוה		1	Eccl 8:13
יָתוֹם		1	Ps 82:2
כָּשֵׁר		1	m. Ned. 1:1
מַשְׂכִּיל		1	Dan 12:10
נָקִי		1	Exod 23:7
קֹוֵי בִיהוה		1	Ps 37:10
רָשׁ		1	Ps 82:2
שָׁבֵי פֶּשַׁע		1	1QH^a VI, 35
תֹּם		1	Prov 10:30

Observations

רָשָׁע (wicked) has a strong bias towards associations of opposition (71.1% vs. 40.0%). This is primarily driven by its antonymic relationship to צַדִּיק (righteous) which itself occurs 54.9% of the time that רָשָׁע exhibits

MAPPING THE LEXICAL SEMANTIC DOMAINS OF רַע 117

one or more semantic association.[30] In terms of associations of similarity, its primary ties are to רַע and אָוֶן (villainy), with a slightly less frequent association with חָמָס (violence). This indicates that it is likely to form part of the semantic domains of רַע.

Terms which did not appear as main terms for רַע, but occurred three or more times with רָשָׁע include: עָרִיץ (ruthless); אוֹיֵב (enemy); לֵץ (scoffer); בּוֹגֵד (traitor); גּוֹי (nation); חָנֵף (impious); מֵרַע (evildoer); שׂוֹנֵא (hater); חַטָּא (sin); שָׁוְא (worthlessness); and שֶׁקֶר (lie). Of these terms, עָרִיץ, אוֹיֵב, מֵרַע, חַטָּא, שָׁוְא, and שֶׁקֶר were found to occur in an association of similarity with רַע at least once and so will be analysed in the second round of analysis.

3.2.2 חֶרֶב (sword)

חֶרֶב occurs 465 times in the analysed texts [415;[31] 3; 40; 7]. In total, חֶרֶב has 123 occurrences (27%)[32] with at least one semantic association. Its occurrence with semantic associations by corpus is shown in Table 3.7 below. Tables 3.8 and 3.9 show the semantic associations of similarity and opposition respectively.

Table 3.7. Number of Identifiable Lexical and
Phrasal Semantic Associations with חֶרֶב by Type of Association[33]

Corpus	Similarity		Opposition		Total
	n.	%	n.	%	n.
Hebrew Bible	108	97.3	5	4.5	110
Ben Sira	2	100.0	0	–	2
Judean Desert	8	100.0	0	–	8
Inscriptions	0	–	0	–	0
Mishnah	2	100.0	0	–	2
Total	120	97.6	5	4.1	123

[30] It may co-occur with other associations of opposition and or with associations of similarity.

[31] Three uses from the Samaritan Pentateuch and the Judean Desert were added: Deuteronomy 2:8 (SP); 4Q51 3a–e, 33 [1 Sam 2:33]; 1QpHab VI, 8 [Hab 1:17].

[32] Four occurrences were eliminated under the conditions specified in §3.1.1.1.

[33] While column totals are simple addition, row totals are not. This is because a certain use of a word may exhibit both associations of similarity as well as associations of opposition.

118 CHAPTER 3

Table 3.8. חֶרֶב in Associations of Similarity

Lexeme	Association	No.	Location
רָעָב		48	Deut 32:25; Isa 51:19; Jer 5:12; 11:22; 14:12, 13, 15 (×2), 16, 18; 15:2; 16:4; 18:21; 21:7, 9; 24:10; 27:8, 13; 29:17, 18; 32:24, 36; 34:17; 38:2; 42:16, 17, 22; 44:12 (×2), 13, 18, 27; Ezek 5:12, 17; 6:11, 12; 7:15 (×2); 12:16; 14:17, 21; Lam 4:9; 1 Chr 21:12; 2 Chr 20:9; 4Q162 2, 1; 4Q171 1–2 II, 1; 4Q504 1–2 III, 8*; m. 'Abot 5:8
דֶּבֶר		37	Exod 5:3; Lev 26:25; Deut 28:22; Jer 14:12; 21:7, 9; 24:10; 27:8, 13; 29:17, 18; 32:24, 36; 34:17; 38:2; 42:17, 22; 44:13; Ezek 5:12, 17; 6:11, 12; 7:15 (×2); 12:16; 14:17, 21; 33:27; 38:21; Amos 4:10; 1 Chr 21:12; 2 Chr 20:9; Sir 39:30; 40:9*; 4Q171 1–2 2 II, 1; 4Q504 1–2 III, 8; m. 'Abot 5:8
קֶשֶׁת	חֶרֶב –	14	Gen 48:22; Josh 24:12; 2 Sam 1:22; 1 Kgs 6:22; Isa 21:15; 41:2; Hos 1:7; 2:20; Zech 9:13; Ps 7:13; 37:14, 15; 44:7; Neh 4:7
דּוֹרֵךְ קֶשֶׁת	נוֹשֵׂא מָגֵן וְחֶרֶב –	1	1 Chr 5:18
רֶשֶׁף קֶשֶׁת	חֶרֶב –	1	Ps 76:4
חֲנִית		12	1 Sam 13:19, 22; 17:45, 47; 21:9; Isa 2:4; Nah 3:3; Ps 57:5; Job 41:18; 1QM XI, 2; 1QHᵃ XIII, 13; 2Q23 1, 5
רָעָה		10	Deut 32:25; Jer 5:12; 11:22; 42:17; 44:18; 49:37; Ezek 6:11; 14:21; 2 Chr 20:9; Sir 40:9
חַיָּה		1	Ezek 33:27
חַיָּה רָעָה		6	Lev 26:6; Ezek 5:17; 14:17, 21; m. Taʿan. 3:5; m. 'Abot 5:8
חַיַּת שֵׁן		1	Sir 39:30
מִלְחָמָה	חֶרֶב –	3	Hos 1:7; 2:20; Ps 76:4
אִישׁ מִלְחָמָה	שׁוֹלֵף חֶרֶב –	1	Judg 20:17
כְּבֵד מִלְחָמָה	חֶרֶב נְטוּשָׁה –	1	Isa 21:15
מְלוּמֵּד מִלְחָמָה	אֲחוּז חֶרֶב –	1	Song 3:8
מֵת מִלְחָמָה	חֲלַל חֶרֶב –	1	Isa 22:2
לְמוּדֵי מִלְחָמָה	נוֹשֵׂא מָגֵן וְחֶרֶב –	1	1 Chr 5:18

MAPPING THE LEXICAL SEMANTIC DOMAINS OF רַע 119

Lexeme	Association	No.	Location
חֵץ		7	Deut 32:25; 32:42; Isa 49:2; Ps 7:13; 57:5; 64:4; Prov 25:18
מָוֶת	חֶרֶב –	5	Jer 15:2; 18:21; 43:11; Job 27:14; Sir 40:9
	יַד חֶרֶב –	1	Job 5:20
כְּלִי מָוֶת	חֶרֶב –	1	Ps 7:13
שְׁבִי		5	Jer 15:2; 43:11; Dan 11:33; Ezra 9:7; 4Q169 3–4 II, 5
דָּם		4	Ezek 5:17; 14:17; 38:21 Sir 40:9
חַרְחֻר		3	Deut 28:22; Sir 40:9; 4Q169 3–4 II, 5
מָגֵן		3	Deut 33:29; Ps 76:4; 1 Chr 5:18
רֹמַח		3	1 Kgs 18:28; Joel 4:10; Neh 4:7
אִישׁ חַיִל	שׁוֹלֵף חֶרֶב –	2	Judg 20:46; 2 Sam 24:9
אֵשׁ		2	Sir 39:30; Ezek 38:21
בְּהֱמַת אֶרֶץ		1	Jer 15:3
שֵׁן בְּהֵמָה		1	Deut 32:25
בִּזָּה		2	Dan 11:33; Ezra 9:7
גָּלוּת		2	4Q169 3–4 II, 5; m. 'Abot 5:8
חַלְחָלָה		2	Ezek 30:4; 4Q385b 1, 3
יֵרָקוֹן		2	Deut 28:22; m. Ta'an. 3:5
כֶּלֶב		1	Jer 15:3
יַד כֶּלֶב		1	Ps 22:21
כְּלִי		1	1 Sam 21:9
רַע	חֶרֶב –	1	Sir 39:30
	יַד חֶרֶב –	1	Job 5:20
שֶׁבֶר		2	Isa 51:19; Sir 40:9
שֹׁד		2	Isa 51:19; Sir 40:9
שִׁדָּפוֹן		2	Deut 28:22; m. Ta'an. 3:5
אֶבֶן אֶלְגָּבִישׁ		1	Ezek 38:21
אַרְבֶּה		1	m. Ta'an. 3:5
בַּז		1	4Q169 3–4 II, 5
בָּרָד		1	Sir 39:30

CHAPTER 3

Lexeme	Association	No.	Location
בֹּשֶׁת		1	Ezra 9:7
גָּפְרִית		1	Ezek 38:21
גֶּשֶׁם שׁוֹטֵף		1	Ezek 38:21
דַּלֶּקֶת		1	Deut 28:22
הָרוּג	מְטֹעֲנֵי חֶרֶב –	1	Isa 14:19
הָרַע	קוֹרֵא חֶרֶב –	1	Jer 25:29
חֳלִי רַע		1	4Q504 1–2 III, 8
חֵמַת זוֹחֵל עָפָר		1	Deut 32:25
חָסִיל		1	m. Taʿan. 3:5
טֶבַח		1	Isa 65:12
יָד		1	Ps 17:13
כִּידוֹן		1	1 Sam 17:45
לֶהָבָה		1	Dan 11:33
מַאֲכֶלֶת		1	Prov 30:14
מַסָּע		1	Job 41:18
מֵפִיץ		1	Prov 25:18
נֶשֶׁק		1	Job 39:22
סוּס		1	Hos 1:7
סֹלְלָה		1	Jer 33:4
עָוֹן		1	Ezek 32:27
עוֹף שָׁמַיִם		1	Jer 15:3
עַקְרָב		1	Sir 39:30
פֶּרֶשׁ		1	Hos 1:7
פֶּתֶן		1	Sir 39:30
צָמָא		1	4Q504 1–2 III, 8
צָרָה		1	2 Chr 20:9
קַדַּחַת		1	Deut 28:22
קֶטֶב		1	Deut 32:25
רֶשֶׁף		1	Deut 32:25
שֶׁלַח		1	Neh 4:12
שַׁחֶפֶת		1	Deut 28:22
שִׁרְיָה		1	Job 41:18

MAPPING THE LEXICAL SEMANTIC DOMAINS OF רַע 121

Table 3.9. חֶרֶב in Associations of Opposition

Lexeme	Association	No.	Location
שָׁלוֹם		3	Lev 26:6; Jer 14:13; 34:4
בֶּטַח		1	Hos 2:20
טוֹב		1	Jer 44:18

Observations

חֶרֶב (sword) occurs almost exclusively in associations of similarity (97.6% vs. 4.1%). Its most frequent associates are רָעָב (famine), and דֶּבֶר (plague). These terms co-occur in associations of similarity 29 times. The decision was made to split the occurrences of רַע into different groups depending on which term it modified. This was primarily driven by the discovery of two out of eight occurrences of חַיָּה (animal) in an association of similarity with חֶרֶב where it was not in the phrase חַיָּה רָעָה. This suggests the term רַע is optional but could be part of the standard form when חַיָּה is used in association with חֶרֶב, רָעָב, and דֶּבֶר.[34]

The connection חֶרֶב, רָעָב, and דֶּבֶר have with רַע appears to be through the phrase חַיָּה רָעָה.[35] However, there are two frequent co-associates between חֶרֶב and רַע which are not associated with רַע primarily through the phrase חַיָּה רָעָה: רָעָה (evil); and מָוֶת (death). This suggests further analysis is required to determine the location of חֶרֶב in relation to the semantic domains of רַע.

The remaining frequent associates of חֶרֶב include (in order of frequency): קֶשֶׁת (bow); חֲנִית (spear); מִלְחָמָה (war); חֵץ (arrow); שְׁבִי (captivity); דָּם (blood); חַרְחֻר (burning); מָגֵן (sword); and רֹמַח (spear). Apart from דָּם which is part of the round one analysis, none of these words appear in associations of similarity with רַע.

---

[34] For statistics of רָעָב and דֶּבֶר with רַע see sections 2.8 and 2.5 respectively. Keeping in mind that the Ancient Hebrew and Mishnaic Hebrew corpus is not uniform in dialect and time of completion, it is possible that later uses were heavily influenced by the potentially early use in Torah (Lev 26:6; this depends on how one dates the Torah). It is notable that Ezekiel which contains the most uses of the standard phrase also includes the one use where חַיָּה receives no modification (Ezek 33:27).

[35] The one occurrence of רַע with חֶרֶב in Sir 39:29 is disputed with the Old Greek's λιμος, suggesting the reading רָעָב (famine).

122 CHAPTER 3

3.2.3 רֹעַ (badness)

רֹעַ occurs 30 times in the analysed texts [20;[36] 7; 3; 0; 0]. In total, רֹעַ
has 24 occurrences (80%) with at least one semantic association. Its occurrence with semantic associations by corpus is shown in Table 3.10 below.
Tables 3.11 and 3.12 show the semantic associations of similarity and
opposition respectively.

Table 3.10. Number of Identifiable Lexical and
Phrasal Semantic Associations with רֹעַ by Type of Association[37]

Corpus	Similarity		Opposition		Total
	n.	%	n.	%	n.
Hebrew Bible	15	93.8	5	31.3	16
Ben Sira	1	20.0	4	80.0	5
Judean Desert	3	100	0	0	3
Inscriptions	0	–	0	–	0
Mishnah	0	–	0	–	0
Total	19	79.2	9	37.5	24

Table 3.11. רֹעַ in Associations of Similarity

Lexeme	Association	No.	Location
רַע	רֹעַ –	7	Jer 23:22; 24:2, 3, 8; 25:5; 26:3; 1QHᵃ XV, 6
רַע תֹּאַר	רֹעַ –	1	Gen 41:19
פָּנִים רָעִים	רֹעַ לֵב –	1	Neh 2:2
רָעָה	רֹעַ אִשָּׁה –	1	Sir 25:17
	רֹעַ מַעֲלָל –	3	Ps 28:4; Hos 9:15; 11Q19 LIX, 7
דָּם	רֹעַ מַעֲלָל –	1	Isa 1:16
	מַחְשֶׁבֶת רֹעַ –	1	1QHᵃ XV, 6
דַּל		1	Gen 41:19
זָדוֹן	רֹעַ לֵבָב –	1	1 Sam 17:28
חֹשֶׁךְ	עָרְמַת רֹעַ –	1	1QS IV, 11
חָמוֹץ	רֹעַ מַעֲלָל –	1	Isa 1:16

[36] One occurrence has been added from the Judean Desert corpus: 1QIsaᵃ I, 19 [Isa 1:16].
[37] While column totals are simple addition, row totals are not. This is because a certain
use of a word may exhibit both associations of similarity as well as associations of
opposition.

MAPPING THE LEXICAL SEMANTIC DOMAINS OF רַע

Lexeme	Association	No.	Location
מֵרַע	רֹעַ מַעֲלָל –	1	Isa 1:16
עָוֹן	רֹעַ מַעֲלָל –	1	1QIsaᵃ I, 19
פֹּעַל	רֹעַ מַעֲלָל –	1	Ps 28:4
רָע	רֹעַ לֵב –	1	Neh 2:2
רַק בָּשָׂר		1	Gen 41:19
שֹׁעָר		1	Jer 29:17
תּוֹעֵבָה	רֹעַ מַעֲלָל –	1	Jer 44:22

Table 3.12. רֹעַ in Associations of Opposition

Lexeme	Association	No.	Location
טוֹב [38]	רֹעַ –	1	Sir 31:24
	רֹעַ אִישׁ –	2	Sir 42:14 (×2)[39]
טוֹב		2	Jer 24:2, 3
הֵיטִיב	רֹעַ מַעֲלָל –	1	Isa 1:16
	רֹעַ אִישׁ –	1	Sir 42:14[40]
יְפֵה תֹאַר		1	Gen 41:19
בְּרִיאַת בָּשָׂר		1	Gen 41:19
מִשְׁפָּט	רֹעַ מַעֲלָל –	1	Isa 1:16
יָטַב	רֹעַ פָּנִים –	1	Eccl 7:3

Observations

רֹעַ has a strong bias towards associations of similarity (79.2% vs. 37.5%). These associations of similarity are taken up primarily by רַע (47.4%). Additionally, the only words that רֹעַ occurred with three or more times in associations of similarity were from the same word family: רַע and רָעָה. Together these made up 63.2% of associations of similarity. The primary opposition was טוֹב (goodness), with other words in its word family also occurring (albeit less than three times). These initial observations indicate that רֹעַ should be considered within the semantic domains of רַע.

---

[38] Occurrences of טוֹב (good) in Ben Sira may actually represent additional occurrences of טוֹב (good) as the lack of pointing renders them indistinguishable.

[39] Manuscripts Mas 1H IV, 25 and Sir B 12r4.

[40] Manuscript Sir B 12r4.

124 CHAPTER 3

3.2.4 רָעָה (evil)

רָעָה occurs 367 times in the analysed texts [317; 31; 11; 1; 7]. In total
רָעָה occurs 143 times (40%)[41] with at least one semantic association. Its
occurrence with semantic associations by corpus is shown in Table 3.13
below. Tables 3.14 and 3.15 show the semantic associations of similarity
and opposition respectively.

Table 3.13. Number of Identifiable Lexical and
Phrasal Semantic Associations with רָעָה by Type of Association

Corpus	Similarity		Opposition		Total
	n.	%	n.	%	n.
Hebrew Bible	78	66.7	43	36.8	117
Ben Sira	9	55.3	8	50.0	16
Judean Desert	5	100.0	0	0.0	5
Inscriptions	0	–	0	–	0
Mishnah	0	0.0	5	100.0	5
Total	92	64.3	56	39.2	143

Table 3.14. רָעָה (evil) in Associations of Similarity

Lexeme	Association	No.	Location
חֶרֶב		10	Deut 32:23; Jer 5:12; 11:23; 42:17; 44:17; 49:37; Ezek 6:10; 14:22; 2 Chr 20:9; Sir 40:9
רָעָב		8	Deut 32:23; Jer 5:12; 11:23; 42:17; 44:17; Ezek 6:10; 14:22; 2 Chr 20:9
עָוֹן		7	Isa 13:11; Jer 36:31; Hos 7:1; Ps 40:13; Job 22:5; Sir 7:1; 4Q171 1–2 II, 3
צָרָה		7	Deut 31:17, 21; 1 Sam 10:19; Jer 15:11; Ps 71:20; 2 Chr 20:9; Sir 6:10
רַע		5	Deut 31:29; 1 Kgs 21:21; Jer 32:32; Ps 52:3; Eccl 8:11
דֶּרֶךְ רַע		2	Ezek 20:43; Jonah 3:10
דֶּבֶר		6	Jer 28:8; 42:17; Ezek 6:10; 14:22; 2 Chr 20:9; Sir 40:9*

[41] Five occurrences were eliminated under the conditions specified in §3.1.1.1.

MAPPING THE LEXICAL SEMANTIC DOMAINS OF רַע   125

Lexeme	Association	No.	Location
אָוֶן מַחְשֶׁבֶת אָוֶן		3 2	Ps 28:3; 41:8; 94:23 Jer 4:14; Prov 6:18
תּוֹעֵבָה		5	Jer 7:12; 44:5; Ezek 6:9; 16:23; Sir 15:13
רֹעַ אִשָּׁה רֹעַ מַעֲלָל		1 3	Sir 25:19 Ps 28:3; Hos 9:15; 11Q19 LIX, 8
בְּלִיַּעַל דְּבַר בְּלִיַּעַל		2 1	Nah 1:11; 4Q398 14–17 II, 5* Ps 41:8
חַטָּאת		3	Gen 50:17; 1 Sam 12:19; Sir 40:9
יָגוֹן אֵבֶל יָגוֹן		2 1	Gen 44:29; Ps 107:39 1QS IV, 13
מְבַקְשֵׁי נֶפֶשׁ	דּוֹרְשֵׁי רָעָה – חֲפֵצֵי רָעָה –	1 2	Ps 38:13 Ps 40:15; 70:3
מָוֶת		3	Prov 14:32;[42] Sir 37:18; 40:9
פֶּשַׁע		3	Gen 50:17; 1 Sam 24:12; Lam 1:22
שֶׁבֶר		3	Jer 4:6; 6:1; Sir 40:9
שֶׁקֶר לְשׁוֹן שֶׁקֶר		2 1	Ps 52:3; 4Q397 14–21, 9 Prov 6:18
דָּם		2	2 Sam 16:8; Sir 40:9
הֹוָה הֹוַת חֹשֶׁךְ		1 1	Isa 47:11 1QS IV, 13
חֶרְפָּה		2	Jer 24:9; Neh 1:3
מְזִמָּה		2	Jer 11:14; Ps 21:12
מִלְחָמָה		2	Jer 28:8; Ps 140:3
מִרְמָה		2	Ps 50:19; 52:3
שֹׁד		2	Jer 6:7; Sir 40:9
שִׂנְאָה		2	Ps 109:5; Prov 26:26

---

[42] בְּרָעָתוֹ יִדָּחֶה רָשָׁע וְחֹסֶה בְמוֹתוֹ צַדִּיק (The wicked is thrust down in his evil, but the righteous seeks refuge in his death). While some amend the text (e.g. Fox), those who treat
the text as it is have a variety of approaches to whose death the second half of the text
refers to (either to the death of the righteous or the wicked). If the death refers to the
death of the wicked it is possible that there is a semantic association here: רָעָה can
be used to refer to the punishment for doing רָעָה, such as in 2 Sam 16:8, וְהִנְּךָ בְּרָעָתֶךָ
כִּי אִישׁ דָּמִים אָתָּה (and behold you in your evil because you are a man of blood; see also
Isa 13:11). Michael V. Fox, *Proverbs 10–31: A New Translation with Introduction and
Commentary*, AB 18B (New Haven: Yale University Press, 2009), 585–86; William
McKane, *Proverbs: A New Approach* (London: SCM, 1992), 475; Bruce K. Waltke, *The
Book of Proverbs: Chapters 1–15*, NICOT (Grand Rapids, MI: Eerdmans, 2004), 607–8.

Lexeme	Association	No.	Location
שְׁנַת פְּקֻדָּה		2	Jer 11:23; 23:12
אָבְדָן		1	Esth 8:6
אוֹיֵב	מְבַקְשֵׁי רָעָה –	1	Esth 9:2
אֵיד		1	Jer 48:16
בֶּלַע		1	Ps 52:3
בֶּן חַיִל		1	1 Kgs 1:52
דֶּרֶךְ		1	Ezek 20:43
הֶבֶל		1	Eccl 2:21
הַוָּה		1	Ps 52:3
זַוְעָה		1	Jer 24:9
זְנוּת		1	Jer 3:2
חַיָּה רָעָה		1	Ezek 14:22
חֳלִי		1	Jer 6:7
חָמָס		1	Jer 6:7
חֲמַת זוֹחֵל עָפָר		1	Deut 32:23
חֵץ		1	Deut 32:23
חֲרוֹן אַף		1	Jer 49:37
חַרְחֻר		1	Sir 40:9
כָּזָב		1	Prov 6:18
כַּחַשׁ		1	Hos 7:3
כַּעַס		1	Eccl 11:10
מַחְשָׁבָה		1	Jer 18:11
מַכָּה		1	Jer 6:7
מַעַל		1	4Q397 14–21, 9
מַעֲלָל		1	Hos 7:2
מְשׁוּבָה		1	Jer 2:19
מָשָׁל		1	Jer 24:9
נֶאֱנָח		1	Lam 1:21
נְבָלָה		1	2 Sam 13:16
נֶגַע		1	Ps 91:10
סַעַר		1	Jer 25:32
עֶבְרָה		1	Sir 31:6

MAPPING THE LEXICAL SEMANTIC DOMAINS OF רַע   127

Lexeme	Association	No.	Location
עֵינַיִם רָמוֹת		1	Prov 6:18
עֲלִילָה		1	Ezek 20:43
עֲלִילָה הַנִּשְׁחָתָה		1	Ezek 20:43
עֹצֶר		1	Ps 107:39
עֹשֶׁק		1	Jer 6:7
צְפִירָה		1	Ezek 7:5
קֶטֶב		1	Deut 32:23
קְלָלָה		1	Jer 24:9
קֵץ		1	Ezek 7:5
רְמִיָּה		1	Ps 52:3
רְעָבוֹן		1	Ps 37:19
רֶשֶׁף		1	Deut 32:23
שָׁוְא		1	Ps 41:8
שׁוֹאָה		1	Isa 47:11
שׂוֹנֵא	מְבַקְשֵׁי רָעָה –	1	Esth 9:2
שֵׁן בְּהֵמָה		1	Deut 32:23
שְׁנִינָה		1	Jer 24:9
תַּאֲוַת נֶפֶשׁ		1	Sir 5:2
תַּזְנוּת		1	Ezek 16:23

Table 3.15. רָעָה in Associations of Opposition

Lexeme	Association	No.	Location
טוֹבָה		30	Gen 44:4; 50:20; Num 24:13; 1 Sam 24:18; 25:21; Jer 18:8, 20; 21:10; 32:42; 39:16; 44:27; Amos 9:4; Ps 35:12; 38:21; 109:5; Prov 17:13; Eccl 7:14; Neh 2:10; 2 Chr 18:7; Sir 6:11; 11:25 (×2)*; 12:5, 8, 9; m. Ber. 9:3 (×2), 5; m. Sanh. 1:6 (×2)
טוֹב		11	Gen 26:29; 1 Sam 20:13; 25:17; 29:6; Jer 44:17; Mic 3:2; Prov 11:27; 13:21; 17:20; Lam 3:38; Sir 37:18
שָׁלוֹם		8	1 Sam 20:13; 2 Kgs 22:20; Isa 57:1; Jer 23:17; 28:8; 29:11; 38:4; 2 Chr 34:28

Lexeme	Association	No.	Location
צֶדֶק		2	Ps 52:3; Eccl 7:15
אַהֲבָה		1	Ps 109:5
בְּחוּרָה		1	Eccl 12:1
בֶּטַח		1	Prov 1:33
הֵיטִיב		1	Sir 39:27
חַיִּים		1	Sir 37:18
כֵּן		1	Jer 23:10
צְדָקָה		1	Prov 11:19

Observations

רָעָה (evil) has a strong bias towards associations of similarity (64.3% vs. 39.2%). However, its strongest associations are those of opposition, with טוֹבָה (goodness) being its strongest associate followed by טוֹב (good), and שָׁלוֹם (peace) which occurs more frequently than all but one of the associations of similarity.

Words or phrases that occurred three or more times in an association of similarity with רָעָה are: חֶרֶב (sword); רָעָב (famine); עָוֹן (iniquity); צָרָה (distress); רַע (bad); דֶּבֶר (plague); אָוֶן (villainy); תּוֹעֵבָה (abomination); רֹעַ (badness); בְּלִיַּעַל (worthlessness); חַטָּאת (sin); יָגוֹן (grief); מְבַקְשֵׁי נֶפֶשׁ (people who seek [to take] life); מָוֶת (death); פֶּשַׁע (transgression); שֶׁבֶר (destruction); and שֶׁקֶר (lie). Because it has many associations with words associated with רַע, רָעָה should be considered within the semantic domains of רַע.

Words that did not appear in the main associations of רַע, but were associated with it at least once include: צָרָה; חַטָּאת; פֶּשַׁע; שֶׁבֶר, and שֶׁקֶר. These will be analysed in the second round of analysis.

3.2.5 דֶּבֶר (plague)

דֶּבֶר occurs 59 times in the analysed texts [50;[43] 2; 3; 4]. In total, דֶּבֶר occurs 48 times (81%) with at least one semantic association. It lacks any associations of opposition. Table 3.16 displays the number of occurrences with semantic associations of similarity by corpus. Table 3.17 lists all semantic associations of similarity.

---

[43] One occurrence was excluded: 2 Chronicles 6:28 = 1 Kings 8:37. Two occurrences in the Samaritan Pentateuch were added: Exodus 9:5, 19.

MAPPING THE LEXICAL SEMANTIC DOMAINS OF רַע   129

Table 3.16. Number of Identifiable Lexical and
Phrasal Semantic Associations with דֶּבֶר

Corpus	Similarity
	n.
Hebrew Bible	41
Ben Sira	2
Judean Desert	3
Inscriptions	0
Mishnah	2
Total	48

Table 3.17. דֶּבֶר in Associations of Similarity

Lexeme	Association	No.	Location
חֶרֶב		37	Exod 5:3; Lev 26:25; Deut 28:21; Jer 14:12; 21:7, 9; 24:10; 27:8, 13; 29:17, 18; 32:24, 36; 34:17; 38:2; 42:17, 22; 44:13; Ezek 5:12, 17; 6:11, 12; 7:15 (×2); 12:16; 14:19, 21; 33:27; 38:22; Amos 4:10; 1 Chr 21:12; 2 Chr 20:9; Sir 39:29; 40:9*; 4Q171 1–2 2 II, 1; 4Q504 1–2 III, 8; m. 'Abot 5:8
רָעָב		33	2 Sam 24:13; 1 Kgs 8:37; Jer 14:12; 21:7, 9; 24:10; 27:8, 13; 29:17, 18; 32:24, 36; 34:17; 38:2; 42:17, 22; 44:13; Ezek 5:12, 17; 6:11, 12; 7:15 (×2); 12:16; 14:19, 21; 1 Chr 21:12; 2 Chr 6:28; 20:9; 4Q171 1–2 II, 1; 1ı3 4 III, 4; 4Q504 1–2 III, 8; m. 'Abot 5:8
חַיָּה חַיָּה רָעָה חַיַּת שֵׁן		1 4 1	Ezek 33:27 Ezek 5:17; 14:19, 21; m. 'Abot 5:8 Sir 39:29
רָעָה		6	Jer 28:8; 42:17; Ezek 6:11; 14:21; 2 Chr 20:9; Sir 40:9*
דָּם		4	Ezek 5:17; 28:22; 38:22; Sir 40:9*
יֵרָקוֹן		3	Deut 28:21; 1 Kgs 8:37; 2 Chr 6:28
שִׁדָּפוֹן		3	Deut 28:21; 1 Kgs 8:37; 2 Chr 6:28
אַרְבֶּה		2	1 Kgs 8:37; 2 Chr 6:28
אֵשׁ		2	Ezek 28:22; Sir 39:29

130   CHAPTER 3

Lexeme	Association	No.	Location
חָסִיל		2	1 Kgs 8:37; 2 Chr 6:28
חַרְחֻר		2	Deut 28:21; Sir 40:9*
מַחֲלָה		2	1 Kgs 8:37; 2 Chr 6:28
נֶגַע		2	1 Kgs 8:37; 2 Chr 6:28
קֶטֶב		2	Hos 13:14; Ps 91:6
אֶבֶן אֶלְגָּבִישׁ		1	Ezek 28:22
בָּרָד		1	Sir 39:29
גָּלוּת		1	'Abot 5:8
גָּפְרִית		1	Ezek 28:22
גֶּשֶׁם שׁוֹטֵף		1	Ezek 28:22
דַּלֶּקֶת		1	Deut 28:21
חֳלִי רַע		1	4Q504 1–2 III, 8
מָוֶת		1	Sir 40:9*
מִלְחָמָה		1	Jer 28:8
מַפּוֹלֶת		1	m. Taʿan 3:4
עַקְרָב		1	Sir 39:29
פַּח יָקוּשׁ		1	Ps 91:3
פֶּתֶן		1	Sir 39:29
צָמָא		1	4Q504 1–2 III, 8
צָרָה		1	2 Chr 20:9
קַדַּחַת		1	Deut 28:21
רַע		1	Sir 39:29
רֶשֶׁף		1	Hab 3:5
שֶׁבֶר		1	Sir 40:9*
שֹׁד		1	Sir 40:9*
שַׁחֶפֶת		1	Deut 28:21

Observations

דֶּבֶר (plague) occurs exclusively in associations of similarity. Nearly all its main associations are found as main associations of חֶרֶב (sword). These are: רָעָב (evil) and חַיָּה רָעָה / חַיָּה (animal); רָעָב (famine); חֶרֶב;

MAPPING THE LEXICAL SEMANTIC DOMAINS OF רַע 131

דָּם (blood). Four out of the six associations with חַיָּה occur in the phrase חַיָּה רָעָה. This phrase forms the main link between דֶּבֶר and רַע.

There were two frequent associates which are not frequent associates of רַע. However, they both occurred at least once with רַע: יֵרָקוֹן (rust) and שִׁדָּפוֹן (blight). Due to their low frequency they are both analysed in Appendix B.1.

3.2.6 אָוֶן (villainy)

אָוֶן occurs 83 times in the analysed texts [75;[44] 2;[45] 6; 0; 0]. In total אָוֶן occurs 61 times (73%) with at least one semantic association. Its occurrence with semantic associations by corpus is shown in Table 3.18 below. Tables 3.19 and 3.20 show the semantic associations of similarity and opposition respectively.

Table 3.18. Number of Identifiable Lexical and
Phrasal Semantic Associations with אָוֶן by Type of Association

Corpus	Similarity		Opposition		Total
	n.	%	n.	%	n.
Hebrew Bible	53	93.0	22	38.6	57
Ben Sira	0	–	0	–	0
Judean Desert	3	75.0	1	25.0	4
Inscriptions	0	–	0	–	0
Mishnah	0	–	0	–	0
Total	56	91.8	23	37.7	61

Table 3.19. אָוֶן in Associations of Similarity

Lexeme	Association	No.	Location
עָמָל		11	Num 23:21; Isa 10:1; 59:4; Hab 1:3; Ps 7:15; 10:7; 55:11; 90:10; Job 4:8; 5:6; 15:35

---

[44] Seven times (Josh 7:2; 18:12; 1 Sam 13:5; 14:23; Hos 4:15; 5:8; 10:5) it occurred as a place name in the phrase בֵּית אָוֶן (Beth Aven). In three other locations context indicated it was being used on its own as the place name "Aven" (or "On" if emended; Ezek 30:17; Hos 10:8; Amos 1:5). These ten occurrences were excluded from the count.

[45] All four occurrences in Sirach 41:10 are the work of correctors. There are two versions of the same phrase in which the only difference is plural versus singular nouns. It was opted to count this as two occurrences rather than four.

CHAPTER 3

Lexeme	Association	No.	Location
רָשָׁע	אִישׁ אָוֶן –	1	Isa 55:7
	בַּעַל אָוֶן –	1	4Q418 126 II, 6
	מְתֵי אָוֶן –	1	Job 22:18
	פּוֹעֲלֵי אָוֶן –	6	Ps 28:3; 36:13; 92:8; 94:4; 101:8; 141:9
אוֹיֵב	פּוֹעֲלֵי אָוֶן –	5	Ps 6:9; 59:3; 64:3; 92:10; 4Q88 X, 12–13
מִרְמָה	אָוֶן –	4	Ps 10:7; 36:4; 55:11; Job 15:35
אִישׁ מִרְמָה	פּוֹעֲלֵי אָוֶן –	1	Ps 5:6[46]
רַע		4	Isa 59:6; Mic 2:1; Ps 36:5; Prov 12:21
עֲצַת רַע		1	Ezek 11:2
שָׁוְא		4	Isa 59:4; Hos 12:12; Ps 41:7; Job 11:11
חֲלוֹם שָׁוְא		1	Zech 10:2
רָעָה	אָוֶן –	3	Ps 28:3; 41:7; 94:23
	מַחְשֶׁבֶת אָוֶן –	2	Jer 4:14; Prov 6:18
שֶׁקֶר	אָוֶן –	3	Isa 59:4; Zech 10:2; Ps 7:15
דּוֹבֵר שֶׁקֶר	פּוֹעֲלֵי אָוֶן –	1	Ps 101:8
לְשׁוֹן שֶׁקֶר	מַחְשֶׁבֶת אָוֶן –	1	Prov 6:18
חָמָס		4	Isa 59:6; Hab 1:3; Ps 55:11; 1QIsaᵃ XLVIII, 18
מֵרַע	פּוֹעֲלֵי אָוֶן –	4	Isa 31:2; Ps 64:3; 92:10; 94:16
דָּם		3	Isa 59:3; Ps 5:6;[47] 59:3
עַוְלָה		3	Isa 59:4; Job 11:14; Prov 22:8
כָּזָב	מַחְשֶׁבֶת אָוֶן –	1	Prov 6:18
דּוֹבֵר כָּזָב	פּוֹעֲלֵי אָוֶן –	1	Ps 5:6
רִיב		2	Hab 1:3; Ps 55:11
שֹׁד		2	Isa 59:7; Hab 1:3
תֹּהוּ		2	Isa 41:29; 59:4
תֹּךְ		2	Ps 10:7; 55:11
אָדָם בְּלִיַּעַל	אִישׁ אָוֶן –	1	Prov 6:12
אִישׁ מֵטֶּה	מְדַבֵּר אָוֶן –	1	1QS XI, 2
אִישׁ רֶשַׁע	פּוֹעֲלֵי אָוֶן –	1	Job 34:8

---

[46] This occurrence is part of the phrase אִישׁ דָּמִים וּמִרְמָה (a man of bloodshed and deceit). It has been split into two phrases in order to better represent the occurrences of דָּם (blood) and מִרְמָה (deceit) in association with פּוֹעֲלֵי אָוֶן (doers of iniquity).

[47] See note above on occurrence with מִרְמָה (deceit) in Psalm 5:6.

MAPPING THE LEXICAL SEMANTIC DOMAINS OF רַע 133

Lexeme	Association	No.	Location
אֶפֶס		1	Isa 41:29
גַּאֲוָה	פּוֹעֲלֵי אָוֶן –	1	Ps 36:13
גְּדוּד	פּוֹעֲלֵי אָוֶן –	1	Hos 6:8
הֶבֶל		1	Zech 10:2
הֹוָה		1	Prov 17:4
הוֹלֵל		1	Ps 5:6
חַטַּאת קֶסֶם		1	1 Sam 15:23
חֹנֶף		1	Isa 32:6
לֵץ	שׁוֹקֵד אָוֶן –	1	Isa 29:20
מָדוֹן		1	Hab 1:3
מַקְנֵי הוֹן	מְדַבֵּר אָוֶן –	1	1QS XI, 2
מְתְקוֹמָם	פּוֹעֲלֵי אָוֶן –	1	Ps 59:3
עַוָּל	פּוֹעֲלֵי אָוֶן –	1	Job 31:3
עָוֹן		1	Isa 59:4
עוֹשֵׂה רְמִיָּה		1	Ps 101:8
עֵינַיִם רָמוֹת	מַחְשְׁבֹת אָוֶן –	1	Prov 6:18
עָרִיץ	שׁוֹקֵד אָוֶן –	1	Isa 29:20
עֹשֶׁק		1	Ps 119:113
פֹּעַל		1	Job 36:10
פֶּשַׁע		1	Job 36:10
קָם		1	Ps 92:10
רוּחַ		1	Isa 41:29
שֶׁבֶר		1	Isa 59:7
שׁוֹלֵחַ אֶצְבַּע	מְדַבֵּר אָוֶן –	1	1QS XI, 2
שׁוּר		1	Ps 92:10
תְּרָפִים		1	1 Sam 15:23

Table 3.20. אָוֶן in Associations of Opposition

Lexeme	Association	No.	Location
טוֹב	אָוֶן – פּוֹעֲלֵי אָוֶן –	1 1	Ps 36:5 Ps 125:5

134 CHAPTER 3

Lexeme	Association	No.	Location
מִשְׁפָּט		2	Isa 59:7; Prov 19:28
צַדִּיק	פּוֹעֲלֵי אָוֶן –	2	Ps 125:5; Prov 21:15
אֶבְיוֹן	שׁוֹקֵד אָוֶן –	1	Isa 29:20
יְשַׁר בְּלֵב	פּוֹעֲלֵי אָוֶן –	1	Ps 125:5
עָנָו	שׁוֹקֵד אָוֶן –	1	Isa 29:20
קֹדֶשׁ		1	11Q19 XLIII, 16
שָׁלוֹם		1	Isa 59:7
תֹּם	פּוֹעֲלֵי אָוֶן –	1	Prov 10:29

Observations

אָוֶן (villainy) occurs primarily in associations of similarity (91.8% vs. 37.7%). It has no frequent (three or more) associations of opposition. Its frequent associates in order of frequency are: עָמָל (trouble); רָשָׁע (wicked); אוֹיֵב (enemy); מִרְמָה (deceit); רַע (bad); שָׁוְא (worthlessness); רָעָה (evil); שֶׁקֶר (lie); חָמָס (violence); מֵרַע (evildoer); דָּם (blood); and עַוְלָה (injustice). The connection between רַע and אָוֶן can be seen both through their frequency of association and their frequent co-associations with רָשָׁע, מִרְמָה, חָמָס, רָעָה, and דָּם.

Words that were not frequently associated with רַע, but were associated with it at least once include: עָמָל; אוֹיֵב; שָׁוְא; שֶׁקֶר; מֵרַע; and עַוְלָה. These will be analysed in the second round of analysis.

3.2.7 מָוֶת (death)

מָוֶת occurs 203 times in the analysed texts [153;[48] 23; 15; 0; 12]. In total, מָוֶת occurs 79 times (39%)[49] with at least one semantic association. Its occurrence with semantic associations by corpus is shown in Table 3.21 below. Tables 3.22 and 3.23 show the semantic associations of similarity and opposition respectively.

---

[48] One occurrence was added: Genesis 50:5 (Samaritan Pentateuch).
[49] Two occurrences were eliminated under the conditions specified in §3.1.1.1.

MAPPING THE LEXICAL SEMANTIC DOMAINS OF רַע

135

Table 3.21. Number of Identifiable Lexical and
Phrasal Semantic Associations מָוֶת by Type of Association

Corpus	Similarity		Opposition		Total
	n.	%	n.	%	n.
Hebrew Bible	37	65.1	22	39.3	56
Ben Sira	9	69.2	6	45.2	13
Judean Desert	6	100.0	0	0.0	6
Inscriptions	0	–	0	–	0
Mishnah	0	0.0	4	100.0	4
Total	52	65.8	32	40.5	79

Table 3.22. מָוֶת in Associations of Similarity

Lexeme	Association	No.	Location
שְׁאוֹל		21	2 Sam 22:6; Isa 28:15, 18; 38:18; Hos 13:14 (×2); Hab 2:5; Ps 6:6; 18:6; 89:49; 116:3; Prov 5:5; 7:27; Song 8:6; Sir 14:12; 48:5; 51:2, 6; 1QHª XI, 10; XVII, 4; 11Q5 XIX, 9
חֶרֶב	מָוֶת –	5	Jer 15:2; 18:21; 43:11; Job 27:15; Sir 40:9
	כְּלִי מָוֶת –	1	Ps 7:14
יַד חֶרֶב	מָוֶת –	1	Job 5:20
רַע		4	Deut 30:15; Job 5:20 Sir 11:14; 37:18
דְּבָר רַע		1	2 Kings 4:40
בְּלִיַּעַל		3	2 Sam 22:5; Ps 18:5; 1QHª XI, 29
רָעָה		3	Prov 14:32;[50] Sir 37:18; 40:9
אַחֲרִית		2	Num 23:10; Sir 11:28
בּוֹר		2	Isa 38:18; Ezek 31:14
חֵץ	מָוֶת –	1	Prov 26:18
	כְּלִי מָוֶת –	1	Ps 7:14
רָעָב		2	Jer 15:2; 18:21
שְׁבִי		2	Jer 15:2; 43:11
אֲבַדּוֹן		1	Job 28:22
אֶרֶץ תַּחְתִּית		1	Ezek 31:14

[50] See footnote to Table 3.14, §3.2.4.

136 CHAPTER 3

Lexeme	Association	No.	Location
אַשְׁמַת פֶּשַׁע		1	4Q184 1, 9
דֶּבֶר		1	Sir 40:9*
דָּם		1	Sir 40:9
זֵק		1	Prov 26:18
חַטָּאת		1	4Q184 1, 9
חֶרֶג		1	Prov 24:11
חַרְחֻר		1	Sir 40:9
יָגוֹן	חֶבְלֵי מָוֶת –	1	Ps 116:3
יוֹם עֶבְרָה		1	Prov 11:4
לוֹט		1	Isa 25:8
מַסֵּכָה		1	Isa 25:8
מְשַׁכֶּלֶת		1	2 Kings 2:21
עָוֶל		1	4Q184 1, 9
צַלְמָוֶת		1	Job 38:17
צָרָה	חֶבְלֵי מָוֶת –	1	Ps 116:3
קֶבֶר		1	Job 3:21
קְלָלָה		1	Deut 30:19
קֶשֶׁת	כְּלֵי מָוֶת –	1	Ps 7:14
רֵישׁ		1	Sir 11:14
רְפָאִים		1	Prov 2:18
שֶׁבֶר		1	Sir 40:9
שֹׁד		1	Sir 40:9
שַׁחַת		1	Sir 51:2

Table 3.23. מָוֶת in Associations of Opposition

Lexeme	Association	No.	Location
חַיִּים		25	Deut 30:15, 19; 31:27; Judg 16:30; 2 Sam 1:23; 15:21; Isa 38:18; Jer 8:3; Jonah 4:3, 8; Job 30:23; Prov 8:36; 11:19; 12:28; 13:14; 14:27; 18:21; Sir 11:14; 15:17; 33:14; 37:18; m. Ketub. 9:1; m. B. Qam. 9:10; m. 'Ohal 3:5 (×2)
חָיָה		3	Ezek 18:23; 32; 33:11
טוֹב		3	Deut 30:15; Sir 11:14; 37:18

MAPPING THE LEXICAL SEMANTIC DOMAINS OF רַע 137

Lexeme	Association	No.	Location
בְּרָכָה		1	Deut 30:15
הַיֶּלֶד		1	Eccl 7:1
נֶפֶשׁ		1	Sir 41:1

Observations

מָוֶת (death) shows a bias towards associations of similarity (65.8% vs. 40.5%). However, its primary association is with its antonym חַיִּים (life). This is closely followed by its association of similarity with שְׁאוֹל (Sheol). Still occurring three or more times, but much less frequent are its associations of similarity with חֶרֶב (sword), רַע (bad), בְּלִיַּעַל (worthlessness), and רָעָה (evil).

In a closer examination of its associations with רַע, its primary association appears to be with חַיִּים, while the primary association of רַע appears to be with טוֹב (good).

3.13. Deuteronomy 30:15

רְאֵה נָתַתִּי לְפָנֶיךָ הַיּוֹם אֶת־הַחַיִּים וְאֶת־הַטּוֹב וְאֶת־הַמָּוֶת וְאֶת־הָרָע

See, I have set before you today life and the good and death and the bad.

Furthermore, one of the three occurrences with רָעָה occurs in Sirach B 7v12 which was corrected to רַע and occurs in the same set of contrasts as above. Conversely, one of its uses with רָעָה and most of its uses with חֶרֶב (sword) are in lists of judgements.[51] The evidence appears to weigh in favour of treating מָוֶת as a word primarily outside the semantic domains of רַע. However, some uses indicate the presence of a polyseme which is at home in lists of judgement.[52]

3.2.8 עָוֹן (iniquity)

עָוֹן occurs 315 times in the analysed texts [234;[53] 17;[54] 53; 0; 11]. In total, עָוֹן occurs 135 times (43%)[55] with at least one semantic association.

---

[51] Except for the use in Psalm 7:14, where it appears to connect to the implement concept of חֶרֶב rather than the concept of judgement.

[52] This use is also identified as the fifth use in DCH (Clines, "מָוֶת 5," *DCH* 5:200).

[53] Three occurrences were added: Numbers 14:8; 23:21 (Samaritan Pentateuch); 1QIsaᵃ I, 19 [Isa 1:15].

[54] Sirach 7:2 is included twice because of a significant variation between manuscripts A 2v7 and C 3r9.

[55] Two occurrences were eliminated under the conditions specified in §3.1.1.1.

138   CHAPTER 3

Its occurrence with semantic associations by corpus is shown in Table 3.24
below. Tables 3.25 and 3.26 show the semantic associations of similarity
and opposition respectively.

Table 3.24. Number of Identifiable Lexical and
Phrasal Semantic Associations with עָוֹן by Type of Association

Corpus	Similarity		Opposition		Total
	n.	**%**	**n.**	**%**	**n.**
Hebrew Bible	96	93.2	11	10.7	103
Ben Sira	4	80.0	2	40.0	5
Judean Desert	26	100.0	3	11.5	26
Inscriptions	0	–	0	–	0
Mishnah	1	100.0	0	0.0	1
Total	127	94.1	16	11.9	135

Table 3.25. עָוֹן in Associations of Similarity

Lexeme	Association	No.	Location
חַטָּאת		55	Exod 34:9; Lev 16:21; Deut 19:15; 1 Sam 20:1; Isa 6:7; 27:9; 40:2; 43:24; 59:2, 12; Jer 5:25; 14:10; 16:10, 18; 18:23; 30:14, 15; 31:34; 36:3; 50:20; Ezek 3:19; 21:29; Hos 4:8; 8:13; 9:9; 13:12; Mic 7:18; Ps 32:5; 38:4, 19; 51:4; 59:5; 79:8; 85:3; 109:14; Job 10:6; 13:23; 14:17; Prov 5:22; Lam 4:6, 13, 22; Dan 9:24; Neh 3:37; 9:2; Sir 3:15; 1QS I, 23; III, 8; III, 22; XI, 9; XI, 14; 1QHᵃ IX, 27; 4Q176 1–2 I, 6; 11Q5 XIX, 14; 11Q19 XXVI, 11
פֶּשַׁע		28	Exod 34:7; Lev 16:21; Num 14:18; Isa 43:24; 50:1; 53:5; 59:12; Ezek 14:10; 18:30; 21:29; 39:23; Mic 7:19; Ps 32:2, 5; 51:4; 59:5; 65:4; 89:33; Job 7:21; 13:23; 14:17; 31:33; 33:9; Dan 9:24; CD III, 18; 1QS XI, 9; 1QHᵃ VI, 35; m. Yoma 3:8
פֶּשַׁע אַשְׁמָה		1	1QS I, 23[56]
פֶּשַׁע מַעֲשֶׂה		1	1QS III, 22
דֶּרֶךְ פֶּשַׁע		1	Ps 107:17

[56] It is difficult to determine whether this case belongs here or with אַשְׁמָה (guilt) below. However, regardless of where it is placed both words come out as important to עָוֹן (sin).

MAPPING THE LEXICAL SEMANTIC DOMAINS OF רַע   139

Lexeme	Association	No.	Location
חֵטְא		11	Lev 20:19; Deut 5:9; Isa 53:11; Hos 12:9; Ps 51:4, 7; 103:10; Dan 9:16; 11Q5 XIX, 10; 11Q19 LXI, 6; m. Yoma 3:8
אַשְׁמָה		7	Ezra 9:6, 7, 13; 1QS III, 22; 1QHᵃ XII, 38; 11Q19 XXVI, 11; LVIII, 17
אַשְׁמַת מַעַל		1	1QHᵃ XII, 30
רָעָה		7	Isa 13:11; Jer 36:31; Hos 7:1; Ps 40:13; Job 22:5; Sir 7:2;[57] 4Q171 1–2 II, 4
רַע		2	Prov 16:6; Sir 7:2[58]
דֶּרֶךְ רַע		1	Ezek 36:31
מַעֲשֶׂה רַע		2	Ezra 9:13; 4Q169 3–4 III, 4
דָּם		4	Lev 20:17; 1QIsaᵃ I, 19; Isa 59:3; Ezek 9:9
חַטָּאָה		4	Exod 34:7; Num 14:18;[59] Isa 5:18; 1QHᵃ IX, 24
נִדָּה	עָוֹן –	2	1QS XI, 14; 1QHᵃ IX, 24
נִדַּת טֻמְאָה	עֲוֹן אַשְׁמָה –	1	1QpHab VIII, 12
טֻמְאָה		1	Ezek 39:23
דְּבָר טֻמְאָה		1	11Q19 LVIII, 17
עָמָל		2	Num 23:21;[60] Isa 59:3
רְמִיָּה		2	Ps 32:2; 1QHᵃ IX, 29
תּוֹעֵבָה		2	Ezek 36:31; 44:12
אָוֶן		1	Isa 59:3
אֵיד	עָוֹן קֵץ –	1	Ezek 35:5
אָשָׁם		1	CD I, 8
בְּלִיַּעַל	כַּחַשׁ עָוֹן –	1	1QS X, 22
בֵּן מַשְׁחִית	עַם כֶּבֶד עָוֹן –	1	Isa 1:4
גַּאֲוָה		1	Sir 16:9
גְּבוּרָה		1	Sir 16:9
גּוֹי חוֹטֵא	עַם כֶּבֶד עָוֹן –	1	Isa 1:4
גְּמוּל		1	Jer 51:6
זָדוֹן לֵב		1	Sir 16:9
זִמָּה		1	Job 31:11

---

[57] Manuscript A 2v7.
[58] Manuscript C 3r9.
[59] Samaritan Pentateuch.
[60] Samaritan Pentateuch.

140 CHAPTER 3

Lexeme	Association	No.	Location
זֶרַע מֵרַע	עַם כֶּבֶד עָוֹן –	1	Isa 1:4
חֲטָאָה		1	Ps 32:2
חֶרֶב		1	Ezek 32:27
חֶרְפָּה		1	4Q417 2 I, 23
כָּזָב	כַּחַשׁ עָוֹן –	1	1QS X, 22
כְּלֵי מִלְחָמָה		1	Ezek 32:27
כְּלִמָּה		1	Ezek 44:12
מַטֶּה		1	Ezek 9:9
מַחֲלָה		1	4Q431 2, 5
מַעַל		1	4Q504 1–2 VI, 5
מִרְמָה	כַּחַשׁ עָוֹן –	1	1QS X, 22
מְשׁוּבָה		1	Jer 14:7
מַשְׂטֵמָה		1	Hos 9:7
נַבְלוּת	כַּחַשׁ עָוֹן –	1	1QS X, 22
נֶגַע		1	4Q431 2, 5
עָוֶל		1	Ezek 28:18
עַוְלָה		1	Isa 59:3
עָלוּם		1	Ps 90:8
עֵצָה		1	Ps 106:43
עֶרְוָה		1	11Q19 LVIII, 17
צָבָא		1	Isa 40:2
רֹעַ מַעֲלָל		1	1QIsaᵃ I, 19
רֶשַׁע		1	Jer 14:20
שָׁוְא		1	Isa 59:3
שִׁקּוּץ	כַּחַשׁ עָוֹן –	1	1QS X, 22
שֶׁקֶר		1	Isa 59:3
תֹּהוּ		1	Isa 59:3
תּוֹעָה		1	1QHᵃ IX, 24*

Table 3.26. עָוֹן in Associations of Opposition

Lexeme	Association	No.	Location
צְדָקָה		4	Ps 69:28; Sir 3:15; 1QS I, 23; 1QHᵃ XII, 30
טוֹב		1	Hos 14:3
מַעֲלָל טוֹב		1	Ezek 36:31

MAPPING THE LEXICAL SEMANTIC DOMAINS OF רע 141

Lexeme	Association	No.	Location
צֶדֶק		2	Isa 59:3; Dan 9:24
תָּמִים		2	2 Sam 22:24; Ps 18:24
אֱמוּנָה		1	Isa 59:3
זַךְ		1	Job 33:9
חֵן	מַשָּׂאֵת עָוֹן –	1	Sir 4:21
חַסְדֵי רַחֲמִים		1	1QS I, 23
חַף		1	Job 33:9
טוֹבָה		1	2 Sam 16:12
כָּבוֹד	מַשָּׂאֵת עָוֹן –	1	Sir 4:21
נָקִי		1	2 Sam 14:9
סְלִיחָה		1	Ps 130:3
פְּרִי קֹדֶשׁ	כַּחַשׁ עָוֹן –	1	1QS X, 22

Observations

עָוֹן (iniquity) occurs primarily in associations of similarity (94.8% vs. 11.9%). Its most frequent associate is חַטָּאת (sin) which occurs 41.4% of the time that עָוֹן appears in one or more association of similarity or opposition. Its next most frequent is פֶּשַׁע (transgression) which occurs 23.3% of the time. Other words in frequent associations of similarity in order of frequency are: חֵטְא (sin); אַשְׁמָה (guilt); רָעָה (evil); רַע (bad); דָּם (blood); חַטָּאָה (sin); and נִדָּה (impurity). Some words co-occurred in construct phrases. Effort was made to group them according to the semantic head of the phrase. However, it is possible that טֻמְאָה (impurity) should be added to the above list.[61]

The four most frequent associates of עָוֹן are not frequent associates of רַע. However, the two most frequent associates of עָוֹן, חַטָּאת and פֶּשַׁע, were found in §3.2.4 to be frequent associates of רָעָה. In addition, two frequent associates of רַע do appear in the list. This might suggest a weaker connection to רַע and will need further analysis.

Words in associations of similarity with עָוֹן that did not appear in the frequent associates of רַע, but were associated with רַע at least once include: חַטָּאת; פֶּשַׁע; and אַשְׁמָה. These will be analysed in the second round of analysis.

---

[61] Its exclusion does not affect the list of terms included in the second round of analysis.

142 CHAPTER 3

3.2.9 רָעָב (famine)

רָעָב occurs 112 times in the analysed texts [102;[62] 0; 5; 0; 5]. In total,
רָעָב occurs 64 times (58%)[63] with at least one semantic association. Its
occurrence with semantic associations by corpus is shown in Table 3.27
below. Tables 3.28 and 3.29 show the semantic associations of similarity
and opposition respectively.

Table 3.27. Number of Identifiable Lexical and
Phrasal Semantic Associations with רָעָב by Type of Association

Corpus	Similarity		Opposition		Total
	n.	%	n.	%	n.
Hebrew Bible	53	91.4	8	13.8	58
Ben Sira	0	–	0	–	0
Judean Desert	5	100.0	0	0.0	5
Inscriptions	0	–	0	–	0
Mishnah	1	100.0	0	0.0	0
Total	59	92.2	8	12.5	64

Table 3.28. רָעָב in Associations of Similarity

Lexeme	Association	No.	Location
חֶרֶב		48	Deut 32:24; Isa 51:19; Jer 5:12; 11:22; 14:12, 13, 15 (×2), 16, 18; 15:2; 16:4; 18:21; 21:7, 9; 24:10; 27:8, 13; 29:17, 18; 32:34, 36; 34:17; 38:2; 42:16, 17, 22; 44:12 (×2), 13, 18, 27; Ezek 5:12, 17; 6:11, 12; 7:15 (×2); 12:16; 14:13, 21; Lam 4:9; 1 Chr 21:12; 2 Chr 20:9; 4Q162 II, 1; 4Q171 1–2 II, 1; 4Q504 1–2 III, 8*; m. 'Abot 5:8
דֶּבֶר		33	2 Sam 24:13; 1 Kgs 8:37; Jer 14:12; 21:7, 9; 24:10; 27:8, 13; 29:17, 18; 32:34, 36; 34:17; 38:2; 42:17, 22; 44:13; Ezek 5:12, 17; 6:11, 12; 7:15 (×2); 12:16; 14:13, 21; 1 Chr 21:12; 2 Chr 6:28; 20:9; 4Q171 1–2 II, 1; 1+3–4 III, 4; 4Q504 1–2 III, 8; m. 'Abot 5:8

[62] One occurrence was added: 4Q171 1+3–4 III, 2 [Ps 37:19].
[63] One occurrence was eliminated under the conditions specified in §3.1.1.1.

MAPPING THE LEXICAL SEMANTIC DOMAINS OF רַע 143

Lexeme	Association	No.	Location
רָעָב		8	Deut 32:24; Jer 5:12; 11:22; 42:17; 44:18; Ezek 6:11; 14:21; 2 Chr 20:9
צָמָא		6	Deut 28:48; Isa 5:13; Amos 8:11; Neh 9:15; 2 Chr 32:11; 4Q504 1–2 III, 8
חַיַּת אֶרֶץ חַיָּה רָעָה		1 4	Job 5:20 Ezek 5:17; 14:13, 21; m. 'Abot 5:8
צָרָה		3	Job 5:20; 2 Chr 20:9; 4Q166 II, 12
אַרְבֶּה		2	1 Kgs 8:37; 2 Chr 6:28
חָסִיל		2	1 Kgs 8:37; 2 Chr 6:28
יֵרָקוֹן		2	1 Kgs 8:37; 2 Chr 6:28
מָוֶת		2	Jer 15:2; 18:21
מַחֲלָה		2	1 Kgs 8:37; 2 Chr 6:28
נֶגַע		2	1 Kgs 8:37; 2 Chr 6:28
שֹׁד		2	Isa 51:19; Job 5:20
שִׁדָּפוֹן		2	1 Kgs 8:37; 2 Chr 6:28
גָּלוּת		1	'Abot 5:8
דָּם		1	Ezek 5:17
חֳלִי רַע		1	4Q504 1–2 III, 8
חֹסֶר		1	Deut 28:48
חֵץ		1	Deut 32:24
כָּפָן		1	Job 5:20
מִלְחָמָה		1	Job 5:20
עֵירֹם		1	Deut 28:48
עָרוֹם		1	4Q166 II, 12
קֶטֶב		1	Deut 32:24
רֶשֶׁף		1	Deut 32:24
שְׁבִי		1	Jer 15:2
שֶׁבֶר		1	Isa 51:19

Table 3.29. רָעָב in Associations of Opposition

Lexeme	Association	No.	Location
שָׂבָע		5	Gen 41:30 (×2), 31, 36, 54
טוֹב		2	Gen 41:36; Jer 44:18
טוּב		1	Deut 28:48

144 CHAPTER 3

Lexeme	Association	No.	Location
רָב		1	Deut 28:48
שָׁלוֹם		1	Jer 14:13
שִׂמְחָה		1	Deut 28:48

Observations

רָעָב (famine) occurs primarily in associations of similarity (92.2% vs. 12.5%). It had one frequent association of opposition, שָׂבָע (abundance), which occurred exclusively in Genesis 41. Its strongest associations are with חֶרֶב (sword) and דֶּבֶר (plague). Out of the remaining three frequent associations of similarity, two are shared with חֶרֶב (sword) and דֶּבֶר: רָעָה (evil); and חַיָּה רָעָה (bad animal). The remaining frequent associations of similarity are צָמָא (thirst) and צָרָה (distress). צָמָא co-occurs once with רַע in the phrase חֲלִי רַע (bad sickness). צָרָה occurs twice with רַע and is also a frequent associate of רָעָה. Both will be considered in the second round of analysis.

3.2.10 חָמָס (violence)

חָמָס occurs 80 times in the analysed texts [61;[64] 10; 9; 0; 0]. In total חָמָס occurs 51 times (65%)[65] with at least one semantic association. Its occurrence with semantic associations by corpus is shown in Table 3.30 below. Tables 3.31 and 3.32 show the semantic associations of similarity and opposition respectively.

Table 3.30. Number of Identifiable Lexical and Phrasal Semantic Associations חָמָס by Type of Association

Corpus	Similarity		Opposition		Total
	n.	%	n.	%	n.
Hebrew Bible	37	90.2	9	22.0	41
Ben Sira	3	60.0	3	60.0	5
Judean Desert	4	80.0	3	60.0	5
Inscriptions	0	–	0	–	0
Mishnah	0	–	0	–	0
Total	44	86.3	15	29.4	51

[64] One occurrence was added from the Judean Desert corpus: 1QIsaᵃ XLVIII, 19 [Isa 59:7].
[65] One occurrence was eliminated under the conditions specified in §3.1.1.1.

MAPPING THE LEXICAL SEMANTIC DOMAINS OF רַע 145

Table 3.31. חָמָס in Associations of Similarity

Lexeme	Association	No.	Location
שֹׁד		8	1QIsaᵃ XLVIII, 19; Isa 60:18; Jer 6:7; 20:8; Ezek 45:9; Amos 3:10; Hab 1:3; 2:17
דָּם		4	Judg 9:24; Jer 51:35; Hab 2:8, 17
מִשְׁפַּט דָּם		1	Ezek 7:23
אָוֶן		3	Isa 59:6; Hab 1:3; Ps 55:10
מַחְשֶׁבֶת אָוֶן		1	1QIsaᵃ XLVIII, 19
רַע	חָמָס –	3	Isa 59:6; Jonah 3:8; Ps 140:2
יוֹם רַע	שֶׁבֶת חָמָס –	1	Amos 6:3⁶⁶
שֶׁקֶר		4	Deut 19:16; Mic 6:12; 11Q5 XXII, 6; 11Q19 LXI, 7
אוֹיֵב	חָמָס –	1	2 Sam 22:3
	אִישׁ חָמָס –	2	2 Sam 22:49; Ps 18:49
לֵץ	אִישׁ חָמָס –	3	Prov 3:31; Sir 32:17, 18
מִרְמָה		3	Isa 53:9; Zeph 1:9; Ps 55:10
עָמָל		3	Hab 1:3; Ps 7:17; 55:10
רָשָׁע	אוֹהֵב חָמָס –	1	Ps 11:5
	אִישׁ חָמָס –	2	Ps 140:5; Prov 3:31
עַוְלָה		2	Ezek 28:16; Ps 58:3
קָם	אִישׁ חָמָס –	2	2 Sam 22:49; Ps 18:49
רִיב		2	Hab 1:3; Ps 55:10
שֶׁבֶר		2	1QIsaᵃ XLVIII, 19; Isa 60:18
שָׁוְא		2	Exod 23:1; 1QHᵃ XIV, 8*
תֹּךְ		2	Ps 55:10; 72:14
אִישׁ לָשׁוֹן		1	Ps 140:12
בְּלִיַּעַל		1	Prov 16:29
גַּאֲוָה		1	Ps 73:6
זֵד		1	Sir 32:18
חֳלִי		1	Jer 6:7
חָנֵף		1	Sir 40:15
כָּזָב		1	Ps 58:3
כְּסִיל		1	Prov 3:31
מָדוֹן		1	Hab 1:3

⁶⁶ See footnote to Table 3.2, §3.1.2.

146 CHAPTER 3

Lexeme	Association	No.	Location
מַכָּה		1	Jer 6:7
נָלוֹז		1	Prov 3:31
נִרְגָּן		1	Prov 13:2
עָוֶל		1	11Q5 XXII, 6
עָם	אִישׁ חָמָס –	1	1QpHab VIII, 11
עוֹצֶה עֵינַיִם		1	Prov 16:29
עֹשֶׁק		1	Jer 6:7
קוֹרֵץ שְׂפָתַיִם		1	Prov 16:29
רְמִיָּה		1	Mic 6:12
רָעָה		1	Jer 6:7
רֶשַׁע		1	Prov 4:17
תַּהְפֻּכָה		1	Prov 13:2

Table 3.32. חָמָס in Associations of Opposition

Lexeme	Association	No.	Location
חֶסֶד		3	Sir 49:3; 4Q372 1, 19; 11Q5 XXII, 6
מִשְׁפָּט		3	1QIsa[a] XLVIII, 19; Ezek 45:9; Job 19:7
חָכָם		2	Prov 3:31; Sir 32:17
צַדִּיק		2	Ps 11:5; Prov 3:31
אֱמֶת		1	4Q372 1, 19
דַּל מַשְׂכִּיל		1	Sir 10:23
זַךְ		1	Job 16:17
חַיִּים		1	Prov 10:11
טוֹב		1	Prov 13:2
יָשָׁר		1	Prov 3:31
מַעֲשֵׂה חָסִיד		1	11Q5 XXII, 6
עָנִי		1	Prov 3:31
צְדָקָה		1	Ezek 45:9
קֹדֶשׁ		1	1QH[a] XIV, 8*
רַחֲמִים		1	4Q372 1, 19
שָׁלוֹם		1	1QIsa[a] XLVIII, 19
תָּמִים		1	Ezek 28:15

MAPPING THE LEXICAL SEMANTIC DOMAINS OF רַע

Observations

חָמָס (violence) occurs primarily in associations of similarity (86.3% vs. 29.4%), although this is driven by a strong bias in the Hebrew Bible corpus. Out of its nine most frequent associates, one is רַע (bad) and four are frequent associates of רַע: דָּם (blood); אָוֶן (villainy); מִרְמָה (deceit); and רָשָׁע (wicked). The most frequent associate of חָמָס was שֹׁד (destruction). שֹׁד occurs once as an associate of רַע and so will be analysed in the second round. Out of the remaining four frequent associates of חָמָס, none were frequent associates of רַע, but three were frequent associates of אָוֶן and one, לֵץ (scoffer) was a frequent associate of רָשָׁע. The three that are frequent associates of אָוֶן also occur at least once with רַע and are to be analysed in the second round. They are: שֶׁקֶר (lie); אוֹיֵב (enemy); and עָמָל (trouble).

3.2.11 תּוֹעֵבָה (abomination)

תּוֹעֵבָה occurs 136 times in the analysed texts [117; 4; 15; 0; 0[67]]. In total תּוֹעֵבָה occurs 43 times (32%)[68] with at least one semantic association. Its occurrence with semantic associations by corpus is shown in Table 3.33 below. Tables 3.34 and 3.35 show the semantic associations of similarity and opposition respectively.

Table 3.33. Number of Identifiable Lexical and
Phrasal Semantic Associations תּוֹעֵבָה by Type of Association

Corpus	Similarity		Opposition		Total
	n.	%	n.	%	n.
Hebrew Bible	32	84.2	8	21.1	38
Ben Sira	1	100.0	0	0.0	1
Judean Desert	4	80.0	2	40.0	5
Inscriptions	0	–	0	–	0
Mishnah	0	–	0	–	0
Total	37	84.1	10	22.7	44

---

[67] There were three occurrences in the Mishnah, but they were all quotes and so were removed.
[68] Two occurrences were eliminated under the conditions specified in §3.1.1.1.

148 CHAPTER 3

Table 3.34. תּוֹעֵבָה in Associations of Similarity

Lexeme	Association	No.	Location
דֶּרֶךְ		6	Ezek 7:3, 4, 8, 9; 16:47; 18:24
זִמָּה		6	Lev 18:22; 20:13; Ezek 16:43, 58; 22:11; 11Q19 LXVI, 14
רָעָה		5	Jer 7:10; 44:4; Ezek 6:9; 16:22; Sir 15:13
שִׁקּוּץ		4	Ezek 5:11; 7:20; 11:18, 21
נִבְלַת שִׁקּוּץ		1	Jer 16:18
חַטָּאת		4	Ezek 16:51 (×2); 18:14, 24
רַע		2	2 Kgs 21:2; 2 Chr 33:2
דְּבַר רַע		1	Deut 17:4
דֶּרֶךְ רַע		1	Ezek 36:31
גִּדָּה	תּוֹעֵבָה –	1	11Q19 LXVI, 14
דֶּרֶךְ נִדָּה	מַעֲשֵׂה תּוֹעֵבָה –	1	1QS IV, 10
עָוֹן		2	Ezek 36:31; 44:12
פֶּשַׁע	תּוֹעֵבָה –	1	Ezek 18:24
	תּוֹעֲבַת נִדָּה –	1	1QHᵃ XIX, 14
שָׂנֵא	תּוֹעֲבַת נֶפֶשׁ –	2	Prov 6:16; 4Q418 81+81a, 2*
תֶּבֶל		2	Lev 18:22; 20:13
אִוֶּלֶת	מַעֲשֵׂה תּוֹעֵבָה –	1	1QS IV, 10
אַשְׁמַת מַעַל		1	1QHᵃ XIX, 14
גֵּוָה		1	1QS IV, 10
גִּלּוּל		1	Ezek 14:6
זָר		1	Deut 32:16
חֹנֶף	מַעֲשֵׂה תּוֹעֵבָה –	1	1QS IV, 10
חֶסֶד		1	Lev 20:13
כֹּבֶד אֹזֶן	מַעֲשֵׂה תּוֹעֵבָה –	1	1QS IV, 10
כֹּבֶד לֵב	מַעֲשֵׂה תּוֹעֵבָה –	1	1QS IV, 10
כַּחַשׁ		1	1QS IV, 10
כְּלִמָּה		1	Ezek 44:13
לְשׁוֹן גִּדּוּף	מַעֲשֵׂה תּוֹעֵבָה –	1	1QS IV, 10
מַעַל		1	Ezek 18:24
עָוֶל		1	Ezek 18:24
עִוְּרוֹן עֵינַיִם	מַעֲשֵׂה תּוֹעֵבָה –	1	1QS IV, 10

MAPPING THE LEXICAL SEMANTIC DOMAINS OF רַע 149

Lexeme	Association	No.	Location
קִנְאַת זָדוֹן	מַעֲשֵׂה תוֹעֵבָה –	1	1QS IV, 10
קְצַר אַפַּיִם	מַעֲשֵׂה תוֹעֵבָה –	1	1QS IV, 10
קְשִׁי עֹרֶף	מַעֲשֵׂה תוֹעֵבָה –	1	1QS IV, 10
רְמִיָּה אַכְזָרִי		1	1QS IV, 10
רֹעַ מַעֲלָל		1	Jer 44:22
רֶשַׁע		1	1QS IV, 10
שֶׁקֶר		1	1QS IV, 10
תַּזְנוּת		1	Ezek 16:22

Table 3.35. תוֹעֵבָה in Associations of Opposition

Lexeme	Association	No.	Location
רָצוֹן		6	Prov 11:1, 20; 12:22; 15:8; CD XI, 21
טוֹב		2	Prov 20:23; 1QS IV, 10
מַעֲלָל טוֹב		1	Ezek 36:31
אֶרֶךְ אַפַּיִם		1	1QS IV, 10
בִּינָה		1	1QS IV, 10
דַּעַת		1	1QS IV, 10
חָכְמָה		1	1QS IV, 10
טָהוֹר		1	Prov 15:26
יֵצֶר סָמוּךְ		1	1QS IV, 10
מַחְשֶׁבֶת קֹדֶשׁ		1	1QS IV, 10
עֲנָוָה		1	1QS IV, 10
צְדָקָה		1	Ezek 18:24
קִנְאַת מִשְׁפַּט צֶדֶק		1	1QS IV, 10
רַחֲמִים		1	1QS IV, 10
שֵׂכֶל		1	1QS IV, 10

Observations

תוֹעֵבָה (abomination) primarily occurs in associations of similarity (84.1% vs. 22.7%). One of its strongest associations is one of opposition, with רָצוֹן (will). The other two are of similarity, דֶּרֶךְ (way) and זִמָּה (wickedness). However, דֶּרֶךְ represents an anomaly as a result of the methodology (see

150   CHAPTER 3

below). תּוֹעֵבָה shows some association with רַע through its association with the word itself and with רָעָה (evil). Its other frequent associates are: שִׁקּוּץ (detestable thing); and חַטָּאת (sin). Both זִמָּה and חַטָּאת occur in association with רַע at least once and will be analysed in the second round.

An Anomaly: דֶּרֶךְ (way)

There is some clear evidence which points to the exclusion of דֶּרֶךְ from further analysis: it can be modified by both רַע (bad) and by its antonym טוֹב (good).[69] An example text can demonstrate how this word made its way into the frequent associations of תּוֹעֵבָה.

3.14. Ezekiel 7:3b

וּשְׁפַטְתִּיךְ כִּדְרָכָיִךְ וְנָתַתִּי עָלַיִךְ אֵת כָּל־תּוֹעֲבֹתָיִךְ

I will judge you according to your ways and I will bring upon you all your abominations.

In example 3.14 the two words are in semantic parallel. However, a negative sense is imposed on דֶּרֶךְ (way) through the discourse. Immediately preceding this verse the Lord is pronouncing through Ezekiel the coming judgement in response to the תּוֹעֲבוֹת רָעוֹת (evil abominations) of Israel (Ezek 6:11). The semantic parallel can occur then because דֶּרֶךְ can be modified through discourse context. This conclusion can be confirmed through examining the other texts where דֶּרֶךְ stands alone in parallel and through examining the following verse where it does not.

3.15. Ezekiel 36:31

וּזְכַרְתֶּם אֶת־דַּרְכֵיכֶם הָרָעִים וּמַעַלְלֵיכֶם אֲשֶׁר לֹא־טוֹבִים וּנְקֹטֹתֶם בִּפְנֵיכֶם עַל עֲוֹנֹתֵיכֶם וְעַל תּוֹעֲבוֹתֵיכֶם

You shall remember your bad ways and your deeds which were not good and you will be loathsome in your sight because of your iniquities and your abominations.

In example 3.15 the preceding discourse is different to that of example 3.14. The prophecy is discussing how the people will be changed such that they live obedient lives (Ezek 36:27). Similarly, the use of דֶּרֶךְ has changed. Here the adjective רַע is used to create a more specific reference. Instead of referring to דַּרְכֵיכֶם (your ways) the prophecy refers to דַּרְכֵיכֶם הָרָעִים (your bad ways).

[69] Examples include 1 Samuel 12:23 and 1 Kings 13:33.

MAPPING THE LEXICAL SEMANTIC DOMAINS OF רַע   151

3.2.12 בְּלִיַעַל (worthlessness)

בְּלִיַעַל occurs 72 times in the analysed texts [27; 1; 44; 0; 0]. In total, בְּלִיַעַל occurs 33 times (49%)[70] with at least one semantic association. Its occurrence with semantic associations by corpus is shown in Table 3.36 below. Tables 3.37 and 3.38 show the semantic associations of similarity and opposition respectively.

Table 3.36. Number of Identifiable Lexical and
Phrasal Semantic Associations בְּלִיַעַל by Type of Association

Corpus	Similarity		Opposition		Total
	n.	%	n.	%	n.
Hebrew Bible	12	92.3	1	7.7	13
Ben Sira	1	100.0	0	0.0	1
Judean Desert	8	42.1	13	68.4	19
Inscriptions	0	–	0	–	0
Mishnah	0	–	0	–	0
Total	21	63.6	14	42.4	33

Table 3.37. בְּלִיַעַל in Associations of Similarity

Lexeme	Association	No.	Location
מָוֶת		3	2 Sam 22:5; Ps 18:5; 1QHᵃ XI, 30
רַע	בְּלִיַעַל –	1	1 Sam 30:22
	אִישׁ בְּלִיַעַל –	1	Sir 11:32
	דְּבַר בְּלִיַעַל –	1	Ps 101:3
רָעָה	בְּלִיַעַל –	2	Nah 1:11; 4Q398 14–17 II, 5*
	דְּבַר בְּלִיַעַל –	1	Ps 41:9
רָשָׁע	בְּלִיַעַל –	2	Job 34:18; Prov 19:28
	אִישׁ בְּלִיַעַל –	1	Sir 11:32
כָּזָב		2	1QS X, 21; 1QHᵃ XII, 11
אֹיֵב	גְּדוּד בְּלִיַעַל –	1	1QM XI, 8
אָוֶן		1	Prov 6:12
דָּם		1	2 Sam 16:7
חָמָס		1	Prov 16:27
חֹשֶׁךְ		1	1QM I, 1

[70] Five occurrences were eliminated under the conditions specified in §3.1.1.1.

152 CHAPTER 3

Lexeme	Association	No.	Location
כַּחַשׁ עָוֹן		1	1QS X, 21
כְּסִיל	עֵד בְּלִיַּעַל –	1	Prov 19:28
לֵבָב עִקֵּשׁ	דְּבַר בְּלִיַּעַל –	1	Ps 101:3
לֵץ	עֵד בְּלִיַּעַל –	1	Prov 19:28
מִרְמָה		1	1QS X, 21
נַבְלוּת		1	1QS X, 21
נֶעֱזָב		1	1QHᵃ XI, 29
נֶעְלָם		1	1QHᵃ XI, 29
נִרְגָּן		1	Prov 16:27
עוֹצֶה עֵינָיִם		1	Prov 16:27
עֹשֵׂה סֵטִים	דְּבַר בְּלִיַּעַל –	1	Ps 101:3
קוֹרֵץ שְׂפָתַיִם		1	Prov 16:27
רֵיק		1	2 Chr 13:7
שִׁבְעַת גּוֹיֵ הֶבֶל	גְּדוּד בְּלִיַּעַל –	1	1QM XI, 8
שָׁוְא		1	1QHᵃ X, 24*
שִׁקּוּץ		1	1QS X, 21
תַּהְפּוּכָה		1	Prov 16:27

Table 3.38. בְּלִיַּעַל in Associations of Opposition

Lexeme	Association	No.	Location
אֵל		6	1QS I, 18; II, 5; 1QM I, 5; IV, 2; XVIII, 1; 1QHᵃ XII, 14
אֵל יִשְׂרָאֵל		2	1QM XIII, 2*; XIII, 4
אוֹר		2	1QM I, 1; I, 13
שַׂר הָאוֹרִים		1	CD V, 18
שַׂר מָאוֹר		1	1QM XIII, 11
חַיִל	בְּנֵי בְלִיַּעַל –	1	1 Sam 10:27
פְּרִי קֹדֶשׁ		1	1QS X, 21

Observations

בְּלִיַּעַל (worthlessness) shows a bias towards associations of similarity (63.6% vs. 42.4%). Its associations of opposition are driven by the Qumran sectarian texts where it is a frequent associate of אֵל (God), אוֹר (light)

MAPPING THE LEXICAL SEMANTIC DOMAINS OF רַע 153

or variations of these. These uses align with the common use of בְּלִיַּעַל to refer to a personification or angel of evil in sectarian texts.[71]

In other uses of בְּלִיַּעַל, it associates frequently with רַע and three frequent associates of רַע: מָוֶת (death); רָעָה (evil); and רָשָׁע (wicked). The uses with מָוֶת appear more in line with the association of מָוֶת with שְׁאוֹל (Sheol). In these uses בְּלִיַּעַל may refer to the place of the dead:

> 3.16. 2 Samuel 22:5
>
> כִּי אֲפָפֻנִי מִשְׁבְּרֵי־מָוֶת נַחֲלֵי בְלִיַּעַל יְבַעֲתֻנִי
>
> For the waves of death have surrounded me and the torrents of Belial[72] terrify me.

Despite this, the associations with רַע, רָעָה, and רָשָׁע indicate that the non-personified use should be considered within the semantic domains of רַע.

3.2.13 דָּם (blood)

דָּם occurs 757 times in the analysed texts [363;[73] 7; 54; 0; 333]. In total, דָּם occurs 74 times (10%)[74] with at least one semantic association. Its occurrence with semantic associations by corpus is shown in Table 3.39 below. Tables 3.40 and 3.41 show the semantic associations of similarity and opposition respectively.

Table 3.39. Number of Identifiable Lexical and Phrasal Semantic Associations דָּם by Type of Association

Corpus	Similarity		Opposition		Total
	n.	%	n.	%	n.
Hebrew Bible	58	96.7	4	6.7	60
Ben Sira	3	100.0	0	0.0	3
Judean Desert	6	100.0	0	0.0	6
Inscriptions	0	—	0	—	0
Mishnah	5	100.0	0	0.0	5
Total	72	97.3	4	5.4	74

---

[71] Corrado Martone, "Evil or Devil? Belial Between the Bible and Qumran," *Hen* 26 (2004): 115–27.

[72] DCH also lists 2 Samuel 22:5 with the personified uses (Clines, "בְּלִיַּעַל 3," *DCH* 2:178–79).

[73] Two occurrences were added from the Samaritan Pentateuch: Exodus 7:18; and Leviticus 4:17. One occurrence was added from the Judean Desert corpus: 1QIsaᵃ I, 18 [Isa 1:15].

[74] Thirteen occurrences were eliminated under the conditions specified in §3.1.1.1.

154 CHAPTER 3

Table 3.40. דָּם in Associations of Similarity

Lexeme	Association	No.	Location
בָּשָׂר		13	Deut 12:27 (×2); 32:42; Isa 49:26; Ezek 39:18, 19; Ps 50:13; Sir 14:18; m. Naz. 9:5 (×2); m. Soṭah 8:1; m. Menaḥ. 2:1; m. Parah 4:3
חֵלֶב		11	Exod 23:18; Lev 3:17; 7:26; 2 Sam 1:22; Isa 34:6 (×2), 7; Ezek 39:19; CD IV, 2; 4Q270 1a II, 1; 11Q19 XVI, 15
נֶפֶשׁ	דָּם –	8	Gen 9:4, 5; Lev 17:14 (×2); Deut 12:23; Ezek 22:27; Prov 1:18; 11Q19 LIII, 6
	דָּם נָקִי –	1	Deut 27:25
חָמָס		5	Judg 9:24; Jer 51:35; Ezek 7:23; Hab 2:8, 17
דֶּבֶר		4	Ezek 5:17; 28:23; 38:22; Sir 40:9*
חֶרֶב		4	Ezek 5:17; 14:19; 38:22; Sir 40:9
עָוֹן		4	Lev 20:16; 1QIsaᵃ I, 18; Isa 59:3; Ezek 9:9
אָוֶן		3	Isa 59:3; Ps 5:7; 59:3
עַוְלָה		3	Isa 59:3; Mic 3:10; Hab 2:12
אֵשׁ		2	Ezek 38:22; Joel 3:3
מִרְמָה		2	Ps 5:7; 55:24
רַע		2	Isa 33:15; 1QHᵃ XV, 6
רֹעַ מַעֲלָל מַחֲשֶׁבֶת רֹעַ		1 1	Isa 1:15 1QHᵃ XV, 6
רָעָה		2	2 Sam 16:8; Sir 40:9
שֶׁקֶר		2	Isa 59:3; 1QpHab X, 10
אֶבֶן אֶלְגָּבִישׁ		1	Ezek 38:22
אוֹיֵב		1	Ps 59:3
בֶּגֶד		1	Sir 39:26
בְּלִיַּעַל	אִישׁ דָּם –	1	2 Sam 16:7
בֶּן פָּרִיץ	שֹׁפֵךְ דָּם –	1	Ezek 18:10
גָּפְרִית		1	Ezek 38:22
גֶּשֶׁם שׁוֹטֵף		1	Ezek 38:22
דְּבַשׁ	דַּם עֵנָב –	1	Sir 39:26
דּוֹבֵר כָּזָב	אִישׁ דָּם –	1	Ps 5:7

MAPPING THE LEXICAL SEMANTIC DOMAINS OF רע

Lexeme	Association	No.	Location
דִּין		1	Deut 17:8
הוֹלֵל		1	Ps 5:7
זְעָקָה		1	Job 16:18
חַטָּא	אִישׁ דָּם –	1	Ps 26:9
חַיָּה רָעָה		1	Ezek 5:17
חָלָב	דַּם עֵנָב –	1	Sir 39:26
חֶמֶר	דַּם עֵנָב –	1	Deut 32:14
חַרְחֻר		1	Sir 40:9
חֹשֶׁךְ		1	Joel 3:4
יַיִן	דַּם עֵנָב –	1	Gen 49:11
יִצְהָר		1	Sir 39:26
לָחוּם		1	Zeph 1:17
מָוֶת		1	Sir 40:9
מֶטֶה		1	Ezek 9:9
מִתְקֹמֵם		1	Ps 59:3
נֶגַע		1	Deut 17:8
נוֹאֵף	שׁוֹפֵךְ דָּם –	1	Ezek 23:45
נֶפֶשׁ צַדִּיק	דָּם נָקִי –	1	Ps 79:10
עָמָל		1	Isa 59:3
עֶצֶם		1	1QHª XIII, 9*
עָר	אִישׁ דָּם –	1	Ps 139:19
צֹאָה		1	Isa 4:4
רָעָב		1	Ezek 5:17
רָשָׁע	אִישׁ דָּם –	1	Ps 139:19
שֶׁבֶר		1	Sir 40:9
שֹׁד		1	Sir 40:9
שָׁוְא		1	Isa 59:3
שֹׁחַד		1	Isa 33:15
שִׁקּוּץ		1	Zeph 9:7
תֹּהוּ		1	Isa 59:3
תִּימָרַת עָשָׁן		1	Joel 3:3

156 CHAPTER 3

Table 3.41. דָּם in Associations of Opposition

Lexeme	Association	No.	Location
אֱמוּנָה		1	Isa 59:3
יָשָׁר	אִישׁ דָּם –	1	Prov 29:10
צַדִּיק	אִישׁ דָּם –	1	Ps 55:24
צֶדֶק		1	Isa 59:3
תָּם	אִישׁ דָּם –	1	Prov 29:10

Observations

דָּם (blood) occurs almost exclusively in associations of similarity (97.3% vs. 5.4%). It also shows an unusually low frequency of association compared to other words analysed so far. Its three most frequent associations, בָּשָׂר (flesh), חֵלֶב (fat), and נֶפֶשׁ (soul), do not occur in association with רַע.[75] Furthermore, once occurrences of חַיָּה רָעָה (bad animal) are separated out from רַע it appears that דָּם is only loosely connected to רַע. Despite this, it cannot be excluded from the domains of רַע as it contains frequent associations with five frequent associates of רַע: חָמָס (violence); דֶּבֶר (plague); חֶרֶב (sword); עָוֹן (iniquity); and אָוֶן (villainy). It seems likely that one or more polysemes of דָּם are within or related to the semantic domains of רַע while the polyseme that occurs most frequently in semantic associations is not.

It has one frequent associate עַוְלָה (injustice) which occurs at least once in association with רַע and is a frequent associate of אָוֶן. עַוְלָה will be analysed in the second round of analysis.

3.2.14 חֹשֶׁךְ (darkness)

חֹשֶׁךְ occurs 131 times in the analysed texts [85;[76] 1; 45; 0; 0]. In total חֹשֶׁךְ occurs 82 times (65%)[77] with at least one semantic association. Its occurrence with semantic associations by corpus is shown in Table 3.42 below. Tables 3.43 and 3.44 show the semantic associations of similarity and opposition respectively.

---

[75] While בָּשָׂר is found in some phrases associated with phrases containing רַע, it is parallel to מַרְאֶה (appearance) or תֹּאַר (form) each time.

[76] Three occurrences were added from the Judean Desert corpus: 1QIsaᵃ XXIII, 29 [Isa 29:18]; 1QIsaᵃ XXXVIII, 12 [Isa 45:7]; 11Q5 XX, 4 [Ps 139:12]. One occurrence was added from the Samaritan Pentateuch and multiple Judean Desert manuscripts: Deuteronomy 5:22 [Deuteronomy 5:19 SP]; 4Q41 V, 2; 4Q129 1, 10; XQ2 I, 1.

[77] Four occurrences were eliminated under the conditions specified in §3.1.1.1.

MAPPING THE LEXICAL SEMANTIC DOMAINS OF רַע 157

Table 3.42. Number of Identifiable Lexical and
Phrasal Semantic Associations חֹשֶׁךְ by Type of Association

Corpus	Similarity		Opposition		Total
	n.	%	n.	%	n.
Hebrew Bible	38	65.5	35	60.3	58
Ben Sira	1	100.0	0	0.0	1
Judean Desert	6	25.1	20	87.0	23
Inscriptions	0	–	0	–	0
Mishnah	0	–	0	–	0
Total	45	54.9	55	67.1	82

Table 3.43. חֹשֶׁךְ in Associations of Similarity

Lexeme	Association	No.	Location
צַלְמָוֶת		9	Isa 9:1; Ps 107:10, 14; Job 3:5; 10:21; 12:22; 24:16; 28:3; 34:22
אֲפֵלָה		6	1QIsaᵃ XXIII, 29; Isa 58:10; 59:9; Joel 2:2; Zeph 1:15; 4Q392 1, 4
אֹפֶל		5	Isa 29:18; Amos 5:20; Job 10:21; 23:17; 28:3
עֲרָפֶל		5	Deut 4:11; Deut 5:22;[78] Isa 60:2; Joel 2:2; Zeph 1:15
לַיְלָה		4	Ps 139:11, 12; Job 5:14; Job 17:12
עָנָן		4	Deut 4:11; Deut 5:22;[79] Joel 2:2; Zeph 1:15
רַע	חֹשֶׁךְ –	2	Isa 5:20; 45:7
	דֶּרֶךְ חֹשֶׁךְ –	1	Prov 2:13
אָסוּר	יוֹשֵׁב חֹשֶׁךְ –	2	1QIsaᵃ XXXV, 17; Isa 49:9
אַשְׁמָה		1	1QM XIII, 15
רֶשַׁע אַשְׁמָה		1	1QS II, 7
אֲבַדּוֹן		1	Ps 88:13
אֵבֶל יָגוֹן	הוַת חֹשֶׁךְ –	1	1QS IV, 13
אַסִּיר	יוֹשֵׁב חֹשֶׁךְ –	1	Isa 42:7
בְּלִיַּעַל		1	1QM I, 1
דָּם		1	Joel 3:4

[78] Variant in multiple manuscripts: 4Q41 V, 2; 4Q129 1, 10; XQ2 I, 1; Deut 5:19 (SP).
[79] Variant in multiple manuscripts: 4Q41 V, 2; 4Q129 1, 10; XQ2 I, 1; Deut 5:19 (SP).

158   CHAPTER 3

Lexeme	Association	No.	Location
חֲלַקְלַקּוֹת		1	Ps 35:6
חֲשֵׁכָה		1	Ps 139:12
כַּמְרִיר		1	Job 3:5
מִסְתָּר		1	Isa 45:3
מְצוּקָה		1	Zeph 1:15
מַר		1	Isa 5:20
מְשׁוֹאָה		1	Zeph 1:15
נְשִׁיָּה		1	Ps 88:13
סֵתֶר	אֶרֶץ חֹשֶׁךְ –	1	Isa 45:19
עָב שַׁחַק		1	2 Sam 22:12
עֵיפָה		1	Job 10:21
עֲנָנָה		1	Job 3:5
עָרְמַת רֹעַ	דֶּרֶךְ חֹשֶׁךְ –	1	1QS IV, 11
צַר		1	Isa 5:30
צָרָה		1	Zeph 1:15
קֶבֶר		1	Ps 88:13
רָעַת מָרוֹר	הֹוַת חֹשֶׁךְ –	1	1QS IV, 13
שְׁאוֹל		1	Job 17:13
שׁוֹאָה		1	Zeph 1:15
שִׂכְלוּת		1	Sir 11:16*

Table 3.44. חֹשֶׁךְ in Associations of Opposition

Lexeme	Association	No.	Location
אוֹר		47	Gen 1:4, 5, 18; Exod 10:22; Isa 5:20, 30; 9:1; 45:7; 58:10; 59:9; 60:2; Ezek 32:8; Amos 5:18, 20; Mic 7:8; Ps 112:4; 139:11; 11Q5 XX, 4; Job 12:22, 25; 17:12; 18:18; 26:10; 29:3; 38:19; Eccl 2:13; 11:8; Lam 3:2; 1QS I, 10; III, 3; III, 19; III, 25; X, 2; 1QM I, 1; I, 10; I, 11; XIII, 5; XIII, 15; 1QHᵃ XVII, 26; XX, 9; XXI, 15; 1Q27 1 I, 5*; 4Q392 1, 4; 1, 6; 4Q462 1, 10; 11Q11 V, 7; 11Q17 X, 5
יוֹם		4	Ps 139:12; Job 5:14; 17:12; 24:16
אֱמֶת		2	1QS III, 21; 1QM XIII, 15

MAPPING THE LEXICAL SEMANTIC DOMAINS OF רע 159

Lexeme	Association	No.	Location
טוֹב		2	Isa 5:20; 1QIsaᵃ XXXVIII, 12
נֵר		2	Ps 18:29; Job 29:3
צָהֳרַיִם		2	Isa 58:10; Job 5:14
אוֹרָה		1	Ps 139:12
יָשָׁר	דֶּרֶךְ חֹשֶׁךְ –	1	Prov 2:13
מָתוֹק		1	Isa 5:20
נֹגַהּ		1	Amos 5:20
נְגֹהָה		1	Isa 59:9
נְהָרָה		1	Job 3:4
צְדָקָה		1	11Q11 V, 7
שָׁלוֹם		1	Isa 45:7

Observations

חֹשֶׁךְ (darkness) occurs fairly evenly in associations of similarity and opposition in the Hebrew Bible corpus (65.5% vs. 60.3%). However, in the Judean Desert corpus there is a strong bias against associations of similarity (21.7% vs. 87.0%). The frequent associations of similarity with חֹשֶׁךְ are: צַלְמָוֶת (deep darkness); אֲפֵלָה (darkness); אֹפֶל (darkness); עֲרָפֶל (thick cloud); לַיְלָה (night); עָנָן (cloud); and רַע.

חֹשֶׁךְ shares no frequent associates (of similarity) with רַע (bad) despite appearing three times in an association of similarity with רַע itself. The evidence points to an active metaphor as opposed to words that share a semantic domain. This can be highlighted further by examining two of the times חֹשֶׁךְ occurs in an association of similarity with רַע.

3.17. Isaiah 5:20

הוֹי הָאֹמְרִים לָרַע טוֹב וְלַטּוֹב רָע שָׂמִים חֹשֶׁךְ לְאוֹר וְאוֹר לְחֹשֶׁךְ שָׂמִים מַר לְמָתוֹק וּמָתוֹק לְמָר

Woe to those who call bad good and good bad, who change darkness to light and light to darkness, who change bitter to sweet and sweet to bitter!

3.18. Isaiah 45:7

יוֹצֵר אוֹר וּבוֹרֵא חֹשֶׁךְ עֹשֶׂה שָׁלוֹם וּבוֹרֵא רָע אֲנִי יְהוָה עֹשֶׂה כָל־אֵלֶּה

[I] form light and create darkness, make peace, and create bad; I the LORD make all these.

160 CHAPTER 3

In examples 3.17–3.18, the pairs are similar to each other with respect to their opposition. That is, the most prominent similarity between חֹשֶׁךְ and רַע is the way they oppose the terms light and good/peace respectively.[80]

Although there are no examples of חֹשֶׁךְ and רַע in an association of similarity in the Judean Desert corpus, there is an example from that corpus which suggests the metaphor may still be active.

3.19. 1Q27 1 I, 5b–6

וגלה הרשע מפני הצדק כגלות [ח]ושך מפני אור

... and wickedness disappears from before righteousness as [da]rkness disappears from before light.

Example 3.19 functions in a similar way to examples 3.17–3.18. The similarity between the terms is seen in their oppositions. Therefore, despite the frequency of phrases such as בְּנֵי חֹשֶׁךְ (children of darkness) in the Judean Desert corpus, it seems likely from texts such as example 3.19, and the low frequency of association with terms associated with רַע that the metaphor is still active. Therefore, the evidence is in favour of חֹשֶׁךְ being considered outside the semantic domains of רַע although it is of metaphoric importance.

3.2.15 מִרְמָה (deceit)

מִרְמָה occurs 46 times in the analysed texts [39; 1; 6; 0; 0]. In total מִרְמָה occurs 32 times (70%) with at least one semantic association. Its occurrence with semantic associations by corpus is shown in Table 3.45 below. Tables 3.46 and 3.47 show the semantic associations of similarity and opposition respectively.

Table 3.45. Number of Identifiable Lexical and Phrasal Semantic Associations מִרְמָה by Type of Association

Corpus	Similarity		Opposition		Total
	n.	%	n.	%	n.
Hebrew Bible	20	80.0	9	36.0	25
Ben Sira	1	100.0	0	0.0	1

---

[80] The variant in 1QIsaᵃ XXXVIII, 12 uses טוב (good) instead of שָׁלוֹם (peace).

MAPPING THE LEXICAL SEMANTIC DOMAINS OF רע   161

Corpus	Similarity		Opposition		Total
	n.	%	n.	%	n.
Judean Desert	5	83.3	2	33.3	6
Inscriptions	0	–	0	–	0
Mishnah	0	–	0	–	0
Total	26	81.3	11	34.4	32

Table 3.46. מִרְמָה in Associations of Similarity

Lexeme	Association	No.	Location
אָוֶן	מִרְמָה –	4	Ps 10:7; 36:4; 55:12; Job 15:35
פֹּעֲלֵי אָוֶן	אִישׁ מִרְמָה –	1	Ps 5:7
שֶׁקֶר		4	Ps 52:6; 109:2; Sir 51:6; 4Q169 3–4 II, 8
חָמָס		3	Isa 53:9; Zeph 1:9; Ps 55:12
כָּזָב	מִרְמָה –	2	1QS X, 22; 4Q169 3–4 II, 8
דּוֹבֵר כָּזָב	אִישׁ מִרְמָה –	1	Ps 5:7
עָמָל		3	Ps 10:7; 55:12; Job 15:35
רַע		2	Ps 34:14; 52:6
דְּבַר רַע		1	Jer 5:27
דָּם		2	Ps 5:7; 55:12
כַּחַשׁ		1	Hos 12:1
כַּחַשׁ עָוֹן		1	1QS X, 22
הַוָּה		2	Ps 38:13; 52:6
רְמִיָּה		2	Ps 52:6; 1QHᵃ XII, 21
רָעָה		2	Ps 50:19; 52:6
שָׁוְא		2	Ps 24:4; Job 31:5
תֹּךְ		2	Ps 10:7; 55:12
אֶבֶן וָאֶבֶן	מֹאזְנֵי מִרְמָה –	1	Prov 20:23
אָלָה		1	Ps 10:7
בְּלִיַּעַל		1	1QS X, 22
בֶּלַע		1	Ps 52:6
הוֹלָל		1	1QHᵃ XII, 21
זִמָּה		1	Sir 51:6
חֹזֵה תָעוּת	אִישׁ מִרְמָה –	1	1QHᵃ XII, 21

162 CHAPTER 3

Lexeme	Association	No.	Location
חוֹלֵל	אִישׁ מִרְמָה –	1	Ps 5:7
חָלָק		1	4Q185 1–2 II, 14
נַבְלוּת		1	1QS X, 22
נֵכֶל		1	1QpHab III, 5
עַוְלָה		1	Ps 43:1
רִיב		1	Ps 55:12
רָשָׁע		1	Ps 109:2
רֶשַׁע		1	Mic 6:11
שָׂנֵא		1	Ps 109:2
שִׁקּוּץ		1	1QS X, 22

Table 3.47. מִרְמָה in Associations of Opposition

Lexeme	Association	No.	Location
טוֹב		2	Ps 34:14; 52:6
צֶדֶק		2	Ps 52:6; Prov 12:17
שָׁלוֹם		2	Ps 34:14; 35:20
אֶבֶן שְׁלֵמָה		1	Prov 11:1
בֹּר כַּפַּיִם		1	4Q525 2 II+3,3
מִשְׁפָּט		1	Prov 12:5
פְּרִי קֹדֶשׁ		1	1QS X, 22
צַדִּיק		1	Ps 55:24
שִׂמְחָה		1	Prov 12:20
תֻּמָּה		1	Job 31:5

Observations

מִרְמָה (deceit) has a strong bias towards associations of similarity. All but one of its five frequent associates share some association with רַע and two (אָוֶן; villainy; and חָמָס; violence) are frequent associates of רַע. It can be considered as within the semantic domains of רַע. The three frequent associates that share some association with רַע are שֶׁקֶר (lie), כָּזָב (falsehood) and עָמָל (trouble). They will be analysed in the second round.

MAPPING THE LEXICAL SEMANTIC DOMAINS OF רַע   163

3.2.16 שָׂטָן (accuser/Satan)

שָׂטָן occurs 31 times in the analysed texts [27; 0; 4; 0; 0]. In total שָׂטָן occurs five times (17%)[81] with at least one semantic association. Its occurrence with semantic associations by corpus is shown in Table 3.48 below. Tables 3.49 and 3.50 show the semantic associations of similarity and opposition respectively.

Table 3.48. Number of Identifiable Lexical and
Phrasal Semantic Associations שָׂטָן by Type of Association

Corpus	Similarity		Opposition		Total
	n.	%	n.	%	n.
Hebrew Bible	2	100.0	0	0.0	2
Ben Sira	0	–	0	–	0
Judean Desert	3	100.0	1	33.3	3
Inscriptions	0	–	0	–	0
Mishnah	0	–	0	–	0
Total	5	100.0	1	20.0	5

Table 3.49. שָׂטָן in Associations of Similarity

Lexeme	Association	No.	Location
יֵצֶר רַע פֶּגַע רַע		1 2	11Q5 XIX, 15 1 Kgs 5:18; 4Q504 1–2 IV, 12*
מַכְאוֹב		1	11Q5 XIX, 15
מַשְׁחִית		1	1QHᵃ XXIV, 23*
רוּחַ טְמֵאָה		1	11Q5 XIX, 15
רָשָׁע		1	Ps 109:6

Table 3.50. שָׂטָן in Associations of Opposition

Lexeme	Association	No.	Location
בְּרָכָה		1	4Q504 1–2 IV, 12
שָׁלוֹם		1	4Q504 1–2 IV, 12

---

[81] One occurrence was eliminated under the conditions specified in §3.1.1.1.

164   CHAPTER 3

Observations

שָׂטָן (accuser/Satan) rarely occurs with semantic associations. Due to its overall low frequency of occurrence this causes problems in determining its status within the semantic domains of רַע. It may be that its low frequency of association masks its participation in the domain. In favour of this possibility is its one association with רָשָׁע (wicked) which is a frequent associate of רַע. It is likely, at the very least, that שָׂטָן is related in some important way to רַע and רָשָׁע. It is treated as related to, but not part of, the domains of רַע.

3.2.17 Discussion: First Round

In the first round of analysis חֹשֶׁךְ (darkness) and מָוֶת (death) were determined to be outside the semantic domains of רַע. Additionally, it was decided to treat the rare term שָׂטָן (accuser/Satan) as a term outside, but related to, the domains of רַע. דָּם (blood) has frequent and important associations which were not found with other terms frequently associated with רַע. However, it seemed likely that this was based on the semantic associations of different polysemes.

In the case with חֶרֶב (sword) polysemy may also be an issue. חֶרֶב demonstrated a number of frequent associations not associated with other terms that are frequently associated with רַע. It seems likely that חֶרֶב can, at minimum, refer to an implement (i.e. sword) and or the action commonly carried out with such an implement (i.e. war).[82]

Another potential issue with the רָעָב (famine) – דֶּבֶר (plague) – חֶרֶב triad of terms is that their seemingly close association with רַע is driven by the rare phrase חַיָּה רָעָה (bad animal; [7; 0; 1; 0; 2]).[83] However, חֳלִי רַע (bad sickness) is also associated with the triad, and רָעָה (evil) has a frequent association with the triad.[84] Overall, this indicates the need to consider these terms further.

At the conclusion of the first round of analysis, 19 words were found to be frequent associates of at least one frequent associate of רַע in addition to being associated with רַע at least once themselves. Two of these,

---

[82] This is supported in the findings of Koller, although Koller prefers to list them as homonyms brought about through a metonymous extension. Koller, *The Semantic Field of Cutting Tools*, 162–66.

[83] Gen 37:20, 33; Lev 26:6; Ezek 5:17; 14:15, 21; 34:25; 11Q14 1 II, 11; m. Ta'an. 3:5; m. 'Abot 5:8..

[84] רַע may also be associated with it once, although it is more likely an error, with the scribe of Sir B 9v1 missing a final ב.

MAPPING THE LEXICAL SEMANTIC DOMAINS OF רַע 165

יֵרָקוֹן (rust) and שִׁדָּפוֹן (blight) occur ten times or less, and so are discussed in Appendix B.1.[85] The remaining 17 words have been selected for analysis in the second round. שֶׁקֶר (lie) frequently occurs with five frequent associates of רַע. Three words occur frequently with three frequent associates of רַע: אוֹיֵב (enemy); חַטָּאת (sin); and עָמָל (trouble). Five words occur frequently with two frequent associates of רַע: מֵרַע (evildoer); עַוְלָה (injustice); פֶּשַׁע (transgression); צָרָה (distress); and שָׁוְא (worthlessness). The remaining eight words occur frequently with just one frequent associate of רַע: אַשְׁמָה (guilt); זִמָּה (wickedness); חַטָא (sin); כָּזָב (falsehood); עָרִיץ (ruthless); צָמָא (thirst); שֶׁבֶר (destruction); and שֹׁד (destruction).

3.3 ASSOCIATION ANALYSIS: ROUND 2

3.3.1 שֶׁקֶר (lie)

שֶׁקֶר occurs 144 times in the analysed texts [114;[86] 6; 17; 0; 7]. In total שֶׁקֶר occurs 58 times (41%)[87] with at least one semantic association. Its occurrence with semantic associations by corpus is shown in Table 3.51 below. Tables 3.52 and 3.53 show the semantic associations of similarity and opposition respectively.

Table 3.51. Number of Identifiable Lexical and
Phrasal Semantic Associations שֶׁקֶר by Type of Association

Corpus	Similarity		Opposition		Total
	n.	%	n.	%	n.
Hebrew Bible	35	81.4	12	27.9	43
Ben Sira	3	100.0	0	0.0	3
Judean Desert	11	100.0	2	18.2	11
Inscriptions	0	–	0	–	0
Mishnah	1	100.0	0	0.0	1
Total	50	86.2	14	24.1	58

---

[85] They are found to demonstrate significant links with one domain of use of רַע. However, due to their rarity and the particular domain, analysis of their use does not contribute significantly to understanding רַע.

[86] One occurrence was added from the Judean Desert corpus: XQ3 I, 28 [Deut 5:20].

[87] Three occurrences were eliminated under the conditions specified in §3.1.1.1.

166 CHAPTER 3

Table 3.52. שֶׁקֶר in Associations of Similarity

Lexeme	Association	No.	Location
כָּזָב	שֶׁקֶר –	4	Isa 28:15; Sir 15:20; 1QpHab X, 12; 4Q371 1a–b, 13*
	אָמַר שֶׁקֶר –	1	4Q171 1–2 I, 19
	לְשׁוֹן שֶׁקֶר –	1	Prov 6:17
	עֵד שֶׁקֶר –	2	Prov 19:5, 9
לְשׁוֹן כָּזָב	תַּלְמוּד שֶׁקֶר –	1	4Q169 3–4 II, 8
שָׁוְא		5	Isa 59:3; Ps 144:8, 11; Sir 15:20[88]; 1QpHab X, 11*
חֲלוֹם שָׁוְא		1	Zech 10:2
אָוֶן	שֶׁקֶר –	3	Isa 59:3; Zech 10:2; Ps 7:15
מַחֲשֶׁבֶת אָוֶן	לְשׁוֹן שֶׁקֶר –	1	Prov 6:17
פּוֹעֲלֵי אָוֶן	דּוֹבֵר שֶׁקֶר –	1	Ps 101:7
רְמִיָּה	שֶׁקֶר –	4	Mic 6:12; Ps 52:5; 120:2; 1QS IV, 9
עוֹשֵׂה רְמִיָּה	דּוֹבֵר שֶׁקֶר –	1	Ps 101:7
הֶבֶל		4	Jer 16:19; Jer 51:17; Zech 10:2; Prov 31:30
חָמָס		4	Deut 19:18; Mic 6:12; 11Q5 XXII, 6; 11Q19 LXI, 9
מִרְמָה	שֶׁקֶר –	2	Sir 51:5; Ps 109:2
לְשׁוֹן מִרְמָה	שֶׁקֶר –	1	Ps 52:5
שְׂפַת מִרְמָה	תַּלְמוּד שֶׁקֶר –	1	4Q169 3–4 II, 8
כַּחַשׁ		3	Sir 41:18; 1QS IV, 9; 4Q169 3–4 II, 2
רָעָה	שֶׁקֶר –	2	Ps 52:5; Prov 6:17
	לְשׁוֹן שֶׁקֶר –	1	4Q397 14–21, 9
רָשָׁע	שֶׁקֶר –	1	Ps 109:2
	דּוֹבֵר שֶׁקֶר –	1	Ps 101:7
	שִׂפְתֵי שֶׁקֶר –	1	Ps 31:19
בֶּצַע		2	Jer 6:13; 8:10
דָּם		2	Isa 59:3; 1QpHab X, 10
זִמָּה	אִמְרֵי שֶׁקֶר –	1	Isa 32:7
	טוֹפְלֵי שֶׁקֶר –	1	Sir 51:5
חִנָּם		2	Ps 35:19; 69:5
מַעַל		2	Sir 41:18; 4Q397 14–21, 9
סָרָה	שֶׁקֶר –	1	CD VI, 1
	דִּבֶּר שֶׁקֶר –	1	Isa 59:13

[88] Manuscript B 2v5

MAPPING THE LEXICAL SEMANTIC DOMAINS OF רַע

Lexeme	Association	No.	Location
עָמָל		2	Isa 59:3; Ps 7:15
פֶּשַׁע		2	Isa 57:4; Sir 41:18
רַע	שֶׁקֶר –	1	Ps 52:5
	אֹרַח שֶׁקֶר –	1	Ps 119:104
אִוֶּלֶת		1	1QS IV, 9
אֱלִיל	חֲזוֹן שֶׁקֶר –	1	Jer 14:14
גֵּוָה		1	1QS IV, 9
דְּבַר בֶּלַע		1	Ps 52:5
דֶּרֶךְ נִדָּה		1	1QS IV, 9
הַוָּה		1	Ps 52:5
הָמוֹן		1	Jer 3:23
זְנוּת		1	Sir 41:18
חָלָק		1	Prov 26:28
חֹנֶף		1	1QS IV, 9
יָד		1	Sir 41:18
יֶתֶר		1	Prov 17:7
כֹּבֶד אֹזֶן		1	1QS IV, 9
כֹּבֶד לֵב		1	1QS IV, 9
כֹּהֵן גָּדוֹל		1	m. Sanh. 1:5
לְשׁוֹן גִּדּוּף		1	1QS IV, 9
מְגַלֶּה סוֹד		1	Sir 15:20[89]
מַעֲשֵׂה תוֹעֵבָה		1	1QS IV, 9
מֵרַע		1	Prov 17:4
נְשׂוֹא פָנִים	מוֹרֶה שֶׁקֶר –	1	Isa 9:14
עָוֶל		1	11Q5 XXII, 6
עַוְלָה		1	Isa 59:3
עָוֹן		1	Isa 59:3
עִוְּרוֹן עֵינַיִם		1	1QS IV, 9
עֵינַיִם רָמוֹת	לְשׁוֹן שֶׁקֶר –	1	Prov 6:17
עֹשֶׁק	דְּבַר שֶׁקֶר –	1	Isa 59:13
פַּחַז		1	Sir 41:18*

[89] Manuscript B 2v5

168 CHAPTER 3

Lexeme	Association	No.	Location
פְּחֲזוּת		1	Jer 23:32
קִנְאַת זָדוֹן		1	1QS IV, 9
קֶסֶם	– חֲזוֹן שֶׁקֶר	1	Jer 14:14
קְצַר אַפַּיִם		1	1QS IV, 9
קְשִׁי עֹרֶף		1	1QS IV, 9
רוּחַ		1	Mic 2:11
רֶשַׁע		1	1QS IV, 9
שֵׁבֶט		1	m. Sanh. 1:5
שִׂנְאָה		1	Ps 109:2
תֹּהוּ		1	Isa 59:3
תַּרְמוּת	– חֲזוֹן שֶׁקֶר	1	Jer 14:14[90]
תַּרְמִית		1	Jer 23:26

Table 3.53. שֶׁקֶר in Associations of Opposition

Lexeme	Association	No.	Location
אֱמוּנָה	– שֶׁקֶר	4	Isa 59:3; Jer 9:2; Ps 119:29; Prov 14:5
	– עֵד שֶׁקֶר	1	Prov 12:17
עוֹשֵׂה אֱמוּנָה	– שִׂפְתֵי שֶׁקֶר	1	Prov 12:22
אֱמֶת	– שֶׁקֶר	2	Jer 9:4; Prov 12:19
	– דְּבַר שֶׁקֶר	1	Isa 59:13
שֶׂכֶר אֱמֶת	– פְּעֻלַּת שֶׁקֶר	1	Prov 11:18
טוֹב		2	Ps 52:5; 1QS IV, 9
מִשְׁפָּט	– דְּבַר שֶׁקֶר	1	Isa 59:13
קִנְאַת מִשְׁפָּט צֶדֶק		1	1QS IV, 9
צֶדֶק		2	Isa 59:3; Ps 52:5
אֹרֶךְ אַפַּיִם		1	1QS IV, 9
בִּינָה		1	1QS IV, 9
דַּעַת		1	1QS IV, 9
חָכְמָה		1	1QS IV, 9
חֶסֶד		1	11Q5 XXII, 6
יֵצֶר סָמוּךְ		1	1QS IV, 9
מַחְשֶׁבֶת קֹדֶשׁ		1	1QS IV, 9
מַעֲשֵׂה חָסִיד		1	11Q5 XXII, 6

[90] Qere: תַּרְמִית

MAPPING THE LEXICAL SEMANTIC DOMAINS OF רַע   169

Lexeme	Association	No.	Location
גֶּאֱמַן אֶרֶץ	דּוֹבֵר שֶׁקֶר –	1	Ps 101:7
נָכֹחַ		1	Isa 59:13
עֲנָוָה		1	1QS IV, 9
צְדָקָה	דְּבַר שֶׁקֶר –	1	Isa 59:13
רַחֲמִים		1	1QS IV, 9
שֵׂכֶל		1	1QS IV, 9

Observations

שֶׁקֶר (lie) has a strong bias towards associations of similarity. However, it does have notable oppositions with the masculine feminine word pair אֱמֶת (truth) / אֱמוּנָה (faithfulness). Although its most frequent associates, כָּזָב (falsehood) and שָׁוְא (worthlessness), are not frequent associates of רַע, they do have associations with רַע and are frequently associated with מִרְמָה, and אָוֶן and רָשָׁע respectively. Additionally, one of its third most frequent associates is אָוֶן (villainy), a frequent associate of רַע. Furthermore, out of its ten frequent associates, five (אָוֶן; חָמָס, violence; מִרְמָה, deceit; רָעָה, evil; רָשָׁע, wicked) are frequent associates of רַע. All but one (כַּחַשׁ, falsity) of the frequent associates of שֶׁקֶר are associated at least once with רַע. The accumulated evidence is strongly in favour of the inclusion of שֶׁקֶר within the domains of רַע.

3.3.2 אוֹיֵב (enemy)

אוֹיֵב occurs 332 times in the analysed texts [285;[91] 4; 39; 0; 4]. In total אוֹיֵב occurs 128 times (39%)[92] with at least one semantic association. Its occurrence with semantic associations by corpus is shown in Table 3.54 below. Tables 3.55 and 3.56 show the semantic associations of similarity and opposition respectively.

Some of the lexeme/phrase combinations in Table 3.52 were made due to the similarity of reference. For example, מֶלֶךְ בָּבֶל (king of Babylon), חֵיל מֶלֶךְ בָּבֶל (the army of the king of Babylon), and נְבוּכַדְרֶאצַּר (Nebuchadrezzar) are combined because they have an identical or close to identical referent within the discourse. This combination is not problematic for the

---

[91] Three occurrences were added from the Samaritan Pentateuch and Judean Desert corpuses: Genesis 24:60 (SP); Numbers 14:41 (SP); and 4Q44 5 II, 5 [Deut 32:42].
[92] Four occurrences were eliminated under the conditions specified in §3.1.1.1.

170 CHAPTER 3

current analysis as these words/phrases are not closely related to רַע and
so their combination is a matter of convenience.

Table 3.54. Number of Identifiable Lexical and
Phrasal Semantic Associations אוֹיֵב by Type of Association

Corpus	Similarity		Opposition		Total
	n.	%	n.	%	n.
Hebrew Bible	113	96.6	9	7.7	117
Ben Sira	2	100.0	0	0.0	2
Judean Desert	7	87.5	1	12.5	8
Inscriptions	0	–	0	–	0
Mishnah	0	0.0	1	100.0	1
Total	122	95.3	11	8.6	128

Table 3.55. אוֹיֵב in Associations of Similarity

Lexeme	Association	No.	Location
צַר		23	Num 10:9; Deut 32:27; 42; Isa 1:24; 9:10; 59:18; Mic 5:9; 7:10; Ps 13:5; 27:2; 81:15; 89:23, 43; 106:10; Lam 1:5, 9; 2:4, 17; 4:12; Esth 7:6; 1 Chr 21:12; Sir 12:16; 1QM XII, 11
שׂוֹנֵא		19	Exod 23:4; Lev 26:17; Num 10:35; Deut 30:7; 2 Sam 22:18, 41; Ps 18:18; 21:9; 35:19; 38:20; 41:6; 69:5; 106:10, 42; Esth 9:1, 5, 16; 11Q19 LIX, 11; LIX, 19
פְּלִשְׁתִּי		10	1 Sam 4:3; 12:10; 14:30, 47; 18:25; 2 Sam 3:18; 5:20; 19:10; Isa 9:10; 1 Chr 14:11
מְבַקֵּשׁ נֶפֶשׁ		9	Jer 19:7, 9; 21:7; 34:20, 21; 44:30 (×2); 49:37; 11Q19 LIX, 19
מְשַׂנֵּא		8	4Q44 5 II, 5; Ps 18:41; 55:13; 68:2; 81:15; 83:3; 89:23; 139:22
אֵל/מְשַׂנֵּא צֶדֶק		1	1QM III, 5
גּוֹי		6	Deut 28:48; Ps 9:7; 106:42; Neh 5:9; 6:16; 1QM XII, 11
שִׁבְעַת גּוֹי הֶבֶל		1	1QM XI, 8
עַם		4	Ezek 39:27; Ps 45:6; 89:52; Lam 3:46
עַם אַחֵר		1	Deut 28:31
עַם נָבָל		1	Ps 74:18

MAPPING THE LEXICAL SEMANTIC DOMAINS OF רֵע 171

Lexeme	Association	No.	Location
צוֹרֵר		6	Exod 23:22; Ps 7:6; 8:3; 69:19; 74:3; 143:12
רָשָׁע		6	Ps 3:8; 9:7; 17:9; 37:20; 55:4; 92:10
פּוֹעֲלֵי אָוֶן		5	Ps 6:11; 59:2; 64:2; 92:10; 4Q88 X, 11*
שָׁאוּל		5	1 Sam 24:5; 26:8; 2 Sam 4:8; 22:1; Ps 18:1
מוֹאָב מֶלֶךְ מוֹאָב		3 1	Judg 3:28; 1 Sam 14:47; 4Q434 7b, 3* 1 Sam 12:10
מֶלֶךְ בָּבֶל חֵיל מֶלֶךְ בָּבֶל נְבוּכַדְרֶאצַּר		1 1 2	Jer 20:4 Jer 34:21 Jer 21:7; Jer 44:30
קָם		4	Exod 15:6; 2 Sam 22:49; Ps 18:49; 92:10
בְּנֵי עַמּוֹן נָחָשׁ מֶלֶךְ בְּנֵי עַמּוֹן		2 1	Judg 11:36; 1 Sam 14:47 1 Sam 12:11
בֶּן עַוְלָה		3	2 Sam 7:9; Ps 89:23; 1 Chr 17:8
חָמָס אִישׁ חָמָס		1 2	2 Sam 22:4 2 Sam 22:49; Ps 18:49
מֵרַע		3	Ps 27:2; 64:2; 92:10
אֱדוֹם		2	1 Sam 14:47; 4Q434 7b, 3*
מִתְנַקֵּם		2	Ps 8:3; 44:17
מִתְקוֹמֵם		2	Ps 59:2; Job 27:7
אַבְשָׁלוֹם		1	2 Sam 18:32
אוֹרֵב		1	Ezra 8:31
אִישׁ דָּם		1	Ps 59:2
אַכְזָרִי		1	Jer 30:14
אֱמֹרִי		1	Josh 7:8
אֲרָם		1	Isa 9:10
בָּחִיר		1	Sir 46:1
בְּשַׂר אַשְׁמָה		1	1QM XII, 11
גְּדוּד בְּלִיַּעַל		1	1QM XI, 8
גֶּשֶׁם		1	Neh 6:1
הָמָן הָרָע		1	Esth 7:6
חָלָל		1	1QM XII, 11
טוֹבִיָּה		1	Neh 6:1

Lexeme	Association	No.	Location
מְבַקֵּשׁ רָעָה		1	Esth 9:1
מְגַדֵּף		1	Ps 44:17
מְהוֹלֵל		1	Ps 102:9
מַחֲרִיב אֶרֶץ		1	Judg 16:24
מְחָרֵף		1	Ps 44:17
מַלְכֵי צוֹבָה		1	1 Sam 14:47
מְלַמֵּד		1	Ps 119:98
מַצְמִית		1	Ps 69:5
נֵכָר		1	Isa 62:8
סִיסְרָא		1	1 Sam 12:10
סַנְבַּלַּט		1	Neh 6:1
עָר		1	Ps 139:22
צִי		1	Ps 72:9
רוֹדֵף		1	Ps 31:16
שׁוּר		1	Ps 92:10
שִׁמְשׁוֹן		1	Judg 16:23
תְּקוֹמֵם		1	Ps 139:22

Table 3.56. אוֹיֵב in Associations of Opposition

Lexeme	Association	No.	Location
אוֹהֵב		3	Judg 5:31; Lam 1:2; 4Q525 10, 5
עֶבֶד		2	Isa 66:14; Ps 89:52
שָׁכֵן		2	Ps 80:7; 89:43
אָח		1	m. Soṭah 8:1
אִישׁ שָׁלוֹם		1	Ps 41:6
אַלּוּף		1	Ps 55:13
אֱנוֹשׁ		1	Ps 55:13
מְיוּדָּע		1	Ps 55:13
עֶרֶךְ		1	Ps 55:13
רֵעַ		1	Lam 1:2
שׁוֹלֵם		1	Ps 7:6

MAPPING THE LEXICAL SEMANTIC DOMAINS OF רַע 173

Observations

אוֹיֵב (enemy) rarely occurs with associations of opposition. Additionally, many of its associations of similarity are with individuals, people groups, and nations. These associations are not of interest in establishing the semantic domains of רַע. Eliminating these from consideration, we see the following highly important associates, occurring 9 times or more: צַר (adversary); שׂוֹנֵא (hater); מְבַקֵּשׁ נֶפֶשׁ (seeker of life); מְשַׂנֵּא (hater). Of the seven remaining words and phrases that occur in associations of similarity between 3 and 6 times, there are three words with frequent associations with רַע and three with infrequent associations. The pattern of associations suggests that this word is related to, but outside the semantic domains of רַע. Strengthening this conclusion is the fact that the one association of אוֹיֵב with רַע is when רַע modifies a name.

3.3.3 חַטָּאת (sin)

חַטָּאת occurs 680 times in the analysed texts [294;[93] 5; 31; 0; 350]. In total חַטָּאת occurs 334 times (49%)[94] with at least one semantic association. Its occurrence with semantic associations by corpus is shown in Table 3.57 below. Tables 3.58 and 3.59 show the semantic associations of similarity and opposition respectively.

There was some difficulty deciding how to group the phrases אַשְׁמַת פֶּשַׁע (guilt of transgression) and פֶּשַׁע אַשְׁמָה (transgression of guilt) because both words within the phrases are also important associates on their own. In Table 3.58 the two phrases are included together in their own row rather than being classed with either פֶּשַׁע or אַשְׁמָה.

Table 3.57. Number of Identifiable Lexical and
Phrasal Semantic Associations חַטָּאת by Type of Association

Corpus	Similarity		Opposition		Total
	n.	%	n.	%	n.
Hebrew Bible	155	96.9	9	5.6	160
Ben Sira	2	50.0	3	75.0	4
Judean Desert	21	100.0	0	0.0	21
Inscriptions	0	–	0	–	0
Mishnah	149	100.0	0	0.0	149
Total	327	97.9	12	3.6	334

[93] One occurrence was added from the Samaritan Pentateuch: Numbers 28:30 (SP).
[94] One occurrence was eliminated under the conditions specified in §3.1.1.1.

174   CHAPTER 3

Table 3.58. חַטָּאת in Associations of Similarity

Lexeme	Association	No.	Location
עֹלָה		132	Lev 4:29; 5:7, 8; 6:18; 7:7, 37; 9:2, 3, 7, 15, 22; 10:19; 12:6, 8; 14:13, 19, 22, 31; 15:15, 30; 16:3, 5; 16:25; 23:19; Num 6:11, 14, 16; 7:16, 22, 28, 34, 40, 46, 52, 58, 64, 70, 76, 82, 87; 8:12; 15:24; 28:15, 22, 30; 29:5, 11(×2), 16, 19, 22, 25, 28, 31, 34, 38; Ezek 40:39; 43:19, 22, 25; 45:17, 23, 25; Ezra 8:35; Neh 10:34; 2 Chr 29:24; 11Q19 XVII, 14; XXV, 15; XXVI, 9; m. Šeqal. 6:5; 7:3; m. Ned. 1:4; m. Naz. 4:4 (×2), 6 (×2); 6:7, 8 (×2); 8:1 (×3); m. Hor. 2:6; m. Zebaḥ. 1:3; 4:4; 6:2, 6, 7 (×2); 7:1 (×5), 2 (×4), 3, 4 (×4); 8:4; 10:2 (×2), 4; m. ʿArak. 5:6; m. Tem. 5:6 (×3); m. Meʿil. 3:2; m. Qinnim 1:1 (×3), 2 (×2), 4; 2:5 (×7); 3:3 (×2), 4; m. Neg. 14:7 (×2); m. Parah 1:4; m. Yad. 4:2
אָשָׁם		67	Lev 6:10; 7:7, 37; 14:13 (×2); Num 6:11; 18:9; 2 Kgs 12:17; Ezek 40:39; 42:13; 44:29; 46:20; 11Q19 XXXV, 11; XXXV, 12; m. Ḥal. 4:11; m. Yoma 8:8; m. Ḥag. 1:4; m. Zebaḥ. 1:1 (×4); 4:6; 8:2, 11; 10:2, 6; 11:1; 14:3 (×2); m. Menaḥ. 9:6 (×2); m. Ḥul. 2:10; m. Tem. 1:1 (×4); 7:6; m. Ker. 1:2; 2:3, 4, 6; 3:1, 4; 4:2 (×3); 5:5 (×2), 6 (×2), 7 (×6), 8 (×4); 6:4; m. Meʿil. 2:5; m. Neg. 14:7 (×2), 11; m. Parah 1:4; m. Yad. 4:2
עָוֹן		54	Lev 16:21; Deut 19:15; 1 Sam 20:1; Isa 6:7; 27:9; 40:2; 43:24; 59:2, 12; Jer 5:25; 14:10; 16:10, 18; 18:23; 30:14, 15; 31:34; 36:3; 50:20; Ezek 3:20; 21:29; Hos 4:8; 8:13; 9:9; 13:12; Mic 7:19; Ps 32:5; 38:4, 19; 51:4; 59:4; 79:9; 85:3; 109:14; Job 10:6; 13:23; 14:16; Prov 5:22; Lam 4:6, 13, 22; Dan 9:24; Neh 3:37; 9:2; Sir 3:14; 1QS I, 23; III, 8; III, 22; XI, 9; XI, 15; 1QHᵃ IX, 27; 4Q176 1–2 I, 6; 11Q5 XIX, 13; 11Q19 XXVI, 12

MAPPING THE LEXICAL SEMANTIC DOMAINS OF רַע 175

Lexeme	Association	No.	Location
מִנְחָה		51	Lev 5:11; 7:7, 37; 9:3, 15; 14:31; 23:19; Num 6:14, 16; 7:16, 22, 28, 34, 40, 46, 52, 58, 64, 70, 76, 82, 87; 8:8; 15:24; 18:9; 28:22, 30; 29:5, 11(×2), 16, 19, 22, 25, 28, 31, 34, 38; Ezek 42:13; 44:29; 45:17, 23, 25; 46:20; Neh 10:34; 11Q19 XVII, 14; XXVIII, 8; XXVIII, 11; m. Ned. 1:4; m. Zebaḥ. 6:2; 14:3
שֶׁלֶם		20	Lev 9:3, 22; Num 6:14, 16; Ezek 43:25; 45:17; m. Ned. 1:4; m. Naz. 4:4 (×2), 6 (×2); 6:7 (×2), 8 (×2); m. Zebaḥ. 10:6; 11:1; m. ʿArak. 5:6; m. Meʿil. 2:5; 3:2
זֶבַח שֶׁלֶם		19	Lev 4:29, 34; 7:37; 9:15; 23:19; Num 7:16, 22, 28, 34, 40, 46, 52, 58, 64, 70, 76, 82, 87; m. Šeqal. 7:3
פֶּשַׁע		29	Gen 31:36; 50:17; Lev 16:16, 21; Josh 24:19; Isa 43:25; 44:22; 58:1; 59:12; Ezek 18:21; 21:29; 33:10, 14; Amos 5:12; Mic 1:5; 3:8; 6:7; Ps 25:7; 32:5; 51:4, 5; 59:4; Job 13:23; 14:16; 34:37; Dan 9:24; 1QS XI, 9; 11Q5 XXIV, 11
פֶּשַׁע מַעֲשֶׂה		1	1QS III, 22
נֶסֶךְ		19	Lev 23:19; Num 6:14, 16; 15:24; 28:15, 30; 29:5, 11, 16, 19, 22, 25, 28, 31, 34, 38; 11Q19 XVII, 14; XXVIII, 8; XXVIII, 11
תְּרוּמָה		13	Ezek 44:29; m. Ḥag. 2:5, 6, 7; m. Ḥul. 2:10; m. Parah 10:6 (×5); 11:2 (×3)
פֶּסַח		12	m. Zebaḥ. 1:1 (×3), 2, 3, 4; 2:4; 3:6; m. Menaḥ. 9:6; m. Yad. 4:2 (×3)
אַשְׁמָה		10	2 Chr 28:13; 1QS III, 22; 11Q19 XXVI, 12; XXXV, 14; m. Maʿaś. Š. 1:7; m. Šeqal. 1:5; 2:5; m. Ned. 4:3; m. Zebaḥ. 10:5; m. ʿArak. 5:6
קֹדֶשׁ		9	Neh 10:34; m. Ḥag. 2:5, 6, 7 (×2); m. Parah 10:6 (×3); 11:2
בְּכוֹר		7	m. Ḥag. 1:4; m. Menaḥ. 9:6; m. Ḥul. 2:10; m. Tem. 1:1 (×4)
כָּרֵת		6	m. Hor. 2:3 (×2), 6; m. Ker. 1:2; 2:6; 6:3

176 CHAPTER 3

Lexeme	Association	No.	Location
קָרְבָּן		5	Lev 9:7; Num 15:25; 18:9; m. Ned. 1:4; m. Naz. 6:10
קָרְבָּן עֵץ		1	Neh 10:34
מַעֲשֵׂר		5	m. Ḥag. 2:5, 6, 7; m. Menaḥ. 9:6; m. Ḥul. 2:10
נְדָבָה		5	m. Šeqal. 2:3, 5; m. Naz. 4:4, 6; m. Zebaḥ. 6:2
אִשֶּׁה		4	Lev 6:10; Num 15:25; 28:22; 29:16
לֶחֶם		4	m. Naz. 4:4 (×2), 6 (×2)
קִנֵּי זָבוֹת		4	m. Maʿaś. Š. 1:7; m. Šeqal. 1:5; 2:5; m. Ned. 4:3
קִנֵּי זָבִים		4	m. Maʿaś. Š. 1:7; m. Šeqal. 1:5; 2:5; m. Ned. 4:3
קִנֵּי יוֹלֶדֶת		4	m. Maʿaś. Š. 1:7; m. Šeqal. 1:5; 2:5; m. Ned. 4:3
תּוֹעֵבָה		4	Ezek 16:51, 52; 18:14, 24
אַשְׁמַת פֶּשַׁע	חַטָּאת –	1	4Q184 1, 9
פֶּשַׁע אַשְׁמָה	מַעַל חַטָּאת –	1	1QS IX, 4
	חַטָּאת –	1	1QS I, 23
חֹל		3	m. Ḥag. 2:5, 6, 7
עָוֶל		3	Ezek 18:24; 33:14; 4Q184 1, 9
רָעָה		3	Gen 50:17; 1 Sam 12:19; Sir 47:24
שֶׁקֶל		3	m. Šeqal. 2:3, 4 (×2)
דֶּרֶךְ		2	Ezek 18:21; 33:10
חַטָּאָה		2	Exod 32:30; 2 Kgs 17:22
נִדָּה		2	Zech 13:1; 1QS XI, 15
רַע		1	11Q5 XXIV, 7
דֶּרֶךְ רַע		1	Ezek 33:10
רֶשַׁע		2	Deut 9:27; Ezek 33:14
אָוֶן	חַטָּאת קֶסֶם –	1	1 Sam 15:23
אָלָה	חַטָּאת פֶּה –	1	Ps 59:13
בָּמוֹת אָוֶן	חַטָּאת יִשְׂרָאֵל –	1	Hos 10:8
דְּבַר שְׂפָתַיִם	חַטָּאת פֶּה –	1	Ps 59:13
זֶבַח		1	m. Zebaḥ. 8:1
זְעָקָה		1	Gen 18:20

MAPPING THE LEXICAL SEMANTIC DOMAINS OF רע

Lexeme	Association	No.	Location
חֹדֶשׁ		1	Neh 10:34
חָזֶה		1	m. Ḥag. 1:4
חֵטְא		1	Deut 19:15
טֻמְאָה		1	Lev 16:16
כַּחַשׁ	חַטַּאת פֶּה –	1	Ps 59:13
לֶחֶם מַעֲרֶכֶת		1	Neh 10:34
לֶחֶם פָּנִים		1	m. Zebaḥ. 14:3
מוֹעֵד		1	Neh 10:34
מָוֶת		1	4Q184 1, 9
מִלֻּאִים		1	Lev 7:37
מַעַל		1	Ezek 18:24
עֲבֵרָה		1	m. Yoma 8:9
עֵגֶל		1	Deut 9:21
עֹמֶר		1	m. Zebaḥ. 14:3
צָבָא		1	Isa 40:2
קָדְשֵׁי קָדָשִׁים		1	m. Zebaḥ. 14:3
קָדָשִׁים קַלִּים		1	m. Zebaḥ. 14:3
קְשִׁי		1	Deut 9:27
שַׁבָּת		1	Neh 10:34
שׁוֹק		1	m. Ḥag. 1:4
שְׁתֵּי לֶחֶם		1	m. Zebaḥ. 14:3
תּוֹדָה		1	m. Ned. 1:4
תְּרָפִים	חַטַּאת קֶסֶם –	1	1 Sam 15:23

Table 3.59. חַטָּאת in Associations of Opposition

Lexeme	Association	No.	Location
צְדָקָה		9	Ezek 18:21, 24; 33:14, 16; Prov 13:6; 14:34; Sir 3:14, 15, 30
מִשְׁפָּט		3	Ezek 18:21; 33:14, 16
דֶּרֶךְ טוֹב		2	1 Kgs 8:36; 2 Chr 6:27
חַיִּים		1	Prov 10:16
צֶדֶק		1	Dan 9:24

178   CHAPTER 3

Observations

חַטָּאת (sin) rarely occurs with associations of opposition. חַטָּאת appears
to occur in two distinct domains: sacrifice and sin. Its fairly strong opposition with צְדָקָה (righteous) occurs with occurrences in the domain of sin.

Although its most frequent associates are other sacrifices, it also has
very frequent links with words in the domain of sin indicating clear polysemy. Occurrences within the domain of sin may be of interest in an examination of the semantic domains of רע. The frequent associates of חַטָּאת
when used as part of the "sin" domain are: עָוֹן (iniquity); פֶּשַׁע (transgression); אַשְׁמָה (guilt);[95] תּוֹעֵבָה (abomination); עָוֶל (injustice); רָעָה (evil).
Three of these were identified as frequent associates of רע and two were
selected for second round analysis. There appears sufficient evidence to
retain חַטָּאת in its sense of "sin" as a part of the semantic domains of רע.

3.3.4 מֵרַע (evildoer)

The Hiphil participle מֵרַע occurs 23 times in the analysed texts. Of
these, 2 occurrences appear to act verbally.[96] The remaining 21 function
syntactically as nouns and so are of interest in the present study [18; 2;
1; 0; 0]. In total, the substantive uses of מֵרַע occur 18 times (86%) with
at least one semantic association. Its occurrence with semantic associations by corpus is shown in Table 3.60 below. Tables 3.61 and 3.62 show
the semantic associations of similarity and opposition respectively.

Table 3.60. Number of Identifiable Lexical and
Phrasal Semantic Associations מֵרַע by Type of Association

Corpus	Similarity		Opposition		Total
	n.	%	n.	%	n.
Hebrew Bible	15	100.0	3	20.0	15
Ben Sira	2	100.0	1	50.0	2
Judean Desert	0	0.0	1	100.0	1
Inscriptions	0	–	0	–	0
Mishnah	0	–	0	–	0
Total	17	94.4	5	27.8	18

---

[95] Excluding the 6 uses from the Mishnah where it occurs in reference to sacrifice.
[96] The two occurrences are from Daniel 11:27 in the Hebrew Bible, and m. Sanhedrin 7:10
in the Mishnah. Note that Daniel 11:27 is often considered to be a hapax noun; however,
that discussion is not relevant for the current analysis as it has already been excluded from
further analysis.

MAPPING THE LEXICAL SEMANTIC DOMAINS OF רַע   179

Table 3.61. מֵרַע in Associations of Similarity

Lexeme	Association	No.	Location
פּוֹעֲלֵי אָוֶן		4	Isa 31:2; Ps 64:3; 92:12; 94:16
רָשָׁע		4	Ps 26:5; 37:9; Job 8:20; Prov 24:19
אוֹיֵב		3	Ps 27:2; 64:3; 92:12
רָע	מֵרַע –	1	Prov 24:19
	מֵרַע אוֹהֵב –	1	Sir 37:4
דּוֹבֵר נְבָלָה		1	Isa 9:16
חוֹטֵא		1	Isa 1:4
חָנֵף		1	Isa 9:16
כֶּלֶב	עֲדַת מֵרַע –	1	Ps 22:17
מַשְׁחִית		1	Isa 1:4
נֶעְלָם		1	Ps 26:5
סֵעֵף		1	Ps 119:115
עוֹשֵׂה עַוְלָה		1	Ps 37:1
עַם כֶּבֶד עָוֹן	זֶרַע מֵרַע –	1	Isa 1:4
פּוֹשֵׁעַ		1	Sir 11:16
צַר		1	Ps 27:2
קָם		1	Ps 92:12
רֵעַ	מֵרַע אוֹהֵב –	1	Sir 37:4
שָׁוְא		1	Ps 26:5
שׂוֹנֵא		1	Job 8:20
שׁוּר		1	Ps 92:12
שֶׁקֶר		1	Prov 17:4

Table 3.62. מֵרַע in Associations of Opposition

Lexeme	Association	No.	Location
אוֹהֵב טוֹב	מֵרַע אוֹהֵב –	1	Sir 37:4
חָבֵר	מֵרַע אוֹהֵב –	1	Sir 37:4
יְשַׁר לֵב		1	Ps 94:16
מֵיטִיב		1	1Q27 1 II, 3
עָנָו		1	Ps 37:9
צֶדֶק		1	Ps 94:16
קֹוֵי יהוה		1	Ps 37:9
תָּם		1	Job 8:20

180 CHAPTER 3

Observations

מֵרַע (evildoer) occurs infrequently and so, as with all infrequent words, any conclusions must remain tentative. מֵרַע rarely occurs in associations of opposition. Out of its three frequent associates, two are frequent associates of רַע and the other, אוֹיֵב (enemy), was found to have many associations with associates of רַע. In addition, although it occurs infrequently, it still occurs as an associate of רַע twice. Being a Hiphil participle which is usually substantive and of the same word family as רַע, it is unsurprising to find it shares important associates with רַע. There is strong evidence that the infrequent term מֵרַע is within the semantic domains of רַע.

3.3.5 עָמָל (trouble)

עָמָל occurs 65 times in the analysed texts [56;[97] 3; 5; 0; 1]. In total עָמָל occurs 35 times (54%) with at least one semantic association. Its occurrence with semantic associations by corpus is shown in Table 3.63 below. Tables 3.64 and 3.65 show the semantic associations of similarity and opposition respectively.

Table 3.63. Number of Identifiable Lexical and
Phrasal Semantic Associations עָמָל by Type of Association

Corpus	Similarity		Opposition		Total
	n.	%	n.	%	n.
Hebrew Bible	29	100.0	2	6.9	29
Ben Sira	0	0.0	1	100.0	1
Judean Desert	4	100.0	0	0.0	4
Inscriptions	0	–	0	–	0
Mishnah	1	100.0	0	0.0	1
Total	34	97.1	3	8.6	35

Table 3.64. עָמָל in Associations of Similarity

Lexeme	Association	No.	Location
אָוֶן		11	Num 23:21; Isa 10:1; 59:4; Hab 1:3 Ps 7:15; 10:7; 55:11; 90:10; Job 4:8; 5:6; 15:35

---

[97] One occurrence was added: Numbers 23:21 (Samaritan Pentateuch).

MAPPING THE LEXICAL SEMANTIC DOMAINS OF רַע 181

Lexeme	Association	No.	Location
חָמָס		3	Hab 1:3; Ps 7:17; 55:11
מִרְמָה		3	Ps 10:7; 55:11; Job 15:35
עֳנִי		3	Gen 41:51; Deut 26:7; Ps 25:18
הַוָּה	עָמָל –	1	Ps 55:11
כְּסֵה הַוָּה	יוֹצֵר עָמָל –	1	Ps 94:20
לַחַץ		2	Deut 26:7; 4Q504 1–2 VI, 12
מַעֲשֶׂה		1	Eccl 2:11
כִּשְׁרוֹן מַעֲשֶׂה		1	Eccl 4:4
מְצוּקָה		2	Ps 25:18; 107:12
עָוֹן		2	Num 23:21 (SP); Isa 59:4
רִיב		2	Hab 1:3; Ps 55:11
שֹׁד		2	Hab 1:3; Prov 24:2
שָׁוְא		2	Isa 59:4; Job 7:3
שֶׁקֶר		2	Isa 59:4; Ps 7:15
תֹּךְ		2	Ps 10:7; 55:11
אֵבֶל		1	1QHᵃ XIX, 22
אָלָה		1	Ps 10:7
אֱמוּנָה		1	1QpHab VIII, 2
דָּם		1	Isa 59:4
הוֹן		1	1QS IX, 22
חַיִּים		1	Eccl 9:9
יָגוֹן		1	Jer 20:18
כַּעַס		1	Ps 10:14
מָדוֹן		1	Hab 1:3
מָזוֹן		1	m. B. Meṣ. 5:4
עַוְלָה		1	Isa 59:4
צַר		1	Ps 107:12
צָרָה		1	Ps 25:18
רֵישׁ		1	Prov 31:7
רַע		1	Hab 1:13
רְעוּת רוּחַ		1	Eccl 4:6
רַעְיוֹן לֵב		1	Eccl 2:22
תֹּהוּ		1	Isa 59:4

182   CHAPTER 3

Table 3.65. עָמָל in Associations of Opposition

Lexeme	Association	No.	Location
אֱמוּנָה		1	Isa 59:4
דִּין		1	Isa 10:1
לֵב טוֹב	מַחְשֶׁבֶת עָמָל –	1	Sir 13:26
מִשְׁפָּט		1	Isa 10:1
צֶדֶק		1	Isa 59:4

Observations

עָמָל (trouble) has a strong bias towards associations of similarity. Its
most frequent associate is אָוֶן (villainy). However, as noted in DCH, some
of these uses appear to be from separate polysemes which may not be
related to רַע (עֳנִי). With the presence of חָמָס (violence) and מִרְמָה (deceit)
as two of the remaining three frequent associates it seems likely that עָמָל
is within the semantic domains of רַע.

3.3.6 עַוְלָה (injustice)

עַוְלָה occurs 64 times in the analysed texts [33; 2; 27; 0; 2]. In total
עַוְלָה occurs 42 times (71%)[98] with at least one semantic association. Its
occurrence with semantic associations by corpus is shown in Table 3.66
below. Tables 3.67 and 3.68 show the semantic associations of similarity
and opposition respectively.

Table 3.66. Number of Identifiable Lexical and
Phrasal Semantic Associations עַוְלָה by Type of Association

Corpus	Similarity		Opposition		Total
	n.	%	n.	%	n.
Hebrew Bible	21	84.0	10	40.0	25
Ben Sira	1	100.0	0	0.0	1
Judean Desert	11	73.3	8	53.3	15
Inscriptions	0	–	0	–	0
Mishnah	1	100.0	0	0.0	1
Total	34	81.0	18	42.9	42

---

[98] Five occurrences were eliminated under the conditions specified in §3.1.1.1.

MAPPING THE LEXICAL SEMANTIC DOMAINS OF רע　　　183

Table 3.67. עַוְלָה in Associations of Similarity

Lexeme	Association	No.	Location
רְמִיָּה	עַוְלָה –	4	Job 13:7; 27:4; 1QHᵃ XXI, 35; 1QHᵃ VI, 26
מַעֲשֵׂה רְמִיָּה	עַוְלָה –	1	1QS IV, 23
	יֵצֶר עַוְלָה –	1	1QHᵃ XXI, 30
אוֹיֵב	בֶּן עַוְלָה –	3	2 Sam 7:10; Ps 89:23; 1 Chr 17:9
אָוֶן		3	Isa 59:3; Job 11:14; Prov 22:8
דָּם		3	Isa 59:3; Mic 3:10; Hab 2:12
רֶשַׁע	עַוְלָה –	2	Hos 10:13; 1QHᵃ VI, 26*
	מַמְשֶׁלֶת עַוְלָה –	1	1QS IV, 19
אַשְׁמָה		2	1QHᵃ XIII, 10; 4Q181 2, 4
חָמָס		2	Ezek 28:15; Ps 58:3
כָּזָב		2	Zeph 3:13; Ps 58:3
מִקַּח שֹׁחַד		2	2 Chr 19:7; m. ʾAbot 4:22
מַשֹּׂא פָנִים		2	2 Chr 19:7; m. ʾAbot 4:22
שָׁוְא		2	Isa 59:3; Sir 16:1
אֱוִיל לֵב	בֶּן עַוְלָה –	1	4Q418 69 II, 8
אִוֶּלֶת		1	4Q525 2 II+3,2
אוֹפִיר		1	Job 22:23
בֶּצֶר		1	Job 22:23
גֵּזֶל		1	Isa 61:8
דְּבַר רָע		1	Ps 64:7
הַוָּה		1	Job 6:30
כַּחַשׁ		1	Hos 10:13
כֶּסֶף תּוֹעֵפוֹת		1	Job 22:23
מַחֲזִיק רִשְׁעָה		1	4Q418 69 II, 8
מִרְמָה		1	Ps 43:1
מֵרַע	עוֹשֵׂה עַוְלָה –	1	Ps 37:1
מִשְׂגָּא		1	Ps 89:23
נִדָּה		1	1QS IV, 20
עָוֹן		1	Isa 59:3
עָמָל		1	Isa 59:3
צַר		1	Ps 89:23
שַׁחַת		1	1QS X, 20

184 CHAPTER 3

Lexeme	Association	No.	Location
שִׁכְחָה		1	'Abot 4:22
שֶׁקֶר		1	Isa 59:3
תֹּהוּ		1	Isa 59:3
תַּרְמִית		1	Zeph 3:13

Table 3.68. עַוְלָה in Associations of Opposition

Lexeme	Association	No.	Location
אֱמֶת	עַוְלָה –	4	Mal 2:6; 1QS IV, 17; IV, 20; 1QHᵃ VI, 26
דֶּרֶךְ אֱמֶת	שֹׁרֶשׁ עַוְלָה –	1	4Q416 2 III, 14
מִשְׁפָּט	עַוְלָה –	3	Isa 61:8; Mic 3:10; Zeph 3:5
	מֶמְשֶׁלֶת עַוְלָה –	1	1QS IV, 19
יָשָׁר		2	Ps 92:16; 107:42
צְדָקָה		2	Hos 10:13; 1QHᵃ VI, 26
תָּמִים		2	Ezek 28:15; 4Q525 5, 11
אֱמוּנָה		1	Isa 59:3
דַּעַת		1	1QS IV, 9
חֶסֶד		1	Hos 10:13
חָסִיד		1	Ps 43:1
חֹק		1	4Q525 2 II+3,2
צֶדֶק		1	Isa 59:3
קֹדֶשׁ		1	1QS IV, 20

Observations

עַוְלָה (injustice) has a strong bias towards associations of similarity. Two of its five frequent associates (אָוֶן; villainy; and דָּם; blood) are frequent associates of רע. Its most frequent associate (רְמִיָּה; treachery), is found as a frequent associate of שֶׁקֶר (lie), and as an infrequent associate of רע and a number of words associated with רע. The evidence suggests that עַוְלָה may be on the periphery of the semantic domains of רע.

3.3.7 פֶּשַׁע (transgression)

פֶּשַׁע occurs 133 times in the analysed texts [94;[99] 7; 31; 0; 1]. In total פֶּשַׁע occurs 81 times (61%) with at least one semantic association. Its

[99] One occurrence was added: Numbers 14:18 (Samaritan Pentateuch)

MAPPING THE LEXICAL SEMANTIC DOMAINS OF רַע 185

occurrence with semantic associations by corpus is shown in Table 3.69 below. Tables 3.70 and 3.71 show the semantic associations of similarity and opposition respectively.

Table 3.69. Number of Identifiable Lexical and
Phrasal Semantic Associations פֶּשַׁע by Type of Association

Corpus	Similarity		Opposition		Total
	n.	%	n.	%	n.
Hebrew Bible	56	98.2	6	10.5	57
Ben Sira	3	100.0	0	0.0	3
Judean Desert	19	95.0	3	15.0	20
Inscriptions	0	–	0	–	0
Mishnah	1	100.0	0	0.0	1
Total	79	97.5	9	11.1	81

Table 3.70. פֶּשַׁע in Associations of Similarity

Lexeme	Association	No.	Location
חַטָּאת	פֶּשַׁע –	29	Gen 31:36; 50:17; Lev 16:16, 21; Josh 24:19; Isa 43:25; 44:22; 58:1; 59:12; Ezek 18:22; 21:29; 33:10, 12; Amos 5:12; Mic 1:5, 13; 3:8; 6:7; Ps 25:7; 32:5; 51:3, 5; 59:4; Job 13:23; ; 14:17; 34:37; Dan 9:24; 1QS XI, 9; 11Q5 XXIV, 11
	פֶּשַׁע אַשְׁמָה –	1	1QS I, 23
	פֶּשַׁע מַעֲשֶׂה –	1	1QS III, 22
	אַשְׁמַת פֶּשַׁע –	1	4Q184 1, 10
מַעַל חַטָּאת	אַשְׁמַת פֶּשַׁע –	1	1QS IX, 4
עָוֹן	פֶּשַׁע –	29	Exod 34:7; Lev 16:21; Num 14:18; Isa 43:25; 50:1; 53:5; 59:12; Ezek 18:30; 21:29; 39:24; Mic 6:7; Ps 32:1, 5; 51:3; 59:4; 65:4; 89:33; 103:12; 107:17; Job 7:21; 13:23; 14:17; 31:33; 33:9; Dan 9:24; CD III, 18; 1QS XI, 9; 1QHᵃ VI, 35; m. Yoma 3:8
	פֶּשַׁע אַשְׁמָה –	1	1QS I, 23
	פֶּשַׁע מַעֲשֶׂה –	1	1QS III, 22
עָוֶל	פֶּשַׁע –	5	Ezek 18:22, 28; 33:12; Sir 38:10*; 1QHᵃ XIV, 9
	אַשְׁמַת פֶּשַׁע –	1	4Q184 1, 10

Lexeme	Association	No.	Location
אַשְׁמָה	פֶּשַׁע –	2	1QHᵃ XII, 36; XII, 38
אַשְׁמַת מַעַל	פֶּשַׁע מַעֲשֶׂה –	2	1QS III, 22; 1QHᵃ XIX, 13
דֶּרֶךְ		3	Ezek 18:22, 30; 33:10
חַטָּאָה		3	Ps 32:1; 1QHᵃ XIV, 9; XXII, 33
מַעַל		3	Ezek 18:22; 1QS X, 24; 1QHᵃ XII, 36
נֶעֱוָיָה	פֶּשַׁע –	1	1QS X, 11
	פֶּשַׁע אַשְׁמָה –	1	4Q511 18 I, 9
נַעֲוַיַת לֵבָב	פֶּשַׁע –	1	1QS XI, 9
רָעָה		3	Gen 50:17; 1 Sam 24:12; Lam 1:22
גִּלּוּל		2	Ezek 37:23; 1QHᵃ XII, 20
חֵטְא		2	Ps 103:12; m. Yoma 3:8
חַטָּאָה		2	Exod 34:7; Num 14:18
טֻמְאָה		2	Lev 16:16; Ezek 39:24
רַע		1	Sir 10:6
דֶּרֶךְ רַע		1	Ezek 33:10
שֶׁקֶר		2	Isa 57:4; Sir 41:18
תּוֹעֵבָה		1	Ezek 18:22
תּוֹעֲבַת נִדָּה		1	1QHᵃ XIX, 13
אָוֶן		1	Job 36:9
בָּמָה		1	Mic 1:5
דָּבָר		1	Prov 17:9
דֶּרֶךְ נִדָּה	פֶּשַׁע אֱנוֹשׁ –	1	CD III, 17
זֵד		1	Ps 19:14
זְנוּת		1	Sir 41:18
יָד		1	Sir 41:18
כַּחַשׁ		1	Sir 41:18
מָדוֹן		1	Prov 29:22
מִדְיָן		1	Prov 10:12
מוֹשָׁב		1	Ezek 37:23
מָוֶת	אַשְׁמַת פֶּשַׁע –	1	4Q184 1, 10
מַעַל		1	Sir 41:18
מַצָּה		1	Prov 17:19
מְשׁוּבָה		1	Jer 5:6
נִסְתָּר		1	Ps 19:14
פּוֹשֵׁעַ		1	1QHᵃ X, 11

MAPPING THE LEXICAL SEMANTIC DOMAINS OF רַע 187

Lexeme	Association	No.	Location
פַּחַז		1	Sir 41:18*
פֹּעַל		1	Job 36:9
רְמִיָּה		1	Ps 32:1
רֶשַׁע		1	Ezek 33:12
רִשְׁעָה		1	Ezek 18:28
שְׁגִיאָה		1	Ps 19:14
שִׁקּוּץ		1	Ezek 37:23

Table 3.71. פֶּשַׁע in Associations of Opposition

Lexeme	Association	No.	Location
צְדָקָה	פֶּשַׁע –	3	Ezek 18:22, 28; 33:12
	פֶּשַׁע אַשְׁמָה –	1	1QS I, 23
מִשְׁפָּט		3	Ezek 18:22, 28; 33:12
זַךְ		2	Job 8:4; 33:9
חַסְדֵי רַחֲמִים	פֶּשַׁע אַשְׁמָה –	1	1QS I, 23
חַף		1	Job 33:9
יָשָׁר		1	Job 8:4
יֹשֶׁר לֵבָב		1	1QS XI, 3
נִמְהָר לֵב		1	1QHᵃ X, 11
פֶּתִי		1	1QHᵃ X, 11
צֶדֶק		1	Dan 9:24
תֹּם דֶּרֶךְ		1	1QS XI, 3

Observations

פֶּשַׁע (transgression) rarely occurs with associations of opposition. With עָוֹן (iniquity) and חַטָּאת (sin) it appears to form part of an important triad of terms for sin. On the strength of these associations alone it should be considered within the semantic domains of רַע.

3.3.8 צָרָה (distress)

צָרָה occurs 104 times in the analysed texts [74;[100] 6; 20; 0; 4]. In total צָרָה occurs 43 times (41%) with at least one semantic association. It

---

[100] Two occurrences were added from the Judean Desert corpus: 1QIsaᵃ XXIV, 12 [Isa 30:6]; 1QIsaᵃ XLIII, 1 [Isa 51:14].

188   CHAPTER 3

occurred exclusively with associations of similarity. Its occurrence with semantic associations by corpus is shown in Table 3.72 below. Table 3.73 shows the semantic associations of similarity.

Table 3.72. Number of Identifiable Lexical and
Phrasal Semantic Associations צָרָה

Corpus	Similarity n.
Hebrew Bible	30
Ben Sira	3
Judean Desert	9
Inscriptions	0
Mishnah	1
Total	43

Table 3.73. צָרָה in Associations of Similarity

Lexeme	Association	No.	Location
רָעָה		7	Deut 31:17, 21; 1 Sam 10:19; Jer 15:11; Ps 71:20; 2 Chr 20:9; Sir 6:8
אֵיד		3	Obad 12, 14; Prov 1:27
מְצוּקָה	צָרָה –	1	4Q460 7, 7
	יוֹם צָרָה –	1	Zeph 1:15
	צָרַת לֵבָב –	1	Ps 25:17
צוּקָה	צָרָה –	1	Prov 1:27
	אֶרֶץ צָרָה –	1	Isa 30:6
מְעוּף צוּקָה	צָרָה –	1	Isa 8:22
רָעָב		3	Job 5:19; 2 Chr 20:9; 4Q166 II, 14
אֲפֵלָה	צָרָה –	1	Isa 8:22
	יוֹם צָרָה –	1	Zeph 1:15
חִיל		2	Jer 6:24; Jer 50:43
מְשׁוֹאָה	צָרָה –	1	Sir 51:10
	יוֹם צָרָה –	1	Zeph 1:15
נָאָצָה	יוֹם צָרָה –	2	2 Kgs 19:3; Isa 37:3
נֶגַע	צָרַת נֶפֶשׁ	1	4Q504 1–2 VI, 8
	מוֹעֵד צָרָה –	1	1QS III, 23
עֶבְרָה	צָרָה –	1	Ps 78:49
	יוֹם צָרָה –	1	Zeph 1:15

MAPPING THE LEXICAL SEMANTIC DOMAINS OF רַע 189

Lexeme	Association	No.	Location
עָנִי	צָרַת לֵבָב –	1	Ps 25:17
	צָרַת נֶפֶשׁ –	1	Ps 31:8
עֵת	צָרָה –	1	Prov 17:17
	יוֹם צָרָה –	1	Sir 6:8
פַּחַד		2	Prov 1:27; 1QS X, 15
רַע	יוֹם צָרָה –	1	Sir 51:12
שְׁמוּעָה רָעָה	צָרָה –	1	3Q5 1, 3
שׁוֹאָה	צָרָה –	1	Sir 51:10
	יוֹם צָרָה –	1	Zeph 1:15
תּוֹכֵחָה	יוֹם צָרָה –	2	2 Kgs 19:3; Isa 37:3
אָבַד		1	Obad 12
אֵימָה		1	1QS X, 15
בֶּטֶן שְׁאוֹל		1	Jonah 2:3
בּוּקָה		1	1QS X, 15
גוֹבַאי		1	m. Soṭah 9:15
דֶּבֶר		1	2 Chr 20:9
הֹוָה		1	1QM I, 12
זַעַם		1	Ps 78:49
חֵבֶל		1	Jer 49:24
חֶבְלֵי מָוֶת		1	Ps 116:3
חַיַּת אֶרֶץ		1	Job 5:19
חֶרֶב שָׁפוֹט		1	2 Chr 20:9
חֲרוֹן אַף		1	Ps 78:49
חֹשֶׁךְ		1	Zeph 1:15
חֲשֵׁכָה		1	Isa 8:22
יָגוֹן		1	Ps 116:3
כָּפָן		1	Job 5:19
לַיְלָה		1	Ps 77:3
מְגוֹרָה		1	Ps 34:7
מְהוּמָה		1	2 Chr 15:6
מִלְחָמָה		1	Job 5:19
מְצָרֵי שְׁאוֹל		1	Ps 116:3
מָרוֹר		1	1QHᵃ XIII, 14
נָסוּי		1	4Q504 1–2 VI, 8*

Lexeme	Association	No.	Location
עוֹשֵׂה מִשְׁפָּט	צָרַת מַצְרֵף –	1	1QS VIII, 4
עָמָל		1	Ps 25:17
עֲנוּת נֶפֶשׁ		1	4Q525 2 II+3,6
עָנָן		1	Zeph 1:15
עָרוֹם		1	4Q166 II, 14
עֲרָפֶל		1	Zeph 1:15
צִיָּה		1	1QIsaᵃ XXIV, 12
קוֹל		1	Jer 4:31
רֶטֶט		1	Jer 49:24
שֹׁד		1	Job 5:19
שׁוֹפָר		1	Zeph 1:15
שִׂיחַ		1	Ps 142:3
תְּרוּעָה		1	Zeph 1:15

Observations

צָרָה (distress) occurs most frequently with רָעָה (evil). It also has רָעָב (famine) as a frequent associate. However, it also has a few frequent associates that are not associates of רַע. It may be on the periphery of the semantic domains of רַע.

3.3.9 שָׁוְא (worthlessness)

שָׁוְא occurs 79 times in the analysed texts [53; 7; 6; 0; 13]. In total שָׁוְא occurs 44 times (56%) with at least one semantic association. Its occurrence with semantic associations by corpus is shown in Table 3.74 below. Tables 3.75 and 3.76 show the semantic associations of similarity and opposition respectively.

Table 3.74. Number of Identifiable Lexical and
Phrasal Semantic Associations with שָׁוְא by Type of Association

Corpus	Similarity		Opposition		Total
	n.	%	n.	%	n.
Hebrew Bible	23	85.2	2	7.4	27
Ben Sira	5	100.0	1	20.0	5

MAPPING THE LEXICAL SEMANTIC DOMAINS OF רע 191

Corpus	Similarity		Opposition		Total
	n.	%	n.	%	n.
Judean Desert	5	100.0	0	0.0	5
Inscriptions	0	–	0	–	0
Mishnah	6	85.7	1	14.3	7
Total	39	88.6	4	9.1	44

Table 3.75. שָׁוְא in Associations of Similarity

Lexeme	Association	No.	Location
כָּזָב		8	Ezek 13:6, 7, 8, 9; 21:34; 22:28; Sir 15:7, 20
דְּבַר כָּזָב		1	Prov 30:8
שֶׁקֶר	שָׁוְא –	5	Isa 59:4; Ps 144:8, 11; Sir 15:20[101]; 1QpHab X, 11*
	חֲלוֹם שָׁוְא –	1	Zech 10:2
אָוֶן	שָׁוְא –	3	Isa 59:4; Hos 12:12; Ps 41:7
	חֲלוֹם שָׁוְא –	1	Zech 10:2
	מְתֵי שָׁוְא –	1	Job 11:11
בִּטּוּי		4	m. Šebu. 3:7, 9 (×2), 11
רֶשַׁע	מְתֵי שָׁוְא –	2	Ps 26:4; Sir 15:7
	סוֹד שָׁוְא –	1	1QHᵃ X, 24
חָמָס		2	Exod 23:1; 1QHᵃ XIV, 8*
מִרְמָה		2	Ps 24:4; Job 31:5
נֶעְלָם	מְתֵי שָׁוְא –	1	Ps 26:4
סוֹד נֶעְלָם	עֲדַת שָׁוְא –	1	1QHᵃ XV, 36
עַוְלָה		2	Isa 59:4; Sir 16:1
עָמָל		2	Isa 59:4; Job 7:3
אֵיבָה	שְׁבוּעַת שָׁוְא –	1	m. 'Abot 4:7
אֶפְעֶה		1	1QHᵃ X, 30
בְּלִיַּעַל		1	1QHᵃ X, 24
גָּזֵל	שְׁבוּעַת שָׁוְא –	1	m. 'Abot 4:7
דָּבָר		1	Hos 10:4
דָּם		1	Isa 59:4

---

[101] Manuscript B 2v6.

192   CHAPTER 3

Lexeme	Association	No.	Location
הֶבֶל		1	Zech 10:2
זָדוֹן		1	Sir 15:7
חִילוּל הַשֵּׁם	שְׁבוּעַת שָׁוְא –	1	m. 'Abot 5:9
חָלָק שְׂפַת חֲלָקָה		1 1	Ezek 12:24 Ps 12:3
כְּאֵב נֶאֱמָן כְּאֵב עוֹבֵד		1	Sir 30:17
לֵב וְלֵב		1	Ps 12:3
לֵץ	מְתֵי שָׁוְא –	1	Sir 15:7
מְגַלֶּה סוֹד	עוֹשֵׂה שָׁוְא –	1	Sir 15:20
מַדּוּחִים		1	Lam 2:14
מְזִמָּה		1	Ps 139:20
מֵרַע	מְתֵי שָׁוְא –	1	Ps 26:4
עָוֹן		1	Isa 59:4
עָרִיץ	סוֹד שָׁוְא –	1	1QH[a] X, 24
קֶסֶם		1	Ezek 13:23
רַע		1	Sir 30:17
רָעָה		1	Ps 41:7
תֹּהוּ		1	Isa 59:4
תָּפֵל		1	Lam 2:14

Table 3.76. שָׁוְא in Associations of Opposition

Lexeme	Association	No.	Location
בְּרָכָה		1	Ps 24:4
חָכָם		1	Sir 15:7
יהוה		1	Ps 31:7
עֵדוּת		1	m. Šebu. 7:4
פִּקָּדוֹן		1	m. Šebu. 7:4

Observations

שָׁוְא (worthlessness) has a strong bias towards associations of similarity, with almost no associations of opposition detected. It is frequently

MAPPING THE LEXICAL SEMANTIC DOMAINS OF רַע 193

associated with a two terms frequently associated with רַע: אָוֶן (villainy) and רָשָׁע (wicked). In addition to these associations it has a number of less frequent associations with two other frequent associates of רַע (חָמָס, violence; מִרְמָה, deceit). It is also frequently associated with שֶׁקֶר (lie) which is frequently associated with five words frequently associated with רַע. Its most frequent associate was כָּזָב (falsehood), also found to be a frequent associate of מִרְמָה and the most frequent associate of שֶׁקֶר. The accumulated evidence suggests שָׁוְא should be included as a peripheral term.

In addition, the word בִּיטוּי (vain talk) occurred as a frequent associate of שָׁוְא. However, it was found exclusively in halakhic definition in the Mishnah and is never associated with אָוֶן. Consequently, בִּיטוּי is not analysed further.

3.3.10 אַשְׁמָה (guilt)

אַשְׁמָה occurs 85 times in the analysed texts [19; 1; 54; 0; 11]. In total אַשְׁמָה occurs 43 times (56%)[102] with at least one semantic association. Its occurrence with semantic associations by corpus is shown in Table 3.77 below. Tables 3.78 and 3.79 show the semantic associations of similarity and opposition respectively.

Table 3.77. Number of Identifiable Lexical and
Phrasal Semantic Associations אַשְׁמָה by Type of Association

Corpus	Similarity		Opposition		Total
	n.	%	n.	%	n.
Hebrew Bible	6	100.0	0	0.0	6
Ben Sira	0	–	0	–	0
Judean Desert	24	85.7	4	14.3	28
Inscriptions	0	–	0	–	0
Mishnah	9	100.0	0	0.0	9
Total	39	90.7	4	9.3	43

---

[102] Eight occurrences were eliminated under the conditions specified in §3.1.1.1.

194 CHAPTER 3

Table 3.78. אַשְׁמָה in Associations of Similarity

Lexeme	Association	No.	Location
חַטָּאת	אַשְׁמָה –	11	2 Chr 28:13; 1QS III, 22; 11Q19 XXVI, 12; XXXV, 12; XXXV, 14; m. Maʿaś. Š. 1:7; m. Šeqal. 1:5; 2:5; m. Ned. 4:3; m. Zebaḥ 10:5; m. ʿArak. 5:6
	אַשְׁמַת פֶּשַׁע –	1	4Q184 1, 10
	פֶּשַׁע אַשְׁמָה –	1	1QS I, 23
מַעַל חַטָּאת	אַשְׁמַת פֶּשַׁע –	1	1QS IX, 4
עָוֹן	אַשְׁמָה –	7	Ezra 9:6, 7, 13; 1QS III, 22; 1QHᵃ XII, 38; 11Q19 XXVI, 12; LVIII, 17
	אַשְׁמַת מַעַל –	1	1QHᵃ XII, 31
	פֶּשַׁע אַשְׁמָה –	1	1QS I, 23
פֶּשַׁע	אַשְׁמָה –	3	1QS III, 22; 1QHᵃ XII, 35; XIII, 38
	אַשְׁמַת מַעַל –	1	1QHᵃ XIX, 14
קֵן זָבוֹת		4	m. Maʿaś. Š. 1:7; m. Šeqal. 1:5; 2:5; m. Ned. 4:3
קֵן זָבִים		4	m. Maʿaś. Š. 1:7; m. Šeqal. 1:5; 2:5; m. Ned. 4:3
קֵן יוֹלֵדָה		4	m. Maʿaś. Š. 1:7; m. Šeqal. 1:5; 2:5; m. Ned. 4:3
עֲבֹדַת נִדַּת טֻמְאָה	מִשְׂרַת אַשְׁמָה –	1	1QM XIII, 4
מַחְשֶׁבֶת נִדַּת טֻמְאָה		1	4Q286 7 II, 3*
תּוֹעֲבַת נִדָּה	אַשְׁמַת מַעַל –	1	1QHᵃ XIX, 14
חֵטְא		2	m. Šeqal. 2:5; 6:6
חָלָל	בְּשַׂר אַשְׁמָה –	1	1QM XII, 12
	פֶּגֶר אַשְׁמָה –	1	4Q169 3–4 II, 6
חֹשֶׁךְ	אַשְׁמָה –	1	1QM XIII, 15
	רֶשַׁע אַשְׁמָה –	1	1QS II, 5
מַחְשֶׁבֶת מַשְׂטֵמָה	מִשְׂרַת אַשְׁמָה –	2	1QM XIII, 4; 4Q286 7 II, 3*
מַחְשֶׁבֶת רֶשַׁע	מִשְׂרַת אַשְׁמָה –	2	1QM XIII, 4; 4Q286 7 II, 3
עַוְלָה		2	1QHᵃ XIII, 9; 4Q181 2, 4
עֵינֵי זְנוּת	אַשְׁמָה –	1	1QS I, 6
	יֵצֶר אַשְׁמָה –	1	CD II, 16
אוֹיֵב	בְּשַׂר אַשְׁמָה –	1	1QM XII, 12
אִוֶּלֶת		1	Ps 69:6
אֱלֹהִים		1	Amos 8:14

MAPPING THE LEXICAL SEMANTIC DOMAINS OF רַע   195

Lexeme	Association	No.	Location
אָשָׁם		1	11Q19 XXXV, 12
גּוֹי – בְּשַׂר אַשְׁמָה		1	1QM XII, 12
גְּוִיַּת בָּשָׂר – פֶּגֶר אַשְׁמָה		1	4Q169 3–4 II, 6
דְּבַר טֻמְאָה		1	11Q19 LVIII, 17
דֶּרֶךְ בְּשַׂר שֶׁבַע		1	Amos 8:14
חַטָּאָה		1	1QHᵃ XIX, 24
מָוֶת – אַשְׁמַת פֶּשַׁע		1	4Q184 1, 10
מַעַל		1	1QHᵃ XII, 35
מַעֲשֶׂה רַע		1	Ezra 9:13
נְדָבָה		1	m. Šeqal. 2:5
נַעֲוָיָה – פֶּשַׁע אַשְׁמָה		1	4Q511 18 II, 10
עָוֶל – אַשְׁמַת פֶּשַׁע		1	4Q184 1, 10
עֶרְוָה		1	11Q19 LVIII, 17
צַר – בְּשַׂר אַשְׁמָה		1	1QM, XII, 12
רוּחַ הֹוֶה – בְּנֵי אַשְׁמָה		1	1QHᵃ XV, 14*
רִשְׁעָה		1	1QM XI, 11
שֶׁלֶם		1	m. Zebaḥ 5:5

· Table 3.79. אַשְׁמָה in Associations of Opposition

Lexeme	Association	No.	Location
אֱמֶת		3	1QM XIII, 15; 1QHᵃ XIV, 33; 4Q511 63 III, 4
אוֹר		1	1QM XIII, 15
צְדָקָה – אַשְׁמַת מַעַל		1	1QHᵃ XII, 31
תֹּם דֶּרֶךְ – אַשְׁמַת מַעַל		1	1QHᵃ XII, 31

Observations

אַשְׁמָה (guilt) occurs rarely in associations of opposition. The majority (64%) of its occurrences are within the Judean Desert corpus. In the Mishnah occurrences, it is linked to חַטָּאת (sin) through the sacrifice domain. Elsewhere it has strong links to the חַטָּאת – עָוֹן – פֶּשַׁע triad of sin terms. Its ties with this set of terms mark it for inclusion in the semantic domains of רַע.

196 CHAPTER 3

3.3.11 זִמָּה (wickedness)

זִמָּה occurs 39 times in the analysed texts [29; 2; 5; 0; 3]. In total זִמָּה occurs 23 times (59%) with at least one semantic association. Its occurrence with semantic associations by corpus is shown in Table 3.80 below. Tables 3.81 and 3.82 show the semantic associations of similarity and opposition respectively.

Table 3.80. Number of Identifiable Lexical and
Phrasal Semantic Associations זִמָּה by Type of Association

Corpus	Similarity		Opposition		Total
	n.	%	n.	%	n.
Hebrew Bible	17	94.4	2	11.1	18
Ben Sira	1	100.0	0	0.0	1
Judean Desert	4	100.0	0	0.0	4
Inscriptions	0	–	0	–	0
Mishnah	0	–	0	–	0
Total	22	95.7	2	8.7	23

Table 3.81. זִמָּה in Associations of Similarity

Lexeme	Association	No.	Location
תּוֹעֵבָה		6	Lev 18:17; 20:14; Ezek 16:43, 58; 22:11; 11Q19 LXVI, 15
תַּזְנוּת		3	Ezek 23:21, 29, 35
אִמְרֵי שָׁקֶר		1	Isa 32:7
טוֹפְלֵי שָׁקֶר		1	Sir 51:5
בֶּצַע		2	CD VIII, 7; XIX, 19
הוֹן		2	CD VIII, 7; XIX, 19
זְנוּת		2	Ezek 23:27, 29
תֶּבֶל		2	Lev 18:17; 20:14
אֵשׁ		1	Job 31:11
חֵטְא גִּלּוּל		1	Ezek 23:49
חֶסֶד		1	Lev 20:14

MAPPING THE LEXICAL SEMANTIC DOMAINS OF רַע

Lexeme	Association	No.	Location
כְּלִי רַע		1	Isa 32:7
לְשׁוֹן מִרְמָה		1	Sir 51:5
מוֹרָשֵׁי לְבָב		1	Job 17:11
מַחְשֶׁבֶת		1	1QH^a XII, 14
מִצְהָלוֹת	זִמַּת זְנוּת –	1	Jer 13:27
נְאוּפִים	זִמַּת זְנוּת –	1	Jer 13:27
נְבָלָה		1	Judg 20:6
נִדָּה		1	11Q19 LXVI, 15
נוֹאֶפֶת		1	Ezek 23:44
עָוֹן		1	Job 31:11
שֹׁחַד		1	Ps 26:10
שִׁקּוּץ	זִמַּת זְנוּת –	1	Jer 13:27

Table 3.82. זִמָּה in Associations of Opposition

Lexeme	Association	No.	Location
חָכְמָה		1	Prov 10:23
נְדִיבָה		1	Isa 32:7

Observations

זִמָּה (wickedness) occurs rarely in associations of opposition. Its primary occurrence is with תּוֹעֵבָה (abomination). Because of its low frequency, it is also instructive to note the presence of a few frequent and infrequent associates of רַע among its infrequent associates. It appears that זִמָּה may be at least peripherally part of the semantic domains of רַע.

3.3.12 חָטָא (sin)

חָטָא occurs 20 times in the analysed texts [19; 0; 1; 0; 0]. In total חָטָא occurs 13 times (65%) with at least one semantic association. Its occurrence with semantic associations by corpus is shown in Table 3.83 below. Tables 3.84 and 3.85 show the semantic associations of similarity and opposition respectively.

198   CHAPTER 3

Table 3.83. Number of Identifiable Lexical and
Phrasal Semantic Associations חָטָא by Type of Association

Corpus	Similarity		Opposition		Total
	n.	%	n.	%	n.
Hebrew Bible	11	91.7	3	25.0	12
Ben Sira	0	–	0	–	0
Judean Desert	1	100.0	0	0.0	1
Inscriptions	0	–	0	–	0
Mishnah	0	–	0	–	0
Total	12	92.3	3	23.1	13

Table 3.84. חָטָא in Associations of Similarity

Lexeme	Association	No.	Location
פּוֹשֵׁעַ		3	Isa 1:28; Ps 51:15; 4Q393 1 II–2, 7*
רָשָׁע		3	Ps 1:1, 5; 104:35
אִישׁ דָּם		1	Ps 26:9
בֵּית יַעֲקֹב	מַמְלָכָה הַחַטָּאָה –	1	Amos 9:8
חָנֵף		1	Isa 33:14
לֵץ		1	Ps 1:1
עוֹזֵב יהוה		1	Isa 1:28
עֲמָלֵק		1	1 Sam 15:18
עָנָו		1	Ps 25:8
רַע		1	Gen 13:13

Table 3.85. חָטָא in Associations of Opposition

Lexeme	Association	No.	Location
צַדִּיק		2	Ps 1:5; Prov 13:21
שָׁב		1	Isa 1:28

Observations

חָטָא (sin) occurs infrequently. Out of its two frequent associates, only
רָשָׁע (wicked) is associated with רַע. However, פּוֹשֵׁעַ (sinner) is itself rare,
only occurring 20 times [12; 1; 7; 0; 0] in the analysed text and it occurs
twice in association with רָשָׁע. This indicates the likelihood of a close
association between חָטָא and רָשָׁע.

MAPPING THE LEXICAL SEMANTIC DOMAINS OF רַע   199

3.3.13 כָּזָב (falsehood)

כָּזָב occurs 51 times in the analysed texts [31; 7; 13; 0; 0]. In total, כָּזָב occurs 41 times (80%) with at least one semantic association. Its occurrence with semantic associations by corpus is shown in Table 3.86 below. Tables 3.87 and 3.88 show the semantic associations of similarity and opposition respectively.

Table 3.86. Number of Identifiable Lexical and
Phrasal Semantic Associations כָּזָב by Type of Association

Corpus	Similarity		Opposition		Total
	n.	%	n.	%	n.
Hebrew Bible	20	90.9	2	9.1	22
Ben Sira	6	100.0	1	16.7	6
Judean Desert	11	84.6	3	23.1	13
Inscriptions	0	–	0	–	0
Mishnah	0	–	0	–	0
Total	39	95.1	4	9.8	41

Table 3.87. כָּזָב in Associations of Similarity

Lexeme	Association	No.	Location
שָׁוְא	כָּזָב –	8	Ezek 13:6, 7, 8, 9; 21:34; 22:28; Sir 15:8, 20
	דְּבַר כָּזָב –	1	Prov 30:8
שֶׁקֶר	כָּזָב –	4	Isa 28:15; Sir 15:20[103]; 1QpHab X, 9; 4Q371 1a–b, 13*
אֹמֶר שֶׁקֶר		1	4Q171 1–2 I, 18
לְשׁוֹן שֶׁקֶר		1	Prov 6:19
עֵד שֶׁקֶר		2	Prov 19:5, 9
תַּלְמוּד שֶׁקֶר	לְשׁוֹן כָּזָב –	1	4Q169 3–4 II, 8
מִרְמָה		3	Ps 5:7; 1QS X, 22; 4Q169 3–4 II, 8
עַוְלָה		2	Zeph 3:13; Ps 58:4
רוּחַ		2	CD VIII, 13; XIX, 26
רָשָׁע	אִישׁ כָּזָב –	1	Sir 15:8
	דּוֹבְרֵי כָּזָב –	1	Ps 58:4

---

[103] Manuscript B 2v5

Lexeme	Association	No.	Location
דָּבָר		1	Sir 36:24[104]
דִּבַּת עָם דִּבַּת לָשׁוֹן	שֹׁטֵי כָזָב –	1	Sir 51:2
דָּם		1	Ps 5:7
הֶבֶל		1	Ps 62:10
הוֹלֵל	דּוֹבְרֵי כָזָב –	1	Ps 5:7
זֶבֶד		1	Sir 36:24[105]
זָדוֹן		1	Sir 15:8
חָלָק		1	1QH[a] X, 33
חָמָס		1	Ps 58:4
כַּחַשׁ עָוֹן		1	1QS X, 22
לֵץ	אִישׁ כָזָב –	1	Sir 15:8
לְשׁוֹן תַּרְמִית		1	Zeph 3:13
מְבַקְשֵׁי נֶפֶשׁ	שֹׁטֵי כָזָב –	1	Sir 51:2
מְגַלֶּה סוֹד	אִישׁ כָזָב –	1	Sir 15:20
מִדְיָן		1	Prov 6:19
נַבְלוּת		1	1QS X, 22
סוּפָה		1	CD XIX, 26
סֵתֶר		1	Isa 28:17
עֵינַיִם רָמוֹת		1	Prov 6:19
פּוֹעֲלֵי אָוֶן	דּוֹבֵר כָזָב –	1	Ps 5:7
צוֹפֵי סֶלַע	שֹׁטֵי כָזָב –	1	Sir 51:2
קָם	שֹׁטֵי כָזָב –	1	Sir 51:2
רַהַב	שֹׁטֵי כָזָב –	1	Ps 40:5
רִיק		1	Ps 4:3
רְמִיָּה		1	1QH[a] XII, 11; XII, 17
רַע		1	Hos 7:13
שֹׁד		1	Hos 12:2
שִׁקּוּץ		1	1QS X, 22
תֹּהוּ	מֵימֵי כָזָב –	1	CD I, 15
תָּעוּת		1	1QH[a] XII, 17

[104] Manuscript B 7r1
[105] Manuscript C 1a1

MAPPING THE LEXICAL SEMANTIC DOMAINS OF רַע   201

Table 3.88. כָּזָב in Associations of Opposition

Lexeme	Association	No.	Location
אֱמֶת		1	Prov 14:25
חָכָם	אִישׁ כָּזָב –	1	Sir 15:8
יוֹרֶה יָחִיד	אִישׁ כָּזָב –	1	CD XX, 15
מוֹרֶה צֶדֶק	אִישׁ כָּזָב –	1	1QpHab V, 11
פְּרִי קֹדֶשׁ		1	1QS X, 22
רָשׁ	אִישׁ כָּזָב –	1	Prov 19:22

Observations

כָּזָב (falsehood) has a strong bias towards associations of similarity, with few associations of opposition detected. It is frequently associated with just three terms, one of which is frequently associated with מִרְמָה. The remaining two (שָׁוְא and שֶׁקֶר) were found to be within the semantic domain(s) of רַע (§3.3.1 and §3.3.9). This word should be considered at minimum peripheral to the semantic domains of רַע.

3.3.14 עָרִיץ (ruthless)

עָרִיץ occurs 26 times in the analysed texts [21;[106] 0; 5; 0; 0]. In total עָרִיץ occurs 22 times (85%) with at least one semantic association. Its occurrence with semantic associations by corpus is shown in Table 3.89 below. Tables 3.90 and 3.91 show the semantic associations of similarity and opposition respectively.

Table 3.89. Number of Identifiable Lexical and
Phrasal Semantic Associations עָרִיץ by Type of Association

Corpus	Similarity		Opposition		Total
	n.	%	n.	%	n.
Hebrew Bible	18	94.7	2	10.5	19
Ben Sira	0	–	0	–	0
Judean Desert	2	66.7	2	66.7	3
Inscriptions	0	–	0	–	0
Mishnah	0	–	0	–	0
Total	20	90.9	4	18.2	22

[106] One occurrence was added from the Judean Desert corpus: 1QIsaᵃ XLI, 25 [Isa 49:24].

202 CHAPTER 3

Table 3.90. עָרִיץ in Associations of Similarity

Lexeme	Association	No.	Location
זָר	עָרִיץ –	3	Isa 25:5; 29:5; Ps 54:5
	עָרִיץ גּוֹי –	3	Ezek 28:7; 30:11; 31:12
רָשָׁע		6	Isa 13:11; Ps 37:35; Job 15:20; 27:13; 1QH^a X, 13; 4Q434 1 I, 5*
גִּבּוֹר	עָרִיץ –	2	1Qisa^a XLI, 25; Isa 49:25
	עָרִיץ גּוֹי –	1	Ezek 32:12
זֵד		2	Isa 13:11; Ps 86:14
לֵץ		2	Isa 29:20; 1QH^a X, 13
רַע	עָרִיץ –	1	Jer 15:21
	עָרִיץ גּוֹי –	1	Ezek 30:11
אַיִל		1	Ezek 31:12
בּוֹגֵד		1	1QH^a X, 13
נְבוּכַדְרֶאצַּר	עָרִיץ גּוֹי –	1	Ezek 30:11
עַם עָז	גּוֹי עָרִיץ –	1	Isa 25:3
פּוֹשֵׁעַ		1	1QH^a X, 13
צַר		1	Job 6:23
שׁוֹקֵד אָוֶן		1	Isa 29:20
תֵּבֵל		1	Isa 13:11

Table 3.91. עָרִיץ in Associations of Opposition

Lexeme	Association	No.	Location
אֶבְיוֹן		1	Isa 29:20
אֵשֶׁת חֵן		1	Prov 11:16
יְשַׁר דֶּרֶךְ		1	1QH^a X, 13
עוֹשֵׂה הַתּוֹרָה	עָרִיץ הַבְּרִית –	1	4Q171 1–2 II, 13
עָנָו		1	Isa 29:20

Observations

עָרִיץ (ruthless) is a low frequency word which rarely occurs in associations of opposition. However, it has strong associations with זָר (stranger) and רָשָׁע (wicked). Its association with זָר introduces some doubt as to its position in relation to the semantic domains of רַע. However, it does occur with רַע twice, one of those times (Ezek 30:11) being a joint association

MAPPING THE LEXICAL SEMANTIC DOMAINS OF רַע   203

with זָר. This, in addition to low frequency associations with other associates of רַע and רָשָׁע suggests the presence of עָרִיץ within the semantic domains of רַע.

3.3.15 צָמָא (thirst)

צָמָא occurs 23 times in the analysed texts [17; 0; 3; 0; 3]. In total צָמָא occurs 9 times (39%) with at least one semantic association. Its occurrence with semantic associations by corpus is shown in Table 3.92 below. Tables 3.93 and 3.94 show the semantic associations of similarity and opposition respectively.

Table 3.92. Number of Identifiable Lexical and
Phrasal Semantic Associations צָמָא by Type of Association

Corpus	Similarity		Opposition		Total
	n.	%	n.	%	n.
Hebrew Bible	8	100.0	1	12.5	8
Ben Sira	0	–	0	–	0
Judean Desert	1	100.0	0	0.0	1
Inscriptions	0	–	0	–	0
Mishnah	0	–	0	–	0
Total	9	100.0	1	11.1	9

Table 3.93. צָמָא in Associations of Similarity

Lexeme	Association	No.	Location
רָעָב		6	Deut 28:48; Isa 5:13; Amos 8:11; Neh 9:15; 2 Chr 32:11; 4Q504 1–2 III, 8*
אֶרֶץ צִיָּה		2	Ezek 19:13; Hos 2:5
בָּרוּת		1	Ps 69:22
דֶּבֶר		1	4Q504 1–2 III, 8
חֲלִי רַע		1	4Q504 1–2 III, 8
חֹסֶד		1	Deut 28:48
חֶרֶב		1	4Q504 1–2 III, 8
מִדְבָּר		1	Hos 2:5
עֵירֹם		1	Deut 28:48

204 CHAPTER 3

Table 3.94. צָמָא in Associations of Opposition

Lexeme	Association	No.	Location
טוּב לֵבָב		1	Deut 28:48
רֹב		1	Deut 28:48
שִׂמְחָה		1	Deut 28:48

Observations

צָמָא (thirst) occurs rarely in the analysed texts. Its only frequent associate is רָעָב (famine). While it has one association with each of חֶרֶב (sword), דֶּבֶר (plague) and חֳלִי רַע (bad sickness), these all occur in the same location (4Q504 1–2 III, 8) and so only represent one use in this fashion. This provides scant evidence for inclusion in the semantic domains of רַע although it is obvious that there is a very close association with רָעָב.

3.3.16 שֶׁבֶר (destruction)

שֶׁבֶר occurs 60 times in the analysed texts [44;[107] 2; 0; 0; 14]. In total שֶׁבֶר occurs 29 times (48%) with at least one semantic association. Its occurrence with semantic associations by corpus is shown in Table 3.95 below. Tables 3.96 and 3.97 show the semantic associations of similarity and opposition respectively.

Table 3.95. Number of Identifiable Lexical and
Phrasal Semantic Associations שֶׁבֶר by Type of Association

Corpus	Similarity		Opposition		Total
	n.	%	n.	%	n.
Hebrew Bible	22	95.7	3	13.0	23
Ben Sira	1	100.0	0	0.0	1
Judean Desert	0	–	0	–	0
Inscriptions	0	–	0	–	0
Mishnah	4	80.0	1	20.0	5
Total	27	93.1	4	13.8	29

---

[107] One occurrence was added from the Judean Desert corpus: 1QIsaᵃ XLVIII, 19 [Isa 59:8]. In Judges 7:15 the word is either a homograph or a polyseme that refers to "interpretation." Either way it can be considered irrelevant to the current analysis and so is excluded. Joshua 7:5 appears to refer to a place, so it is also excluded.

MAPPING THE LEXICAL SEMANTIC DOMAINS OF רַע 205

Table 3.96. שֶׁבֶר in Associations of Similarity

Lexeme	Association	No.	Location
מַכָּה		5	Isa 30:26; Jer 10:19; 14:17; 30:12; Nah 3:19
שֹׁד		5	Isa 51:19; 59:7; 60:18; Jer 48:3; Sir 40:9
רָעָה		3	Jer 4:6; 6:1; Sir 40:9
אֲבֵדָה		2	m. B. Meṣ. 7:8; m. Šebu. 8:1
גְּנֵבָה		2	m. B. Meṣ. 7:8; m. Šebu. 8:1
חָמָס		2	Isa 59:7; 60:18
חֶרֶב		2	Isa 51:19; Sir 40:9
מוּם	שֶׁבֶר –	1	Lev 24:20
	שֶׁבֶר רֶגֶל/יָד –	1	Lev 21:19
מִיתָה		2	m. B. Meṣ. 7:8; m. Šebu. 8:1
שְׁבוּיָה		2	m. B. Meṣ. 7:8; m. Šebu. 8:1
אָוֶן		1	Isa 59:7
גִּבֵּן	שֶׁבֶר רֶגֶל/יָד –	1	Lev 21:19
גָּרָב	שֶׁבֶר רֶגֶל/יָד –	1	Lev 21:19
גרוטי		1	m. Kelim 11:3
דֶּבֶר		1	Sir 40:9*
דָּם		1	Sir 40:9
דַּק	שֶׁבֶר רֶגֶל/יָד –	1	Lev 21:19
חֳלִי		1	Jer 10:19
חָרוּם	שֶׁבֶר רֶגֶל/יָד –	1	Lev 21:19
חַרְחֻר		1	Sir 40:9
טֻמְאָה		1	m. Ṭ. Yom 4:7
יְלָלָה		1	Zeph 1:10
יַלֶּפֶת	שֶׁבֶר רֶגֶל/יָד –	1	Lev 21:19
כְּאֵב לֵב	שֶׁבֶר רוּחַ –	1	Isa 65:14
כִּשָּׁלוֹן		1	Prov 16:18
מָוֶת		1	Sir 40:9
מָזוֹר		1	Jer 30:12
מַכְאוֹב		1	Jer 30:15
מַסְמֵר		1	m. Kelim 11:3
מַצָּה		1	Prov 17:19
מְרוֹחַ אֶשֶׁךְ	שֶׁבֶר רֶגֶל/יָד –	1	Lev 21:19

206 CHAPTER 3

Lexeme	Association	No.	Location
מְשַׁמָּה		1	Isa 15:5
עִוֵּר	שֶׁבֶר רֶגֶל/יָד –	1	Lev 21:19
עַיִן		1	Lev 24:20
פַּחַד		1	Lam 3:47
פַּחַת		1	Lam 3:47
פִּסֵּחַ	שֶׁבֶר רֶגֶל/יָד –	1	Lev 21:19
פֶּרֶץ		1	Isa 30:13
קוֹל מִלְחָמָה		1	Jer 50:22
קוֹל צְעָקָה		1	Zeph 1:10
רַע		1	Isa 59:7
רָעָב		1	Isa 51:19
שֵׂאת		1	Lam 3:47
שֵׁן		1	Lev 24:20
שְׁפִיכָה		1	m. Ṭ. Yom 4:7
שָׂרוּעַ	שֶׁבֶר רֶגֶל/יָד –	1	Lev 21:19
תְּבַלֻּל בְּעַיִן	שֶׁבֶר רֶגֶל/יָד –	1	Lev 21:19

Table 3.97. שֶׁבֶר in Associations of Opposition

Lexeme	Association	No.	Location
טוֹב לֵב	שֶׁבֶר רוּחַ –	1	Isa 65:14
כָּבוֹד		1	Prov 18:12
מִשְׁפָּט		1	Isa 59:7
שָׁלוֹם		1	Isa 59:7
שָׁלֵם		1	m. Kelim 14:7

Observations

שֶׁבֶר (destruction) occurs rarely in associations of opposition. It has three frequent associates, two of which occurred at least once as associates of רַע.[108] It appears to have a loose connection to רַע, perhaps being at the periphery of its semantic domains.

---

[108] מַכָּה (wound) technically occurs with רַע as well, but in all the associations it is primarily associated with another noun that רַע modifies. In these cases רַע is primarily associated with גָּדוֹל (great) which modifies מַכָּה.

MAPPING THE LEXICAL SEMANTIC DOMAINS OF רַע
207

3.3.17 שֹׁד (destruction)

שֹׁד occurs 28 times in the analysed texts [27;[109] 1; 0; 0; 0]. In total שֹׁד occurs 17 times (61%) with at least one semantic association. Its occurrence with semantic associations by corpus is shown in Table 3.98 below. Tables 3.99 and 3.100 show the semantic associations of similarity and opposition respectively.

Table 3.98. Number of Identifiable Lexical and
Phrasal Semantic Associations שֹׁד by Type of Association

Corpus	Similarity		Opposition		Total
	n.	%	n.	%	n.
Hebrew Bible	15	93.8	3	18.8	16
Ben Sira	1	100.0	0	0.0	1
Judean Desert	0	–	0	–	0
Inscriptions	0	–	0	–	0
Mishnah	0	–	0	–	0
Total	16	94.1	3	17.6	17

Table 3.99. שֹׁד in Associations of Similarity

Lexeme	Association	No.	Location
חָמָס		8	Isa 59:7; 60:18; Jer 6:7; 20:8; Ezek 45:9; Amos 3:10; Hab 1:3; 2:17
שֶׁבֶר		5	Isa 51:19; 59:7; 60:18; Jer 48:3; Sir 40:9
אָוֶן		2	Isa 59:7; Hab 1:3
חֶרֶב		2	Isa 51:19; Sir 40:9
עָמָל		2	Hab 1:3; Prov 24:2
רָעָב		2	Isa 51:19; Job 5:21
רָעָה		2	Jer 6:7; Sir 40:9
אֲנָקָה		1	Ps 12:6
דֶּבֶר		1	Sir 40:9*
דָּם		1	Sir 40:9
חַיַּת אֶרֶץ		1	Job 5:22
חֲלִי		1	Jer 6:7
חַרְחֻר		1	Sir 40:9

[109] One occurrence was added from the Judean Desert corpus: 1QIsaᵃ XLVIII, 18 [Isa 59:7].

Lexeme	Association	No.	Location
כָּזָב		1	Hos 12:2
כָּפָן		1	Job 5:22
מָדוֹן		1	Hab 1:3
מָוֶת		1	Sir 40:9
מִלְחָמָה		1	Job 5:21
מַכָּה		1	Jer 6:7
צָרָה		1	Job 5:21
רִיב		1	Hab 1:3
רַע		1	Isa 59:7

Table 3.100. שֹׁד in Associations of Opposition

Lexeme	Association	No.	Location
מִשְׁפָּט		3	Isa 59:7; Ezek 45:9; Prov 21:7
צְדָקָה		1	Ezek 45:9
שָׁלוֹם		1	Isa 59:7

Observations

שֹׁד (destruction) occurs with relatively low frequency. It appears to have a very strong association to חָמָס (violence) and a strong association with שֶׁבֶר (destruction). It may be on the periphery of the semantic domains of רַע.

3.3.18 Discussion: Second Round

In the second round אוֹיֵב (enemy) and צָמָא (thirst) were determined to be outside the semantic domains of רַע. For אוֹיֵב this was due to the large number of frequent associates it had which were not associated with רַע. Nevertheless, its frequent association with three frequent associates of רַע may indicate an important relation between אוֹיֵב and the semantic domains of רַע. For צָמָא, there was obviously a close relationship with רָעָב (famine), but beyond that there was little evidence of sharing a semantic domain with רַע.

A number of words were noted as words that may be on the periphery of the semantic domains of רַע. These words (in order of analysis) include: עַוְלָה (injustice); כָּזָב (falsehood); צָרָה (distress); זִמָּה (wickedness); שֶׁבֶר (destruction); and שֹׁד (destruction).

MAPPING THE LEXICAL SEMANTIC DOMAINS OF רַע   209

A number of words were noted for inclusion within the semantic domains of רַע. These words include: שֶׁקֶר (lie); חַטָּאת (sin); מֵרַע (evildoer); עָמָל (trouble); פֶּשַׁע (transgression); שָׁוְא (worthlessness); אַשְׁמָה (guilt); חֵטְא (sin); and עָרִיץ (ruthless).

3.4 ASSOCIATION ANALYSIS: ROUND 3

Two words were selected for round three analysis: לֵץ (scoffer) and חָנֵף (impious). Both occurred as frequent associates of רָשָׁע (wicked).[110] These words occurred in 10 and 7 unique associations respectively with words analysed in the first and second rounds of analysis. In addition they are both infrequent words, occurring 28[111] and 16 times respectively in the analysed texts.

3.4.1 לֵץ (scoffer)

לֵץ occurs 28 times in the analysed texts [17; 10; 1; 0; 0]. In total לֵץ occurs 18 times (64%) with at least one semantic association. Its occurrence with semantic associations by corpus is shown in Table 3.101 below. Tables 3.102 and 3.103 show the semantic associations of similarity and opposition respectively.

Table 3.101. Number of Identifiable Lexical and
Phrasal Semantic Associations לֵץ by Type of Association

Corpus	Similarity		Opposition		Total
	n.	**%**	**n.**	**%**	**n.**
Hebrew Bible	7	53.8	9	69.2	13
Ben Sira	4	100.0	3	75.0	4
Judean Desert	1	100.0	1	100.0	1
Inscriptions	0	–	0	–	0
Mishnah	0	–	0	–	0
Total	12	66.7	13	72.2	18

---

[110] לֵץ also occurred as a frequent associate of חָמָס (violence).

[111] Although לֵץ occurs 28 times it is still of relatively low frequency. Its occurrence as a frequent associate of both רָשָׁע and חָמָס was considered enough evidence to warrant examination at this frequency.

210 CHAPTER 3

Table 3.102. לֵץ in Associations of Similarity

Lexeme	Association	No.	Location
רָשָׁע		6	Ps 1:1; Prov 3:34; 9:7; 19:29; Sir 15:8; 1QHᵃ X, 13
אִישׁ חָמָס		3	Prov 3:34; Sir 32:18 (×2)
כְּסִיל		3	Prov 1:22; 3:34; 19:29
עָרִיץ		2	Isa 29:20; 1QHᵃ X, 13
אִישׁ זָדוֹן		1	Sir 15:8
אִישׁ כָּזָב		1	Sir 15:8
בּוֹגֵד		1	1QHᵃ X, 13
הוֹמֶה		1	Prov 20:1
זֵד		1	Sir 32:18
חַטָּא		1	Ps 1:1
לוֹטֵשׁ		1	Sir 31:26
מְתֵי שָׁוְא		1	Sir 15:8
נָלוֹז		1	Prov 3:34
עֵד בְּלִיַּעַל		1	Prov 19:29
פּוֹשֵׁעַ		1	1QHᵃ X, 13
פֶּתִי		1	Prov 1:22
שׁוֹקֵד אָוֶן		1	Isa 29:20

Table 3.103. לֵץ in Associations of Opposition

Lexeme	Association	No.	Location
חָכָם		6	Prov 3:34; 9:7, 8; 15:12; 21:11; Sir 15:8
אִישׁ חָכָם		2	Sir 32:18 (×2)
בֶּן חָכָם		1	Prov 13:1
יָשָׁר		1	Prov 3:34
יְשַׁר דֶּרֶךְ		1	1QHᵃ X, 13
נָבוֹן		2	Prov 14:6; 19:25
צַדִּיק		2	Prov 3:34; 9:8
אֶבְיוֹן		1	Isa 29:20
עָנָו		1	Isa 29:20
עָנִי		1	Prov 3:34

MAPPING THE LEXICAL SEMANTIC DOMAINS OF רַע 211

לֵץ (scoffer) occurs most frequently in associations of opposition with חָכָם (wise). Its most frequent association of similarity is with רָשָׁע (wicked). It also shares frequent associations with חָמָס (violence) and כְּסִיל (fool). Because two of its three associations are frequent associates of רַע and it shares 10 unique associations with frequent associates of רַע, the evidence is in favour of inclusion within the semantic domains of רַע.

3.4.2 חָנֵף (impious)

חָנֵף occurs 16 times in the analysed texts [13; 3; 0; 0; 0]. In total חָנֵף occurs 9 times (56%) with at least one semantic association, 2 of these being in Ben Sira. It occurs once with a semantic association of opposition.[112] Table 3.104 shows the semantic associations of similarity.

Table 3.104. חָנֵף in Associations of Similarity

Lexeme	Association	No.	Location
רָשָׁע		4	Job 20:5; 27:8; Prov 11:9; Sir 16:6
חַטָּא		1	Isa 33:14
מֵרַע		1	Isa 9:16
חָמָס		1	Sir 40:15
עֶבְרָה		1	Isa 10:6
עַוָּל		1	Job 27:8
פֶּה דּוֹבֵר נְבָלָה		1	Isa 9:16
שׁוֹכְחֵי אֵל		1	Job 8:13

The only frequent associate of חָנֵף (impious) is רָשָׁע (wicked). Because of this and its occurrence in 5 unique associations with frequent associates of רַע and another 2 unique associations with words analysed as being within the semantic domains of רַע in the second round, the evidence is in favour of including חָנֵף within the semantic domains of רַע.

3.4.3 Discussion: Third Round

The analysis of לֵץ (scoffer) and חָנֵף (impious) supports their inclusion in the semantic domains of רַע.

---

[112] The association occurs with צַדִּיק (righteous) in Prov 11:9.

212 CHAPTER 3

3.5 SEMANTIC ASSOCIATION FINDINGS

3.5.1 What Was Found

The goal of the semantic association analysis was to identify and map the semantic domains appropriate to the study of the term רַע (bad). To some extent this goal was achieved. However, certain areas of use of רַע lack representation in the analysis (see §3.5.2).

Figure 3.1 (below) shows a map of the semantic associates found to be within the semantic domain(s) of רַע in the above analysis.[113] Potentially separate domains were linked using different colours. Borders around words from within the word family of רַע are all coloured blue and associations between words within the word family are blue. Likely antonyms (words occurring frequently as the primary opposition of a selected word) are given in red below the word. Words that were noted in the analysis as possible periphery members have dotted lines as borders and double lines connecting them to their associates. The thickness of each line represents the frequency of associations between words. However, only associations that occurred three or more times are displayed. Thick dark lines are used where associations were so frequent that it was impractical to display them to scale. They represent associations that occurred more than 30 times.

Figure 3.1 displays four domains which will be referred to as the רָשָׁע (EVILDOER), אָוֶן (DECEIT), עָוֹן (SIN), and רָעָה (DESTRUCTION) domains.[114] The coloured clouds cover the terms within each domain. The decision was made to only half cover רָעָה with the red cloud because it demonstrates significant links with other domains. Additionally, the decision was made to only include periphery terms in a domain if they were directly linked with a core term. In effect this only meant שֶׁבֶר was left outside the אָוֶן domain. Because דָּם (blood) did not seem to have a close affinity with any particular domain it was not included within any.

---

[113] My method of mapping the semantic domains is inspired by that of Burton. For example see Burton, *The Semantics of Glory*, 255. Haspelmath discusses various uses of semantic maps. Martin Haspelmath, "The Geometry of Grammatical Meaning: Semantic Maps and Cross-Linguistic Comparison," in *The New Psychology of Language*, ed. Michael Tomasello (Mahwah, NJ: Lawrence Erlbaum, 2003), 2:211–42. Linguistic Discovery also produced an issue dedicated to the various aspects of semantic maps. Michael Cysouw, Martin Haspelmath and Andrej Malchukov, "Introduction to the Special Issue 'Semantic Maps: Methods and Applications,'" *Linguistic Discovery* 8 (2010): 1–3.

[114] The Hebrew headwords for each of these domains were selected based on the strength of their association to רַע and the other members of their domain. רָעָה was chosen to represent the רָעָה domain despite its significant links to the עָוֹן domain. It was deemed the best choice as it appears to function as a superordinate of the other terms in the רָעָה domain.

MAPPING THE LEXICAL SEMANTIC DOMAINS OF רַע

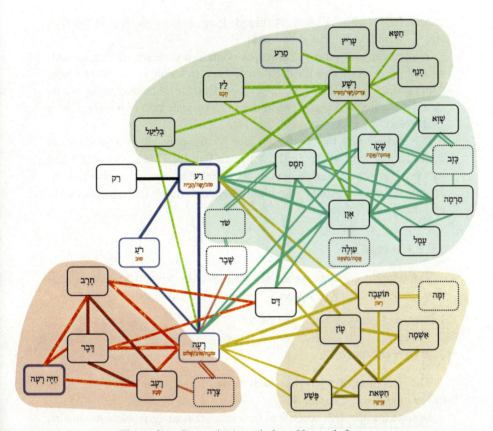

Figure 3.1. Semantic Associations Network for רַע

The רָשָׁע and אָוֶן domains demonstrate extensive interlinking (visualised with overlapping domain clouds). These links occur in contexts where words from the אָוֶן domain occur in phrases which modify the semantics to that of a person who does the action (e.g. פּוֹעֲלֵי אָוֶן; doers of villainy). The need for a phrasal use was deemed sufficient evidence for distinguishing them as separate groups of terms. However, because of the extensive interlinking, the רָשָׁע and אָוֶן domains will be considered as representing one major domain which is split by whether or not a word *as its own phrase* can refer to an evildoer. The rare term רַק (thin) was not found to be connected to any of the domains in Figure 3.1.

Figure 3.1 shows that three terms appear to frequently bridge all major domains. רַע frequently participates in all domains; although its only *frequent* participation in רָעָה is through the phrasal use: חַיָּה רָעָה (bad animal,

214   CHAPTER 3

bottom left). רָעָה (evil) and דָּם (blood) frequently participate in the **רָעָה**
and עָוֹן domains and אָוֶן subdomain.[115]

While both **רָעָה** and עָוֹן domains contain a core set of three words
which are associated with each other very frequently, the other major
domain does not. However, the רָשָׁע subdomain is characterised by its
headword's frequency and use in the antonym pair רָשָׁע (wicked) :: צַדִּיק
(righteous).

It is noteworthy that both **רָעָה** and עָוֹן domains share asymmetrical
relationships with words in the רַע word family. That is, while רַע and
רָעָה (evil) are associated frequently with both domains, these associations
are infrequent compared to the highly frequent trio of associations within
each domain.

3.5.2 Conclusions

Through the association analysis, רַע was found to participate in at least
three major domains of usage. These were identified as:

1. רָשָׁע and אָוֶן (EVILDOER and DECEIT),
2. עָוֹן (SIN),
3. **רָעָה** (DESTRUCTION).

The operation of רַע within each of these major domains is the basis
of the analysis in Chapter 4.

Despite the apparent success of the association analysis, certain domains
of use of רַע are entirely missing from Figure 3.1. For example, as seen
in Chapter 2 (§2.3.4), רַע may be used to describe things such as emotional
states. Additionally, the presence of רַק (thin) in Figure 3.1 draws attention to another area largely missing: COMMODITY (see §2.3.3). Domains
are missing where the use of רַע in such domains does not often occur
in semantic associations of similarity. Although outside the scope of this
project, other methods must be employed to more fully plot the remaining
semantic domains of רַע.

This may appear to some as a failure of the method. However, this
method does an excellent job of eliminating contamination from the
researcher's own conceptual domains. Therefore, while semantic domains
may not be completely mapped using this method, it produces reliable and
valuable results which may provide a critique to other methods.

---

[115] On the association of רָעָה with בְּלִיַּעַל and why this is not considered association with
the רָשָׁע subdomain see §4.7.2.

CHAPTER 4

SEMANTIC DOMAIN ANALYSIS

In Chapter 2 I examined the schematic contribution of רַע to the elements it modifies. It was concluded that, in general, רַע provides a negative qualification to an element. However, it was expected that use in certain domains could lead to variation in the meaning of רַע. This was found in Chapter 2 (§2.3.8) where the meaning of רַע was found to follow a standard pattern in the עָוֹן domain (§4.5). The finding highlighted the importance of the analysis in Chapter 3 and in this chapter (which, in part, led to the finding).

In Chapter 3, an association analysis of רַע was carried out. This was done in order to identify the different domains of use of רַע. In Chapter 3 (§3.5), three major domains of usage were identified: רָשָׁע and אָוֶן; עָוֹן; and רָעָה. In this chapter, the use of רַע in these three major domains is explored. As with Chapter 2, this analysis involves close examination of, primarily, the immediate discourse making up occurrences of words in each domain (the immediate cognitive context, see §1.4.1). Through the analysis רַע is shown to take features of the cognitive categories (§1.4.1) of the domains it operates in.

It must be stressed that the analysis in this chapter *is not* an exploration of the full domains of use of רַע. That would require much additional work beyond the scope of the current study (and additional methods for mapping the domains). Rather, the analysis in this chapter is a partial examination of the semantic domains identified in Chapter 3 with reference to words most likely to provide the greatest interpretive power for understanding רַע in its relation to these domains.

4.1 SCOPE OF DOMAIN ANALYSIS

A full analysis of רַע would deal with all words related to רַע, directly and indirectly. Ultimately this could be stretched to a large portion of the language.[1] However, it is easy to see that the less related a word is to רַע,

---

[1] It might even be argued that a full analysis should take account of the whole language (not to mention world knowledge) because only this would grant a full picture. In terms

216 CHAPTER 4

the less explanatory value it will have. For example, in Chapter 3 (§3.1.2) גָּדוֹל was eliminated from further analysis because it associates with רַע and its antonym טוֹב, and because of the relatively small range of uses in which they co-occur. While the relationship is clearly of interest in understanding רַע, it is of less interest than the relationship between רַע and רָשָׁע (which have extensive links).

Similarly, some of the terms plotted in chapter 3 (§3.5.1) will provide less value for understanding רַע than others. It may be safely assumed that a tangentially related term like זִמָּה provides less value for understanding רַע than the word תּוֹעֵבָה through which it is primarily related. So while it would be preferable to complete a full study of all the words plotted in chapter 3 (§3.5.1), there is not scope in the present work for such an undertaking. It is, therefore, necessary to determine and apply some criteria to limit the close analysis to words which will theoretically provide the most value.

Particularly rare words can be immediately eliminated from this selection because they will not be used enough to derive any meaningful conclusions. This eliminates the frequent associate רַק from further consideration (see section on רַק below). Criteria for further limitation can be profitably derived from criteria used for identifying collocations in corpus linguistics. These criteria include: distance; frequency; exclusivity; directionality; dispersion; type-token distribution; and connectivity.[2] Each criteria along with a brief definition can be seen in Table 4.1.

Table 4.1. Criteria for Identifying Collocations.[3]

Criteria	Definition
1. Distance	Refers to the distance from the word under study.
2. Frequency	Frequency of collocation use.
3. Exclusivity	Refers to the exclusivity of a particular collocation.
4. Directionality	Collocations normally exhibit some form of asymmetric relationship. Directionality takes asymmetry into account.

of taking into account a large variety of words, Sawyer writes "An 'associative field' would include all the words associated in any way with a particular term" and "many linguistic phenomena occur not just in relation to synonyms or the like, but also with opposites. Various types of interference are liable to occur among words associated by any one of the meaning-relations, not just the obvious ones." Sawyer, *Semantics in Biblical Research*, 30, 33.

[2] Brezina, McEnery, and Wattam, "Collocations in Context," 140–41.

[3] Definitions derived from Brezina, McEnery, and Wattam, "Collocations in Context," 140–41.

SEMANTIC DOMAIN ANALYSIS

Criteria	Definition
5. Dispersion	The distribution of the word and collocates across the corpus under investigation.
6. Type-token Distribution	Takes account of the strength of relationship *and* the level of competition a collocate has with other collocates.
7. Connectivity	Collocates may be connected to a word through a particular collocation. Connectivity takes into account collocation networks.

The first criterion, distance, is of little value in the selection of terms in the current analysis. During the association analysis, it was found that some terms exhibited strong semantic relationships across relatively large chunks of discourse. For example, m. 'Abot 2:9 contains a series of sayings using טוֹב, paralleled by a following series using רַע.

> 4.1a. m. 'Abot 2:9a

> אָמַ' לָהֶם צְאוּ וּרְאוּ אֵי זוֹ הִיא דֶרֶךְ טוֹבָה שֶׁיִּדְבַּק בָּהּ [הָ]אָדָם

> He said to them, "Go and see which is the good way that a person should cleave to it."

> 4.1b. m. 'Abot 2:9c

> אָמַ' לָהֶם צְאוּ וּרְאוּ אֵי זוֹ הִיא דֶרֶךְ רָעָה שֶׁיִּתְרַחַק מִמֶּנָּה [הָ]אָדָם

> He said to them, "Go and see which is the bad way that a person should make themselves far from it.

These two words are at a distance of 66 words from each other.[4] Despite this they are related in a strong antonymic relationship. The structure of the sentences and discourse within which they are situated makes this clear. Looking purely at the sentences in examples 4.1a and 4.1b, we can see that the only differences in phrasing in the primary clause consists of the selection of adjective. The relative clause varies on verb selection and preposition choice which clearly varies in conjunction with the adjective selection. Therefore, in this analysis distance is an unreliable proxy for the strength of relationship.

---

[4] This depends on how "words" are counted. If words are counted as groups of letters separated by a space it is 52. If all syntactic and semantic units such as the definite direct object marker, definite article, and pronominal suffixes are counted as words it is 66. If one wanted to count just content words the count would be lower, but still high. See Andersen and Forbes for words as blocks of text separated by a space. Andersen and Forbes, *Biblical Hebrew Grammar Visualized*, 370.

218   CHAPTER 4

The third and sixth criteria, exclusivity and type-token distribution, could be adapted, but applying these criteria would necessitate a thorough analysis which would introduce its own ambiguity. Both require evaluation of the level of competition for a particular slot. To examine the level of competition would require comparing the frequency of association with a certain word to the frequency of association with other words. To correct for domain-related effects, this would need to be done within specific domains of use. However, it would require assigning domains of use to particular instances. Some of these may be clear, but others, such as in the case of רָעָה – which occurs regularly in the **רָעָה** and **עָוֹן** domains – may be less clear and so would require further analysis. The analysis required to implement these criteria would, therefore, defeat the purpose of using the criteria to limit the analysis.

This leaves us with four criteria. These criteria are laid out in Table 4.2 below in terms of semantic associations. No particular weighting is placed on any of the criteria; however, a persuasive case for inclusion of a particular word should be supported across a number of criteria.

Table 4.2. Criteria for Prioritising Analysis of Semantic Associates.

Criteria	Definition
1. Frequency	Frequency of semantic association.
2. Directionality	Semantic associations normally exhibit some form of asymmetric relationship. Directionality takes asymmetry into account.
3. Dispersion	The distribution of use of the semantic association across the corpus under investigation.
4. Connectivity	Semantic associates may be associated through a particular phrase. Connectivity takes into account phrasal uses of lexemes in associations.

Applying the Criteria

The criteria will be applied to all terms identified in Chapter 3 (§3.5.1), Figure 3.1. I briefly describe the rationale for each criterion, then I apply the first criterion, frequency. Each word is then examined against the other criteria in order of frequency.[5]

---

[5] דֶּבֶר, חֶרֶב, and רָעָב are considered together due to the great overlap in their associations with רַע.

SEMANTIC DOMAIN ANALYSIS 219

In terms of frequency, the words that show a strong relationship with רַע are expected to occur more frequently in relationship with רַע. However, a word that demonstrates a lower frequency of association may also be of interest if it is a rarer word. Frequencies of less than 4 are not considered because at such a low rate of association, comments about dispersion and connectivity become next to meaningless.[6] Therefore, such words are removed from consideration for close analysis.

In applying criterion 2, directionality, to the current situation, what is of interest is the explanatory power of analysis for understanding רַע. This means that the comparative frequency of רַע's association with a particular word is more important than the reverse. As such, if there is asymmetry where רַע demonstrates a comparatively strong relationship with a word, but that word does not appear to have a comparatively strong relationship with רַע, it may be still worthy of analysis. Effectively this means criterion 2 is applied in the application of the frequency criterion. However, it may be instructive to note where asymmetry occurs.

In terms of criterion 3, dispersion, the more ubiquitous a use is, the more likely it is to provide greater gains for understanding meaning. It is of interest to note the dispersion in terms of broad text types (wisdom literature, prophecy etc.) and corpus, in addition to across individual works (or books).

Criterion 4, connectivity, is an important criterion to account for. If connectivity of רַע with another word is required for an association to take place, this may influence the usefulness of studying the associate. However, this will depend on other factors as well. Although exclusivity of association was eliminated as a main criterion, it is useful to consider exclusivity of collocation when connectivity is evidenced.

Table 4.3. Association Frequencies of Lexemes and Phrases with רַע
(for frequency ≥ 4)

Frequency	11	9	7	6	5	4
Lexemes and Phrases	רָשָׁע	חֶרֶב רֹעַ	רָעָה	דֶּבֶר	אָוֶן עָוֺן רָעָב רַק	חָמָס תּוֹעֵבָה

---

[6] With lower frequencies, comments about other criteria mean progressively less because there is a greater likelihood of chance variation.

220 CHAPTER 4

רָשָׁע (wicked)

The association with רָשָׁע primarily occurs in psalms and wisdom literature. It is spread over Psalms, Job, Proverbs, Sirach, and m. 'Abot.[7] It also occurs once in Ezekiel. However, this finding should not be unduly emphasised. Much of this effect is due to the general spread of רָשָׁע across the corpuses. In the biblical corpus, רָשָׁע occurs 73% of the time in Psalms and Wisdom Literature. Ezekiel contains the next most frequent use of רָשָׁע. It is notable though, that the association does not once occur in the "extra-biblical" Judean Desert corpus which contains roughly twice the uses of Ben Sira and the Mishnah (both of which demonstrate two associations each).

This finding is suggestive of limited use of the רָשָׁע ‖ רַע association beyond Wisdom Literature. However, the association is ubiquitous in the Wisdom Literature. Additionally, it is dispersed across biblical texts, Ben Sira, and the Mishnah, and it is the most common association of similarity with רַע. In terms of connectivity, רָשָׁע and רַע co-occur with a variety of terms. For example, in Ezekiel 7:21 and 24 the association is between רִשְׁעֵי הָאָרֶץ (the wicked of the earth) and רָעֵי גוֹיִם (the bad of the nations). They also occur in association as individual words (e.g. Ps 10:15). This flexibility of use is suggestive of a greater similarity between the two terms. רָשָׁע should be considered for further analysis.

חֶרֶב (sword), רָעָב (famine), and דֶּבֶר (plague)

The חֶרֶב, רָעָב, and דֶּבֶר associations co-occur across all five of the associations with רָעָב. חֶרֶב and דֶּבֶר co-occur in the remaining דֶּבֶר association. All but three of these uses occur with the phrase חַיָּה רָעָה (bad animal). One of these, where רַע appears on its own, is textually suspect and may be an omission error (Sir 39:29);[8] in another instance it occurs with the phrase חֳלָיִים רָעִים (bad sicknesses, 4Q504 1–2 III, 8). Lastly, it occurs in a poetic line as a superordinate encompassing יַד חֶרֶב and מָוֶת (Job 5:19–20). Although it is dispersed across biblical texts, Ben Sira, the Dead Sea Scrolls, and the Mishnah, as well as across legal, prophetic, and wisdom texts, in six of the eight uses it refers to animals that destroy as part of

---

[7] m. 'Abot is considered an ethical work, although not systematic. It also invites comparison to the books considered wisdom literature. As such I have included it in the category of wisdom literature. See Herford, *Pirkē Aboth*, 8.

[8] רַע instead of רָעָב (famine). This possibility is supported by the Old Greek which translates it as λιμος (famine). Furthermore, the list is specific, but if רַע was used here there is no information to determine the specific referent. See Appendix C.1 for discussion.

SEMANTIC DOMAIN ANALYSIS 221

the phrase חַיָּה רָעָה. Furthermore, although רַע is the most common collo-
cate of חַיָּה in these circumstances, it competes with שֵׁן (Sir 39:30) and
null modification (Ezek 33:27). That is, while חַיָּה רָעָה is the common way
of expressing the idea, it is not necessary for רַע to be present. Although
these associations exhibit dispersion across text-types, they exhibit low
contextual variation, and seem to indicate a standard set of judgements.

4.2. Ezekiel 14:21a[9]

כִּ֣י כֹה֩ אָמַ֨ר אֲדֹנָ֜י יְהֹוִ֗ה אַ֣ף כִּֽי־אַרְבַּ֜עַת שְׁפָטַ֣י ׀ הָרָעִ֗ים חֶ֣רֶב וְרָעָ֤ב וְחַיָּ֤ה רָעָה֙
וְדֶ֔בֶר שִׁלַּ֖חְתִּי

For thus says the Lord God "How much more when I send my four
bad judgements, sword, and famine, and bad beasts, and plague…

Therefore, an analysis of רָעָב, חֶרֶב, and דֶּבֶר is unlikely to contribute
much to our understanding of רַע.

רֹעַ (badness)

The רֹעַ association primarily occurs in Jeremiah (three times elsewhere).
Similarly, רֹעַ occurs in 55% of its biblical uses in Jeremiah. This use in
Jeremiah appears inflated due to two repeated uses: to refer to putrid figs,
and to refer to the people's deeds.[10] It refers to additional areas outside
Jeremiah (animals [Gen 41:3]; appearance [Neh 2:2]; and plans [1QH[a] XV,
6]). It is dispersed between two prophetic books, one poetic, and one narrative. Strikingly, רֹעַ is rare at 30 uses in the analysed texts and yet is the
second most frequent associate of רַע. The rarity of the word will create
difficulties drawing firm conclusions; however, it is not so rare as to assume
it will be unprofitable. Although the רַע ‖ רֹעַ association and the use of רֹעַ
is primarily in Jeremiah, it is adequately dispersed across text-types and
contexts. In terms of connectivity, רֹעַ often occurs in the phrase רֹעַ מַעַלְלֵי-
with a suffixed pronoun (corruption of [possessive pronoun] deeds). However, it also occurs with other terms such as לֵב (heart, Neh 2:2), and מַחְשֶׁבֶת
(thought, 1QH[a] XV, 6). Notably, it never occurs in association with רַע
where neither רֹעַ nor רַע are connected with something. This may be
indicative of either a limited scope of meaning similarity, or may be driven
primarily by the rarity of the word. It is likely that further analysis of רֹעַ
will prove valuable in at least some areas of the use of רַע.

---

[9] Also in §3.1.1.3 as example 3.11.
[10] These two uses also make up the entire set of uses of רֹעַ in Jeremiah. To refer to figs:
Jer 24:2, 3; 24:8; 29:17. To refer to people's deeds: Jer 4:4; 21:12; 23:2, 22; 25:5;
26:3; 44:22.

CHAPTER 4

רָעָה (evil)

The רָעָה association is dispersed across biblical legal, narrative, prophetic, and wisdom texts. Although רָעָה occurred most frequently in Jeremiah (24% of occurrences across all corpora), the רַע ‖ רָעָה association only occurred once in that book (Jer 32:32). While רָעָה occurred 50 times in the extra-biblical corpora (14% of all occurrences), the רַע ‖ רָעָה association did not occur there. Given the association only occurs seven times, we might only expect to see one occurrence in this portion of the corpora,[11] so it is not extraordinary that none occur. In terms of connectivity, when occurring with רַע,רָעָה is often combined with either דֶּרֶךְ (way; e.g. Ezek 20:43) or the verb עָשָׂה (to do), making it something which is done (e.g. Jer 32:30, 32).[12] Similarly, רָעָה is often combined with an action verb such as הָבִיא (to bring; e.g. 1 Kgs 21:21) and עָשָׂה (Jer 32:30, 32). This is suggestive of a specific domain of overlap between the two words. Due to the high frequency of עָשָׂה רַע and דֶּרֶךְ רָעָה phrases – which combined make up 20% of all uses of רַע – further analysis of רָעָה is desirable as it relates to a high proportion of רַע uses.

אָוֶן (villainy)

The אָוֶן association exhibits dispersion across biblical prophetic, wisdom, and poetic texts. This is in line with the dispersion of אָוֶן itself, which occurs 83% of the time in these texts across the entire analysed corpuses. At most we might expect one occurrence in the rest of the texts,[13] so it is not extraordinary that none occur. אָוֶן occurs with רַע in a variety of configurations: in the construct phrase מַעֲשֵׂי־אָוֶן (Isa 59:6); with the participle חוֹשֵׁב (Ezek 11:2; Mic 2:1); and with null connectivity (Ps 36:5; Prov 12:21). Although a less frequent word – occurring only 83 times in the analysed texts – אָוֶן appears to share some important links with רַע. They are frequently associated, this being across a variety of texts and in a variety of configurations. Therefore, further analysis of אָוֶן is desirable.

---

[11] Statistically, the expected rate of occurrence is less than one: 0.95.

[12] One of the instances of association was with חַיָּה רָעָה (Ezek 14:22). This is of interest, but given the argument presented in §4.1 it presents an area that is unlikely to shed much light on רַע. This leaves a frequency of six rather than seven in terms of associations of greater interest for the meaning of רַע.

[13] Statistically, the expected rate of occurrence is less than one: 0.85.

SEMANTIC DOMAIN ANALYSIS

עָוֹן (iniquity)

The עָוֹן association exhibits dispersion across prophetic (and prophetic pesher), wisdom, and historical texts. It occurs across biblical texts, as well as in Ben Sira and the Dead Sea Scrolls. The spread of the עָוֹן ‖ רַע association does not line up with the distribution of עָוֹן across texts. Qumran and Ben Sira receive a greater proportion than we might expect. However, no statistically reliable conclusions can be drawn from this due to the small total size. In terms of connectivity it falls on the side of רַע in this association. It occurs modifying the word דֶּרֶךְ (way; Ezek 36:31) and מַעֲשֶׂה (work; Ezra 9:13; 4Q169 3–4 III, 4). It occurs in conjunction with the verb עָשָׂה (to do) in Ben Sira 7:2, and with -סוּר מֵ (turn from) in Proverbs 16:6. This may suggest it connects with רַע in similar circumstances to when רָעָה connects with רַע (see section on רָעָה above). For the same reasons – the frequent occurrence of רַע in these circumstances – it is desirable to study עָוֹן further.

רַק (thin)

The רַק association exhibits no dispersion. Furthermore, the word occurs exclusively in Genesis 41. No reliable conclusions can be drawn concerning רַע through examining רַק.

חָמָס (violence)

The חָמָס association exhibits dispersion across biblical prophetic and poetic texts. This does not line up with the dispersion of חָמָס itself, which occurs 51% of the time in these texts across the analysed corpuses. However, no statistically reliable conclusions can be drawn from this due to the small total size, and its distribution across corpuses is as may be expected.[14] Its connectivity pattern is fairly similar to what was seen with אָוֶן. This is unsurprising given they appeared closely related in the semantic map (§3.5.1). חָמָס occurs in the phrases פֹּעַל חָמָס (Isa 59:6), חָמָס אֲשֶׁר בְּכַף (Amos 6:3), and אִישׁ חֲמָסִים (Jon 3:8). In the last two cases it occurs with דֶּרֶךְ רָעָה and אָדָם רַע respectively. In one instance the relationship is

---

[14] Statistically, the expected rate of occurrence in Ben Sira and the Judean Desert corpuses is less than one: we might expect 0.95 occurrences.

224 CHAPTER 4

in dispute (Amos 6:3).[15] This association demonstrates lower frequency and lower dispersion than that of אָוֶן. Although an in depth analysis of חָמָס would be of interest for understanding רַע, these factors indicate it is likely of less value than other terms.

תּוֹעֵבָה (abomination)

The תּוֹעֵבָה association is dispersed across biblical legal, historical, and prophetic texts. It exhibits connectivity similar to that associated with רָעָה and עָוֹן. That is, when associated with תּוֹעֵבָה, רַע is connected with the verb עָשָׂה (to do) and noun דֶּרֶךְ (way). This association demonstrates lower frequency than those of רָעָה and עָוֹן. Additionally, two of these associations are identical in phrasing, being a synoptic text (2 Kgs 21:2 // 2 Chr 33:2). Although an in depth analysis of תּוֹעֵבָה would be ideal, it is likely to be of less value than the study of other terms.

Selected Words for Close Analysis

As a result of applying the criteria in Table 4.2, five words were chosen for close analysis. These words are: רָשָׁע, רֹעַ, רָעָה, אָוֶן, and עָוֹן.

4.2 USAGE OF רַע WITHIN CHAPTER 3 DOMAINS

The analysis will be carried out by domain. For each domain and sub-domain, a partial analysis of the domain will first be carried out. This is done with reference to the terms identified (above) as most likely to provide the greatest interpretive power for understanding רַע. This is followed by an application of the findings on each domain to רַע. Last, a comparison is made between רַע and the רעע word family terms (רֹעַ and רָעָה) identified for further analysis in §4.1. Figure 3.1 from Chapter 3 identifies terms considered within each domain. It is reproduced below for ease.

---

[15] The exact meaning of הַמְנַדִּים לְיוֹם רָע וַתַּגִּישׁוּן שֶׁבֶת חָמָס (Oh ones who put away the evil day and you bring near the seat of violence) is disputed (as the different interpretations in the commentaries attest). However, the verbs are in parallel and the two versets are syntactically parallel. At minimum this structure would create a forced semantic parallel. Andersen and Freedman, *Amos*, 555–56; Paul, *Amos*, 204–5.

Figure 4.1. Semantic Associations Network for רַע

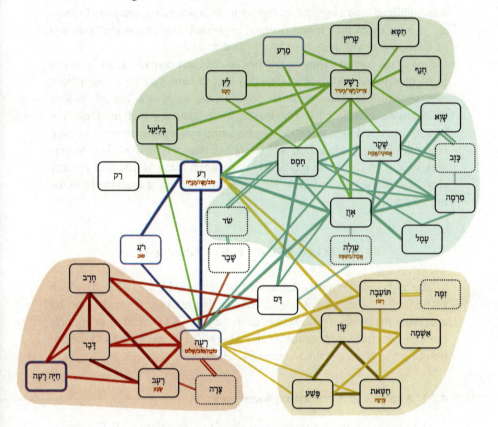

Three major domains were identified:

1. רָשָׁע and אָוֶן or EVILDOER and DECEIT,
2. עָוֹן or SIN,
3. רָעָה or DESTRUCTION.

These domains are analysed in order. Major domain one (רָשָׁע and אָוֶן) is analysed in two sections (§§4.3–4.4). This is followed by an analysis of major domain 2 (עָוֹן; §4.5) and major domain 3 (רָעָה; §4.6). Derivational relationships are analysed in §4.7.

Given the findings of §4.1 which eliminated רָעָב, חֶרֶב, and דֶּבֶר from close consideration, one might wonder about the inclusion of the רָעָה domain in the analysis. This can be explained as follows. While the core

226 CHAPTER 4

triad of terms were not selected for thorough analysis, the **רָעָה** domain was highlighted as a significant feature in the association analysis of Chapter 3. Because of this, it was deemed important to examine the operation of the domain with reference to רָעָה and רַע.

Due to the partial nature of the analysis of each domain, a caveat needs to be mentioned. While it is intended that the analysis be as accurate a representation of each domain as possible, the analysis is biased towards the terms selected in §4.1. This means some features which are argued to be core to their domains below may be found by future analysis to be core features of words identified in §4.1 rather than whole domains. Nevertheless, due to the close relationships between these words and רַע, any such limitations will have less impact on the subsequent assessment of the use of רַע.

4.3 MAJOR DOMAIN 1: רָשָׁע SUBDOMAIN

The **רָשָׁע** subdomain is dominated by the word רָשָׁע (wicked) which fills 65.7% of the uses of **רָשָׁע** words in the analysed texts. I begin by analysing the domain with reference to רָשָׁע (§4.3.1). After drawing preliminary conclusions about the subdomain (§4.3.2), I move on to the operation of רַע in the **רָשָׁע** subdomain (§4.3.3).

4.3.1 Analysis of רָשָׁע (with a focus on רָשָׁע)

The **רָשָׁע** subdomain consists entirely of HUMAN referents.[16] Two broad areas of use are detected in רָשָׁע. These relate to a position in a judicial process: that is, before or after a verdict. These two uses can be seen in Deuteronomy 25:1–2 (example 4.3). Words which indicate a legal case or judicial action are in purple.

4.3. Deuteronomy 25:1–2

כִּי־יִהְיֶה רִיב בֵּין אֲנָשִׁים וְנִגְּשׁוּ אֶל־הַמִּשְׁפָּט וּשְׁפָטוּם וְהִצְדִּיקוּ אֶת־הַצַּדִּיק וְהִרְשִׁיעוּ
אֶת־הָרָשָׁע
וְהָיָה אִם־בִּן הַכּוֹת הָרָשָׁע וְהִפִּילוֹ הַשֹּׁפֵט וְהִכָּהוּ לְפָנָיו כְּדֵי רִשְׁעָתוֹ בְּמִסְפָּר

---

[16] This could perhaps be broadened to include SPIRIT referents and include the special use of בְּלִיַּעַל (Belial). Cases of **רָשָׁע** words which do not have such referents behave in different ways and are not part of the subdomain. For example, see Ezekiel 3:18–19 where רָשָׁע modifies דֶּרֶךְ (way).

SEMANTIC DOMAIN ANALYSIS

> If there is a dispute between men and they approach for judgment, they shall judge them and acquit the righteous and condemn the wicked. If the condemned person is a son of striking [i.e. deserves to be beaten], the judge will cause him to lie down. He [the punisher] will strike him in his [the judge's] presence according to the number his wickedness requires.

In the first use of רָשָׁע it takes the usual role. However, in the second use, רָשָׁע refers not to the wicked person (i.e. the guilty), but to the condemned. An important change in legal status is involved between the uses of רָשָׁע in example 4.3. The first occurs prior to the verdict, the second after the verdict. This distinction can be highlighted by reference to example 4.4.[17]

4.4. Isaiah 5:23

מַצְדִּיקֵי רָשָׁע עֵקֶב שֹׁחַד וְצִדְקַת צַדִּיקִים יָסִירוּ מִמֶּנּוּ

[Woe to those who] acquit the wicked for a bribe and the righteousness of the righteous they turn aside.

This example is valuable because it demonstrates the case of perversion of justice, where the רָשָׁע is declared to be צַדִּיק. This declaration is indicated by use of the Hiphil verb הַצְדִּיק (aquit).[18] Due to its technical nature, this second use of רָשָׁע is unlikely to convey much insight for understanding רַע which does not appear as a technical judicial term. This does, however, demonstrate the close links between רָשָׁע and judicial process, links that are seen for both אָוֶן and עָוֹן.

רָשָׁע appears to be used of those who act contrary to some standard of behaviour: HUMAN(NEGATIVE BEHAVIOUR).[19] This standard is naturally tied to judicial requirements and to religious belief because the worldview represented by the corpus takes God as the ultimate judge of all (e.g. Ps 50:6, אֱלֹהִים שֹׁפֵט הוּא). This link is represented in various semantic associations with those who forsake or love the Lord or his law (examples 4.5 and 4.6). Terms indicating the divine are given in orange here.

4.5. Psalm 119:53

זַלְעָפָה אֲחָזַתְנִי מֵרְשָׁעִים עֹזְבֵי תּוֹרָתֶךָ

Raging seizes me because of the wicked, forsakers of your law.

---

[17] See also Psalm 109:7.

[18] Cf. Clines, "צדק Hi," *DCH* 7:80.

[19] This also holds for the use to refer to the condemned, only in their case they have been *declared* to have acted against some standard, whether or not that is the case.

228 CHAPTER 4

4.6. Psalm 145:20

שׁוֹמֵר יְהוָה אֶת־כָּל־אֹהֲבָיו וְאֵת כָּל־הָרְשָׁעִים יַשְׁמִיד

The LORD keeps all who love him, and all the wicked he destroys.

Use with reference to a human judge can be found in example 4.5. Due to a view of God as ultimate judge, the use with the human sense also often involves reference to God (example 4.5, תוֹרָתֶךָ, *your* law). However, where such reference is not present (example 4.7) it does not mean another standard should necessarily be assumed.[20]

4.7. Exodus 2:13

וַיֵּצֵא בַּיּוֹם הַשֵּׁנִי וְהִנֵּה שְׁנֵי־אֲנָשִׁים עִבְרִים נִצִּים וַיֹּאמֶר לָרָשָׁע לָמָּה תַכֶּה רֵעֶךָ

On the second [i.e. next] day he [Moses] went out, and behold, two Hebrew men were fighting. He said to the guilty one, "Why did you strike your neighbour?"

In the normal use of רָשָׁע, there are a number of collocations with the עָוֹן domain [20; 0; 26; 0; 0] which indicate the רָשָׁע do עָוֹן.[21] However, unlike the אָוֶן subdomain (see Figure 4.1, §4.2; and §4.4.1), combinative semantic associations are rare. In fact, there is only one combinative association between רָשָׁע and עָוֹן, and it is one of contrast rather than similarity.

4.8. 1QHᵃ VI, 35

הסולח לשבי פשע ופוקד עון {ו}{ }ן רשעים

...the one who forgives those who turn [from] transgression and punishes the iniquity of wicked ones.

In example 4.8, the עָוֹן term פֶּשַׁע (transgression) combines with שׁוּב (to turn) to form a phrase that contrasts with רָשָׁע. This example also demonstrates the kind of usage which indicates the רָשָׁע does עָוֹן – that is, through the construct phrase עוון רשעים (iniquity of wicked ones).

Despite the lack of combinative associations, the rate of collocations between רָשָׁע and עָוֹן is significantly more frequent in the Judean Desert corpus compared to that with אָוֶן [20; 0; 1; 0; 0].[22] This is partially

---

[20] The view of God as ultimate judge can be seen as a worldview and need not always be stated.

[21] These are calculated as close proximity collocations (i.e. the collocations occur within the verse). Uses occur in: Isa 13:11; Ezek 3:18, 19; 18:21, 24; 21:30, 34; 33:8, 12, 14; Ps 36:2; Prov 5:22; 10:16; 15:8, 9; 17:15; 21:4, 27; 29:16, 27; 1QpHab IX, 9; XII, 8; 1QHᵃ VI, 35; X, 12; XII, 35; 4Q511 63 III, 4.

[22] These are calculated as close proximity collocations (i.e. the collocations occur within the verse). Uses occur in: Exod 23:1, 7; Isa 53:9; 55:7; Hab 1:13; Ps 11:5; 28:3; 55:4; 58:4; 92:8; 101:8; 109:2; 140:5; Prov 10:6, 11; 11:8; 12:5; 13:5; 19:28;

SEMANTIC DOMAIN ANALYSIS

reflected in a comparatively lower rate of occurrence for אָוֶן than עָוֹן terms between the biblical and the Judean Desert corpus (461:89 or 5.18:1 and 710:182 or 3.90:1 respectively).[23] This could reflect a preoccupation with one domain of behaviour over the other for the communities that produced the Judean Desert texts (rather than a changing meaning). Therefore, although not devoid of relevant associations and collocations, the Judean Desert corpus exhibits few between רָשָׁע and אָוֶן. Example 4.9 is the only use of רָשָׁע in the Judean Desert corpus which is associated with a combinative use of אָוֶן.

4.9. 4Q418 126 II, 6–7

משפט להשיב נקם לבעלי און ופקודת ש[--]
ולסגור בעד רשעים ולהרים ראוש דלים [--]

... judgement to return vengeance on masters of villainy and punishment of [--] to lock up the wicked and to raise the head of the poor [--]

Although this text is somewhat damaged, the semantic association is clear and it follows the general pattern of such associations in the Hebrew Bible (example 4.10).

4.10. Psalm 92:8a

בִּפְרֹחַ רְשָׁעִים ׀ כְּמוֹ עֵשֶׂב וַיָּצִיצוּ כָּל־פֹּעֲלֵי אָוֶן

...When the wicked sprout like grass, and all doers of villainy flourish

4.3.2 Preliminary Conclusion

The analysis of the use of רָשָׁע appears to suggest that the רָשָׁע subdomain refers to a human viewed in terms of negative behaviour: HUMAN(NEGATIVE BEHAVIOUR). Such BEHAVIOUR is usually viewed in terms of JUDICIAL implications. That is, when רָשָׁע is not being used in its specialised judicial use,

29:12; 1QH[a] XV, 15. Two uses were not included: Ezek 13:22 because the רָשָׁע is not the one doing אָוֶן, and Prov 12:21 because the use of אָוֶן relates to a punishment inflicted on the רָשָׁע.

[23] That is, there were 3.90 occurrences of עָוֹן terms in the biblical corpus for every one occurrence in the Judean Desert corpus, whereas there were 5.18 occurrences of אָוֶן in the biblical corpus for every one in the Judean Desert corpus. This was calculated based on a simple frequency of terms found to be within or on the periphery of the domains (710:182 vs 461:89). One correction was introduced in the case of a highly frequent polyseme of חַטָּאת (sin offering). חַטָּאת was associated with another term for an offering at least 77 times in the biblical corpus and 7 times in the Judean Desert corpus. However, the total occurrence of this polyseme is likely to be slightly higher. There are likely some occurrences where it does not associate with another term for an offering.

230   CHAPTER 4

it still relates to the JUDICIAL: the רָשָׁע is someone who deserves to be declared רָשָׁע.

It also has very strong connections to judicial process and strong ties to both the אָוֶן subdomain, and the עָוֹן domain. These ties both indicate the רָשָׁע does NEGATIVE ACTS. Although in the Judean Desert corpus there was strong bias towards uses in which the negative behaviour is עָוֹן, this subdomain may be neutral with respect to whether the behaviour is from אָוֶן or עָוֹן.[24]

4.3.3 רַע as Part of רָשָׁע

Having partially considered how the רָשָׁע subdomain functions, we now turn to the use of רַע within the subdomain. We begin with some straight-forward uses where core relationships are clear.

Examples 4.11 and 4.12 demonstrate two common uses of רַע with רָשָׁע. In both, the uses can be clearly demonstrated to be modifying a HUMAN discourse element. The close semantic association between the words indicate that רַע participates in the רָשָׁע subdomain in these uses. Orange is used to highlight important semantic parallels.

4.11. Proverbs 4:14–16

בְּאֹרַח רְשָׁעִים אַל־תָּבֹא וְאַל־תְּאַשֵּׁר בְּדֶרֶךְ רָעִים
פְּרָעֵהוּ אַל־תַּעֲבָר־בּוֹ שְׂטֵה מֵעָלָיו וַעֲבוֹר
כִּי לֹא יִשְׁנוּ אִם־לֹא יָרֵעוּ וְנִגְזְלָה שְׁנָתָם אִם־לֹא יַכְשׁוֹלוּ

Do not enter into the path of wicked ones, do not proceed in the way of bad ones. Avoid it, do not pass in it, turn away from it and pass on. Because they cannot sleep unless they have done bad, their sleep is robbed if they have not caused [someone] to stumble.

In example 4.11, the pronouns in the second line refer back to אֹרַח (path) and דֶּרֶךְ (way), but in the third line the verbs (and one pronoun) are mas-culine plural, taking רְשָׁעִים and רָעִים as their subject (and referent) and clearly referring to a group of HUMANS. These HUMANS are construed as doing lawless ACTS (e.g. robbing).

4.12. Ben Sira 11:33 (A 4v25–27)

גור מרע כי רע יוליד למה מום מום עולם תשא
לא תדבק לרשע ויסלף דרכך ויהפכך מבריתיך

---

[24] The bias could be due to a preoccupation with one domain over the other, or even a collapse of use of the distinction between the domains, with עָוֹן taking over. Further analysis would need to be conducted of how עָוֹן is used in the Judean desert corpus, comparing it to biblical usage. Such analysis is outside the scope of this project.

SEMANTIC DOMAIN ANALYSIS

231

Fear from a bad one, because he will father bad. Why should you bear an eternal blemish? Do not cling to a wicked one, he will subvert your way and turn you from your covenant.

In example 4.12, we again see the verbs taking up רַע and רָשָׁע as their subjects, making it clear that these words refer to HUMANS. However, the second use of רַע is the object of the verb הוֹלִיד (to father). Thus it refers to something that is brought about, and must modify the element ACT.

How do we treat uses that may be considered as רָשָׁע or אָוֶן? In example 4.13, רַע demonstrates links with both subdomains.

4.13. Psalm 140:2, 5

חַלְּצֵנִי יְהוָה מֵאָדָם רָע מֵאִישׁ חֲמָסִים תִּנְצְרֵנִי {...}
שָׁמְרֵנִי יְהוָה | מִידֵי רָשָׁע מֵאִישׁ חֲמָסִים תִּנְצְרֵנִי אֲשֶׁר חָשְׁבוּ לִדְחוֹת פְּעָמָי

Deliver me, LORD, from the bad man, rescue me from the man of violence {...} Keep me, LORD, from the hand of the wicked, rescue me from the man of violence, who plans to trip my feet.

We may argue from a syntax perspective that it is most likely an example of רַע as רָשָׁע.[25] However, consider the extensive links between רָשָׁע and אָוֶן shown in Figure 4.1 (also see §4.4.1). Such links exist between phrasal uses of אָוֶן terms and רָשָׁע terms, where people who do אָוֶן are conceptualised as being רָשָׁע. It is probably best to see רַע as functioning within both subdomains in this example rather than trying to determine specific function.

HUMAN uses within and outside רָשָׁע

Given the findings above, רַע may operate within this subdomain where it modifies HUMAN(BEHAVIOUR). Therefore, the רָשָׁע subdomain is more specific than simply HUMAN uses of רַע. There is usage which may suggest that רַע+HUMAN can be used generally, simultaneously encompassing meanings within and outside the רָשָׁע subdomain. We first look at some uses of רַע within the subdomain.

---

[25] In this example the question of which subdomain רַע participates in rests on the question of which element רַע combines with. Is it an ACT or a HUMAN? Syntactically speaking, the question hinges on whether רַע modifies אָדָם through attributive or construct relations. It seems most likely that the use is attributive. DCH only identifies one use of אָדָם in construct form in the pre-mishnaic texts (1QS XI, 9; Clines, "אָדָם 2a," *DCH* 1:126–27). This suggests it would be highly unusual. Additionally, the parallel between verses 2 and 5 incorporates אִישׁ חֲמָסִים in the second half of both. This suggests a stronger semantic link between אָדָם רַע and רָשָׁע than between אָדָם רַע and אִישׁ חֲמָסִים.

232 CHAPTER 4

Examples 4.14 and 4.15 may be described as uses of רָשָׁע.

4.14. Jeremiah 12:14

כֹּה ׀ אָמַ֣ר יְהֹוָ֗ה עַל־כָּל־שְׁכֵנַי֙ הָרָעִ֔ים הַנֹּֽגְעִים֙ בַּֽנַּחֲלָ֔ה אֲשֶׁר־הִנְחַ֖לְתִּי אֶת־עַמִּ֣י אֶת־יִשְׂרָאֵ֑ל הִנְנִ֤י נֹֽתְשָׁם֙ מֵעַ֣ל אַדְמָתָ֔ם וְאֶת־בֵּ֥ית יְהוּדָ֖ה אֶת֥וֹשׁ מִתּוֹכָֽם

Thus says the LORD, "Concerning all my bad neighbours who strike the inheritance which I gave to my people Israel: behold, I am uprooting them from their land and I will uproot the house of Judah from their midst.

In this example the "neighbours" are characterised by their NEGATIVE BEHAVIOUR (orange) towards the people of Israel. This indicates that רַע combines with HUMAN(BEHAVIOUR) in this passage and is thus part of the רָשָׁע subdomain. It is also linked with the Lord's JUDICIAL behaviour.

4.15. Genesis 38:7

וַיְהִ֗י עֵ֚ר בְּכ֣וֹר יְהוּדָ֔ה רַ֖ע בְּעֵינֵ֣י יְהֹוָ֑ה וַיְמִתֵ֖הוּ יְהֹוָֽה

Er, Judah's firstborn, was bad in the eyes of the LORD, so the LORD put him to death.

This example is more enigmatic. There is no clear indication from the discourse what it was that the Lord based the judgement on. However, on the basis of the worldview of the text, in which Lord is considered a righteous judge (cf. Gen 18:20–33), we can assess this text. This example has a JUDICIAL context, the Lord executes judgement against Er for being רַע. This indicates to us that whatever was רַע about Er should be considered something requiring judgement. Therefore, this combinative use should be seen as one of HUMAN(NEGATIVE BEHAVIOUR) and part of the רָשָׁע subdomain.

There are some combinative uses of רַע which are HUMAN, but are outside, or partially outside, the רָשָׁע subdomain. Two examples (4.16 and 4.17) are replicated from Chapter 2.

4.16. Genesis 28:8

וַיַּ֣רְא עֵשָׂ֔ו כִּ֥י רָע֖וֹת בְּנ֣וֹת כְּנָ֑עַן בְּעֵינֵ֖י יִצְחָ֥ק אָבִֽיו

Esau saw that the daughters of Canaan [i.e. Esau's Canaanite wives] were bad in the eyes of Isaac his father.

In this example (example 2.30, §2.3.2) it was found that while רַע predicatively modifies a HUMAN group, the modified element is HUMAN(KINSHIP). That is, it is with respect to their KINSHIP, not BEHAVIOUR that Isaac found the Canaanite women to be רַע. Thus it would be wrong to assume on the basis of their evaluation as רַע, that these women deserve JUDGEMENT or do either עָוֹן or אָוֶן.

SEMANTIC DOMAIN ANALYSIS

233

The following example (example 2.33, §2.3.2) is more difficult. An element more specific than HUMAN(אָמָה)[26] was not ultimately identified.

4.17. Exodus 21:7a, 8a, c

וְכִי־יִמְכֹּר אִישׁ אֶת־בִּתּוֹ לְאָמָה {...}
אִם־רָעָה בְּעֵינֵי אֲדֹנֶיהָ אֲשֶׁר־לֹא יְעָדָהּ {...} לְמָכְרָהּ בְּבִגְדוֹ־בָהּ

If a man sells his daughter as a female slave {...} if [she is] bad in the eyes of her lord so that he has not designated her, {...} he has behaved treacherously with her.

It was suggested that the element may be anything applicable to an אָמָה (female slave). This would necessarily include HUMAN(BEHAVIOUR), but is wider than that. Therefore, this example may be superordinate to use within the רָשַׁע subdomain, partially overlapping with it.[27] This use may indicate that different combinative uses of רַע+HUMAN may be considered together in a single domain of HUMAN(ANY-רַע).[28]

4.4 MAJOR DOMAIN 1: אָוֶן SUBDOMAIN

The אָוֶן subdomain is less frequent than both רָשַׁע and עָוֹן. It shows disproportionately low representation in the Mishnah, with words (other than רַע) identified as within or on the periphery of this subdomain occurring just 23 times.[29] I begin by examining the subdomain with a focus on אָוֶן (§4.4.1). After drawing preliminary conclusions about the subdomain (§4.4.2), I move on to examine the operation of רַע in the אָוֶן subdomain (§4.4.3).

4.4.1 Analysis of אָוֶן (with a focus on אָוֶן)

An examination of אָוֶן quickly demonstrates the subdomain revolves around the concept of DECEIT. In many uses of אָוֶן, it is construed as an

---

[26] I.e. Anything applicable to an אָמָה (female slave).

[27] We may *speculate* that if the אָמָה was actually רָשַׁע, the behaviour of the אָדוֹן (master) in this text might not be considered בֶּגֶד (treacherous). Regardless, this use does still suggest a general use of רַע+HUMAN.

[28] For example 4.17 this would be, more specifically, אָמָה(ANY-רַע). This may be an ad hoc domain. People can create what Barsalou terms *ad hoc categories* in order to achieve specific goals. These may include categories (or domains) such as THINGS TO SELL AT A GARAGE SALE or PLACES TO LOOK FOR AN ANTIQUE DESK. Such categories are "not well established in memory," but display prototypicality structures in the same way as entrenched categories such as FRUIT and FURNITURE. Lawrence W. Barsalou, "Ad Hoc Categories," *Memory & Cognition* 11 (1983): 1.

[29] See §3.5.1. Terms within: אָוֶן; חָמָס; מִרְמָה; עָמָל; שָׁוְא; שֶׁקֶר. Terms on periphery: כָּזָב; עַוְלָה; שֹׁד. דָּם was not considered to be within the domain because of its similarly frequent links with other domains.

234   CHAPTER 4

ACT. However, there are some uses where it is construed as an EVENT.
Additionally, אָוֶן appears to be used to refer to PUNISHMENT for doing אָוֶן
(punishment in kind; and may also have been used of GUILT incurred for
doing אָוֶן. אָוֶן can also be construed as a STATE, and has been considered
linked to NOTHINGNESS. Each area will be examined in turn.

אָוֶן, *DECEIT, and SPEECH*

The link between this domain and DECEIT can be illustrated with reference to each of the terms within and on the periphery of the domain (examples 4.18–4.23). Terms which indicate a link with SPEECH are identified
in orange. While SPEECH is not always a feature of the use of these terms,
it helps identify the link with DECEIT. At times the discourse indicates the
NEGATIVE result (or intent) of the DECEIT is to harm. Words which indicate this link are identified in purple. This colour scheme will be retained
throughout §4.4.

4.18.   אָוֶן, שֶׁקֶר, and שָׁוְא (Zech 10:2)

כִּי הַתְּרָפִים דִּבְּרוּ־אָוֶן וְהַקּוֹסְמִים חָזוּ שֶׁקֶר וַחֲלֹמוֹת הַשָּׁוְא יְדַבֵּרוּ הֶבֶל יְנַחֵמוּן
עַל־כֵּן נָסְעוּ כְמוֹ־צֹאן יַעֲנוּ כִּי־אֵין רֹעֶה

For the teraphim have spoken villainy, and the diviners have seen a lie,
and the dreams of worthlessness they speak will comfort vainly. Therefore, they wander like sheep, they are afflicted because there is no
shepherd.

4.19.   שֶׁקֶר and חָמָס (Deut 19:16, 18–19)[30]

כִּי־יָקוּם עֵד־חָמָס בְּאִישׁ לַעֲנוֹת בּוֹ סָרָה {...}
וְדָרְשׁוּ הַשֹּׁפְטִים הֵיטֵב וְהִנֵּה עֵד־שֶׁקֶר הָעֵד שֶׁקֶר עָנָה בְאָחִיו
וַעֲשִׂיתֶם לוֹ כַּאֲשֶׁר זָמַם לַעֲשׂוֹת לְאָחִיו וּבִעַרְתָּ הָרָע מִקִּרְבֶּךָ

If a violent witness arises against a man to testify against him rebel-
liously, {...} The judges will seek well, and behold, the witness is a lying
witness. He testified falsely against his brother. You shall do to him as
he planned to do to his brother. You shall purge the bad from your midst.

4.20.   עָמָל and שֹׁד (Prov 24:1–2)

אַל־תְּקַנֵּא בְּאַנְשֵׁי רָעָה וְאַל־תִּתְאָו לִהְיוֹת אִתָּם
כִּי־שֹׁד יֶהְגֶּה לִבָּם וְעָמָל שִׂפְתֵיהֶם תְּדַבֵּרְנָה

Do not be jealous about men of evil. Do not desire to be with them.
Because their heart mutters destruction, and their lips speak trouble.

---

[30] Although this example does not demonstrate חָמָס as the object of a verb of SPEECH, it is
still closely associated with SPEECH. See also Psalm 27:12.

SEMANTIC DOMAIN ANALYSIS

235

4.21. מִרְמָה (Ps 50:19–20)

פִּיךָ שָׁלַחְתָּ בְרָעָה וּלְשׁוֹנְךָ תַּצְמִיד מִרְמָה
תֵּשֵׁב בְּאָחִיךָ תְדַבֵּר בְּבֶן־אִמְּךָ תִּתֶּן־דֹּפִי

You send your mouth with evil, and your tongue frames deceit. You turn [and] speak against your brother, you set slander on the son of your mother.

4.22. שָׁוְא and כָּזָב (Ezek 13:7)

הֲלוֹא מַחֲזֵה־שָׁוְא חֲזִיתֶם וּמִקְסַם כָּזָב אֲמַרְתֶּם וְאֹמְרִים נְאֻם־יְהוָה וַאֲנִי לֹא דִבַּרְתִּי

Have you not seen a vision of worthlessness and do you not speak a divination of falsehood, saying "declares the LORD"? But I have not spoken.

4.23. שֶׁקֶר, עַוְלָה, and שָׁוְא (Isa 59:3b–4)

שִׂפְתוֹתֵיכֶם דִּבְּרוּ־שֶׁקֶר לְשׁוֹנְכֶם עַוְלָה תֶהְגֶּה
אֵין־קֹרֵא בְצֶדֶק וְאֵין נִשְׁפָּט בֶּאֱמוּנָה בָּטוֹחַ עַל־תֹּהוּ וְדַבֶּר־שָׁוְא הָרוֹ עָמָל וְהוֹלֵיד אָוֶן

Your lips speak a lie, your tongue mutters injustice. No one speaks out righteously. No one enters a case faithfully. [They] trust in emptiness, they speak worthlessness, they conceive trouble and father villainy.

As these examples show, all terms within the אָוֶן subdomain are tied with DECEIT and SPEECH. However, they also demonstrate that the result or intent of such speech is considered harmful. In example 4.23, we also see that the אָוֶן subdomain can, itself, be used to describe ACTS that arise from such SPEECH. This highlights a common use of the subdomain and leads in to considering the use of אָוֶן as ACT.

AS ACT

As a NEGATIVE ACT, אָוֶן is something which is usually directed against humans.[31] Example 4.24 demonstrates some of the actions which may be described as אָוֶן.

4.24. Micah 2:1–2

הוֹי חֹשְׁבֵי־אָוֶן וּפֹעֲלֵי רָע עַל־מִשְׁכְּבוֹתָם בְּאוֹר הַבֹּקֶר יַעֲשׂוּהָ כִּי יֶשׁ־לְאֵל יָדָם
וְחָמְדוּ שָׂדוֹת וְגָזָלוּ וּבָתִּים וְנָשָׂאוּ וְעָשְׁקוּ גֶּבֶר וּבֵיתוֹ וְאִישׁ וְנַחֲלָתוֹ

---

[31] It is sometimes used in ways that suggest an attempt to deceive the divine (e.g. Isa 1:13). This finding suggests that while anti-human behaviour is generally what is occurring, it is not the focus of this domain. This may be contrary to the findings of van Steenbergen in his worldview analysis. His findings for Isaiah suggest the distinction between עָמָל and אָוֶן relates to HUMAN–DIVINE versus HUMAN–HUMAN action. See van Steenbergen, *Semantics, World View and Bible Translation*, 42, 59–72, 157.

236 CHAPTER 4

> Woe to those who plan villainy and do bad upon their beds! In the
> light of the morning they do it, because it is in the power of their
> hand. They covet fields and seize [them], and houses and take [them].
> They oppress a man and his house, and a man and his inheritance.

To do אָוֶן is clearly more than just to deceive someone. The person who
does אָוֶן perpetrates unjust acts. However, the act of DECEIT in SPEECH
should not be separated too firmly from the ACTS listed in example 4.24.
Example 4.19, in reference to false testimony, demonstrated that SPEECH
itself may be the אָוֶן thing. It may be helpful to think of this in terms
of SPEECH ACTS. That is, אָוֶן SPEECH is speech which does something
harmful.

There are two features that stand out in the use of אָוֶן as an ACT. Both
are present in example 4.24. The first is its use in a construct phrase referring to a HUMAN who does אָוֶן (coloured according to the רָשָׁע domain).
The second is its use with reference to PLANNING/PREMEDITATION (coloured
pink). This second shows distinct links with SPEECH.

As ACT: construct HUMAN use

In 34 of the 83 occurrences of אָוֶן (40%) it occurs in a construct HUMAN
use.[32] In such use, it commonly occurs in semantic parallel with רָשָׁע
(9 times) and other רָשָׁע terms (7 times). The most common phrase is
פֹּעֲלֵי אָוֶן (doers of villainy) occurring 23 times. This use can be seen in
example 4.25.

> 4.25. Psalm 28:3–4a
>
> אַל־תִּמְשְׁכֵנִי עִם־רְשָׁעִים וְעִם־פֹּעֲלֵי אָוֶן דֹּבְרֵי שָׁלוֹם עִם־רֵעֵיהֶם וְרָעָה בִּלְבָבָם
> תֶּן־לָהֶם כְּפָעֳלָם וּכְרֹעַ מַעַלְלֵיהֶם
>
> Do not drag me away with the wicked and with doers of villainy, those
> who speak peace with their neighbours, but evil is in their heart. Give
> to them according to their deed, and according to the corruption of
> their deeds…

In this example, we see the wicked in a close semantic parallel with פֹּעֲלֵי
אָוֶן (doers of villainy). This particular group is further qualified as being
deceitful – speaking peace while planning otherwise. Verse 4 makes it clear
that this is more than talk; it involves acts deserving judgement.

---

[32] This use seems most common with אָוֶן, but can be seen with other terms to varying
degrees. For example: חָמָס (Ps 11:5); שֶׁקֶר (Ps 101:7–8). עָמָל and עַוְלָה do not occur
in direct association with רָשָׁע, but do occur in the construct HUMAN use (e.g. Ps 94:20;
2 Sam 7:10). מִרְמָה only once occurs with רָשָׁע and the construct HUMAN use is less
clear than with other terms (Ps 109:2).

SEMANTIC DOMAIN ANALYSIS

As ACT: PREMEDITATION and SPEECH

There is a strong link between אָוֶן and plans. It often occurs in uses that refer to SPEECH and imply PREMEDITATION. However, it appears most clearly in connection with the noun מַחֲשָׁבָה (plan) or verb חָשַׁב (to plan). אָוֶן occurs with at least one of these terms 10 times (12% of occurrences).[33] Example 4.26 demonstrates use with terms of SPEECH and חָשַׁב. Example 4.27 demonstrates use with מַחֲשָׁבָה.

> 4.26. Psalm 36:4–5
>
> דִּבְרֵי־פִיו אָוֶן וּמִרְמָה חָדַל לְהַשְׂכִּיל לְהֵיטִיב
> אָוֶן ׀ יַחְשֹׁב עַל־מִשְׁכָּבוֹ יִתְיַצֵּב עַל־דֶּרֶךְ לֹא־טוֹב רָע לֹא יִמְאָס
>
> The words of his mouth are villainy and deceit, he has ceased acting wisely and doing good. He plans villainy on his bed, he takes his stand in a not-good way, he does not reject bad.

In this example, the first use of אָוֶן is connected to speech terms דָּבָר (word) and פֶּה (mouth). This is expressed in ceasing to act wisely or do good. The second use of אָוֶן is connected with חָשַׁב, being explicitly described as something PLANNED. רַע refers to NEGATIVE BEHAVIOUR. This is clear through the parallel דֶּרֶךְ לֹא־טוֹב ‖ רַע. This example links the אָוֶן subdomain with SPEECH, PLANNING and IMPLEMENTATION of NEGATIVE ACTS.

> 4.27. Isaiah 55:7
>
> יַעֲזֹב רָשָׁע דַּרְכּוֹ וְאִישׁ אָוֶן מַחְשְׁבֹתָיו וְיָשֹׁב אֶל־יְהוָה וִירַחֲמֵהוּ
>
> Let the wicked forsake his way, and the man of villainy his plans. Let him turn to the LORD, that he may show him mercy…

This example illustrates both the link between רָשָׁע and אָוֶן through the construct HUMAN use, and the connection between אָוֶן and PLANNING.[34] In this example, the רָשָׁע is construed as one who *behaves* a certain way, and the אִישׁ אָוֶן as one who *plans*. They act in a manner that is worthy of judgement and are so called to turn to the Lord (the judge) for mercy.[35]

---

[33] Isaiah 55:7; 59:7; Jeremiah 4:14; Ezekiel 11:2; Micah 2:1; Psalm 36:5; Job 22:15; Proverbs 6:12, 18; 4Q174 1–2 I, 9.

[34] Van Steenbergen also notes the importance of this connection with planning, van Steenbergen, *Semantics, World View and Bible Translation*, 137.

[35] The logic of the passage appears to be that God is greater in glory, with the glory term פאר appearing in verse 5 and the conceptual metaphor of GLORY IS HEIGHT appearing in verse 9. Burton has demonstrated that the GLORY IS HEIGHT metaphor is a subset of POWER IS HEIGHT. Therefore, if this analysis is correct, the verse makes a plea to the wicked (and man of villainy) to turn from their behaviour and plans because they are

238   CHAPTER 4

This may suggest that even as the construct HUMAN use presents the person who does אָוֶן as someone who *behaves* a certain way, PREMEDITATION is still implied. Consider example 4.28:

> 4.28. Job 22:15
>
> הַאֹרַח עוֹלָם תִּשְׁמֹר אֲשֶׁר דָּרְכוּ מְתֵי־אָוֶן
>
> Will you keep the way of old which men of villainy have trod?

In this example, PREMEDITATION is not explicit. The construction refers to people characterised by an ACT. However, the type of ACT could comfortably be taken as referring to that which is PREMEDITATED. Regardless of how we explain this, example 4.28 does caution against seeing a hard division between רֶשַׁע and אָוֶן in the construct HUMAN use (cf. example 4.13 §4.3.3). If BEHAVIOUR is profiled by one and PREMEDITATION by the other, there is overlap.

As EVENT

The EVENT use can be seen in example 4.29.

> 4.29. Psalm 55:4
>
> מִקּוֹל אוֹיֵב מִפְּנֵי עָקַת רָשָׁע כִּי־יָמִיטוּ עָלַי אָוֶן וּבְאַף יִשְׂטְמוּנִי
>
> …because of the voice of the enemy, because of the oppression of the wicked, for they drop[36] villainy on me, and in anger they harass me.

In this example, אָוֶן is clearly construed as something that happens to someone: an EVENT. However, there is an ACTOR (the wicked) which brings the EVENT to pass. This use is likely poetic, construing what is essentially an ACT as an EVENT through verb selection.[37] Further uses of אָוֶן as an EVENT are discussed in the following sections.

---

    not what God approves of (verse 8) and because God is all powerful (verse 9), being much higher in glory. Marilyn E. Burton, "Glory in the Heights and the Deep: Some Implications of Semantic Analysis for a Biblical Theology of Glory," in *From Words to Meaning: Studies in OT Language and Theology*, ed. Samuel Hildebrandt, Kurtis Peters and Eric Ortlund (Sheffield: Sheffield Phoenix, forthcoming).

[36] This verb has caused some discussion. However, the text as it stands is understandable and so the meaning "cause to move" (i.e. drop) seems appropriate. Marvin E. Tate, *Psalms 51–100*, WBC 20 (Waco, TX: Word, 1990), 51–52.

[37] This is supported in Tate's translation (although he neglects to comment specifically on this). Tate, *Psalms 51–100*, 50. Dahood translates it with a specific term "invective." Mitchell Dahood, *Psalms II: 51–100*, AB 17 (Garden City, NY: Doubleday, 1968), 32.

SEMANTIC DOMAIN ANALYSIS

MISFORTUNE or PUNISHMENT?

A commonly accepted sense of אָוֶן is MISFORTUNE.[38] Proverbs 22:8 (example 4.30) is considered to be an example of such a use.

4.30. Proverbs 22:8

זוֹרֵעַ עַוְלָה יִקְצָור־אָוֶן וְשֵׁבֶט עֶבְרָתוֹ יִכְלֶה

The sower of injustice will reap villainy and the rod of his wrath will be finished.

On the face of it, this example appears to support such an interpretation. אָוֶן appears to be simply a NEGATIVE EVENT which occurs to the sower of injustice.[39] However, the worldview of the text has the Lord in ultimate control.[40] Just four verses later we read:

4.31. Proverbs 22:12

עֵינֵי יְהוָה נָצְרוּ דָעַת וַיְסַלֵּף דִּבְרֵי בֹגֵד

The eyes of the LORD observe knowledge and he subverts words of a traitor.

In example 4.30, the Lord is understood to cause the sower of עַוְלָה to reap אָוֶן.[41] The concept we are dealing with is PUNISHMENT: PUNISHMENT IN KIND for certain ACTS. This can be seen through examples 4.32 and 4.33.

4.32. Exodus 21:23–24a (cf. Lev 24:17–22)

וְאִם־אָסוֹן יִהְיֶה וְנָתַתָּה נֶפֶשׁ תַּחַת נָפֶשׁ
עַיִן תַּחַת עַיִן שֵׁן תַּחַת שֵׁן

If there is harm, you shall give life for life, eye for eye, tooth for tooth, …

This passage demonstrates the idea with concrete imagery. However, example 4.33 applies the concept to אָוֶן terminology.

---

[38] So with DCH, BDB (TROUBLE), and Gesenius, but HALOT lists DISASTER. See Clines, "אָוֶן," *DCH* 1:154–55; Francis Brown, S. R. Driver and Charles A. Briggs, "אָוֶן," *BDB* 19; F. W. Gesenius, "אָוֶן," 21; Köhler and Baumgartner, "אָוֶן," *HALOT* 1:22.

[39] So the translation given by Murphy: "calamity." However, he goes on to interpret this as retribution. Murphy, *Proverbs*, 163, 165. Waltke takes this to apply to NOTHINGNESS, but see the discussion of that meaning below (point F). Waltke, *The Book of Proverbs: Chapters 15–31*, 208.

[40] So Waltke comments "This subunit [Prov 22:1–9] teaches that the Lord pays back virtue but punishes vice." Waltke, *The Book of Proverbs: Chapters 15–31*, 198.

[41] The tension between the aphorisms of Proverbs and Job's friends, and Job himself is due to this understanding.

240 CHAPTER 4

4.33. Psalm 94:23a

וַיָּ֤שֶׁב עֲלֵיהֶ֨ם ׀ אֶת־אוֹנָ֗ם וּבְרָעָתָ֥ם יַצְמִיתֵ֑ם

He [the LORD] has turned[42] their villainy upon them, he destroys them
for their evil.

The logic of such a phrase requires that the Lord causes אָוֶן to happen
to the ones who do אָוֶן. This implies that אָוֶן can be understood as PUNISH-
MENT for itself. We see this idea in example 4.34 as well.

4.34. Job 4:8–9

כַּאֲשֶׁ֣ר רָ֭אִיתִי חֹ֣רְשֵׁי אָ֑וֶן וְזֹרְעֵ֖י עָמָ֣ל יִקְצְרֻֽהוּ

מִנִּשְׁמַ֣ת אֱל֣וֹהַ יֹאבֵ֑דוּ וּמֵר֖וּחַ אַפּ֣וֹ יִכְלֽוּ

The plower of villainy and the sower of trouble will reap it. By the
breath of God they perish, and by the blast of his nose they are finished.

This example shows that regardless of what form the אָוֶן which comes
upon doers of אָוֶן takes, it is from God. From these examples, the following
pattern appears: [אָוֶן = PUNISHMENT FOR אָוֶן(ACT)]. This semantic pattern
appears to parallel the widely recognised pattern for עָוֹן (§4.5). Seeing
the use of אָוֶן in such a way allows us to approach the following text in a
more nuanced way.[43]

4.35. Jeremiah 4:6, 14–16

שְׂאוּ־נֵ֣ס צִיּ֗וֹנָה הָעִ֙יזוּ֙ אַֽל־תַּעֲמֹ֔דוּ כִּ֣י רָעָ֗ה אָנֹכִ֛י מֵבִ֥יא מִצָּפ֖וֹן וְשֶׁ֥בֶר גָּדֽוֹל {...}

כַּבְּסִ֤י מֵרָעָה֙ לִבֵּךְ֙ יְר֣וּשָׁלִַ֔ם לְמַ֖עַן תִּוָּשֵׁ֑עִי עַד־מָתַ֛י תָּלִ֥ין בְּקִרְבֵּ֖ךְ מַחְשְׁב֥וֹת אוֹנֵֽךְ[44]

כִּ֛י ק֥וֹל מַגִּ֖יד מִדָּ֑ן וּמַשְׁמִ֥יעַ אָ֖וֶן מֵהַ֥ר אֶפְרָֽיִם

הַזְכִּ֣ירוּ לַגּוֹיִ֗ם הִנֵּה֙ הַשְׁמִ֣יעוּ עַל־יְר֣וּשָׁלִַ֔ם נֹצְרִ֥ים בָּאִ֖ים מֵאֶ֣רֶץ הַמֶּרְחָ֑ק וַֽיִּתְּנ֛וּ עַל־עָרֵ֥י יְהוּדָ֖ה קוֹלָֽם

Lift a standard toward Zion. Seek refuge, do not stand, because I am
bringing evil from the North, and great destruction. {...} Wash your
heart from evil, Jerusalem, so that you may be saved. How long will
your plans of villainy lodge within you? For a voice declares from Dan,
and proclaims villainy from Mount Ephraim. Inform to the nations,
behold, proclaim about Jerusalem, besiegers are coming from the distant
land. They set their voice against the cities of Judah.

---

[42] Or read וְיָשֵׁב (he will turn) with the Old Greek's καὶ ἀποδώσει.

[43] Such that it has an extra level not mentioned by Holladay when he says, "If the people
harbour their baneful schemes, then Yahweh has his own bane to bring over the land."
William Lee Holladay, *Jeremiah 1: A Commentary on the Book of the Prophet Jeremiah,
Chapters 1–25*, ed. Paul D. Hanson, Hermeneia (Philadelphia, PA: Fortress, 1986),
158.

[44] On plural abstracts with feminine singular verbs see GKC §145.k.

SEMANTIC DOMAIN ANALYSIS 241

The first use of אָוֶן is the prototypical use seen above. The second use of אָוֶן is more complex. In the mouth of the "voice which declares" (קוֹל מַגִּיד) it refers to the NEGATIVE EVENT of the invasion of Babylon, which is an ACT of אָוֶן (Babylon harming Judah). However, in the mouth of the prophet, it is PUNISHMENT FOR אָוֶן from the Lord (see v.6).[45]

As GUILT

אָוֶן has the semantic pattern ACT/BEHAVIOUR→PUNISHMENT. This pattern is also seen in עָוֹן. However, עָוֹן has the additional pattern ACT/BEHAVIOUR→GUILT. There is one use of אָוֶן which may demonstrate the use [אָוֶן = GUILT FOR אָוֶן(ACT)] pattern if it is accepted as correct.

4.36. 11Q19 XLIII, 15–16

> ואכלוהו בימי המועדים ולוא
> יואכלו ממנו בימי המעשה לאונמה כי קודש הוא
> ובימי הקודש יאכל ולוא יאכל בימי המעשה

> They will eat it [the tithe] on the festival days, but they shall not eat it on days of work because of[46] their villainy, because it is holy. On the holy days it may be eaten, but it may not be eaten on days of work.

In this example, the people's אָוֶן, connected with a work day, contrasts with the holiness of the tithe. As such it appears to refer to a cultic holy–profane distinction. This use is unique in the corpus and may be the result of a scribal error. עָוֹן suits such a cultic context much better, and may have been intended rather than אָוֶן (cf. §4.5.1). However, assuming אָוֶן is correct, it may indicate that אָוֶן could also be used for GUILT. Alternatively, it may indicate semantic bleaching from usage in the עָוֹן domain.

As STATE

אָוֶן is occasionally construed as a STATE. First we will consider example 4.37 from Hosea. Example 4.37 presents an occurrence of אָוֶן used as the predicate in a verbless clause to modify a location.

---

[45] John Calvin has noted the use of אָוֶן to refer to PUNISHMENT here: "The word און, *aun*, does indeed properly signify iniquity [i.e. villainy in the current work]; but it is to be taken here for punishment. But whenever the Prophets use this term, they intimate that evil is not inflicted by God except for just causes; and they remind us that its source or fountain is to be found in the wickedness of men." Where Calvin finds a theological way of explaining the use of this word for punishment, I argue for a linguistic understanding of its use as punishment. John Calvin, *Jeremiah 1–9*, vol. 1 of *Jeremiah & Lamentations*, trans. J. O. Thrussington (Edinburgh: Banner of Truth Trust, 1989), 223.

[46] The ל prefix indicates a causal relationship here. Van der Merwe, Naudé and Kroeze, *A Biblical Hebrew Reference Grammar*, §39.11.6.f.

242 CHAPTER 4

4.37. Hosea 12:12

אִם־גִּלְעָד אָוֶן אַךְ־שָׁוְא הָיוּ

If Gilead is villainy, they are also worthlessness.

It seems likely that this use functions metaphorically, with the key to understanding this use being found in example 4.38 which occurs much earlier in Hosea.[47]

4.38. Hosea 6:8

גִּלְעָד קִרְיַת פֹּעֲלֵי אָוֶן עֲקֻבָּה מִדָּם

Gilead is a town of doers of villainy, tracked with blood.

This example indicates, that in the discourse of the book, the town of Gilead is considered full of people who do אָוֶן. Therefore, in example 4.37, while אָוֶן is being used to describe a STATE in that verse, it refers to the presence of the acts themselves which are carried out by human ACTORS. In this example, אָוֶן as STATE means to be CHARACTERISED BY NEGATIVE ACTS.[48]

The other use of אָוֶן as STATE may be similar. In example 4.39, we see אָוֶן (and עָמָל) used as STATE to describe the best years of the human LIFE.

4.39. Psalm 90:9–10

כִּי כָל־יָמֵינוּ פָּנוּ בְעֶבְרָתֶךָ כִּלִּינוּ שָׁנֵינוּ כְמוֹ־הֶגֶה

יְמֵי־שְׁנוֹתֵינוּ בָהֶם שִׁבְעִים שָׁנָה וְאִם בִּגְבוּרֹת | שְׁמוֹנִים שָׁנָה וְרָהְבָּם עָמָל וָאָוֶן

כִּי־גָז חִישׁ וַנָּעֻפָה

For all our days pass away[49] in your wrath we complete our years as a sigh. The days of our years in themselves[50] are seventy years, or by strength, eighty years, but their pride[51] is trouble and villainy, surely they soon pass and we fly away.

---

[47] Although Stuart sees 12:12 as likely corrupt, he suggests that if correct it "was apparently enough to remind Hosea's audience of the city's bloody reputation (cf. 6:8)." Douglas Stuart, *Hosea–Jonah*, WBC 31 (Waco, TX: Word, 1987), 194.

[48] Macintosh takes it this way, translating it as, "If Gilead was characterised as evil," and comments that, "The phrase is understood to refer to the fuller expression of 6.8." A. A. Macintosh, *A Critical and Exegetical Commentary on Hosea*, ICC (Edinburgh: T&T Clark, 1997), 504.

[49] See Clines, "עֶבְרָה II," *DCH* 6:245.

[50] Following Goldingay who follows Schnocks. John Goldingay, *Psalms 90–150*, vol. 3 of *Psalms*, BCOTWP (Grand Rapids, MI: Baker, 2008), 20. Kraus suggests it should be eliminated due to being a difficult reading. However, this goes against the text critical preference for difficult readings. Hans-Joachim Kraus, *Psalms 60–150*, trans. Hilton C. Oswald, CC (Minneapolis, MN: Fortress, 1993), 213.

[51] Or breadth if the emendation to רֹחַב is accepted. Clines, "רֹחַב 6," *DCH* 7:463. However, breadth seems an unlikely choice to describe a lifetime. Goldingay, *Psalms 90–150*, 20.

SEMANTIC DOMAIN ANALYSIS 243

In this example, the use of אָוֶן is linked to the best years of life,[52] which
the psalmist describes as negative. Should we see it as CHARACTERISED
BY אָוֶן? It seems likely that instead of being characterised by the acts,
it is seen as CHARACTERISED BY PUNISHMENT FOR אָוֶן. This sense of divine
judgement ties in best with the surrounding verses (7–11). In particular,
verse 9 produces another STATE image: "all our days" (כָל־יָמֵינוּ) pass in
(STATE) your wrath (עֶבְרָתֶךָ).

NOTHINGNESS

One final set of examples needs to be mentioned. The ability of אָוֶן to
refer to nothingness or emptiness is often mentioned.[53] The primary passages that appear to convey this idea both occur in Isaiah (examples 4.40
and 4.42).

4.40. Isaiah 41:28–29

וְאֵרֶא וְאֵין אִישׁ וּמֵאֵלֶּה וְאֵין יוֹעֵץ וְאֶשְׁאָלֵם וְיָשִׁיבוּ דָבָר
הֵן כֻּלָּם אָוֶן אֶפֶס מַעֲשֵׂיהֶם רוּחַ וָתֹהוּ נִסְכֵּיהֶם

I look, and there is no one, and from among these there is no counsellor, that I might ask them and they would return a word. Behold all of
them are villainy, their works are nothing, their metal images are wind
and formlessness.

This example is a STATE use in reference to idols, which are described
as אָוֶן.[54] Syntactically, this use is comparable to the use in Hosea 12:12

---

[52] Goldingay argues that it should not be seen as referring to LIFE because the OT does not
"refer to eighty years as a long life." Goldingay, *Psalms 90–150*, 30. However, he fails
to take account of Barzillai in 2 Samuel 19:33 being referred to as eighty and זָקֵן מְאֹד
(very old).

[53] For example Karl-Heinz Bernhardt, "אָוֶן," *TDOT* 1:142; R. Knierim, "אָוֶן," *TLOT* 1:62;
Eugene Carpenter and Michael A. Grisanti, "אָוֶן," *NIDOTTE* 1:308.

[54] Note the textual difficulties in this text: In 1QIsaᵃ XXXV, 8 it reads אַיִן (nothing) in
place of אָוֶן. The translators of the Syriac and Targum Jonathan read "nothing," either
supporting the use of אַיִן or understanding אָוֶן to be able to mean nothing. Baltzer stands
apart as a commentator unwilling to emend אָוֶן to אַיִן. Baltzer argues that "The well-
versed reader knows that Hosea, for example, replaces the word אֵל ('God') in the name
of the sanctuary Beth-El ('house of God') by אָוֶן ('iniquity'). Here DtIsa's proof that
the other gods are no gods at all culminates in the assertion that they are 'iniquity.'"
Klaus Baltzer, *Deutero-Isaiah: A Commentary on Isaiah 40–55*, ed. Peter Machinist,
trans. Margaret Kohl, Hermeneia (Minneapolis, MN: Fortress, 2001), 122. The one use
of אָוֶן in Ben Sira occurs in corrections to the B manuscript of Ben Sira 41:10 (B 11r2).
This could represent a use of אָוֶן to mean NOTHING. However, it is hard to know how
much weight to give this reading. While it may represent a variant, it has multiple corrections. It is also possible it connects more directly to the ACT/BEHAVIOUR→PUNISHMENT
pattern. כל מאפס אל אפס <מאונם א' אונם> <כל מאונים אל אונים> ישוב [ ] כן <בן> חנף

244 CHAPTER 4

(example 4.37). In example 4.37, it was suggested that Gilead was meta-phorically described as being in a STATE of אָוֶן, referring to the occurrence of such acts. So it is here. However, the acts should be seen as those of DECEITFUL SPEECH: the emphasis of the discourse is on the inability of the idols to tell what is to happen (Isa 41:22–23, 25–28). They are unable to inform accurately because they have no power (Isa 41:23).[55]

Thus example 4.40 appears to be saying that the answers people receive when they seek information from the idols are false, they are DECEIT.[56] Support for this interpretation can be found in the following passage.

4.41. Zechariah 10:1–2a

שַׁאֲלוּ מֵיהוָה מָטָר בְּעֵת מַלְקוֹשׁ יְהוָה עֹשֶׂה חֲזִיזִים וּמְטַר־גֶּשֶׁם יִתֵּן לָהֶם לְאִישׁ עֵשֶׂב בַּשָּׂדֶה

כִּי הַתְּרָפִים דִּבְּרוּ־אָוֶן וְהַקּוֹסְמִים חָזוּ שֶׁקֶר וַחֲלֹמוֹת הַשָּׁוְא יְדַבֵּרוּ הֶבֶל יְנַחֵמוּן עַל־כֵּן נָסְעוּ כְמוֹ־צֹאן יַעֲנוּ כִּי־אֵין רֹעֶה

Ask rain from the LORD in the time of the latter rain, the LORD, maker of thunderbolts, and he will give rain showers to them, to each[57] plant in the field. For the teraphim have spoken villainy, and the diviners have seen a lie, and the dreams of worthlessness they speak will comfort vainly. Therefore, they wander like sheep, they are afflicted because there is no shepherd.

In example 4.41, the teraphim (the cult objects consulted by the diviners)[58] speak falsely. Here is a strong link between אָוֶן and SPEECH. This SPEECH contrasts with what the Lord has to offer, because he has power to put it

מתהו אל תהו – Corrector: All [that is] from their villainy [or villainies] is to their villainy [or villainies], so the godless [come] from emptiness to emptiness. Unfortunately Skehan and DiLella fail to comment on this reading. Skehan and Di Lella, *The Wisdom of Ben Sira*, 468.

[55] It might also be suggested that אָוֶן here is being construed similarly to example 4.39, as referring to PUNISHMENT. If this is the case, van Steenbergen's argument that it refers to the disastrous consequences of such behaviour may be correct. This reading seems unlikely, as it requires one to read "All of them are villainy" as "All of them lead to God bringing אָוֶן (i.e. punishment)." This reading thus requires a move beyond that of example 4.39, with the people, not the idols (the grammatical subject) having the true STATE of אָוֶן. Van Steenbergen, *Semantics, World View and Bible Translation*, 137.

[56] This is also how שֶׁקֶר is used in Jeremiah 10:14 and 51:17.

[57] אִישׁ is occasionally used distributively of inanimate things. Clines, "אִישׁ I 1c," *DCH* 1:222.

[58] Teraphim have been taken to refer to household gods. However, this link is questionable. Nevertheless, the link with consultation is undeniable. Van der Toorn makes the argument for seeing them as household gods. Flynn disputes this. Boda notes that "the teraphim is the cult object, while diviners are the cult personnel trained to use the teraphim." See Karel van der Toorn, "The Nature of the Biblical Teraphim in the Light of the Cuneiform Evidence," *CBQ* 52 (1990): 203–22; Shawn W. Flynn, "The Teraphim in Light of Mesopotamian and Egyptian Evidence," *CBQ* 74 (2012): 694–711; Mark J. Boda, *The Book of Zechariah*, NICOT (Grand Rapids, MI: Eerdmans, 2016), 602–3.

SEMANTIC DOMAIN ANALYSIS   245

into action (cf. Zech 9:9–17). So the people are called to ask from the Lord
rather than those who have no power to achieve what they say will happen,
and whose answers are, therefore, DECEIT. Both examples 4.40 and 4.41
function in the same way: idols and teraphim can only give deceitful
answers due to their lack of real power.

> 4.42. Isaiah 66:3b
>
> מַזְכִּיר לְבֹנָה מְבָרֵךְ אָוֶן גַּם־הֵמָּה בָּחֲרוּ בְּדַרְכֵיהֶם וּבְשִׁקּוּצֵיהֶם נַפְשָׁם חָפֵצָה
>
> The one who makes a remembrance offering of frankincense is one who
> blesses villainy. They have themselves chosen their ways, and their
> soul delights in their abominations.

Example 4.42 is the last in a series of metaphors describing the unacceptable nature of the offerings being presented to the Lord. This passage
has been taken to refer to an idol.[59] Carpenter and Grisanti suggest that
this implies worshipping an idol.[60] However, rather than identifying אָוֶן
directly with idols, we should consider the possibility that this use is dysphemistic.[61] That is, it uses intentionally offensive language, calling the
idols אָוֶן because their counsel is אָוֶן due to their lack of power (as in
example 4.40).[62] Such dysphemistic use is exactly what we see in Hosea,
where the prophet calls בֵּית־אֵל (Beth-El; house of God) בֵּית־אָוֶן (house
of villainy).[63]

4.4.2 Preliminary Conclusion

Across the אָוֶן subdomain, words are regularly construed as DECEITFUL
SPEECH, such SPEECH has the effect of harming another. Additionally, אָוֶן
words are used to describe ACTS that arise from אָוֶן SPEECH. The SPEECH

---

[59] Although Oswalt accepts the translation "iniquity" he then equates it with an idol. John
Oswalt, *The Book of Isaiah. Chapters 40–66*, NICOT (Grand Rapids, MI: Eerdmans,
1998), 669. In contrast, Watts translates this as "idol," but describes it in terms of "van-
ity" (i.e. nothingness). John D. W. Watts, *Isaiah 34–66*, WBC 25 (Waco, TX: Word,
1987), 350, 356.

[60] Carpenter and Grisanti, אָוֶן, 308.

[61] "A dysphemism is an expression with connotations that are offensive either about the
denotatum or the audience, or both." Allan and Burridge, *Euphemism & Dysphemism*,
221.

[62] Blenkinsopp favours taking this as dysphemism: "We are now told that those who rou-
tinely carry out this pleasing ceremony in honor of YHVH are also involved in rituals
of a quite different nature involving the recital of blessings over another deity, using
the dysphemism *āven*, "harm," "mischief," but also "idol" (1 Sam 15:23; Hos 10:8;
Zech 10:2)." Joseph Blenkinsopp, *Isaiah 56–66: A New Translation with Introduction
and Commentary*, AB 19B (New York: Doubleday, 2003), 298.

[63] Hosea 4:15; 5:8; 10:5.

246   CHAPTER 4

itself may be considered an ACT, particularly in reference to legal matters. אָוֶן often refers to NEGATIVE ACTS which harm other humans. The link with DECEIT is such that אָוֶן ACTS should generally be understood as the product of DECEIT; that is, אָוֶן connotes DECEIT. ACTS are often presented as PREMEDITATED.

Contrary to previous descriptions of אָוֶן, it does not appear to have a polyseme referring to MISFORTUNE,[64] but instead it follows the semantic pattern ACT/BEHAVIOUR→PUNISHMENT.[65] In some cases, אָוֶן is construed as an EVENT or even a STATE. In EVENT and STATE uses, the meaning is derived from ACT uses and can be understood through discourse indicators. אָוֶן has been argued to refer to NOTHINGNESS. However, uses taken to refer to NOTHINGNESS are better understood as relying on the core domain meaning of DECEIT.

4.4.3 רַע as Part of אָוֶן

Having partially considered how the אָוֶן subdomain functions, we now turn to the use of רַע within the subdomain. We begin with some straightforward uses where core relationships are clear.

4.43. Psalm 34:14–15

נְצֹר לְשׁוֹנְךָ מֵרָע וּשְׂפָתֶיךָ מִדַּבֵּר מִרְמָה
סוּר מֵרָע וַעֲשֵׂה־טוֹב בַּקֵּשׁ שָׁלוֹם וְרָדְפֵהוּ

Keep your tongue from bad, and your lips from speaking deceit. Turn from bad, do good, seek peace and pursue it.

The modified element in the first instance of רַע is SPEECH. In this use it is tied to DECEIT. Example 4.43 continues with description of action similar to what was seen with אָוֶן in example 4.26 (§4.4.1), thus demonstrating the use of רַע as PREMEDITATED ACT, spoken and done. The sense of planning comes through more clearly in the next example with the use of חָשַׁב (to plan) in the discourse.

---

[64] The extent that this applies to the whole אָוֶן subdomain awaits further analysis. עָמָל at least appears to be used for the toil of work and the gain from such toil. However, according to Clines ("עָמָל 3a–b," *DCH* 6:482), in such use it appears almost entirely in Ecclesiastes which uses its own unique language. Samet has effectively argued for the language of Ecclesiastes to be considered its own system. As such it should be considered a philosophical sublanguage. Nili Samet, "Qohelet's Idiolect: The Language of a Jew in a Changing World," (paper presented at the Starr Seminar, Harvard University, 2018); Foster, "Is Everything 'Beautiful' or 'Appropriate' in Its Time?," 43.

[65] It is also possible the pattern ACT/BEHAVIOUR→GUILT exists, as with עָוֹן (§4.5), if the reading in 11Q19 XLIII, 15–16 is accepted as correct and representative of a real, but rare, use.

SEMANTIC DOMAIN ANALYSIS

4.44. Psalm 52:4–6

הַוּוֹת תַּחְשֹׁב לְשׁוֹנֶךָ כְּתַעַר מְלֻטָּשׁ עֹשֵׂה רְמִיָּה

אָהַבְתָּ רָּע מִטּוֹב שֶׁקֶר | מִדַּבֵּר צֶדֶק סֶלָה

אָהַבְתָּ כָל־דִּבְרֵי־בָלַע לְשׁוֹן מִרְמָה

Your tongue plans destructions, like a sharpened razor, doer of treachery. You love bad more than good, a lie more than speaking righteousness. Selah. You love all devouring words, O tongue of deceit.

In this example, the parallel רַע :: רַע ‖ טוֹב :: שֶׁקֶר :: צֶדֶק links רַע with SPEECH.
Furthermore, the link between NEGATIVE SPEECH and NEGATIVE ACT is
apparent here. So we have הַוּוֹת (destructions) in verse 4 and כָל־דִּבְרֵי־בָלַע
(all devouring words) in verse 6. Thus the NEGATIVE SPEECH implies the
process of planning and implementing a NEGATIVE ACT.

The following two examples show associations with the subdomain
while containing less information to specify what is in view. Given the
association between אָוֶן and DECEIT it should be considered to be implied
in these examples.

4.45. Habbakuk 1:13

טְהוֹר עֵינַיִם מֵרְאוֹת רָע וְהַבִּיט אֶל־עָמָל לֹא תוּכָל לָמָּה תַבִּיט בּוֹגְדִים תַּחֲרִישׁ
בְּבַלַּע רָשָׁע צַדִּיק מִמֶּנּוּ

[You who have] eyes too pure to see bad, and you [who] are not able
to look on trouble, why do you look on the treacherous, [and] keep
silent when the wicked swallows one more righteous than he?

This example presents the Lord as a just judge who cannot allow certain
acts to continue. Thus, רַע may be seen as modifying ACT here. The ACTS
are described at the end of the verse: the רָשָׁע harming the צַדִּיק (righteous).
The verse appears to describe a process of ACTING to achieve an unjust
outcome, and so the connotation of PREMEDITATED is relevant here.

4.46. Jonah 3:8

וְיִתְכַּסּוּ שַׂקִּים הָאָדָם וְהַבְּהֵמָה וְיִקְרְאוּ אֶל־אֱלֹהִים בְּחָזְקָה וְיָשֻׁבוּ אִישׁ מִדַּרְכּוֹ
הָרָעָה וּמִן־הֶחָמָס אֲשֶׁר בְּכַפֵּיהֶם

Let them cover themselves in sackcloth, both humans and livestock
and cry out to God forcefully. Let them turn each from his bad way
and from the violence which is in their hands.

In this example רַע modifies BEHAVIOUR.[66] It is associated here with
חָמָס (violence), but there is little detail in the discourse to illuminate what

---

[66] For more examples of דֶּרֶךְ used with רַע see §2.3.5.

248 CHAPTER 4

sort of ACTS are in view. However, aspects of the domain which are not explicitly ruled out may be relevant. Thus we may consider this to refer to the presence of behaviours which include: bearing false witness; unjust legal action; and deceitful behaviour. Such behaviours generally end in the oppression of those lacking power (e.g. Mic 2:1–2, example 4.24 §4.4.1).

Difficult Uses

There are a number of associations for which the meaning is more difficult to determine. In example 4.47, it appears that planning is indicated by the use of חָשַׁב (to plan). However, on examination, another interpretation is apparent.

4.47. Ezekiel 11:2–3

וַיֹּאמֶר אֵלַי בֶּן־אָדָם אֵלֶּה הָאֲנָשִׁים הַחֹשְׁבִים אָוֶן וְהַיֹּעֲצִים עֲצַת־רָע בָּעִיר הַזֹּאת
הָאֹמְרִים לֹא בְקָרוֹב בְּנוֹת בָּתִּים הִיא הַסִּיר וַאֲנַחְנוּ הַבָּשָׂר

He said to me, "Son of man, these are the men who plan villainy and counsel counsel of bad in this city. The ones who say 'It [i.e. the time][67] is not near to build houses. It [i.e. the city] is the pot and we are the flesh.'"

In the discourse, the Lord is showing the prophet Ezekiel the leaders in Jerusalem who are teaching the people that Jerusalem will not fall to the Babylonians. Being the flesh in the pot means being safe from the flames. In this case it means they are saying they will be safe in the city from the Babylonians.[68] It appears that the sense of planning is being overridden by the discourse. They are not so much planning as simply advising. The aspect of אָוֶן that is foregrounded here is the DECEIT. These leaders are producing deceitful counsel in advising the people to remain in the city.[69]

In the following example, רַע is associated with an EVENT use of אָוֶן.

4.48. Proverbs 12:21

לֹא־יְאֻנֶּה לַצַּדִּיק כָּל־אָוֶן וּרְשָׁעִים מָלְאוּ רָע

No villainy happens to the righteous, though[70] the wicked are full of bad.

---

[67] As an adverb of time. Clines, "קָרוֹב 3c," *DCH* 7:321.

[68] John B. Taylor, *Ezekiel: An Introduction and Commentary*, TOTC 22 (Downers Grove, IL: IVP, 1969), 110.

[69] The concurrent prophet, Jeremiah, was urging the people to turn themselves over to the Babylonians (Jer 21:8–10).

[70] Concessive clauses in Hebrew may be marked by the ו followed by the subject. John C. Beckman, "Concessive Clause: Biblical Hebrew," *Encyclopedia of Hebrew Language and Linguistics*.

SEMANTIC DOMAIN ANALYSIS 249

The passive verbal form constructionally removes the ACTOR. Because it is a feature of the passive verb to elide the ACTOR, אָוֶן may still be seen as an EVENT caused by an ACTOR. Conversely, רַע here may refer to a NEGATIVE ACT. Compare the use of מָלֵא (to be full) in example 4.48 with example 4.49.

> 4.49. Micah 6:12

> עֲשִׁירֶיהָ מָלְאוּ חָמָס וְיֹשְׁבֶיהָ דִּבְּרוּ־שָׁקֶר

> Its [the city's] rich ones are **full of** violence, and its dwellers speak a lie.

The parallel structure in this example clearly indicates that to be "full of violence" means to be someone who goes about doing that thing.[71] Therefore, in example 4.48, the proverb appears to be saying that although the wicked go about doing רַע, the righteous are protected from אָוֶן: the wicked do not succeed in their ACTS against the righteous.[72]

Use without אָוֶן

The findings may be applied to certain uses of רַע which appear to contain aspects of the אָוֶן subdomain. Consider the following example:

> 4.50. Psalm 109:20

> זֹאת פְּעֻלַּת שֹׂטְנַי מֵאֵת יְהוֶה וְהַדֹּבְרִים רָע עַל־נַפְשִׁי

> [May] this [curse][73] be the reward for my accusers from the LORD, those who speak bad against my life.

In this example, the speaking of רַע indicates the link with אָוֶן, and the עַל preposition identifies the goal of SPEECH being to harm the psalmist's life: NEGATIVE ACT. The use of רַע here may be identified in connection to the אָוֶן subdomain. This refers not to people who simply say things about the psalmist, but to those who PLAN and ACT to harm the psalmist.

While such application can be fruitful, one must be wary of over-applying findings. Consider the following example which bears similarity to example 4.39 (§4.4.1).

---

[71] Also the wider discourse which consists of a series of accusations (Mic 6:10–12). Waltke writes "'Full of violence,' they abuse the poor and powerless by bending the law to their advantage." Bruce K. Waltke, *A Commentary on Micah* (Grand Rapids, MI: Eerdmans, 2007), 411.

[72] Waltke notes the possibility of this interpretation while preferring to see רַע as referring to "harm." Waltke, *The Book of Proverbs: Chapters 1–15*, 538–39. It may be possible that the proverb intends both interpretations.

[73] "This" refers to a curse (vv. 16–19).

250 CHAPTER 4

4.51. Genesis 47:9b

מְעַט וְרָעִים הָיוּ יְמֵי שְׁנֵי חַיַּי וְלֹא הִשִּׂיגוּ אֶת־יְמֵי שְׁנֵי חַיֵּי אֲבֹתַי בִּימֵי מְגוּרֵיהֶם

The days of the years of my life have been few and bad. They have not reached the days of the years of the lives of my ancestors, in the days of their sojourning.

The main similarity between this example and example 4.39 is the reference to LIFETIME. However, in example 4.39 the context bore implication of PUNISHMENT from God. This example does not. Additionally, it does not appear to bear other features determined to be core to the subdomain such as DECEIT and SPEECH. It seems likely that this use of רַע is outside the אָוֶן subdomain, rather being a negative evaluation of LIFETIME(LENGTH) closer to other uses of רַע with TIME (Appendix A.4) and not associated with the punishment aspect of the אָוֶן subdomain.

4.5 MAJOR DOMAIN 2: עָוֹן

The second major domain is centred around the פֶּשַׁע–חַטָּאת–עָוֹן triad of words. In this section, I begin by analysing the domain with reference to עָוֹן (§4.5.1). After drawing preliminary conclusions about the domain (§4.5.2), I move on to examine the operation of רַע in the עָוֹן domain (§4.5.3).

4.5.1 Analysis of עָוֹן (with a focus on עָוֹן)

The עָוֹן domain appears to relate to infractions against divine rule or an intermediary.[74] Due to the link with divine rule, there are both cultic and non-cultic dimensions.[75] There are broadly three uses of עָוֹן. The primary use appears to be of an ACT or BEHAVIOUR (consisting of certain acts). Building on this use are the senses of GUILT incurred due to the ACT, and PUNISHMENT for the ACT. Some clear uses of the senses ACT/BEHAVIOUR, GUILT, and PUNISHMENT are presented below (a–c).[76] This pattern appears

---

[74] Perhaps simply just against rightful authority; however, it is argued that this is seen as divinely ordained.

[75] The cultic dimension leads to its own semantic developments of words in this domain. Thus we saw, in the semantic association analysis, that חַטָּאת is used to refer to sacrifice for חַטָּאת אַשְׁמָה also appeared in the cultic sense in the Mishnah (see §3.3.3 and §3.3.10). This particular semantic pattern was considered out of scope of the current analysis due to a lack of applicability to the use of רַע

[76] For עָוֹן, this is a pattern recognised in the lexica. BDB, DCH, and HALOT all record all three uses. See Brown, Driver and Briggs, "עָוֹן," *BDB* 730–31; Clines, "עָוֹן," *DCH* 6:307–11; Köhler and Baumgartner, "עָוֹן," *HALOT* 1:800.

SEMANTIC DOMAIN ANALYSIS

251

to be borne out by the עָוֹן–חַטָּאת–פֶּשַׁע triad (b–c). Words identifying the link with infractions against divine rule are in purple. Orange is used to draw attention to example-specific details.

As ACT/BEHAVIOUR

Example 4.52 demonstrates the use referring to an ACT.[77]

4.52. Jeremiah 14:7

אִם־עֲוֺנֵ֙ינוּ֙ עָ֣נוּ בָ֔נוּ יְהֹוָ֕ה עֲשֵׂ֖ה לְמַ֣עַן שְׁמֶ֑ךָ כִּי־רַבּ֣וּ מְשׁוּבֹתֵ֔ינוּ לְךָ֖ חָטָֽאנוּ

Though our iniquities testify against us, LORD, act, for the sake of your name. For our apostasies are many, we have sinned against you.

In this example we can clearly see that עָוֹן is construed as a set of ACTS. This is clear through the parallel with "our apostasies are many." A plurality of ACTS testify rather than an accumulated GUILT. Note the link to infraction of divine rule.

Example 4.53 demonstrates how עָוֹן can refer to BEHAVIOUR:

4.53. 4Q171 1–2 II, 2–4[78]

פשרו על כול השבים
לתורה אשר לוא ימאנו לשוב מרעתם כיא כול הממרים
לשוב מעוונם יכרתו

Its interpretation concerns all those who turn to the Law, who do not refuse to turn from their evil. However, all those who refuse to turn from their iniquity will be cut off.

This example,[79] presents a slight variation of the ACT construal. There are three semantically similar phrases here involving the verb שׁוּב (to turn). The first is "those who turn to the Law." "The Law" is a code of behaviour. One might be considered to do "a law," meaning a single act, but to do "the law" means following the whole code and therefore refers to BEHAVIOUR. This parallel helps us to understand the uses of רָעָה and עָוֹן as similarly referring to a contrary BEHAVIOUR: a pattern that breaches divine law.

The following use of עָוֹן nuances the distinction of understanding of the domain as a breach of divine law to include divinely sanctioned intermediaries. It appears that ACTS against those in divinely-appointed authority are considered as ACTS against the divine.

---

[77] See Isaiah 59:12 for an example with חַטָּאת and פֶּשַׁע. אַשְׁמָה (guilt) has a less frequent ACT use (e.g. Ps 69:6).

[78] A very similar use is seen in Malachi 2:6.

[79] Part of a psalms pesher. This section interprets Psalm 37:8–9a.

250 252 CHAPTER 4

4.54. Ben Sira 10:4–6 (A 3v22–23)

ביד אלהים ממשלת תבל ואיש לעת יעמד עליה
ביד אלהים ממשלת כל גבר ולפני מחוקק ישית הודו
[ב]כל פשע אל תשלֵים רע לריע ואל תהלך בדרך גאוה

The dominion of the world is in the hand of God, and he will establish
a man over it for a time. The dominion of every man is in the hand of
God, and he will place his splendour before the decreed one.
Do not repay bad to a neighbour for any transgression, and do not walk
in the path of pride.

Example 4.54 should be understood as addressing the ruler,[80] a ruler
who is delegated authority by God. God is said to establish this man over
the world. However, the parallel phrase, שִׂית הוֹד לִפְנֵי (to set splendour
before), should be understood as a reference to delegated authority. This
phrase is semantically very similar to the phrase נָתַן הוֹד עַל (set splendour
upon) which Burton has shown refers to the appointment of a legitimate
representative or successor (cf. Num 27:20).[81] Thus פֶּשַׁע, in example 4.54,
refers to action against the divine through the proxy: the divinely appointed
ruler.[82]

---

[80] Skehan and Di Lella, *The Wisdom of Ben Sira*, 224.

[81] The phrase נָתַן הוֹד עַל (set splendour upon) "is used to describe the appointment of one
person as another's representative or successor – the bestowal of glorious authority by
a superior on a subordinate." In 1 Chronicles 29:25, "Solomon is, in a very real sense,
in loco dei, for God has chosen Solomon as *his* king." In Daniel 11:21 we see that not
receiving הוֹד refers to illegitimate rule "strengthening the argument that to set הוֹד upon
someone is in fact to appoint them to a position of authority." Marilyn E. Burton, "'You
Have Bestowed Your Glory upon the Heavens': A Re-Reading of Psalm 8:2b" (paper
presented at the SBL International Meeting, Helsinki, 2018).

[82] This finds support in statements such as in Psalm 2:7b – יְהוָה אָמַר אֵלַי בְּנִי אַתָּה אֲנִי
הַיּוֹם יְלִדְתִּיךָ (The LORD said to me [the anointed king], "You are my son, today I have
fathered you."). This concept is also seen in the anointing of the king by a prophet (e.g.
1 Sam 10:1; 16:12–13; 1 Kgs 1:34). It can even occur for the non-Israelite (1 Kgs 19:15)
because the Lord claims dominion over the whole earth (Sir 10:4–5). It is also indicated
in Deuteronomy 17:12 which refers to the punishment for disobeying the ruling of a priest
or judge in a criminal case. The idea of kingship delegated by the divine was common in
the Ancient Near East. Nili S. Fox, "Kingship and the State in Ancient Israel," in *Behind
the Scenes of the Old Testament: Cultural, Social, and Historical Contexts*, ed. Jonathan
S. Greer, John W. Hilber and John H. Walton (Grand Rapids, MI: Baker, 2018), 475–76.
Clines, "חָטָא," and "פֶּשַׁע," *DCH* 3:198; 6:793, lists five uses of חָטָא and four uses
of פֶּשַׁע against other people. חָטָא: Genesis 31:36; 50:17; Numbers 5:6; 12:11; 1 Samuel 20:1. פֶּשַׁע: Genesis 31:36; 50:17; 1 Samuel 24:12; 25:28. Most may refer to an ACT
against an authority (e.g. ruler or family head) and might be conceived of in terms of delegated divine authority. If Numbers 5:6 (חַטֹּאת הָאָדָם, the sins of the person) is read this
way, it ties it to breaking faith with the Lord, which indicates divine law. 1 Samuel 25:28
may also refer to delegated divine authority, although David is not technically ruler at the
time: כִּי־מִלְחֲמוֹת יְהוָה אֲדֹנִי נִלְחָם (because my lord is fighting the battles of the LORD).

SEMANTIC DOMAIN ANALYSIS 253

As GUILT

The uses of ACT and GUILT in this domain should be seen in terms of continuity of meaning from ACT→GUILT. It is important to remember, that as ACT is not a good translation when עָוֹן is an ACT, GUILT is not necessarily a good translation when referring to the concept GUILT. Therefore examples in this section may appear to connote both GUILT and ACT at times. In example 4.55, עָוֹן is construed as GUILT incurred for an ACT.

> 4.55. 2 Samuel 14:32b
>
> וְעַתָּה אֶרְאֶה פְּנֵי הַמֶּלֶךְ וְאִם־יֶשׁ־בִּי עָוֹן וֶהֱמִתָנִי
>
> Now, let me see the face of the king, and if there is iniquity in me then let him put me to death.

In this example, Absalom requests King David to judge him, and if the king considers him guilty for something that he be put to death. The sense of GUILT fits the construction best here. Absalom is not asking about a specific ACT. The passage concerns his retributive murder of his brother Amnon for raping his sister Tamar (2 Sam 13:32). In this passage Absalom asks the king to judge whether עָוֹן (GUILT) remains in him (cf. Num 15:31); that is, if he is guilty of an ACT against the divinely appointed king (or divine law).[83] The following examples demonstrate the GUILT sense with other עָוֹן words.

> 4.56. אַשְׁמָה (Ezra 9:7a)
>
> מִימֵי אֲבֹתֵינוּ אֲנַחְנוּ בְּאַשְׁמָה גְדֹלָה עַד הַיּוֹם הַזֶּה וּבַעֲוֺנֹתֵינוּ נִתַּנּוּ אֲנַחְנוּ מְלָכֵינוּ כֹהֲנֵינוּ בְּיַד ׀ מַלְכֵי הָאֲרָצוֹת
>
> From the days of our fathers until this day we have been in great guilt. Because of our iniquities we, our kings, [and] our priests have been given into the hand of the kings of the lands…

This example is fairly straightforward. The singular STATE implies a continuity of GUILT. The following clause connects the GUILT (אַשְׁמָה) and the ACTS (עֲוֺנוֹת) to the punishment.

This leaves Genesis 31:36. While this is more difficult, it may be that Jacob is acknowledging the authority of his father-in-law with whose family he has established a strong bond. Matthews and Benjamin, *Social World of Ancient Israel*, 18. There are two uses of the verb חָטָא לְ which may imply the possibility of sinning against someone who is not in authority over the sinner (1 Kgs 8:31 // 2 Chron 6:22; 1 Sam 2:25). However, the Kings // Chronicles use could be seen in light of the comment on Numbers 5:6. 1 Samuel 2:25 could refer to failing an authority.

[83] A similar example is found in 2 Samuel 19:20 where עָוֹן is used to refer to potential GUILT due to cursing the anointed king (2 Sam 19:21).

254 CHAPTER 4

4.57. פֶּשַׁע ,תּוֹעֵבָה, and אַשְׁמָה (1QHᵃ XIX, 13–14)

ולמען⁸⁴ כבודכה טהרתה אנוש מפשע להתקדש
לכה מכול תועבות נדה ואשמת מעל להוחד עֻם בני אמתך⁸⁵

For the sake of your glory, you cleansed man from transgression so
that [he] can purify himself for you from all abominations of impurity
and guilt of sinfulness, to be united with the sons of your truth…

In this example פֶּשַׁע refers to a STATE from which one can be cleansed.
In connection with the semantic pattern in this domain, it seems that this
should be seen as GUILT being absolved. תּוֹעֵבָה (abomination) and אַשְׁמָה
may also refer to GUILT which may be absolved through cultic actions.[86]

4.58. חַטָּאת and עָוֹן (Isa 6:5, 7b)

וָאֹמַר אוֹי־לִי כִּי־נִדְמֵיתִי כִּי אִישׁ טְמֵא־שְׂפָתַיִם אָנֹכִי וּבְתוֹךְ עַם־טְמֵא שְׂפָתַיִם
אָנֹכִי יוֹשֵׁב כִּי אֶת־הַמֶּלֶךְ יְהוָה צְבָאוֹת רָאוּ עֵינָי {…}
וַיֹּאמֶר הִנֵּה נָגַע זֶה עַל־שְׂפָתֶיךָ וְסָר עֲוֹנֶךָ וְחַטָּאתְךָ תְּכֻפָּר

I said, "Woe to me, for I am ruined; because I am a man, unclean of
lips, and I dwell in the midst of a people, unclean of lips; for my eyes
have seen the king, the LORD OF HOSTS." {…} He said, "Behold, this
has touched your lips. Your iniquity has turned aside and your sin is
atoned for.

This example bears similarity to example 4.57. It appears linked with
cultic action.[87] However, the general sense of GUILT is present rather than
reference to any specific ACTS (as demonstrated through the reference to
unclean lips).

As PUNISHMENT

The sense of PUNISHMENT is more easily distinguished because the referent is distinctly different. In example 4.59, עָוֹן is construed as PUNISHMENT
FOR עָוֹן.

4.59. Genesis 19:15b

קוּם קַח אֶת־אִשְׁתְּךָ וְאֶת־שְׁתֵּי בְנֹתֶיךָ הַנִּמְצָאֹת פֶּן־תִּסָּפֶה בַּעֲוֹן הָעִיר

"Rise! Take your wife and your two daughters who are here, lest you
be swept away in the iniquity of the city."

---

[84] Accordance records a scribal correction from לעען to למען.
[85] Accordance records a scribal correction to אמתך.
[86] Cf. 2 Samuel 11:4 for another use of הִתְקַדֵּשׁ מִן (to purify oneself from).
[87] Verse 6 records the use of a coal (רִצְפָּה) from the altar.

SEMANTIC DOMAIN ANALYSIS 255

In this example, the city of Sodom is being destroyed for their sin
(חַטָּאת, Gen 18:20).[88] This appears to be in reference to breach of divine
law.[89] In this example, עָוֹן clearly refers to the thing that threatens the life
of Lot and his family which must be the PUNISHMENT of the city. Such
use can be seen throughout the centre triad of the עָוֹן domain.

4.60. פֶּשַׁע (Isa 24:20)

נוֹעַ תָּנוּעַ אֶרֶץ כַּשִּׁכּוֹר וְהִתְנוֹדְדָה כַּמְּלוּנָה וְכָבַד עָלֶיהָ פִּשְׁעָהּ וְנָפְלָה וְלֹא־תֹסִיף
קוּם

The earth staggers around like a drunk. It sways about like a hut. Its
transgression is heavy upon it. It falls and will not rise again.

In this example, the symptoms of פֶּשַׁע can be understood as the stag-
gering around and swaying, falling and not rising. The surrounding verses
also reinforce this interpretation. Thus פֶּשַׁע refers to PUNISHMENT which
is displayed in different ways throughout the section of discourse.

4.61. חַטָּאת (Zech 14:18b–19)

תִּהְיֶה הַמַּגֵּפָה אֲשֶׁר יִגֹּף יְהוָה אֶת־הַגּוֹיִם אֲשֶׁר לֹא יַעֲלוּ לָחֹג אֶת־חַג הַסֻּכּוֹת
זֹאת תִּהְיֶה חַטַּאת מִצְרָיִם וְחַטַּאת כָּל־הַגּוֹיִם אֲשֶׁר לֹא יַעֲלוּ לָחֹג אֶת־חַג הַסֻּכּוֹת

There will be the plague with which the LORD will strike the nations
who do not go up to celebrate the festival of Sukkot. This will be the
sin of Egypt and the sin of all the nations who do not go up to celebrate
the festival of Sukkot.

This example is quite clear. In this example, חַטָּאת, which is a plague
(מַגֵּפָה),[90] can only be seen as the punishment for failing to observe (cultic)
divine law.

4.5.2 Preliminary Conclusions

Examination of the עָוֹן domain shows that the domain is characterised by ACTS or BEHAVIOURS which breach divine law. This breach may be

---

[88] Which could also be tied to GUILT. Clines, "חַטָּאת 4," *DCH* 3:198.
[89] Cf. Genesis 13:13 – מְאֹד לַיהוָה וְחַטָּאִים רָעִים סְדֹם וְאַנְשֵׁי (The people of Sodom were bad
and great sinners to the LORD). The fact that these people did not recognise the Lord is
not necessarily important. As with Genesis 18:25, the analysed texts regularly argue
for the Lord's sovereignty over the whole world (e.g. Ps 136; Sir 10:4–5). Van Wolde
rightly argues that the Sodom and Gomorrah episode of Genesis 18–19 presents the Lord
as judge of the whole earth. Ellen J. van Wolde, "Cognitive Grammar at Work in Sodom
and Gomorrah," in *Cognitive Linguistic Explorations in Biblical Studies*, ed. Bonnie
Howe and Joel B. Green (Berlin: De Gruyter, 2014), 172–203.
[90] Also probably lack of rain (cf. Zech 14:17–18a).

256 CHAPTER 4

construed as against either the Lord, or his representative (e.g. the king).[91] The semantic patterns ACT/BEHAVIOUR→GUILT and ACT/BEHAVIOUR→PUNISHMENT were found to occur in the domain. Both patterns occur for the core triad of words פֶּשַׁע–חַטָּאת–עָוֹן to varying degrees and it is at least partially represented for other עָוֹן words.

4.5.3 רַע as Part of עָוֹן

Having partially considered how the עָוֹן domain functions, we now turn to the use of רַע within the domain. We begin with some straightforward uses where core relationships are clear.

In a number of uses with רַע, the particular ACT refers to idolatry. This use can be seen in example 4.62.

> 4.62. Deuteronomy 9:16, 18ac
>
> וָאֵרֶא וְהִנֵּה חֲטָאתֶם לַיהוָה אֱלֹהֵיכֶם עֲשִׂיתֶם לָכֶם עֵגֶל מַסֵּכָה סַרְתֶּם מַהֵר מִן־הַדֶּרֶךְ אֲשֶׁר־צִוָּה יְהוָה אֶתְכֶם {...}
>
> וָאֶתְנַפַּל לִפְנֵי יְהוָה כָּרִאשֹׁנָה {...} עַל כָּל־חַטַּאתְכֶם אֲשֶׁר חֲטָאתֶם לַעֲשׂוֹת הָרַע בְּעֵינֵי יְהוָה לְהַכְעִיסֹו
>
> I looked, and behold you had sinned against the LORD your God. You made for yourselves a calf, an image, you had turned quickly from the way which the LORD had commanded you. {...} I threw myself down before the LORD as at first {...} because of all your sin which you sinned by doing the bad in the eyes of the LORD, provoking him to anger.

Elsewhere the ACT is not specified (example 4.63).[92]

> 4.63. 11Q5 XXIV, 6–8
>
> גמולי הרע ישיב ממני דין האמת ✡ ✡ ✡ ✡
> אל תשפטני כחטאתי כי לוא יצדק לפניכה כול חי
> הבינני ✡ ✡ ✡ ✡ בתורתכה ואת משפטיכה למדני
>
> Turn the punishment for the bad from me, Judge of the Truth, LORD. Do not judge me according to my sin, for no living [person] is just before you. Instruct me, LORD, in your law, and teach me your judgements.

In this example, the psalmist requests forgiveness for certain ACTS. The legal language, combined with the request for instruction in the law,

---

[91] See n. 82 §4.5.1 which briefly comments on some difficult uses. While this finding appears to be the case, future research may nuance it further.

[92] Punishment is for an ACT, implying that רַע refers to something done. The parallel with חַטָּאת (sin) reinforces this view.

SEMANTIC DOMAIN ANALYSIS

257

indicate that the ACTS referred to by רַע and חַטָּאת (sin) should be considered as referring to breaches of divine law deserving punishment.

Example 4.64 demonstrates use of רַע in the semantic pattern ACT/BEHAVIOUR→PUNISHMENT in this domain.

> 4.64. Ben Sira 7:1–2 (C 3r8–10;* A 2v6–7)[93]
>
> אל תעש רע ואל יֹשיגך רע
> רחק מֵעָוֹן ויט ממך
>
> Do not do bad, and bad will not overtake you. Be far from iniquity and it will turn aside from you.

In this example the initial use of רַע refers to an ACT. The second use of רַע is construed as an EVENT which happens to the one who does bad. The implication is PUNISHMENT FOR רַע. This parallels the use of עָוֹן, which refers to both ACT and, through its use as subject of נָטָה, as PUNISHMENT.

Use without עָוֹן

As identified in Chapter 2 (§2.3.1), the phrase עָשָׂה רַע (to do bad) is the most common use of רַע in the analysed texts, accounting for 16.3% of the use of רַע. Specific use often links it to the עָוֹן domain. For example, the following use from Kings specifies that the behaviour refers to idolatry.[94]

> 4.65. 1 Kings 11:5–6a
>
> וַיַּעַשׂ שְׁלֹמֹה הָרַע בְּעֵינֵי יְהֹוָה וְלֹא מִלֵּא אַחֲרֵי יְהֹוָה כְּדָוִד אָבִיו
> אָז יִבְנֶה שְׁלֹמֹה בָּמָה לִכְמוֹשׁ שִׁקֻּץ מוֹאָב
>
> Solomon did the bad in the eyes of the LORD. He did not wholly follow[95] the LORD like David his father [did]. Then Solomon built a high place to Chemosh, abomination of Moab…

However, עָשָׂה רַע in example 4.66 appears to be no more specific than to refer to a NEGATIVE ACT.

---

[93] Text is reconstructed from A 2v6–7 which clearly records all the missing forms. The A manuscript uses the variant רעה; however, both readings appear acceptable from other uses of רַע and רָעָה (example 4.54 §4.5.1, and example 4.80 §4.7.2). See Appendix C.1 for side-by-side comparison.

[94] Idolatry reference seen with a parallel to חַטָּאת in example 4.62 above.

[95] For this unusual use of מִלֵּא see Clines, "מלא Pi. 6a," *DCH* 5:281.

CHAPTER 4

4.66. Deuteronomy 19:18–20

וְדָרְשׁוּ הַשֹּׁפְטִים הֵיטֵב וְהִנֵּה עֵד־שֶׁקֶר הָעֵד שֶׁקֶר עָנָה בְאָחִיו

וַעֲשִׂיתֶם לוֹ כַּאֲשֶׁר זָמַם לַעֲשׂוֹת לְאָחִיו וּבִעַרְתָּ הָרָע מִקִּרְבֶּךָ

וְהַנִּשְׁאָרִים יִשְׁמְעוּ וְיִרָאוּ וְלֹא־יֹסִפוּ לַעֲשׂוֹת עוֹד כַּדָּבָר הָרָע הַזֶּה בְּקִרְבֶּךָ

The judges will seek well, and behold, the witness is a lying witness. He testified falsely against his brother. You shall do to him as he planned to do to his brother. You shall purge the bad from your midst. The rest will hear, fear, and no longer do such bad as this in your midst.

In this example, the first use of רַע, in the phrase בִּעֵר רַע, follows the pattern ACT→GUILT (§2.3.8). The second takes as its referent the ACT of testifying falsely. In such use it ties directly with the אָוֶן subdomain. However, while אָוֶן and עָוֹן profile different things, there is an essential link between them. This can be demonstrated with example 4.67.

4.67. Isaiah 59:2–4

כִּי אִם־עֲוֹנֹתֵיכֶם הָיוּ מַבְדִּלִים בֵּינֵכֶם לְבֵין אֱלֹהֵיכֶם וְחַטֹּאותֵיכֶם הִסְתִּירוּ פָנִים מִכֶּם מִשְּׁמוֹעַ

כִּי כַפֵּיכֶם נְגֹאֲלוּ בַדָּם וְאֶצְבְּעוֹתֵיכֶם בֶּעָוֹן שִׂפְתוֹתֵיכֶם דִּבְּרוּ־שֶׁקֶר לְשׁוֹנְכֶם עַוְלָה תֶהְגֶּה

אֵין־קֹרֵא בְצֶדֶק וְאֵין נִשְׁפָּט בֶּאֱמוּנָה בָּטוֹחַ עַל־תֹּהוּ וְדַבֶּר־שָׁוְא הָרוֹ עָמָל וְהוֹלֵיד אָוֶן

But your iniquities have made a separation between you and your God, and your sins have hidden [his] face from you so that [he] does not hear. For your hands are defiled with blood, your fingers with iniquity. Your lips speak a lie, your tongue mutters injustice. No one speaks out righteously. No one enters a case faithfully. [They] trust in emptiness, they speak worthlessness, they conceive trouble and father villainy.

In this example we see that the עָוֹן ACTS are described as what separates the people from God. When the focus shifts between domains between 3a and 3b, the prophet moves to discussing specific PLANNED ACTS (false testimony and its results).[96] This link indicates a conceptual link between domains: the acts against humans cause a broken relationship with God.[97] Given this link in the cognitive context (their worldview), רַע may be referring to עָוֹן domain concepts in example 4.66. This is reinforced by the fact that in the phrase בִּעֵר רַע (to purge bad), רַע appears to follow the

---

[96] Van Steenbergen also notes there is a link between אָוֶן and deliberate planning. Van Steenbergen, *Semantics, World View and Bible Translation*, 138.

[97] Van Steenbergen writes, "The main focus is on broken *Relationship* with other people as a cause of broken *Relationship* with *Causality*." That is, a broken relationship with other humans is the cause of a broken relationship with God. Van Steenbergen, *Semantics, World View and Bible Translation*, 128.

SEMANTIC DOMAIN ANALYSIS

ACT→GUILT pattern. Due to the link between domains, it may be best to see רַע in a general way, referring both to NEGATIVE ACTS and usually implying a breach of relationship with the divine.[98]

4.6 MAJOR DOMAIN 3: רָעָה

The רָעָה domain is centred around the דֶּבֶר-רָעָב-חֶרֶב triad of words. Its links to רַע are primarily through the phrase חַיָּה רָעָה (bad animal)[99] and through the common associate רָעָה. As was mentioned in §4.1, the uses exhibit low contextual variation, and seem to indicate a standard set of judgements. These may be best understood as NEGATIVE EVENTS usually construed as PUNISHMENT. The triad most commonly occurs, as in example 4.68, without רַע or רָעָה.

> 4.68. Jeremiah 14:10b, 12b
>
> וַיהוָה לֹא רָצָם עַתָּה יִזְכֹּר עֲוֹנָם וְיִפְקֹד חַטֹּאתָם {...}
> כִּי בַּחֶרֶב וּבָרָעָב וּבַדֶּבֶר אָנֹכִי מְכַלֶּה אוֹתָם
>
> The LORD is not pleased with them. Now he will remember their iniquity, and he will punish their sins. {...} By the sword, famine, and plague, I am finishing them.

This domain will be examined from two angles: the use of רָעָה in the domain (§4.6.1); and the use of רַע in the domain (§4.6.2).

4.6.1 רָעָה as Part of רָעָה

רָעָה forms a major link between רַע and רָעָה. The evidence tends towards seeing רָעָה as a superordinate of רָעָה. This can be demonstrated with example 4.69, and its use elsewhere.[100]

---

[98] However, this breach (and the link between domains) is dependent on the understanding that God disapproves of רַע and what contains domains such as אָוֶן. Note the use of עֹשֵׂה רָע (doer of bad) in Malachi 2:17. Unless the statement is a false quote and was intended to sound absurd to the listeners, this demonstrates that it was possible for someone to say that one who does רַע is right with God (טוֹב בְּעֵינֵי יהוה).

[99] In one instance the phrase חֳלָיִים רָעִים (bad sicknesses) occurred (4Q504 2 III, 8) and in one instance רַע occurred (Sir 39:29). However, the last may be a scribal error of omission for רָעָב (famine).

[100] Deut 32:23; Jer 5:12; 11:22–23; 42:17; 44:17–18; Ezek 14:21–22; 2 Chr 20:9. The only example which does not support this view is found in Jeremiah 28:8. However, this use appears textually suspect. Multiple Hebrew manuscripts have רָעָב (famine; see BHS Apparatus). This is supported by the Vulgate (*fame*, famine). It is also supported by the specificity of the list. In all other uses, when רָעָה appears in association with

260   CHAPTER 4

4.69. Ezekiel 6:10–11

וְיָדְעוּ כִּי־אֲנִי יְהֹוָה לֹא אֶל־חִנָּם דִּבַּרְתִּי לַעֲשׂוֹת לָהֶם הָרָעָה הַזֹּאת
כֹּה־אָמַר אֲדֹנָי יְהֹוִה הַכֵּה בְכַפְּךָ וּרְקַע בְּרַגְלְךָ וֶאֱמָר־אָח אֶל כָּל־תּוֹעֲבוֹת רָעוֹת
בֵּית יִשְׂרָאֵל אֲשֶׁר בַּחֶרֶב בָּרָעָב וּבַדֶּבֶר יִפֹּלוּ

"They shall know that I am the LORD, I did not say vainly that I would
do this evil to them." Thus says the Lord GOD, "Clap your hands and
stamp your foot and say 'Alas' about all the bad abominations of the
house of Israel who will fall by the sword, by the famine, and by the
plague."

In this example, רָעָה refers to PUNISHMENT which the Lord brings in
response to the abominations of Israel (Ezek 5:6–8). This may indicate a
relationship with the PUNISHMENT aspect of אָוֶן and עָוֹן. This relationship
will be explored more when רָעָה is examined in §4.7.2.

The word צָרָה (distress) was suggested to be on the fringe of the **רָעָה**
domain. In connection with that term, רָעָה appears to indicate something
than other than PUNISHMENT.

4.70. 1 Samuel 10:19

וְאַתֶּם הַיּוֹם מְאַסְתֶּם אֶת־אֱלֹהֵיכֶם אֲשֶׁר־הוּא מוֹשִׁיעַ לָכֶם מִכָּל־רָעוֹתֵיכֶם וְצָרֹתֵיכֶם
וַתֹּאמְרוּ לוֹ כִּי־מֶלֶךְ תָּשִׂים עָלֵינוּ

You today have rejected your God who saves you from all your evils
and your distresses. You have said to him, "Set a king over us."

In example 4.70, the sense of PUNISHMENT does not appear to fit well.
However, רָעָה is still construed as an EVENT. It is linked to the concept of
oppression through the previous verse which says God delivered the people from the ones oppressing them (לָחַץ). It seems here that the pronominal suffix attached to רָעָה does mark the beneficiary (as we would expect
for PUNISHMENT), but the sense is more general, referring to a NEGATIVE
EVENT rather than specifically to PUNISHMENT.

4.6.2 רַע as Part of רָעָה

The three combinative uses of רַע in association with **רָעָה** are given
below (examples 4.71, 4.72, and 4.73).

רָעָה, it appears as a superordinate. In this use, it occurs with more specific things (war
and plague), but other than the possibility of it referring to famine in connection with
war and plague, the text gives us no indication as to what that is. The substitution of the
more common חֶרֶב (sword) for מִלְחָמָה (war) is in line with Koller's discussion of the
polyseme of חֶרֶב meaning "war." Koller, *The Semantic Field of Cutting Tools*, 163–66.

SEMANTIC DOMAIN ANALYSIS

261

4.71. Ezekiel 14:21a

כִּי כֹה אָמַר אֲדֹנָי יְהוִה אַף כִּי־אַרְבַּעַת שְׁפָטַי | הָרָעִים חֶרֶב וְרָעָב וְחַיָּה רָעָה וָדֶבֶר שִׁלַּחְתִּי

For thus says the Lord God "How much more when I send my four bad judgements, sword, and famine, and bad beasts, and plague…

4.72. 4Q504 2 III, 8*

חוליים ‸רעים‸ ורעב וצמא ודבר וחרב

[--] bad sicknesses and famine and thirst and plague and sword [--]

The first two uses, examples 4.71 and 4.72, can be easily identified in line with chapter 2 (§§2.3.10–2.3.11). It was seen there that רַע functioned to emphasise a negative element. In a similar way, in example 4.71, the phrase שְׁפָטַי הָרָעִים (my bad judgements) functions as a superordinate over the list, with רַע emphasising the severity (negative element) of the judgements.[101] These combinative uses seem semantically similar to the PUNISHMENT uses detected in אָוֶן and עָוֹן.

In this final use, רַע appears as a superordinate of מָוֶת (death) and יַד חֶרֶב (power of the sword).[102]

4.73. Job 5:19–20

בְּשֵׁשׁ צָרוֹת יַצִּילֶךָ וּבְשֶׁבַע | לֹא־יִגַּע בְּךָ רָע
בְּרָעָב פָּדְךָ מִמָּוֶת וּבְמִלְחָמָה מִידֵי חָרֶב

In six troubles he will deliver you, and in seven, bad will not touch you. In famine he will redeem you from death, and in war, from the power of the sword.

In the discourse, Eliphaz is speaking. He is describing how God protects those he disciplines. רַע modifies the element EVENT and so refers to NEGATIVE EVENTS that may happen in the circumstances of צָרוֹת (troubles). A clear link with PUNISHMENT is not seen here. If PUNISHMENT is to be found, it must be linked with the צָרוֹת, but not the רַע. Therefore, this use seems to indicate that although רָעָה is often construed as PUNISHMENT, it is not a necessary feature of this domain.

---

[101] The phrase was not listed in the analysis in chapter 3, because it would have led to double-counting individual uses of some words and introduced additional error in the counts.

[102] Note that the list of things continues in the following verses, but due to the way the poetry flows, the only clear associates of רַע are contained in example 4.73 which explicitly lists *effects* of troubles.

262 CHAPTER 4

4.6.3 Preliminary Conclusions

This brief examination of the **רָעָה** domain indicates that it provides little power for the analysis of רַע. רָעָה appears to be a superordinate of the domain, and two uses of רַע also function that way (examples 4.69, 4.71, and 4.73). While there is a link between **רָעָה** and PUNISHMENT, this may be symptomatic of the conceptual link in ancient Israelite thought between certain NEGATIVE EVENTS and DIVINE PUNISHMENT.[103] However, the connection between **רָעָה** and PUNISHMENT is not a necessary feature of the domain. **רָעָה** may more generally encompass certain NEGATIVE EVENTS, which can be construed as PUNISHMENT. It appears that the PUNISHMENT link is a potential element of these terms in the cognitive context (e.g. can be a result of divine punishment), but none necessarily or directly refer to PUNISHMENT. Thus, the **רָעָה** domain contains words referring to NEGATIVE EVENTS related to invasion and siege that are often construed as PUNISHMENTS.[104]

4.7 SOME DERIVATIONAL RELATIONSHIPS OF THE רעע WORD FAMILY: רֹעַ AND רָעָה, רַע

In §4.1, רֹעַ and רָעָה were indicated as words requiring further analysis. Because they have not turned up as core terms to any particular domain,[105] they are analysed separately here. As derivational sense relations, they are expected to share important, "partly systematic, partly idiosyncratic"[106] relations to רַע. In §4.7 orange is used to draw attention to example-specific details (additional colours are used as required).

---

[103] This concept comes through in the cycles of apostasy and oppression in Judges, the connections in Kings and Chronicles between service to God and events and elsewhere. It is also seen in m. 'Abot 5:8–9 which begins שִׁבְעָה מִינֵי פוּרְעָנִיּוֹת בָּאִים עַל שִׁבְעָה גוּפֵי עֲבֵירוֹת (Seven kinds of punishments come for seven kinds of transgressions) and goes on to list different infractions of divine law and a corresponding NEGATIVE EVENT (including חֶרֶב, דֶּבֶר, רָעָב and רָעָה חַיָּה).

[104] It may have begun as an ad-hoc domain. The first uses of at least two of the core triad together occur in Exodus 5:3, Leviticus 26:25, Deuteronomy 28:22 and Deuteronomy 32:25. All refer to divine PUNISHMENT. However, it is taken up frequently in oracles of judgement. The majority of later occurrences are found in the Latter Prophets (71.7%) in such oracles (see Tables 3.8, 3.17, and 3.28 in §3.2.2, §3.2.5, and §3.2.9). As Skehan and Di Lella have said, "Famine and pestilence were the usual accompaniments of a prolonged siege." Skehan and Di Lella, *The Wisdom of Ben Sira*, 460–61. That is, this domain appears centred on words that relate to warfare.

[105] רָעָה is superordinate to **רָעָה**, but should not be properly considered one of the core terms as it is less frequent than the core triad דֶּבֶר–רָעָב–חֶרֶב and shares frequent links with the other domains as well, particularly with עָוֹן.

[106] Cruse, *Meaning in Language*, 133–34.

SEMANTIC DOMAIN ANALYSIS   263

4.7.1 רַע and רֹעַ

In Chapter 2 (§2.3.2, example 2.31), רֹעַ was seen to behave in a similar manner to רַע. In Chapter 3 (§3.2.3), רֹעַ was found to only frequently
associate with words from its own word family: רַע and רָעָה.[107] In §4.1,
it was noted that the most common associations between רֹעַ and רַע are
in reference to the quality of figs and of people's deeds.[108] The use to
refer to people's deeds is the most common (13 occurrences, 43.3%) and
always occurs in the phrase ־רֹעַ מַעַלְלֵי (the badness of [POSS.PRON] deeds).
However, other areas of use were identified as well. רֹעַ appears to function as an abstract noun used to qualify various other things with respect
to badness. Example 4.74 demonstrates the uses with reference to deeds.

> 4.74. Jeremiah 26:3
>
> אוּלַי יִשְׁמְעוּ וְיָשֻׁבוּ אִישׁ מִדַּרְכּוֹ הָרָעָה וְנִחַמְתִּי אֶל־הָרָעָה אֲשֶׁר אָנֹכִי חֹשֵׁב
> לַעֲשׂוֹת לָהֶם מִפְּנֵי רֹעַ מַעַלְלֵיהֶם
>
> Perhaps they will listen and turn each from his bad (רַע) way. Then I
> would relent of the evil (רָעָה) which I am planning to do to them because
> of the badness (רֹעַ) of their deeds.

In example 4.74, there is a clear semantic association between רַע and
רֹעַ, which modify BEHAVIOUR and ACTS respectively. Additionally, this
example demonstrates a use of רָעָה as a PUNISHMENT for רַע and רֹעַ. While
רַע is commonly used to modify both BEHAVIOUR and ACTS (§2.3.1 and
§2.3.5), of these two רֹעַ is only ever used to modify ACTS. Similarly, רֹעַ
never occurs in reference to PUNISHMENT.

There is a similar use of רֹעַ found in Ben Sira. However, in this use
(example 4.75), it modifies a human with reference to his behaviour:
HUMAN(BEHAVIOUR). This is similar to what was seen with רַע modifying
HUMAN in Chapter 2 (§2.3.2), but with different syntax – as would be
expected of an abstract noun.

> 4.75. Ben Sira 31:24 (B 4v6)
>
> רע על לחם ירגז בשער [ ] דעת ‹עדות› רועו נאמנה
>
> A person who is bad (רַע) concerning bread [i.e. stingy] will tremble
> in the gate. Knowledge ‹witness› of his badness is sure.

---

[107] This leaves out associations of opposition, which demonstrated frequent association with
the words טוב/טוב (goodness/good) – it is difficult to distinguish which word is used at
times.

[108] These two uses also make up the entire set of uses of רֹעַ in Jeremiah. To refer to figs:
Jer 24:2, 3; 24:8; 29:17. To refer to people's deeds: Jer 4:4; 21:12; 23:2, 22; 25:5;
26:3; 44:22. Additional uses to refer to people's deeds occur in: Deut 28:20; Isa 1:16;
Hos 9:15; Ps 28:4; 11Q19 LIX, 7.

264   CHAPTER 4

רֹעַ behaves like other abstract nouns such as בֶּטַח (confidence) and רֹב (abundance), taking the preposition לְ to indicate a qualitative relationship (example 4.76).[109]

> 4.76. Genesis 41:19
>
> וְהִנֵּה שֶׁבַע־פָּרוֹת אֲחֵרוֹת עֹלוֹת אַחֲרֵיהֶן דַּלּוֹת וְרָעוֹת תֹּאַר מְאֹד וְרַקּוֹת בָּשָׂר לֹא־רָאִיתִי כָהֵנָּה בְּכָל־אֶרֶץ מִצְרַיִם לָרֹעַ
>
> Behold, seven other cows came up after them, very poor and bad (רַע) of appearance, and thin of flesh. I had not seen such as these in all the land of Egypt with respect to badness (רֹעַ).

In this use, as in other uses, it seems to function in a semantically similar way to רַע in combination with the element it modifies.

Thus רֹעַ behaves as an abstract noun, but qualifies things in a similar manner to רַע. There appears to be little semantic difference between them; in areas where both are used the difference is likely mostly (or completely) syntactic.[110]

4.7.2   רַע and רָעָה

Uses of רָעָה have been referred to from time to time in this chapter during the analysis of the domains. Where רָעָה does appear to have semantic associations with the רָשַׁע subdomain, they are always with בְּלִיַּעַל (worthlessness), and it always refers to an ACT. רָעָה has less ties than רַע with the אָוֶן subdomain. Conversely, it has more extensive links with the עָוֹן domain than רַע does. As seen in §4.6, while רָעָה is used a number of times as a superordinate of רָעָה, רַע was only found twice.

The following example demonstrates the apparent use of רָעָה with רָשַׁע.

> 4.77. Nahum 1:11
>
> מִמֵּךְ יָצָא חֹשֵׁב עַל־יְהוָה רָעָה יֹעֵץ בְּלִיָּעַל
>
> One who planned evil against the LORD came from you, a counsellor of worthlessness.

This association is not properly with רָשַׁע because here neither רָעָה nor בְּלִיַּעַל refer to a HUMAN. Thus, given the presence of חָשַׁב and יָעַץ (to plan

---

[109] For בֶּטַח see 1 Kgs 5:5; for רֹב see 1 Kgs 1:19. Van der Merwe, Naudé and Kroeze, *A Biblical Hebrew Reference Grammar*, §39.11.6.b. In a similar kind of use – modifying a clause – it takes the preposition מִן to indicate the reason for a state of affairs (Jer 24:2).

[110] This is not to say that they can always be differentiated with ease. There are uses of the letters רע which could syntactically be either adjective or noun (e.g. Sir B 12r4 appears to record a variant, having רוע with the correcter writing רע).

SEMANTIC DOMAIN ANALYSIS

265

and to counsel), the association is linked to DECEIT and PLANNING, and should probably be considered as within the אָוֶן subdomain (cf. example 4.47 §4.4.3). Compare this with example 4.78. In both uses it refers to a PLANNED ACT or BEHAVIOUR towards someone (divine or human).

> 4.78. Psalm 38:13
>
> וַיְנַקְשׁוּ ׀ מְבַקְשֵׁי נַפְשִׁי וְדֹרְשֵׁי רָעָתִי דִּבְּרוּ הַוֹּות וּמִרְמֹות כָּל־הַיֹּום יֶהְגּוּ
>
> Those who seek my life lay snares [for me]. Those who seek my evil speak destruction; they mutter deceits all day.

It can also refer to an ACT for which a person deserves punishment as in the following example.

> 4.79. Psalm 94:23
>
> וַיָּשֶׁב עֲלֵיהֶם ׀ אֶת־אֹונָם וּבְרָעָתָם יַצְמִיתֵם יַצְמִיתֵם יְהוָה אֱלֹהֵינוּ
>
> He will return[111] upon them their villainy and will destroy them for their evil. The LORD our God will destroy them.

When רָעָה associates with the עָוֶן domain, it often refers to an ACT or EVENT. In the EVENT use, it may be construed as PUNISHMENT (example 4.80).

> 4.80. Jeremiah 44:2–5
>
> כֹּה־אָמַר יְהוָה צְבָאֹות אֱלֹהֵי יִשְׂרָאֵל אַתֶּם רְאִיתֶם אֵת כָּל־הָרָעָה אֲשֶׁר הֵבֵאתִי
> עַל־יְרוּשָׁלִַם וְעַל כָּל־עָרֵי יְהוּדָה וְהִנָּם חָרְבָּה הַיֹּום הַזֶּה וְאֵין בָּהֶם יֹושֵׁב
> מִפְּנֵי רָעָתָם אֲשֶׁר עָשׂוּ לְהַכְעִסֵנִי לָלֶכֶת לְקַטֵּר לַעֲבֹד לֵאלֹהִים אֲחֵרִים אֲשֶׁר לֹא
> יְדָעוּם הֵמָּה אַתֶּם וַאֲבֹתֵיכֶם
> וָאֶשְׁלַח אֲלֵיכֶם אֶת־כָּל־עֲבָדַי הַנְּבִיאִים הַשְׁכֵּים וְשָׁלֹחַ לֵאמֹר אַל־נָא תַעֲשׂוּ אֵת
> דְּבַר־הַתֹּעֵבָה הַזֹּאת אֲשֶׁר שָׂנֵאתִי
> וְלֹא שָׁמְעוּ וְלֹא־הִטּוּ אֶת־אָזְנָם לָשׁוּב מֵרָעָתָם לְבִלְתִּי קַטֵּר לֵאלֹהִים אֲחֵרִים
>
> Thus says the LORD of Hosts, God of Israel, "You have seen all the evil which I brought upon Jerusalem, and upon all the cities of Judah – behold they are a waste this day, and no one dwells in them – because of their evil which they did, angering me by going and offering sacrifices and serving other gods which they did not know, neither them, you, nor your fathers. I sent – persistently sent – to you all my servants, the prophets, saying, 'Do not do this abominable thing which I hate!' But they did not listen, they did not incline their ear, to turn from their evil, to not offer to other gods.

In this example, the first use of רָעָה (v.2), refers to PUNISHMENT. The second and third uses (v.3) refer to an ACT which breaches divine law: idolatry. While it is acknowledged that רָעָה is used for negative events,

---

[111] Following the Old Greek ἀποδώσει=וְיָשֶׁב and keeping the tense consistent.

266 CHAPTER 4

given the links with the עָוֹן domain and the semantic patterns present in
that domain, this should be seen in terms of PUNISHMENT FOR רָעָה (rather
than the more semantically bland NEGATIVE EVENT).

The GUILT sense of the עָוֹן domain is also a possible sense for רָעָה, as
seen in example 4.81 (and the use of בִּעֵר רָעָה).[112]

> 4.81. 1 Samuel 25:28
>
> שָׂא נָא לְפֶ֫שַׁע אֲמָתֶ֫ךָ כִּי עָשֹׂה־יַעֲשֶׂה יְהוָה לַאדֹנִי בַּ֫יִת נֶאֱמָן כִּי־מִלְחֲמוֹת יְהוָה
> אֲדֹנִי נִלְחָם וְרָעָה לֹא־תִמָּצֵא בְךָ מִיָּמֶֽיךָ
>
> Please bear the transgression of your female slave. For the Lord will
> certainly make my lord a sure house, because my lord is fighting the
> battles of the LORD, and evil will not be found in you all your days.

This example is very similar to example 4.55 §4.5.1, which is a prime
example of עָוֹן being used to refer to GUILT in a judicial context. The
judicial frame is evoked with the request to forgive (נָשָׂא, lift) her פֶּ֫שַׁע
(transgression).[113] By declaring that she has פֶּ֫שַׁע against David she is saying that he is divinely appointed (rather than a rebel; cf. 1 Sam 25:10).
Furthermore, his house will be sure, in contrast to Saul's house, because
he fights the Lord's battles and because רָעָה will not be found in him. That
is, the Lord will not find reason to remove him from the throne.

רָעָה may also be used with the בְּ preposition to describe the mode[114]
of an action (example 4.82). It also appears in this use in the אָוֶן subdomain with terms for SPEECH (example 4.21 §4.4.1) and may indicate a
link between the following use and DECEIT.

> 4.82. Exodus 32:12
>
> לָמָּה יֹאמְרוּ מִצְרַיִם לֵאמֹר בְּרָעָה הוֹצִיאָם לַהֲרֹג אֹתָם בֶּהָרִים וּלְכַלֹּתָם מֵעַל פְּנֵי
> הָאֲדָמָה שׁוּב מֵחֲרוֹן אַפֶּ֫ךָ וְהִנָּחֵם עַל־הָרָעָה לְעַמֶּֽךָ
>
> Why should the Egyptians say, "He brought them out with evil, to kill
> them in the mountains, and to finish them from upon the face of the
> ground"? Turn from your anger, and relent of the evil to your people.

---

[112] Judges 20:12b–13a, given as example 2.79 in §2.3.8. See also the use in Jeremiah 4:14
where it may function in this sense while in association with אָוֶן.

[113] The identity of the פֶּ֫שַׁע is disputed. Although McCarter takes it to be simply a polite
request, it seems best to take this as related to the wrong her husband has done to David.
P. Kyle McCarter, *I Samuel: A New Translation with Introduction, Notes and Commentary*, AB 8 (Garden City, NY: Doubleday, 1980), 398; David Toshio Tsumura, *The
First Book of Samuel*, NICOT (Grand Rapids, MI: Eerdmans, 2007), 589; Baldwin,
1 and 2 Samuel, 161.

[114] This is a frequent use of the preposition. See van der Merwe, Naudé and Kroeze, *A
Biblical Hebrew Reference Grammar*, §39.6.4.

SEMANTIC DOMAIN ANALYSIS

4.7.3 Preliminary Conclusions

There is a great degree of overlap in the usage of רֹעַ and רָעָה with רַע. רֹעַ appears to operate as an abstract noun across many areas of use of רַע. It should likely be seen in light of how רַע operates in each of its areas of use. Thus רֹעַ provides little information for understanding the use of רַע. רָעָה, on the other hand, provides more. It appears to be the preferred term for use in connection with the עָוֹן domain, while רַע appears to be the preferred term in connection with the רֶשַׁע and אָוֶן subdomains. Out of the two, רַע shows greater versatility, occurring across all identified domains, and much more widely. Due to the influence of the עָוֹן domain, the semantic patterns ACT/BEHAVIOUR→PUNISHMENT and ACT/BEHAVIOUR→GUILT appear to occur for both רַע and רָעָה. This should not be seen as a primary sense of the terms, but a development related to their use in specific domains. Both רַע and רָעָה can also be used in similar ways to simply refer to a NEGATIVE ACT/BEHAVIOUR/EVENT (as seen in §4.6). This use nuances our understanding of the impact of the semantic patterns from אָוֶן and עָוֹן. Use of רָעָה or רַע to refer to PUNISHMENT should not be seen everywhere a NEGATIVE EVENT is meant, but only under specific conditions.[115] Under such conditions, the semantic pattern of domains אָוֶן and עָוֹן could be reasonably expected to impose the sense of PUNISHMENT over the more general use.[116]

Finally, רָעָה was also demonstrated to be used to describe the mode of an action. That example (4.82) bears similarity to example 4.83, and may help us understand the use of רַע there.

> 4.83. Exodus 5:14, 19
>
> וַיֻּכּוּ שֹׁטְרֵי בְּנֵי יִשְׂרָאֵל אֲשֶׁר־שָׂמוּ עֲלֵהֶם נֹגְשֵׂי פַרְעֹה לֵאמֹר מַדּוּעַ לֹא כִלִּיתֶם חָקְכֶם לִלְבֹּן כִּתְמוֹל שִׁלְשֹׁם גַּם־תְּמוֹל גַּם־הַיּוֹם {...}
> וַיִּרְאוּ שֹׁטְרֵי בְנֵי־יִשְׂרָאֵל אֹתָם בְּרָע לֵאמֹר לֹא־תִגְרְעוּ מִלִּבְנֵיכֶם דְּבַר־יוֹם בְּיוֹמוֹ
>
> The foremen of the children of Israel whom the oppressors of Pharaoh had set over them were beaten, saying, "Why have you not completed your quota of bricks today or yesterday as in the past?" {...}

---

[115] Such as where explicit semantic associations are made. Such as in example 4.80 above, or example 4.54 §4.5.1 for רַע. It may also occur where semantic associations are not explicit, but there is a strong presence of language associated with one of the domains (e.g. language of punishment due to infraction against divine law).

[116] This finding is reinforced by the demonstrated presence of the pattern ACT/BEHAVIOUR→GUILT for both רַע and רָעָה.

268 CHAPTER 4

> The foremen of the children of Israel understood[117] they [the Egyptians] were with bad, saying, "You shall not reduce your [quantity of] bricks, the daily quota.[118]

Although the preposition בְּ is often used to mark the object of the verb רָאָה, in this example there is another object marked by אֶת.[119] This is often taken to refer children of Israel (בְּנֵי־יִשְׂרָאֵל), which forms part of the construct phrase describing the foremen.[120] However, it seems more likely the pronominal suffix is anaphoric, referring to the Egyptian speakers in verse 14 and 16. It is difficult to establish whether a link with אָוֶן and DECEIT should be understood here.

4.8 CONCLUSION

In this chapter, the domains identified in Chapter 3 were partially analysed. This was done with particular reference to words which were identified as being most likely to provide the greatest interpretive power for רַע. In addition, the two semantic associates רֹעַ and רָעָה were analysed with reference to רַע. The results from the analysis was applied to understanding the use of רַע.

It was found that, in connection with its use with רָשָׁע, רַע refers to HUMANS who deserve judicial action against them. Such people are people who do both אָוֶן and עָוֹן ACTS/BEHAVIOURS. In connection with its use with אָוֶן, רַע may be linked with DECEITFUL SPEECH and ACTS/BEHAVIOURS. In connection with its use with עָוֹן, רַע may be linked with ACTS/BEHAVIOURS that breach divine law.

For both אָוֶן and עָוֹן the semantic pattern ACT/BEHAVIOUR→PUNISHMENT was identified. In addition, for עָוֹן, the semantic pattern ACT/BEHAVIOUR→

---

[117] Literally "saw." While רָאָה generally is used with כִּי in this use, it does occur without כִּי or another discourse marker, and also occasionally with two objects. Clines, "ראה I 10.d–e," *DCH* 7:355.

[118] "A thing of a day in its day."

[119] A number of times רָאָה is used with two objects to mean "understand someone/something is." Clines, *DCH* 7:355. Note also the use of בְּרַע with the verb דִּבֶּר (to speak) in Psalm 73:8. While this use is not the same, it does indicate the use of בְּרַע to describe the mode of SPEECH. The standard interpretation has led Propp to declare "Because it is so awkward, I suspect the first half of v 19 is corrupt," and argues that it should be emended to read בְּרָעָתָם (in their רָעָה) rather than אֹתָם בְּרָע. William Henry Propp, *Exodus 1–18: A New Translation with Introduction and Commentary*, AB 2 (New York: Doubleday, 1999), 244.

[120] This is how Propp takes it. However, Durham takes it to refer to the foremen. Propp, *Exodus 1–18*, 244; John I. Durham, *Exodus*, WBC 3 (Waco, TX: Word, 1987), 67.

SEMANTIC DOMAIN ANALYSIS 269

GUILT was identified. רַע and רָעָה were both found to participate in these semantic patterns at times. However, it was also noted in connection with the EVENT use of רַע and רָעָה that they are not limited to the PUNISHMENT use of the אָוֶן and עָוֹן domains. Rather, they both can refer more generally to a NEGATIVE EVENT.

Because רַע is a general term providing a negative qualification to an element (Chapter 2), where direct semantic associations do not exist, care must be taken in linking its use with the connotations of a particular semantic domain. Nevertheless, a number of examples have been given where language associated with the analysed domains provides enough to link רַע with the domain.[121] Additionally, some examples were provided to demonstrate where application should be avoided.

---

[121] Note the specific definition of semantic association being used here is of associations identified in Chapter 3. If we were to define "semantic association" more broadly we would consider verbs of speech (for example) to be semantic associations too.

CHAPTER 5

CONCLUSION

The current work sits within a flourishing body of scholarly work in Ancient Hebrew semantics. In this area it draws particular inspiration from the work of Reinier de Blois on the SDBH and the work of Marilyn Burton on the semantic domain of GLORY in Ancient Hebrew.[1]

As is often the case, the original goal of the current work was overly ambitious. I had originally planned to analyse the entire רעע word family within their domains of operation. It soon became apparent that such a wide scope of analysis with such fine detail of analysis would be impractical and that something had to be sacrificed. This led to numerous limitations of scope. The focus shifted to the word רַע (bad), and each stage of analysis was reduced in scope. Thus the aim of the current work focused on *presenting a more accurate picture of the meaning and use of* רַע.

While not rigorously adhering to any specific linguistic theory, this work draws on lexical and cognitive semantic theory to analyse רַע in Ancient and Mishnaic Hebrew. Although analysis involved the different stages feeding in to each other, it began with an analysis of the contribution of רַע to the discourse elements it modifies (Chapter 2). This was followed by the mapping of some of the lexical semantic domains of רַע in its combinative use (Chapter 3). Lastly, the mapped domains and part of the רעע word family were partially analysed with the findings applied to understanding the use of רַע (Chapter 4).

Although it does not receive much mention during Chapters 2–4, the various stages of Hebrew represented in the analysed texts were a consideration during the analysis. However, there appeared to be no clear evidence of diachronic change in the meaning of רַע. For this reason there is little mention of meaning change.[2]

The main findings of each chapter are summarised and integrated below (§5.1). This is followed by a brief examination of how the findings

---

[1] In particular see de Blois, *Towards a New Dictionary*; UBS, "SDBH"; Burton, *The Semantics of Glory*.

[2] However, during the analysis, evidence of change for other terms was detected at times. For example, טוֹב (good) and יָפֶה (beautiful) were found to vary over time. This was not analysed in the current work, but has been published elsewhere. Foster, "Is Everything 'Beautiful' or 'Appropriate' in Its Time?"

relate to previous research (§5.2) and a suggestion towards an improved lexical entry for רַע (§5.3). Lastly, some areas are highlighted for future research (§5.4).

5.1 Main Findings

In Chapter 2, the null hypothesis[3] for the schematic meaning of רַע was taken to be: רַע provides a general negative modification to the discourse element it modifies. This was largely found to be the case. However, there were some variations in use which were uncovered. רַע was found to be able to operate as the negative direction of a continuous scale, or the negative side in a two-category (good-bad) system (Figure 2.1, as 5.1 below). Additionally, it can be used to modify discourse elements that are prosodically neutral as well as those that are prosodically negative. For example, when modifying the neutral element ACT, it construes the ACT as NEGATIVE, and when modifying the negative element HARMFUL TO HUMANS, it foregrounds the negative element. רַע was also found to be used in both objective and subjective uses.

Figure 5.1. Category Versus Scalar Use of רַע

Finally, in Chapter 2 (§2.3.8), a use was examined which could only be properly understood with reference to the domain mapping and analysis of Chapters 3–4. In summary, the findings of Chapter 2 indicate that, where semantic patterns of certain domains do not affect its use, רַע forms a general NEGATIVE qualification of an element which can be used in both objective and subjective descriptions.

In Chapter 3, some of the semantic domains of רַע were mapped through a semantic association analysis. The method of analysis did not produce a map of all the domains of operation of רַע. Rather, it led to a map of the domains of use where the combinative use of רַע occurred in semantic

---

[3] The null hypothesis comes from statistics and refers to the hypothesis that there is no distinction between groups. It is the hypothesis for which one seeks to find disconfirming evidence.

CONCLUSION

association with other words. From this mapping process, three major domains of use were identified (Figure 3.1, as Figure 5.2):

1. רָשָׁע and אָוֶן (EVILDOER and DECEIT),
2. עָוֺן (SIN),
3. רָעָה (DESTRUCTION).

Figure 5.2. Semantic Associations Network for רַע

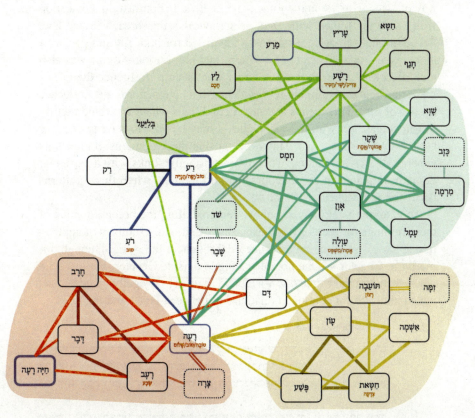

In Chapter 4, a shortlist of words were selected for thorough examination in the semantic domain analysis. These were: רָשָׁע (wicked), רַע (badness), רָעָה (evil), אָוֶן (villainy), and עָוֺן (iniquity). While uses of other domain-specific words were analysed, these words received a full analysis and greater focus in Chapter 4. While this may lead to a skewed picture of the identified domains, it was deemed that such bias, while regrettable, would be in favour of information that would aid in the interpretation of רַע (the words were selected on the basis of their links with רַע). Thus, Figure 5.2 should be viewed as a רַע-centric map of semantic associations,

274 CHAPTER 5

and the domain analyses should be seen as skewed towards words used
with רַע.

The analysis of Chapter 4 indicated that in connection with the רָשָׁע subdomain, רַע refers to HUMANS who deserve judicial action against them. Such
people are people who do both אָוֶן and עָוֹן ACTS or BEHAVIOURS. However,
not all uses of רַע+HUMAN should be seen as within the רָשָׁע subdomain.

In connection with אָוֶן, רַע is characterised by DECEIT. It is used in this
way of SPEECH, ACTS, BEHAVIOURS, and EVENTS. In contrast, in connection
with עָוֹן, רַע is linked with ACTS or BEHAVIOURS that breach divine law.
An additional semantic pattern was identified for both אָוֶן and עָוֹן: ACT/
BEHAVIOUR→PUNISHMENT. The pattern ACT/BEHAVIOUR→GUILT was also
identified for עָוֹן. Both these patterns were seen to influence the use of
רַע. Reinforcing this finding was evidence that both patterns also influence
the use of רָעָה. This means that under conditions where רַע would modify
ACT in connection with these domains, it may be used to refer to GUILT or
PUNISHMENT for a רַע ACT. However, outside these domains, רַע takes its
general NEGATIVE meaning. Therefore, substantive links with a particular
domain indicated in the discourse should indicate when these patterns
occur for any particular use of רַע.

An example is explained below, demonstrating the potential value of
these findings for theology and exegesis. Additional examples of application to exegesis can be found scattered throughout the work, although primarily in Chapter 4. One notable example outside Chapter 4 is in §2.3.8
where בַּעֵר הָרַע *purge the bad* was found to refer to a legally mandated act
which allows for a continued relationship between Israel and the Lord.

5.1 Isaiah 31:1–3

הוֹי הַיֹּרְדִים מִצְרַיִם לְעֶזְרָה עַל־סוּסִים יִשָּׁעֵנוּ וַיִּבְטְחוּ עַל־רֶכֶב כִּי רָב וְעַל פָּרָשִׁים
כִּי־עָצְמוּ מְאֹד וְלֹא שָׁעוּ עַל־קְדוֹשׁ יִשְׂרָאֵל וְאֶת־יהוה לֹא דָרָשׁוּ
וְגַם־הוּא חָכָם וַיָּבֵא רָע וְאֶת־דְּבָרָיו לֹא הֵסִיר וְקָם עַל־בֵּית מְרֵעִים וְעַל־עֶזְרַת
פֹּעֲלֵי אָוֶן
וּמִצְרַיִם אָדָם וְלֹא־אֵל וְסוּסֵיהֶם בָּשָׂר וְלֹא־רוּחַ וַיהוָה יַטֶּה יָדוֹ וְכָשַׁל עוֹזֵר וְנָפַל
עָזֻר וְיַחְדָּו כֻּלָּם יִכְלָיוּן

Woe to those who go down to Egypt for help. They rely on horses, and
they trust in chariots, because they are many, and in horsemen, because
they are very strong, but they do not look upon the Holy One of Israel,
they do not seek the LORD. He, also, is wise. He brings bad and he does
not turn his words aside. He rises against the house of evildoers and
against the help of doers of villainy. Egypt is human, and not God. Their
horses are flesh and not spirit. The LORD will stretch out his hand and
the helper will stumble and the helped will fall. They will all perish
together.

CONCLUSION   275

In this example we see the pattern ACT/BEHAVIOUR→PUNISHMENT. This is clear from the presence of language indicating the authoritative position of the Lord over Israel who has turned aside from him to seek help from Egypt. The oracle of punishment argues that those who do what is רַע will not find help (from Egypt) from the רַע facing them. This is because the רַע is brought by the Lord as PUNISHMENT for their actions as evildoers and "doers of villainy." Rather than turning to the Lord, they turn to Egypt for help, sealing their fate. Egypt, by attempting to prevent God's action, also comes under God's judgement. An understanding of the semantics of the domains of רַע means that the text should be interpreted as depicting the Lord as both the sovereign to whom one *should* turn for help, and a righteous judge. He is one who punishes deceitful, oppressive action, and watches over his judgement to see that it is enacted. Yet the text implies an offer of mercy: if they were to look upon the Holy One of Israel, if they were to seek the Lord, then this רַע need not come upon them.

In addition to these findings in relation to רַע, the current research found a certain conceptual distance between the אָוֶן subdomain and עָוֹן domain. While each domain requires further research to be thoroughly mapped, this distance is unlikely to be disconfirmed. Therefore, words from each of these domains should not be considered synonyms in future. Efforts should be made where possible to avoid translating words with the same word in the target language (e.g. using "iniquity" for both אָוֶן and עָוֹן), and exegetical work must consider them as referring to different concepts.

The semantic association method was found to not provide a complete map of the domains of use of רַע. Various reasons could account for this including: a preference to use semantic associates with particular domains and not others; a lack of close associates in some domains; lower frequency of use of some domains due to the specific concerns of the texts. This draws attention to a potential source of error for studies using semantic associations to map domains: domains may be incomplete, and potentially missed in some cases. However, despite this, and the time cost, the method does present valuable findings which can positively identify paradigmatic relations between many words in a more reliable manner than other methods may produce.

5.2 COMPARISON WITH PREVIOUS RESEARCH ON רַע

A brief overview of research on רַע was given in the introduction (§1.2). In comparison to the definitions given by both Dohmen and Myhill, the current analysis suggested some variations. The definitions given by both are reproduced here.

276 CHAPTER 5

> Dohmen: [T]he semantic spectrum of r^{cc} and its derivatives is well defined by its usage…. Each of these terms covers the most varied aspects of everything not good or negative; they do not make a distinction between "bad" and "evil," and so the exact meaning of r^{cc} in each instance can be determined only from contextual clues. Semantic foci come to light only in specific types of usage.[4]

> Myhill: Something is ra‘ if it causes a negative subjective reaction on the part of some being, and it involves seeing this ra‘ thing from the point of view of that being.[5]

Contrary to both were the findings of the use of רַע as influenced by the domains אָוֶן and עָוֹן to refer to GUILT and PUNISHMENT. In support of Dohmen against Myhill, it was found that רַע could be used in either objective or subjective uses (i.e. does not distinguish "bad" and "evil").

In the area of semantic domains we can note a significant departure from the domains suggested by NIDOTTE. In NIDOTTE words from the אָוֶן subdomain and עָוֹן domain are regularly listed in the same domains.[6] In contrast, the findings partially support the finding of van Steenbergen in his study of Isaiah. Van Steenbergen found two subdomains of NEGATIVE MORAL BEHAVIOUR: subdomain A, חטא (sin), עָוֹן (sin), and פשע (transgression); and subdomain B, אָוֶן (iniquity), רעע, and רשע (wicked). Although van Steenbergen relies on analysis of roots, we can see this finding replicated in the separation between major domains 1 (רָשָׁע and אָוֶן) and 2 (עָוֹן). In addition, his worldview explanation appears to have some relevance for the difference between אָוֶן and עָוֹן. He argued that words found within אָוֶן are more closely linked to relationships between humans, and that words found within עָוֹן are more closely linked with a relationship to the divine.[7] His definition of רעע behaviour may make a reasonable definition of its use in reference to אָוֶן and עָוֹן; "A deliberate form of negative moral behaviour of various degrees of specificity, regularly associated with active involvement in specific kinds of unacceptable behaviour."[8] However, van Steenbergen places רעע within his second subdomain. In contrast, the current research shows that רַע (and רָעָה) operate across the domains. It is possible that this was masked in his study by considering whole word families (רעע and רשע) as single units rather than related-but-different words.

---

[4] C. Dohmen and D. Rick, *TDOT* 13:562.

[5] Myhill, "Subjective Hebrew Ra‘," 5.

[6] "Iniquity," "Sin, guilt, rebellion, transgression, wrong," and "Transgression." VanGemeren, *NIDOTTE* 5:108, 174, 197.

[7] Van Steenbergen, *Semantics, World View and Bible Translation*, 157.

[8] Van Steenbergen, *Semantics, World View and Bible Translation*, 186.

CONCLUSION

277

In relation to my previous work on the word family רעע,[9] the current work investigated the link with חֶרֶב and רָעָב, words within the third domain (רָעָה). רַע and רָעָה were found to operate as superordinates of this highly specific domain. Their use as part of the domain was not considered to be fruitful for understanding רַע further.

Ingrid Faro recently completed her monograph titled *Evil in Genesis: A Contextual Analysis of Hebrew Lexemes for Evil in the Book of Genesis.* Unfortunately, her lexical work on the root רעע suffers from the paucity of data that is found in taking such a small sample size (i.e. Genesis only). It is unsurprising, then, that her lexical definition does not vary much from that of Dohmen. She finds that רַע is a general term for anything perceived as bad (a definition which sounds like it may agree with Myhill's subjective use argument).[10] However, Faro does add to this with an exegetical examination of the role of good and evil in Genesis, a look at related concepts, and a theological definition. The merits of these portions cannot be easily judged from the current work, but they could perhaps be rounded out by beginning with the more comprehensive definition of רַע that this work offers.[11]

5.2.1 A Brief Comparison with the Lexica

The findings of this study highlight a consistent weakness in the lexica: the reliance on glosses. This unfortunately creates a blunt instrument that struggles to handle the nuance indicated in the use of רַע, particularly in connection with the אָוֶן subdomain and עָוֹן domain. It appears that the connection with GUILT and PUNISHMENT has not been noted previously. Indeed, it is exactly the nuance found there that the lexica struggle to describe.

Furthermore, the lexica struggle to account for the wide range of use of רַע, often splitting into multiple senses where it simply forms a NEGATIVE qualification of differing elements (so with HALOT and BDB).[12] DCH performs better on this score, with less senses and a wide range of

---

[9] Foster, "A Delimitation."

[10] Faro, *Evil in Genesis*, 195–96.

[11] Faro, *Evil in Genesis*, 196. It is worth noting that Faro's theological definition is a definition of the concept rather than the lexemes. This means that definitions like this should not be read back into the lexeme in all uses. Her theological definition is "evil is anything that departs from God and his good ways as established in creation and in covenant." We should not read this back into the marketplace cry "רַע רַע" of the buyer in Proverbs 20:14 which is not motivated by a concern for theological description, but is, rather, a pragmatic description of quality.

[12] Köhler and Baumgartner, "רַע," *HALOT* 1:1251–3; Brown, Driver and Briggs, "רַע," *BDB* 948–9.

278   CHAPTER 5

glosses (e.g. sense 2 = "bad, evil, i.e. displeasing, disagreeable, unpleasant, unsatisfactory, distressing").[13] However, DCH lacks further description necessary to make sense of the array of glosses provided.

5.2.2 The Semantic Dictionary of Biblical Hebrew

While this book was being written, the SDBH was updated to include an entry on רַע. This is certainly a welcome addition to the SDBH and begs the question: "Is the current work still of value?" In this section I will attempt to briefly summarise the information presented on רַע in the SDBH and point to some areas the results of the current work may add value or even question the entries.

The entry in the SDBH suggests six broad areas of use for רַע. These are presented below in the form found on the website, which includes glosses followed by Hebrew Bible frequency numbers:

a) Bad
b) Bad > Evil
c) Bad > Ferocious
d) Bad > Grieve
e) Bad > Unsafe
f) Bad > Wrong[14]

The first entry, "bad," refers to a series of ways an object may be evaluated as bad. This shows a fairly close overlap with COMMODITY uses (§2.3.3). The lexical domain attached to this use could be improved with the inclusion of רַע.

The second entry, "evil," refers to the condition of a human or spirit. This use appears to overlap with uses of רַע in the רֶשַׁע subdomain. That is, where רַע modifies HUMAN(BEHAVIOUR). However, it also is extended to uses to describe the עַיִן (eye) of a person and to spirits. The inclusion of these two into the entry do not seem to fit well with the apparent character of the רֶשַׁע subdomain (§4.3.2), particularly with respect to the judicial implications. The halakhic use of עַיִן רָעָה in m. Terumot 4:3 appears to indicate the possibility of a non-moral meaning to the phrase.[15] Additionally, the use of רַע with רוּחַ (spirit) may not carry judicial implications.[16] The lexical domain may need to be examined with reference to the רֶשַׁע subdomain to determine if some additional words need to be added.

---

[13] Clines, "רַע I 2," *DCH* 7:505.
[14] UBS, "SDBH," 2021, http://semanticdictionary.org/.
[15] Although this could be forced rather than standard use.
[16] Although this might be a peculiarity with the SPIRIT use.

CONCLUSION

279

The third entry, "ferocious," refers to uses modifying חַיָּה (animal) and חֶרֶב (sword). Although I may dispute the inclusion of "not useful" in the definition,[17] this entry seems sound and roughly corresponds to uses which modify prosodically negative discourse elements.

The fourth entry, "grieve," refers to uses which relate to grief. These were primarily dealt with in §2.3.4 (although Neh 2:1 was dealt with in example 2.31, §2.3.2). This entry is fairly straightforward.

The fifth entry, "unsafe," is defined as: "state of an event or an object that is very difficult or painful or harmful; also used to describe the attitude or emotion in reaction to such an event."[18] This entry relates to general negative uses (primarily seen in §4.7.2 when discussing the relation between רָעָה and רַע). However, this entry includes אָוֶן in the lexical domain. This conflicts with the tentative findings concerning the אָוֶן subdomain. While the entry may be correct in including אָוֶן in the lexical domain, the current work casts doubt on this.

The sixth entry, "wrong," is fairly straightforward. It refers to the vast number of cases where רַע modifies an ACT or BEHAVIOUR. However, there is a significant concern with the items identified in the lexical domain attached to this use. Specifically, אָוֶן and עַוְלָה are included with תּוֹעֵבָה.[19] The אָוֶן subdomain and עָוֹן domain were found in this work to be lacking any frequent links between them. This result seriously questions the inclusion of these words together in a lexical domain. In addition, a word closely related to the use of רַע in this domain, עָוֹן, is missing.[20] It seems that two domains of use may be conflated here.

The sixth entry also lists the uses of רַע which occur in the phrase בִּעֵר הָרַע (purge the bad) which was established to refer to GUILT rather than an ACT (§2.3.8 and §4.5). This highlights an issue with the SDBH entry: it fails to identify the uses of רַע which follow the semantic patterns in the עָוֹן domain (ACT/BEHAVIOUR→PUNISHMENT and ACT/BEHAVIOUR→ GUILT). This could, perhaps be included as an implication, as is done for the entry on עָוֹן, "resulting in a state of guilt which often leads to punishment."[21]

---

[17] As of May 2021, the definition reads "condition of an animal that is untamed and dangerous, or of an object that is not useful and dangerous." However, the use of רַע to modify חֶרֶב (Ps 144:10; example 2.94) does not appear to warrant the inclusion of the description "not useful."

[18] UBS, "SDBH," 2021, http://semanticdictionary.org/.

[19] In addition, the verb פשע is included here. While only פֶּשַׁע was studied (and does not yet have an entry in SDBH) we might wonder if the verb should be included.

[20] רַע is also missing from the lexical domains in the entry on עָוֹן.

[21] UBS, "SDBH," 2021, http://semanticdictionary.org/.

280   CHAPTER 5

Finally, the SDBH lacks explicit observation of the scalar/categorical uses of רַע. It also lacks explicit observation of subjective versus objective use. Introduction of both of these at relevant points would be a good improvement.

In conclusion, the SDBH entry on רַע is a welcome addition, but lacks some important features. These features include: scalar versus categorical usage; subjective versus objective usage; and potentially faulty identification of the domains mapped in the current work. This identification of domains is perhaps most problematic when it comes to the potential for רַע to follow semantic patterns from the עָוֹן domain.[22]

5.3 Towards a New Entry for רַע

Future lexicographical entries on רַע may be improved in a number of ways. Here I will attempt to sketch out information relevant to an entry for רַע from the findings of this work.

רַע is an adjective of the word family רעע. It often occurs without modifying a noun. In such use it can be considered to modify some feature (or element) arising from the discourse. רַע is used as a general term to qualify something as negative. Its opposite is טוֹב (as well as יָפֶה in post-Biblical and especially Mishnaic Hebrew). רַע most often provides a general negative modification to the discourse element it modifies. Where such an element is negative already, it emphasises the negative quality.

רַע may be used objectively (where the writer expects everyone to immediately agree with the assessment), or subjectively (where the writer specifies a certain point of view). It may be construed as part of a bi-polar scale from טוֹב (or יָפֶה) to רַע, or as part of a two-category system (as in the case of moral objective use).

רַע occurs across a wide selection of domains and does not appear to cede ground in any domains to any other words across the periods studied. Furthermore, in some domains (which are of particular interest to the authors of the biblical text) רַע takes on semantic patterns of the domain.

In particular, the semantic patterns identified for the עָוֹן domain (characterised by breach of divinely delegated authority) and the אָוֶן subdomain (characterised by deceit) were seen for רַע. These included the patterns: ACT/BEHAVIOUR→GUILT and ACT/BEHAVIOUR→PUNISHMENT. That is, רַע could be used as a member of these domains to refer to either GUILT (עָוֹן

---

[22] This issue with the semantic domains is curious. In personal correspondence with de Blois I gained the impression that our methods for mapping domains are not so different.

CONCLUSION 281

only) or PUNISHMENT (both domains) as a result of a רַע ACT or BEHAVIOUR. Uses to refer to these things may be indicated by discourse context, such as where רַע is done to someone as a judicial response to רַע done by that person. Similarly, where רַע describes something that needs to be removed as a result of רַע (or עָוֹן) actions it may refer to GUILT.

5.4 AREAS FOR FUTURE RESEARCH

Throughout the analysis, areas for future research have been indicated. These generally relate to areas of limitation in scope. For example, it would be of benefit to analyse the entire רעע word family as has been done for רַע. Another area where this study is lacking is in relation to the domains of opposites. Thus, a study of טוֹב may be instructive to gaining a full understanding of the use of both רַע and טוֹב.

There were some limitations in relation to Chapters 3–4 which could be addressed through future research. With respect to the domains within which רַע functions, it may be instructive to investigate the domains where regular semantic associations did not arise. While the use of רַע in these domains could be limited to the general NEGATIVE use identified, it cannot be known unless it is examined.

In addition, the domains mapped in Chapter 3 are in need of further analysis. First, each domain should be established from the perspective of its core terms rather than its relationship to רַע. This will give a clearer picture of the extent of each domain. The interrelations of words in each domain should then be examined to display the shades of meaning found within each domain. That would also display which features highlighted in this study are true domain features, and which are artefacts of the scope of analysis. Additionally, such research may provide a clearer picture of discourse features which identify the use of these domains, thus making it clearer how רַע is being used at any particular time.

Two important areas for further research concern the אָוֶן subdomain and עָוֹן domain. For the אָוֶן subdomain, the current work suggested that MISFORTUNE is not properly a feature of the subdomain, but that it is also used for PUNISHMENT of אָוֶן ACTS. This should be treated as a tentative finding pending a full study of the אָוֶן subdomain. For the עָוֹן domain, the current work found it referred to a breach of divine law. This builds on van Steenbergen's analysis which found the group of terms referred to a breach of relationship with "causality" (i.e. the divine).[23] However, as

---

[23] Van Steenbergen, *Semantics, World View and Bible Translation*, 157.

282 CHAPTER 5

with אָוֶן, this finding, and the exact interrelations between the words within the domain await a full study of the עָוֹן domain.

Finally, an area for future research is the theological implications of the current work. This has been left relatively unexplored. The findings of this work can provide further clarity for interpreting the text which will have implications for exegesis and theology. However, the extent to which current theological understandings may be impacted (whether substantially, or simply nuanced) by these findings awaits future analysis.

APPENDICES

A. רַע AND SCHEMA: ADDITIONAL ANALYSIS

As mentioned in Chapter 2 (§2.2.2), groups of uses of רַע with less than ten occurrences presented in Table 2.1 (except for the ANIMAL group) are analysed here.

A.1 רוּחַ (spirit)

There are 9 occurrences of רַע modifying רוּחַ (spirit) in the analysed texts [7; 0; 0; 0; 2]. This use appears to exist in very specific circumstances, always in the phrase רוּחַ רָעָה and primarily in 1 Samuel.

Occurrences: Judg 9:23; 1 Sam 16:14, 15, 16, 23; 18:10; 19:9; m. Šabb. 2:5; m. ʿErub. 4:1.

In all extant uses of רוּחַ רָעָה, it appears that the modified element is SPIRIT.

A.1. Judges 9:23

וַיִּשְׁלַח אֱלֹהִים רוּחַ רָעָה בֵּין אֲבִימֶלֶךְ וּבֵין בַּעֲלֵי שְׁכֶם וַיִּבְגְּדוּ בַעֲלֵי־שְׁכֶם בַּאֲבִימֶלֶךְ

God sent a bad spirit between Abimelech and the leaders of Shechem, and the leaders of Shechem dealt treacherously with Abimelech.

While DCH lists רוּחַ as being able to refer to temper or anger, in this occurrence the spirit is *sent*.[1] Although non-sentient things can be sent (e.g. דָּגָן, grain in Joel 2:19), in all other uses when רוּחַ is sent it refers to a spirit. God sends his spirit (Isa 48:16) and withdraws it (example A.2).

A.2. 1 Samuel 16:14

וְרוּחַ יְהוָה סָרָה מֵעִם שָׁאוּל וּבִעֲתַתּוּ רוּחַ־רָעָה מֵאֵת יְהוָה

The Spirit of the LORD turned from Saul and a bad spirit from the LORD terrified him.

---

[1] Although DCH classifies this use of רוּחַ as "temper, anger," when considering חלשׁ, DCH lists it as "spirit." See Clines, "רוּחַ 3.b.8," and "חלשׁ 6.e," *DCH* 7:432; 8:380. Commentators take it as evil spirit without referring to the possibility of another meaning. For example, Trent C. Butler, *Judges*, WBC 8 (Nashville, TN: Thomas Nelson, 2009), 244; Barry G. Webb, *The Book of Judges*, NICOT (Grand Rapids, MI: Eerdmans, 2012), 280–81.

284   APPENDICES

A.3. m. Šabbat 2:5

הַמְכַבֶּה אֶת הַנֵּר מִפְּנֵי שֶׁהוּא מִתְיָרֵא מִפְּנֵי גוֹיִם מִפְּנֵי לִיסְטִים מִפְּנֵי **רוּחַ רָעָה**
אִם בִּשְׁבִיל הַחוֹלֶה שֶׁיִּישַׁן פָּטוּר

The one who puts out the [Sabbath] lamp [on the night of the Sabbath]
from fear of gentiles, of robbers, of a bad spirit, or so that a sick person
might sleep is exempt [from punishment].

Given the modified element is SPIRIT, there is no reason to suspect that
רַע contributes anything other than a negative evaluation.

A.2 DEED

There are 8 occurrences where רַע modifies one of three synonyms
(מַעֲלִיל, מַעֲשֶׂה, or מַעֲלָל) referring to a DEED through attributive, predicative, or construct relations [6; 0; 2; 0; 0]. One of these (1QHᵃ V, 20) was
too damaged to be analysed further here.

Occurrences: 1 Sam 25:3; Zech 1:4; Eccl 2:17; 4:3; 12:14; Ezra 9:13;
Neh 9:35; 1QHᵃ V, 20*; 4Q169 3–4 III, 3.

These occurrences bear close similarities to the use of רַע in conjunction
with עָשָׂה (§2.3.1). All uses appear to modify the element BEHAVIOUR.[2]

A.4. 1 Samuel 25:3b

וְהָאִישׁ קָשֶׁה וְרַע מַעֲלָלִים

…and the man was severe and bad of deeds.

It was shown in Chapter 2 (§2.1.3, example 2.2) that in this example
the primary relationship is between רַע and מַעֲלָלִים (deeds). As was mentioned there, the discourse shows Nabal acting in a harsh and inhospitable manner to David and his men who protected his shepherds and sheep
(1 Sam 25:10–11, 15–16). Thus this specific use in the discourse indicates
that Nabal is prone to doing רַע acts and therefore the reader/hearer should
expect him to act in that way. Because the text is indicating Nabal's pattern of behaviour, the modified element should be taken to be BEHAVIOUR
rather than ACT. Thus, רַע provides a negative qualification of BEHAVIOUR.
This use should be considered an objective use of רַע. There are no markers of subjectivity in the text and the text simply labels him in this way
setting up expectations for the following discourse which displays the truth
of the claim.

---

[2] Although, as discussed in §2.3.5, there may be some difficulty determining the boundary
between BEHAVIOUR and ACT.

APPENDICES   285

Examples A.5 and A.6, below, demonstrate some additional uses. In these uses the modified element may be ACT, referring to things done rather than a pattern of behaviour. However, this is complicated by the parallel with דֶּרֶךְ (way) in example A.5.

A.5. Zechariah 1:4

כֹּה אָמַר יְהוָה צְבָאוֹת שׁוּבוּ נָא מִדַּרְכֵיכֶם הָרָעִים וּמַעַלְלֵיכֶם הָרָעִים וְלֹא שָׁמְעוּ וְלֹא־הִקְשִׁיבוּ אֵלַי נְאֻם־יְהוָה

Thus says the LORD of Hosts, "Turn from your bad ways and your bad deeds." But they did not obey and did not listen to me declares the LORD.

A.6. 4Q169 3–4 III, 3–4

פשרו על דורשי החלקות אשר באחרית הקץ יגלו מעשיהם הרעים לכול ישראל ורבים יבינו בעוונם ושנאום

Its interpretation concerns the seekers of flattery: in the end time their bad deeds will be revealed to all Israel. Then many will perceive their iniquity and hate them.

Example A.7 is a little bit different.

A.7. Ecclesiastes 4:3

וְטוֹב מִשְּׁנֵיהֶם אֵת אֲשֶׁר־עֲדֶן לֹא הָיָה אֲשֶׁר לֹא־רָאָה אֶת־הַמַּעֲשֶׂה הָרָע אֲשֶׁר נַעֲשָׂה תַּחַת הַשָּׁמֶשׁ

Better than both is the one who is not yet, who has not seen the bad work that is occurring[3] under the sun.

At first glance it appears that the modified element is ACT. However, Qohelet may be lamenting the oppressive acts that occur on earth, as well as events such as the lack of comforters for the oppressed (Eccl 4:1–2).[4] Whether ACT or incorporating both ACT and EVENT, this is described here as רַע, again a negative qualification. Thus, in modifying DEED, רַע applies a negative qualification to the element.

---

[3] Samet shows that the participle is likely represented by the pointing here, with the vowel pattern being confused with a third א form. Nili Samet, "The Validity of the Masoretic Text as a Basis for Diachronic Linguistic Analysis of Biblical Texts: Evidence from Masoretic Vocalisation," *JS* 25 (2016): 1069–70.

[4] Fox argues that events are in view. Schoors suggests it remains unclear. However, Qohelet's unusual use of language renders Fox's suggestion likely. Michael V Fox, *Qoheleth and His Contradictions*, BLS 18 (Sheffield: Almond Press, 1989), 202; A. Schoors, *The Preacher Sought to Find Pleasing Words: A Study of the Language of Qoheleth Part II Vocabulary*, OLA 143 (Leuven: Peeters, 2004), 146; Samet, "Qohelet's Idiolect"; Foster, "Is Everything 'Beautiful' or 'Appropriate' in Its Time?," 42–43.

286　　　　　　　　　　　　　　APPENDICES

A.3 מַיִם (water)

There are 7 occurrences where רַע modifies מַיִם (water) [1; 0; 0; 0; 6]. In three of the mishnaic uses מַיִם is elided.

Occurrences: 2 Kgs 2:19; m. Ber. 3:5; m. Šabb. 22:4; m. ʾAbot 1:11; m. Ḥul. 3:5; m. Miqw. 10:6 (×2).

It seems likely that in all uses the good–bad quality of water is in view. Consider the following examples.

A.8.　2 Kings 2:19, 21–22

וְהַמַּיִם רָעִים וְהָאָרֶץ מְשַׁכָּלֶת...

וַיֵּצֵא אֶל־מוֹצָא הַמַּיִם וַיַּשְׁלֶךְ־שָׁם מֶלַח וַיֹּאמֶר כֹּה־אָמַר יְהֹוָה רִפִּאתִי לַמַּיִם הָאֵלֶּה

לֹא־יִהְיֶה מִשָּׁם עוֹד מָוֶת וּמְשַׁכָּלֶת

וַיֵּרָפוּ הַמַּיִם עַד הַיּוֹם הַזֶּה

"…the water is bad and the land unfruitful."… He went out to the source of the water and cast salt there. Then he said, "Thus says the Lord: 'I have healed this water, death and unfruitfulness will no longer come from there.'" So the water has been healed until this day…

A.9.　m. ʾAbot 1:11

אַבְטַלְיוֹן אוֹ׳ חֲכָמ׳ הִיזָּהֲרוּ בְדִיבְרֵיכֶם שֶׁמָּא תָחוֹבוּ חוֹבַת גָּלוּת וְתִיגְלוּ לִמְקוֹם

הַמַּיִם הָרָעִים וְיִשְׁתּוּ הַתַּלְמִידִים הַבָּאִים אַחֲרֵיכֶם וְיָמוּתוּ

Abtallion says, "Sages be careful what you say, lest you incur the penalty of exile and you go into exile to a place of bad water, and the disciples who follow you drink and die…

Bad water may lead to unproductive land (example A.8), or human (example A.9) or animal death (m. Ḥul. 3:5). The element in view, therefore, appears to be WATER QUALITY. Good quality water would be water that can be safely consumed by humans and animals, and produces crops. This does not mean bad quality water has no use. For example, it can be used to keep other things cool:

A.10.　m. Šabbat 22:4

נוֹתְנִין... וְאֶת הַמַּיִם הַיָּפִים בָּרָעִים בִּשְׁבִיל שֶׁיֵּיצַּנוּ

They put… good water into bad to keep it cool.

When modifying WATER QUALITY, רַע applies a negative qualification to the element. In the cognitive context the positive–negative scale appears to concern whether the water has life-sustaining quality or not.

A.4 TIME

There are six occurrences where רַע modifies יוֹם (day) [5; 1; 0; 0; 0]. Two of these occur in construct. There were an additional seven occurrences where רַע may modify TIME [5; 1; 1; 0; 0]. These all occur in the syntactically ambiguous phrase עֵת רָעָה and are dealt with in §A.4.2.

A.4.1 יוֹם רַע

Occurrence: Gen 47:9; Amos 6:3; Ps 49:6; 94:13; Prov 15:15; Sir 40:23 (Sir B 10r15).

More than one element may be modified when considering TIME.

> A.11. Genesis 47:9
>
> וַיֹּאמֶר יַעֲקֹב אֶל־פַּרְעֹה יְמֵי שְׁנֵי מְגוּרַי שְׁלֹשִׁים וּמְאַת שָׁנָה מְעַט וְרָעִים הָיוּ יְמֵי
> שְׁנֵי חַיַּי וְלֹא הִשִּׂיגוּ אֶת־יְמֵי שְׁנֵי חַיֵּי אֲבֹתַי בִּימֵי מְגוּרֵיהֶם
>
> Jacob said to Pharaoh, "The days of the years of my sojourning are one hundred and thirty years. The days of the years of my life have been few and bad. They have not reached the days of the years of the lives of my ancestors, in the days of their sojourning.

In this example, the modified element appears to be LIFETIME. From the context it appears that Jacob is labelling it as negative due to the length of his life in comparison to the length of his ancestors. In this use we may say that רַע is subjective, with Jacob classifying his life as such based on a comparison which does not hold for many others.

> A.12. Proverbs 15:15
>
> כָּל־יְמֵי עָנִי רָעִים וְטוֹב־לֵב מִשְׁתֶּה תָמִיד
>
> All the days of the afflicted are bad, but the good of heart has a continual feast.

In this example, the modified element is LIFETIME(AFFLICTED HUMAN). The contrast is between the lives of the afflicted and the good of heart. עָנִי should be understood as *afflicted* rather than *poor* here because the poor can be good of heart, but the afflicted, or one with a sorrowful heart has a broken spirit (Prov 15:13). רַע provides a negative qualification. Although it does not explicitly feature in Jacob's explanation, this may perhaps be seen as true from his evaluation of his life (example A.11). That is, Jacob sees them as bad because of his perspective on his life, a number of years of which he spent mourning for Joseph (Gen 44:27–29).

288   APPENDICES

A.13. Psalm 94:12–13

אַשְׁרֵי ׀ הַגֶּבֶר אֲשֶׁר־תְּיַסְּרֶנּוּ יָּהּ וּמִתּוֹרָתְךָ תְלַמְּדֶנּוּ
לְהַשְׁקִיט לוֹ מִימֵי רָע עַד יִכָּרֶה לָרָשָׁע שָׁחַת

Blessed is the man whom you discipline O LORD, and [whom] you instruct from your law, to quiet him during[5] days of bad until a pit is dug for the wicked.

This example refers not to LIFETIME, but to TIME(PERIOD). The instruction from the Lord is intended to help the person to endure a certain time which will end when the pit is dug for the wicked. רַע again provides a negative qualification, not specifying how the TIME(PERIOD) is bad, although the implication from the discourse is that it is due to the activities of the רָשָׁע (wicked).

A.4.2 עֵת רָעָה

Occurrence: Jer 15:11; Amos 5:13; Mic 2:3; Ps 37:19; Eccl 9:12; Sir 11:27 (Sir A 4v15); and 11Q5 XVIII, 15.

In the case of TIME, there is some difficulty in determining the exact number of uses within this group. This is because the phrase עֵת רָעָה (bad time/ time of bad) is ambiguous. It could either be a construct phrase employing the noun רָעָה, or רַע modifying the feminine noun עֵת (time). Example A.14 (below) highlights the issue well.

A.14. Amos 5:13

לָכֵן הַמַּשְׂכִּיל בָּעֵת הַהִיא יִדֹּם כִּי עֵת רָעָה הִיא

Therefore, the prudent one – in that time – will be silent because it is a bad time [time of evil?].

At this point it is worth considering Ecclesiastes 12:1.

A.15. Ecclesiastes 12:1

וּזְכֹר אֶת־בּוֹרְאֶיךָ בִּימֵי בְּחוּרֹתֶיךָ עַד אֲשֶׁר לֹא־יָבֹאוּ יְמֵי הָרָעָה וְהִגִּיעוּ שָׁנִים אֲשֶׁר תֹּאמַר אֵין־לִי בָהֶם חֵפֶץ

Remember your creator in the days of your youth, before the days of the evil come and the years arrive of which you say, "I have no delight in them."

---

[5] On the translation of the verb and מִן preposition see Marvin E. Tate, *Psalms 51–100*, 484. This interpretation makes the most sense of following temporal clause. In view here is the sustaining of the blessed man through days of bad until the cause of them (the wicked) is removed.

APPENDICES   289

This example uses the noun רָעָה. In this passage, the days "of the evil" are days in which a person does not have delight. From all appearances, its meaning is indistinguishable from when רַע is used. It appears to have applied a negative qualification to the element TIME(PERIOD). In this use it contrasts with חֵפֶץ (delight), indicating the modification is subjective. Example A.15 is, then, similar to example A.13. This indicates it is unlikely to be semantically possible to differentiate syntactically ambiguous uses.

A.16. Jeremiah 15:11

אָמַר יְהֹוָה אִם־לֹא שֵׁרוֹתִךָ לְטֶוֹב אִם־לֹוא | הִפְגַּעְתִּי בְךָ בְּעֵת־רָעָה וּבְעֵת צָרָה אֶת־הָאֹיֵב

The LORD says, "Have I not set you free for good? Have I not pleaded for you with the enemy in a bad time and a time of distress?

A.17. Ecclesiastes 9:12

כִּי גַּם לֹא־יֵדַע הָאָדָם אֶת־עִתּוֹ כַּדָּגִים שֶׁנֶּאֱחָזִים בִּמְצוֹדָה רָעָה וְכַצִּפֳּרִים הָאֲחֻזוֹת בַּפָּח כָּהֵם יוּקָשִׁים בְּנֵי הָאָדָם לְעֵת רָעָה כְּשֶׁתִּפּוֹל עֲלֵיהֶם פִּתְאֹם

For the person does not know his time. Like the fish that are caught in a bad trap and like the birds caught in the trap, like them the children of man are snared at a bad time, when it suddenly falls upon them.

In example A.16, one might argue that the noun is used because it is in parallel with a noun. However, it is not necessary for a noun to be in parallel with a noun, and we might make the opposite argument with Ecclesiastes 9:12 (example A.17), where there is a parallel phrase using an adjective. Therefore, with no other guide to go off, the practice of Even-Shoshan is followed, categorising these as uses of רָעָה.[6] Despite this, they are considered further in this section as relevant to the use of רַע.

In examples A.16–A.17 above, the modified element is TIME(PERIOD) as it was in example A.13. Similarly, the qualification is a negative one. The time is considered bad in the sense that it causes distress (example A.16), or is a negative change in fortunes (which may also imply distress, example A.17).

A.18. 11Q5 XVIII, 13–15

הנה
עיני ∾ צ צ ∾ על טובים תחמל ועל מפאריו יגדל חסדו
מעת רעה יציל נפש[ו]ם

Behold, the eyes of the LORD have compassion on the good. His mercy increases on those who glorify him. From a bad time he will deliver [their] soul.

---

[6] Abraham Even-Shoshan, *A new concordance of the Bible*, 1085–6.

290 APPENDICES

In example A.18, the same pattern is seen. This example is similar to example A.13 above. The one who trusts in the Lord will be delivered through the רַע TIME(PERIOD). However, the time itself is nondescript. As with the other uses, a negative qualification is in view, likely referring to times which cause distress.

A.4.3 *Conclusion*

The element TIME when modified by רַע is always viewed in terms of the passing of events with reference to some human. When רַע modifies TIME, it provides a negative qualification encompassing the occurrence of things in life that are considered distressing (example A.16). This could be due to one's own attitude to life (example A.12). Distressing things may include the behaviour of others (example A.13), a short life (example A.11) among others.

A.5 יֵצֶר (inclination)

There are six occurrences where רַע modifies יֵצֶר [2; 0; 2; 0; 2]. These occur in attributive, predicative, and construct relations.

Occurrences: Gen 6:5; 8:21; 4Q417 1 II, 12; 11Q5 XIX, 16; m. Ber. 9:5; m. 'Abot 2:11.

Elements and Modification

The use of יֵצֶר in the analysed texts needs to be addressed. In earlier texts it can be used of something that is formed.[7] However, in later use it is more technical, becoming "*the* focal point of (at least one part of) Tannaitic anthropology."[8] In this part of Tannaitic anthropology, the use of יֵצֶר alone accounts for human sinfulness. However, in Qumran it is a more marginal concept, while having some role in accounting for human sinfulness.[9] Despite the variation in meaning of יֵצֶר, the term's use with רַע is most likely derived from its use in Genesis 6:5 and 8:21.[10]

---

[7] Clines, "יֵצֶר," *DCH* 4:270–71.

[8] Ishay Rosen-Zvi, "Two Rabbinic Inclinations? Rethinking a Scholarly Dogma," *JSJ* 39 (2008): 530.

[9] Rosen-Zvi, "Two Rabbinic Inclinations," 530.

[10] If יֵצֶר later becomes negative in itself, it may be a natural development of such use. Nevertheless, the discussion here is concerned with the use of רַע, not the specifics of יֵצֶר. See Rosen-Zvi, "Two Rabbinic Inclinations," 529n48.

APPENDICES
291

A.19. Genesis 6:5

וַיַּרְא יְהוָה כִּי רַבָּה רָעַת הָאָדָם בָּאָרֶץ וְכָל־יֵצֶר מַחְשְׁבֹת לִבּוֹ רַק רַע כָּל־הַיּוֹם

The LORD saw that the badness of man on the earth was great, and every inclination of the thoughts of his heart was only bad every day.

A.20. Genesis 8:21

וַיָּרַח יְהוָה אֶת־רֵיחַ הַנִּיחֹחַ וַיֹּאמֶר יְהוָה אֶל־לִבּוֹ לֹא־אֹסִף לְקַלֵּל עוֹד אֶת־הָאֲדָמָה בַּעֲבוּר הָאָדָם כִּי יֵצֶר לֵב הָאָדָם רַע מִנְּעֻרָיו וְלֹא־אֹסִף עוֹד לְהַכּוֹת אֶת־כָּל־חַי כַּאֲשֶׁר עָשִׂיתִי

The LORD smelt the pleasing smell and said in his heart, "I will not again curse the ground because of humanity, although the inclination of the human heart is bad from his youth. Never again will I strike all life as I have done.

In examples A.19–A.20, the element refers to human INCLINATION, what a person purposes to do.[11] It is declared by the Lord here as רַע. This negative qualification has features suggesting objective use. The Lord observes it as something objectively verifiable through action (example A.19). The inclination may be viewed in a somewhat similar way in example A.21.

A.21. 11Q5 XIX, 15–16

סלחה *צצצ* לחטאתי
וטהרני מעווני רוח אמונה ודעת חונני אל אתקלה
בעווה אל תשלט בי שטן ורוח טמאה מכאוב ויצר
רע אל ירשו בעצמי כי אתה *צצצ* שבחי ולכה קויתי
כול היום

Forgive me, LORD, my sin and cleanse me from my iniquity. Favour me with a spirit of faithfulness and knowledge. Let me not dishonour myself in ruin. Do not let Satan rule in me, or an unclean spirit. Let neither pain nor a bad inclination possess my body. Because you, LORD, are my praise, and I hope in you every day.

In this example, the psalmist is requesting that the Lord not allow a series of things to rule or possess him. It seems that the inclination may be something beyond an inherent part of him, rather referring to something that may drive him to act against God; this would place it in line with the other things mentioned (pain and spirits).[12] Viewing it in this way would also make sense of the following fragmentary text.

---

[11] See B. Otzen, "יֵצֶר," *TDOT* 6:264–65.

[12] This may also see some similarity with the discussion of the two spirits and their operations in 1QS IV and Paul's discussion of the σαρκος (flesh) in Romans 7.

292 APPENDICES

A.22. 4Q417 1 II, 12

אל תפתכה מחשבת יצר רע

Do not let a thought of a bad inclination deceive you...

This suggests something more than something inherent to a person. It appears as something which can deceive a person. In both this example and example A.21, רַע may be seen as providing a negative qualification – the INCLINATION is negative in that it leads a person to a negative outcome. A similar use of רַע is seen in mishnaic literature (example A.23)

A.23. m. 'Abot 2:11

ר׳ יְהוֹשֻׁעַ אוֹ׳ עַיִן רָעָה וְיֵצֶר הָרַע וְשִׂנְאַת הַבְּרִיּוֹת מוֹצִיאִין אֶת הָאָדָם מִן הָעוֹלָם

Rabbi Joshua says, "A bad eye, the bad inclination, and hatred of people puts a person out of the world."[13]

In this example, the inclination is something to be resisted. However, regardless of the exact meaning of יֵצֶר – whether it is seen as a thing residing in a person or not[14] – the schematic contribution of רַע may still be seen as a negative qualification.

The following example must be discussed, as it is unique in Tannaitic literature, being the only occurrence with a dualistic model of "two opposing yetzarim."[15]

A.24. m. Berakot 9:5

שֶׁנֶּ׳ וְאָהַבְתָּ אֵת יְיָ אֱלֹהֶיךָ בְּכָל לְבָבְךָ וּבְכָל נַפְשְׁךָ וּבְכָל מְאוֹדֶךָ בְּכָל לְבָבְךָ בִּשְׁנֵי יְצָרֶיךָ בְּיֵצֶר טוֹב וּבְיֵצֶר רָע

As it is said, "You shall love the Lord your God with all your heart, with all your soul, and with all your might." With all your heart [means] with your two inclinations, with the good inclination and the bad inclination.

To explain this use of יֵצֶר, Rosen-Zvi offers a plausible suggestion that it relates to the focus in m. Berakot 9 on praising "God for bad and good events alike" and thus grafts "an external dualistic model onto the single yetzer doctrine (subjecting it to human will)."[16] In such a model the יֵצֶר רַע has to be supressed, "Sin is caused by the evil yetzer that dwells within people, who nonetheless have the ability to fight it and prevail."[17]

---

[13] Herford comments that "to drive a man from the world... means exclusion from human fellowship." Herford, Pirkē Aboth, 58.

[14] Rosen-Zvi, "Two Rabbinic Inclinations," 514n1.

[15] Rosen-Zvi, "Two Rabbinic Inclinations," 526–27.

[16] Rosen-Zvi, "Two Rabbinic Inclinations," 531.

[17] Rosen-Zvi, "Two Rabbinic Inclinations," 530.

APPENDICES   293

However the use of יֵצֶר רַע is interpreted, רַע forms a negative qualification (whether it be something that needs to be suppressed, or turned to
good action).[18]

Summary

Although the use of יֵצֶר has a somewhat complicated history, particularly in the Rabbinic period, the use of רַע with it appears to provide a
negative qualification of the element. We are concerned with this feature
here, and not with determining the anthropological significance of the יֵצֶר
רַע to the Rabbis.

A.6 כֹּחַ (strength)

There are six occurrences in the analysed texts where רַע modifies כֹּחַ,
all occurring in the Mishnah [0; 0; 0; 0; 6].
Occurrences: m. ʿOr. 1:5; m. ʾOhal. 18:6; m. Zabim 3:1 (×2);
m. Zabim 4:3 (×2).
In all uses of כֹּחַ modified by רַע, the context implies physical
strength is in view. This may relate to the health of a vine or strength of
a tree or branch (examples A.25–A.26) or of a person or animal (example A.27).

A.25. m. ʿOrlah 1:5

ר' מֵאִיר אוֹ' [מקום שכוחה יפה מותר] מְקוֹם שֶׁכּוֹחָהּ רַע אָסוּר

Rabbi Meir says, "[If the grafting was on] a place where its [the vine's]
strength is good, it is released [from the law of *Orlah*], [but if it was on]
a place where its strength is bad, it is subject.

A.26. m. ʾOhalot 18:6

הַמְהַלֵּךְ בֵּית [הַ]פְּרָס עַל אֲבָנִים שֶׁאֵינוּ יָכוֹל לַהֲסִיטָן עַל הָאָדָם וְעַל הַבְּהֵמָה
[שֶׁכֹּחָן יָפֶה טָהוֹר עַל אֲבָנִים שֶׁהוּא יָכוֹל לַהֲסִיטָן עַל הָאָדָם וְעַל הַבְּהֵמָה][19] שֶׁכֹּ
וחָן רַע טָמֵא

---

[18] Although the יֵצֶר רַע could be seen as used for a good purpose in Amoraic literature
(Ber. Rab. 9:7), it does not appear that way in Tannaitic literature. M. Berakot 9:5 is the
only potential candidate for such interpretation. Myhill relies on such examples in making
his case for a purely subjective רַע. John Myhill, "Subjective Hebrew Raʿ," 16; Rosen-
Zvi discusses such cases, finding them to be fringe uses of יֵצֶר in Rabbinic literature,
Rosen-Zvi, "Two Rabbinic Inclinations."
[19] This bracketed section is missing from the Kaufmann manuscript, but is present in
Eshkol. The text does not make sense without it.

294 APPENDICES

The one who moves through a graveyard on stones which he is not able to move, or on a person, or on a domestic animal[20] whose strength was good is clean, [but if it was] on stones which he is able to move, or on a person or domestic animal whose strength was bad, is unclean.

A.27. m. Zabim 3:1

הַזָּב וְהַטָּהוֹר... עָלוּ בָאִילָן שֶׁכּוֹחוֹ רַע בַּסּוּכָה שֶׁכּוֹחָהּ רַע וּבְאִילָן יָפֶה... טְמֵאִין

If a Zab and a clean one… go up on a tree whose strength was bad, [or] on a branch whose strength was bad on a good tree… they are unclean.

In all these examples it is clear that רַע provides a negative qualification to the element STRENGTH[21] specified by כֹּחַ and the discourse. In such use it evokes a bi-polar view of כֹּחַ from יָפֶה (positive = sufficient) to רַע (negative = insufficient).

B. Mapping the Lexical Semantic Domains of רַע

In Chapter 3 (§3.1.1.5), analysis of words occurring ten times or less in the analysed texts with at least one semantic association of similarity with רַע was relegated to Appendix B.1. Analysis of these words was done for completeness.

Additionally, it was noted in Chapter 3 (§3.1.1.5) that some associations of opposition (i.e. words/phrases with positive prosody) were identified for further analysis. This analysis prompted a paper on semantic change in טוֹב and יָפֶה.[22] However, it provided no results which were expected to contribute much to our understanding of the meaning of רַע. The selection and analysis of these words is presented in §B.2.

B.1 Words Occurring 10 Times or Less

Words occurring 10 times or less in the analysed texts, occurring at least once in a semantic association of similarity (i.e. similar prosody) with רַע include: בֶּלַע (swallowing); הוֹלֵלוֹת (madness); זוֹעֵף (being angry); חָסִיל (locust); יֵרָקוֹן (rust); נֶאָצָה (reviling); סִכְלוּת (folly); תַּהְפֵּכָה (perversity); פִּיד (misfortune); פָּרִיץ (violent one); and שִׁדָּפוֹן (blight).

---

[20] Jastrow, בְּהֵמָה.

[21] While in English *constitution* is considered with regard to humans, the concept seems an appropriate description of how כֹּחַ is being used in the Mishnah.

[22] Foster, "Is Everything 'Beautiful' or 'Appropriate' in Its Time?"

APPENDICES

295

Two of these, בֶּלַע and נָאָצָה, only occur with semantic associates once and so need not be considered further. זוֹעֵף only occurs twice (Gen 40:6; Dan 1:10).[23] The occurrence in Genesis 40:6 is in semantic association with רַע, and the occurrence in Daniel 1:10 is in an association of opposition with מַרְאֶה טוֹב (good appearance) and בְּרִיא בָּשָׂר (fat of flesh). הוֹלֵלוֹת and פִּיד only occur four times. הוֹלֵלוֹת appears each time with at least one semantic associate. It is associated in associations of similarity with סִכְלוּת,[24] רַע,[25] and the phrase רֶשַׁע כֶּסֶל (wickedness of folly),[26] and in opposition with חָכְמָה (wisdom).[27] פִּיד occurs in semantic associations three times. It occurs twice in associations of similarity: once with רַע in Job 31:29; and once with אֵיד (disaster) in Proverbs 24:20. It also appears once (Job 12:5) in associations of opposition with שַׁאֲנָן (at ease), and בַּטְחוֹת (security).

שִׁדָּפוֹן and פָּרִיץ, תַּהְפֻּכָה, סִכְלוּת, יֵרָקוֹן, חָסִיל occur more than four times and have their associations presented in tables below.

B.1.1 חָסִיל (locust)

חָסִיל occurred seven times in the analysed texts [6; 0; 0; 0; 1]. It occurred with associations of similarity in every occurrence. These can be seen in Table B.1.

Table B.1. חָסִיל in Associations of Similarity

Lexeme	Association	No.	Location
אַרְבֶּה		6	1 Kgs 8:37; Joel 1:4; 2:25; Ps 78:46; 2 Chr 6:28; m. Taʿan. 3:5
יֵרָקוֹן		3	1 Kgs 8:37; 2 Chr 6:28; m. Taʿan. 3:5
שִׁדָּפוֹן		3	1 Kgs 8:37; 2 Chr 6:28; m. Taʿan. 3:5
גָּזָם		2	Joel 1:4; 2:25
דֶּבֶר		2	1 Kgs 8:37; 2 Chr 6:28
יֶלֶק		2	Joel 1:4; 2:25
מַחֲלָה		2	1 Kgs 8:37; 2 Chr 6:28
נֶגַע		2	1 Kgs 8:37; 2 Chr 6:28

---

[23] In the relevant form: Qal participle. It occurs three other times.

[24] Ecclesiastes 1:17; 2:12.

[25] Ecclesiastes 9:3

[26] Ecclesiastes 7:25 as part of the phrase הַסִּכְלוּת הוֹלֵלוֹת (the foolishness that is madness).

[27] Ecclesiastes 1:17; 2:12; 7:25.

Lexeme	Association	No.	Location
רָעָב		2	1 Kgs 8:37; 2 Chr 6:28
גֵּב		1	Isa 33:4
חַיָּה רָעָה		1	m. Taʿan. 3:5
חֶרֶב		1	m. Taʿan. 3:5

חָסִיל demonstrates its closest connection to other words for locusts: יֶלֶק; גָּזָם; אַרְבֶּה; and גֵּב. It occurs with אַרְבֶּה in six of its seven occurrences. However, it also shows some association with lists of destructive judgements.

B.1.2 יֵרָקוֹן (rust)

יֵרָקוֹן occurs 10 times in the analysed texts [6; 0; 2; 0; 2]. In total יֵרָקוֹן occurs 9 times (90%) with at least one semantic association. It occurred exclusively with associations of similarity. Table B.2 shows the semantic associations of similarity.

Table B.2. יֵרָקוֹן in Associations of Similarity

Lexeme	Association	No.	Location
שִׁדָּפוֹן		8	Deut 28:22; 1 Kgs 8:37; Amos 4:9; Hag 2:17; 2 Chr 6:28; 11Q14 1 II, 12; m. Taʿan. 3:5; m. ʿArak. 9:1
אַרְבֶּה		3	1 Kgs 8:37; 2 Chr 6:28; m. Taʿan. 3:5
דֶּבֶר		3	Deut 28:22; 1 Kgs 8:37; 2 Chr 6:28
חָסִיל		3	1 Kgs 8:37; 2 Chr 6:28; m. Taʿan. 3:5
חֶרֶב		2	Deut 28:22; m. Taʿan. 3:5
מַחֲלָה		2	1 Kgs 8:37; 2 Chr 6:28
נֶגַע		2	1 Kgs 8:37; 2 Chr 6:28
רָעָב		2	1 Kgs 8:37; 2 Chr 6:28
בָּרָד		1	Hag 2:17
דַּלֶּקֶת		1	Deut 28:22
חַיָּה רָעָה		1	m. Taʿan. 3:5
חַרְחֻר		1	Deut 28:22
קַדַּחַת		1	Deut 28:22
קֶרַח		1	4Q473 2, 6

APPENDICES

Lexeme	Association	No.	Location
שַׁחֶפֶת		1	Deut 28:22
שֶׁלֶג		1	4Q473 2, 6

יֵרָקוֹן occurs with very low frequency across the analysed texts. Its associations are with forms of disaster or affliction of which it appears to almost always form a part. It may be associated with רַע through the rare phrase חַיָּה רָעָה (bad animal). The likelihood of association is reinforced if one considers the two texts 4Q285 8, 8–10 and 11Q14 1 II, 12–14. 4Q285 and 11Q14 are both copies of the same text and combining their text leads to the discovery of an additional association of similarity between יֵרָקוֹן, חַיָּה רָעָה and דֶּבֶר (plague).

B.1.3 סִכְלוּת *(folly)*

סִכְלוּת[28] occurred nine times in the analysed texts [7; 1; 1; 0; 0]. It occurred with associations of similarity (Table B.3) and associations of opposition (Table B.4).

Table B.3. סִכְלוּת **in Associations of Similarity**

Lexeme	Association	No.	Location
הוֹלֵלוֹת		2	Eccl 1:17; 2:12
חֹשֶׁךְ		2	Eccl 2:13; Sir 11:16*
הוֹלֵלוּת רָעָה		1	Eccl 10:13
רֶשַׁע כֶּסֶל	סִכְלוּת הוֹלֵלוֹת –	1	Eccl 7:25

Table B.4. סִכְלוּת **in Associations of Opposition**

Lexeme	Association	No.	Location
חָכְמָה		4	Eccl 2:12, 13; 7:25; 10:1
אוֹר		1	Eccl 2:13
חֶשְׁבּוֹן		1	Eccl 7:25
כָּבוֹד		1	Eccl 10:1

סִכְלוּת occurs once outside Ecclesiastes (Sir 11:16). It has only one frequent associate: חָכְמָה (wisdom).

---

[28] Twice as שִׂכְלוּת: Ecclesiastes 1:17; Ben Sira 11:16.

298 APPENDICES

B.1.4 תַּהְפֻּכָה *(perversity)*

תַּהְפֻּכָה occurs ten times in the analysed texts [10; 0; 0; 0; 0]. It occurred with associations of similarity (Table B.5) and associations of opposition (Table B.6).

Table B.5. תַּהְפֻּכָה in Associations of Similarity

Lexeme	Association	No.	Location
גֵּאָה		1	Prov 8:13
גָּאוֹן		1	Prov 8:13
דֶּרֶךְ רַע	פִּי תַּהְפֻּכָה –	1	Prov 8:13
זֵר		1	Prov 23:33
נִרְגָּן	אִישׁ תַּהְפֻּכָה –	1	Prov 16:28
רָעָה		1	Prov 16:30
רָשָׁע		1	Prov 10:31

Table B.6. תַּהְפֻּכָה in Associations of Opposition

Lexeme	Association	No.	Location
אָמֵן		1	Deut 32:20
צַדִּיק		1	Prov 10:31
רָצוֹן		1	Prov 10:32

תַּהְפֻּכָה occurs once outside Proverbs (Deut 32:20). It has no frequent associates.

B.1.5 פָּרִיץ *(violent one)*

פָּרִיץ occurs eight times in the analysed texts [6; 0; 1; 0; 1]. It occurred exclusively with associations of similarity (Table B.7).

Table B.7. פָּרִיץ in Associations of Similarity

Lexeme	Association	No.	Location
אַרְיֵה	פָּרִיץ חַיּוֹת –	1	Isa 35:9
זֵר		1	Ezek 7:22
טָמֵא		1	1QHª XIV, 23
עָרֵל		1	1QHª XIV, 23

APPENDICES   299

Lexeme	Association	No.	Location
רָעֵי גּוֹיִם		1	Ezek 7:22
רִשְׁעֵי הָאָרֶץ		1	Ezek 7:22
שׁוֹפֵךְ דָּם	בֶּן פָּרִיץ –	1	Ezek 18:10

פָּרִיץ only occurs in parallel four times and has no associates that occur
more than once.

B.1.6 שִׁדָּפוֹן *(blight)*

שִׁדָּפוֹן occurs 9 times in the analysed texts [5; 0; 1; 0; 3]. In total שִׁדָּפוֹן
occurs 8 times (89%) with at least one semantic association. It occurred
exclusively with associations of similarity. Table B.8 shows the semantic
associations of similarity.

Table B.8. שִׁדָּפוֹן in Associations of Similarity

Lexeme	Association	No.	Location
יֵרָקוֹן		8	Deut 28:22; 1 Kgs 8:37; Amos 4:9; Hag 2:17; 2 Chr 6:28; 11Q14 1 II, 12; m. Taʿan. 3:5; m. ʿArak. 9:1
אַרְבֶּה		3	1 Kgs 8:37; 2 Chr 6:28; m. Taʿan. 3:5
דֶּבֶר		3	Deut 28:22; 1 Kgs 8:37; 2 Chr 6:28
חָסִיל		3	1 Kgs 8:37; 2 Chr 6:28; m. Taʿan. 3:5
חֶרֶב		2	Deut 28:22; m. Taʿan. 3:5
מַחֲלָה		2	1 Kgs 8:37; 2 Chr 6:28
נֶגַע		2	1 Kgs 8:37; 2 Chr 6:28
רָעָב		2	1 Kgs 8:37; 2 Chr 6:28
בָּרָד		1	Hag 2:17
דַּלֶּקֶת		1	Deut 28:22
חַיָּה רָעָה		1	m. Taʿan. 3:5
חַרְחֻר		1	Deut 28:22
קַדַּחַת		1	Deut 28:22
שַׁחֶפֶת		1	Deut 28:22

Like יֵרָקוֹן (rust), שִׁדָּפוֹן occurs with very low frequency across the analysed texts. Additionally, their very close relationship leads to the same

300   APPENDICES

conclusion: It may be associated with רַע through the rare phrase חַיָּה רָעָה (bad animal).[29]

B.1.7 *Discussion*

The words occur too few times to say much about their use. However, יֵרָקוֹן and שִׁדָּפוֹן demonstrated some connection with רַע through the **רָעָה** domain. חָסִיל (locust) also showed some connection through this domain. As noted in Chapter 4 (§4.6), words within this domain are unlikely to provide much help in understanding the meaning and use of רַע.

B.2 Selection and Analysis of Associations of Opposition

B.2.1 *Selection for Analysis*

The initial list for association analysis in the "opposition" group is taken from Table 3.3 (§3.1.2). It includes all of the frequent associates of רַע in associations of opposition: טוֹב (good); יָפֶה (beautiful); הֲנָיָיה (benefit); שָׁלוֹם (peace); צַדִּיק (righteous); בָּרִיא (fat); אוֹר (light); חַיִּים (life); and מִשְׁפָּט (judgement).

However, for further analysis, the word needs to show a certain important link with רַע such that its oppositions can highlight the boundaries of meaning of רַע. The sort of information that is of importance is like that which can be seen for טוֹב. Through this initial analysis it appears טוֹב cedes some areas of opposition to רַע in Mishnaic Hebrew. The frequency of the יָפֶה :: רַע opposition in the Mishnah for areas such as agriculture to the exclusion of טוֹב :: רַע oppositions in this area suggest that טוֹב is no longer the conventional opposition for רַע in these areas.[30]

Turning back to the selection method, in addition to occurring with רַע, we need to have some confidence that the word or phrase occurs in this opposition in conventional use. The frequency of occurrence should give some indication of this. That is, high frequency words that occur three times with רַע are unlikely to be demonstrating a conventional opposition, whereas low frequency words that occur three times may be. Not only this, but we need to determine its use as the *primary opposition* for רַע. For

---

[29] See §B.1.2.

[30] Further investigation led to the following conclusion: "In the Mishnah, יָפֶה does not have the conventional use of something aesthetically pleasing to the senses. It is, however, conventionally used of things that are considered of good quality in the agricultural context. In this sense it appears to have completely displaced טוֹב." Foster, "Is Everything 'Beautiful' or 'Appropriate' in Its Time?," 52.

APPENDICES   301

example, it is not very illuminating to say that צַדִּיק (righteous) occurs in opposition to רַע if רַע is also in an association of similarity with רָשָׁע (wicked) in those occurrences. This is because צַדִּיק :: רָשָׁע appear to form an antonym pair (see §3.2.1).

From the outset it is clear that טוֹב (good), and יָפֶה (beautiful) will require further analysis. Their frequency of occurrence and variation of use between corpuses are particularly of interest. Notably, both occur as primary oppositions of רַע. הֲנָיָיה (benefit) is also of interest. However, its occurrence with רַע is limited to m. Sanhedrin 8:5. According to the criterion of dispersion (Table 4.2, §4.1), it seems unlikely that pursuing further analysis of this word is worthwhile.[31]

The next most frequent, שָׁלוֹם (peace), can be eliminated. It occurs approximately 452 times[32] and only occurs clearly as the primary opposition to רַע in Isaiah 45:7 [MT] and Proverbs 12:20. It occurs once where it may or may not be the primary opposition (4Q504 1–2 IV, 13), twice where טוֹב is the primary opposition (Ps 34:15; 4Q525 14 II, 12), and once as part of a large list of similarities and oppositions (Isa 59:7). This does not mean שָׁלוֹם is of no interest in the analysis of רַע, but rather that it is unlikely that an association analysis of the word will illuminate the meaning of רַע.

The case of צַדִּיק (righteous) is more complex. It occurs three times with רַע as the primary opposition (Ps 34:17; Prov 11:21; 29:6). In particular in these cases רַע is semantically human. However, צַדִּיק occurs an estimated 307 times[33] and occurs 129 times in association with its antonym רָשָׁע (wicked). The fact that רַע only occurs where רָשָׁע would also be an appropriate choice, and that it does so comparatively rarely indicates that the analysis of רָשָׁע in §3.2.1 has already filled in the information that an association analysis of צַדִּיק would be likely to give.

בָּרִיא (fat) only occurs an estimated 30 times.[34] It is only associated with רַע in Genesis 41 in reference to פָּרָה (cow). This might indicate importance; however, the primary opposition with רַע three of the four times is יָפֶה (beautiful), and the one time it is not present, the word רַק (thin) which elsewhere in Genesis 41 forms the primary opposition for בָּרִיא is also in semantic association. Therefore, בָּרִיא is excluded.

---

[31] הֲנָיָיה occurs 84 times in the analysed texts; all occurrences are in the Mishnah. It only occurs ten times in an association of opposition. All of these are within m. Sanhedrin 8:5 and involve an opposition with רַע.

[32] DCH lists 399 occurrences. Clines, "שָׁלוֹם," DCH 8:365. The Accordance tagging of the Kaufmann manuscript contains 53 occurrences.

[33] DCH lists 284 occurrences. Clines, "צַדִּיק," DCH 7:75. The Accordance tagging of the Kaufmann manuscript contains 23 occurrences.

[34] DCH lists 14 occurrences. Clines, "בָּרִיא," DCH 2:263. The Accordance tagging of the Kaufmann manuscript contains 16 occurrences.

302　　　　　　　　　　　　　　APPENDICES

מִשְׁפָּט has an estimated 871 occurrences,[35] only three are found in opposition to רַע and none could convincingly be said to be of primary opposition. Additionally, neither אוֹר (light) nor חַיִּים (life) occur as the primary opposition of רַע. Therefore, they are excluded.

Words for inclusion in the analysis are now reduced to two: טוֹב (good), and יָפֶה (beautiful).

B.2.2 *Analysis of Associations of Opposition*

B.2.2.1 טוֹב (good)

טוֹב occurs 743[36] times in the analysed texts [502;[37] 40; 38; 5; 158]. Table B.9 shows its occurrence in associations of opposition.

Table B.9. טוֹב in Associations of Opposition

Lexeme	Association	No.	Location
רַע	טוֹב –	87	Gen 2:9, 17; 3:5, 22; 24:50; 31:24, 29; 41:26; Lev 27:10, 12, 14, 33; Num 13:19; Deut 1:39; 30:15; Josh 23:15; 1 Sam 29:6; 2 Sam 13:22; 14:17; 19:36; 1 Kgs 3:9; 22:8, 18; 2 Kgs 2:19; Isa 3:10; 5:20; 7:15, 16; 1Qisaᵃ XXXVIII, 13; Jer 24:2, 3, 5; 40:4; 42:6; Ezek 36:31; Amos 5:14, 15; Mic 1:12; Mal 2:17; Ps 34:15; 36:5; 37:27; 52:5; Job 2:10; 30:26; Prov 14:19, 22; 15:3; 31:12; Eccl 12:14; 2 Chr 18:17; Sir 11:14, 31; 12:4; 13:24, 25; 14:10; 31:23; 37:18, 28; 39:25 (×2)*, 27*, 33*; 1QS I, 5; II, 3; X, 18; 4Q303 8; 4Q365 32, 6; 4Q367 3, 10; 4Q380 1 II, 5*; 4Q410 1, 6; 4Q416 1, 15*; 4Q417 1 I, 18*; 4Q418 2+2a–c, 7; 4Q423 1–2 I, 7; 5, 6*; 4Q525 14 I, 13; 11Q5 XVIII, 14; 11Q19 LV, 14; m. Ber. 9:2, 5; m. 'Abot 2:9 (×5); 5:19
	אוֹהֵב טוֹב –	1	Sir 37:5
דָּבָר רַע	שְׁמוּעָה טוֹבָה –	1	1 Sam 2:24

[35] DCH lists 861 occurrences. Clines, "מִ,שְׁפָּט," *DCH* 5:556. The Accordance tagging of the Kaufmann manuscript contains 10 occurrences.
[36] Differentiation of adjective and verb can be very difficult. For example one can refer to the case of Judges 11:25. See Miller-Naudé and Naudé, "A Re-Examination," 292.
[37] Eight occurrences were added from the Samaritan Pentateuch: Genesis 41:26; Exodus 6:8; 18:24; Numbers 20:12 (×2); Deuteronomy 8:7; 13:19; and 28:11. Two occurrences were added from the Judean Desert corpus: 1QIsaᵃ XXXVIII, 13 [Isa 45:6]; and 11Q5 XVI, 5 [Ps 118:9].

APPENDICES

Lexeme	Association	No.	Location
רָעָה		10	Gen 26:29; 1 Sam 20:12; Jer 44:17; Mic 3:2; Ps 52:5; Prov 3:27; 11:27; 13:21; 17:20; Lam 3:38
רֹעַ		5	Jer 24:2, 3, 5; Sir 42:14 (×2)
דַּק		4	Gen 41:5, 22, 24, 26
רָשָׁע		4	Prov 14:19; Eccl 9:2; 1QHª VI, 23; 11Q5 XVIII, 14
חוֹטֵא		3	Prov 13:22; Eccl 7:26; 9:2
מָוֶת		3	Deut 30:15; Sir 11:14; 37:18
שְׁדוּף קָדִים		3	Gen 41:5, 22, 26
תּוֹעֵבָה		2	Ezek 36:31; Prov 20:23
מַעֲשֵׂה תּוֹעֵבָה		1	1QS IV, 3
אָוֶן		1	Ps 36:5
פּוֹעֲלֵי אָוֶן		1	Ps 125:4
בְּעָתָה		2	Jer 8:15; 14:19
חֹשֶׁךְ		2	Isa 5:20; 1Qisaª XXXVIII, 13
עָוֹן		2	Ezek 36:31; Hos 14:3
רְמִיָּה		1	Ps 52:5
רְמִיָּה אַכְזָרִי		1	1QS IV, 3
שֶׁקֶר		2	Ps 52:5; 1QS IV, 3
אֵבֶל		1	Esth 9:22
אִוֶּלֶת		1	1QS IV, 3
אִישׁ מְזִמָּה		1	Prov 12:2
שֵׂכֶל טוֹב – בּוֹגְדִים		1	Prov 13:15
בֶּלַע		1	Ps 52:5
גֵּוָה		1	1QS IV, 3
דֶּרֶךְ נִדָּה		1	1QS IV, 3
הַוָּה		1	Ps 52:5
זֵד		1	11Q5 XVIII, 14
דֶּרֶךְ טוֹב – חַטָּאת		1	1 Kgs 8:36
חָמָס		1	Prov 13:2
חֹנֶף		1	1QS IV, 3
טָמֵא		1	Eccl 9:2
יָגוֹן		1	Esth 9:22

304 APPENDICES

Lexeme	Association	No.	Location
כֹּבֶד אֹזֶן		1	1QS IV, 3
כֹּבֶד לֵב		1	1QS IV, 3
כַּחַשׁ		1	1QS IV, 3
לְשׁוֹן גִּדּוּף		1	1QS IV, 3
מוּם		1	Dan 1:4
מַחֲשֶׁבֶת עָמָל	לֵב טוֹב –	1	Sir 13:26
מַר		1	Isa 5:20
מִרְמָה		1	Ps 52:5
מֵרַע		1	Sir 37:5
נִמְבְזֶה		1	1 Sam 15:9
נָמֵס		1	1 Sam 15:9
סוּג לֵב		1	Prov 14:14
עֶבְרָה		1	Prov 11:23
עִוְרוֹן עֵינַיִם		1	1QS IV, 3
עָנִי		1	Prov 15:15
פַּחַד		1	4Q525 14 II, 13
צָנֻם		1	Gen 41:22
קִנְאַת זָדוֹן		1	1QS IV, 3
קֹצֶר אַפַּיִם		1	1QS IV, 3
קְשִׁי עֹרֶף		1	1QS IV, 3
רֵיק		1	Gen 41:26
רֵישׁ		1	Sir 11:14
רָעָב		1	Gen 41:35
רַק		1	Gen 41:26
רֶשַׁע		1	1QS IV, 3

טוֹב (good) occurred most frequently with רַע. However, it also demonstrated frequent associations with רָעָה (evil); רֹע (evil); דַּק (thin); רֶשַׁע (wicked); חוֹטֵא (sinner); מָוֶת (death); שְׁדוּף קָדִים (scorched by the east wind); and תּוֹעֵבָה (abomination).

The טוֹב :: רָעָה opposition occurs ten times, exclusively in the Hebrew Bible. In nine occurrences, רָעָה is the only opposition (in Ps 52:5 the main opposition is with רַע). Without further analysis it is impossible to know whether this use is an acceptable and uncommon opposition used

APPENDICES 305

in place of the more common רַע :: טוֹב opposition, or if there is a difference in meaning.

Except for in Ben Sira, the uses of רֹע occur in passages where the
primary opposition is with רַע. Furthermore, because Ben Sira is unpointed,
it is possible these may be misidentified uses of טוֹב (good).[38]

Although דַּק and שְׁדוּף קָדִים occur only four and three times respectively and are limited in occurrence to Genesis 41, the three overlapping
occurrences do not occur with רַע and are the only occurrences in the
analysed texts where שִׁבֹּלֶת (ear of grain) is qualified. This may indicate
a limitation to the use of רַע with respect to agriculture.

רָשָׁע occurs once (1QH[a] VI, 23) as the only opposition of טוֹב and three
times with at least one other term, two of which the main opposition is
with צַדִּיק (righteous).

חוֹטֵא (sinner) occurs each time with טוֹב as its primary opposition. The
Qal participle only occurs 43 times [17; 3; 0; 0; 23] across the analysed
texts. As such, it may indicate an uncommon use and/or limitation to the
meaning of רַע.

מָוֶת and תוֹעֵבָה need not be considered antonyms of טוֹב as מָוֶת always
occurs in primary opposition with חַיִּים (life), and תוֹעֵבָה only occurs once
as the primary opposition.

B.2.2.2 יָפֶה (beautiful)

יָפֶה occurs 152 times in the analysed texts [43; 3; 8; 0; 98]. Its most
frequent occurrence is in Mishnaic Hebrew.

Table B.10. יָפֶה in Associations of Opposition

Lexeme	Association	No.	Location
רַע		29	Gen 41:2, 4, 18; m. Ter. 2:6 (×4); 4:3; 6:6; m. ʿOr. 1:5; Šabb. 22:4; m. Ketub. 13:10 (×3); m. Ned. 9:8 (×2); m. B. Meṣ. 4:1 (×2); m. B. Bat. 5:6 (×4); m. ʿArak. 9:2; m. ʾOhal. 18:6; m. Miqw. 10:6 (×2); m. Zabim 2:2; 3:1; 4:3
דַּק בָּשָׂר – יָפֶה מַרְאֶה		2	Gen 41:2, 4
מוּם		2	2 Sam 14:25; Song 4:7

---

[38] Unless there is a spelling error they are not misidentified uses of רַע because in the
B manuscript it is written רוע.

306 APPENDICES

Lexeme	Association	No.	Location
רַק בָּשָׂר	יָפֶה מַרְאֶה –	2	Gen 41:4, 18
דַּל		1	Gen 41:18
רַע		1	Gen 41:18

יָפֶה occurred in frequent association with רַע only. This was primarily driven by 26 associations in the Mishnah. It occurred with no other frequent oppositions. The comparatively rare occurrence of the יָפֶה :: רַע opposition in the Hebrew Bible suggests a linguistic movement in the use of יָפֶה. In the Mishnah, it appears to have overtaken functions that were reserved for טוֹב in the Biblical corpus.

B.2.3 *Discussion*

Three oppositions were found which may deserve future analysis and comparison to the טוֹב :: רַע opposition. These are טוֹב :: חוֹטֵא ;טוֹב :: רָעָה; and רַע :: יָפֶה. These oppositions may indicate areas of limitation of meaning and/or use for רַע. However, the most frequent opposition occurs with רָעָה, which behaves in very similar ways to רַע, and its use may represent where they overlap in meaning. The טוֹב :: חוֹטֵא opposition is of low frequency and unlikely to greatly influence the picture of רַע presented in this work. Finally, the יָפֶה :: רַע opposition was analysed elsewhere[39] and did not provide additional information to nuance our understanding of רַע. The opposition טוֹב :: שָׂדוּף קָדִים + דַּק was also detected, it only occurred in Genesis 41. It provides too little data to draw any conclusions.

Despite the above conclusions, further analysis of the טוֹב :: רָעָה and טוֹב :: חוֹטֵא oppositions may be of some value in rounding out our understanding of רַע.

C. TEXTUAL MATTERS

This appendix provides a list of portions of text which were analysed despite textual damage. These are organised by corpus. They were identified with an asterisk (*) when mentioned in the body of this work. Where possible links are provided to where the images of the manuscripts can be viewed.[40]

---

[39] Foster, "Is Everything 'Beautiful' or 'Appropriate' in Its Time?"
[40] Links valid as of May 2021.

APPENDICES
307

C.1 Ben Sira

Ben Sira 7:1–2 (A 2v6b–7 / C 3r8b–10)

A: אל תעש לך רעה ואל ישיגך רעה
C: אל תעש רע [ואל]ישיגך רע
A: הרחק מעון ויט ממך
C: רחק מעון [ויט]ממך

Links: https://www.bensira.org/images/Manuscripts/A/A_II_Verso.jpg;
https://www.bensira.org/images/Manuscripts/C/C_IV_Recto.jpg

The gaps in the C manuscript are of sufficient size to include the reconstructed letters. The variant manuscript and the Old Greek also support the reconstruction.

Ben Sira 11:16 (A 4v5b–6)

שכלות
וחושֶׁך לפשעים נוצרה ומרעים רעה עמם

Link: https://www.bensira.org/images/Manuscripts/A/A_IV_Verso.jpg
The final two letters of חושך are heavily damaged. However, there is physical evidence for their existence.

Ben Sira 11:25 (A 4v14b–15)

טובָ͏ת͏ יום תְשַׁכַּח רעָה͏ה ורעת
י[ום] תשׁכֹח טובֹה ואחרית אאד͏ם תהיה עליו

Link: https://www.bensira.org/images/Manuscripts/A/A_IV_Verso.jpg
The second occurrence of טובה has damage to the ב and final ה. However, there is still adequate physical evidence for the existence of the letters.

Ben Sira 38:10 (B 8r16)

[סו]ר מֹעוֹל ומהכר <הֹסיר מ' והכר> פנים [ ] ומכל פשעים טהר לב

Link: https://www.bensira.org/images/Manuscripts/B/B_VIII_Recto.jpg
Although there is extensive damage to the phrase, the verse most likely begins with סור מֵעָוֶל (turn from injustice). The visible parts of the letters in the preposition phrase render the existence of מֵעָוֶל (from injustice)

308   APPENDICES

certain. There is also some physical evidence for סור (to turn). This is enough to be confident of the existence of a parallel.

Ben Sira 39:25 (B 9r13)

‏] -- לט[וב חלק מראש] [כן לרעים טוב ורע <לרע>

Link: https://www.bensira.org/images/Manuscripts/B/B_IX_Recto.jpg

The first occurrence of טוב (good) in this verse is damaged. However, although difficult to detect in the colour photograph, the final two letters וב survive. The evidence for this association is sufficient: there is some physical evidence; it is an extremely common association; and the Old Greek supports the reading with ἀγαθὰ τοῖς ἀγαθοῖς where the Hebrew text is lost.

Ben Sira 39:27 (B 9r16)

כל °] --]ל[ט]וֹּבִֿֿ֛ם ייטיבו] [כן לרעים לרעה <לזרא> נהפכו

Link: https://www.bensira.org/images/Manuscripts/B/B_IX_Recto.jpg

לַטּוֹבִים (to the good) is heavily damaged. The initial letter ט is missing, and there is damage to the initial ל and the letters ובי (although some evidence of these letters can be seen). The physical evidence for the word, the regularity of this association and the support of the Old Greek renders this word certain. The Old Greek supports this parallel with τοῖς εὐσεβέσιν εἰς ἀγαθά. Although unusual, there is precedent for טוב being translated εὐσεβής in Ben Sira (Sir 12:4).

Ben Sira 39:29–30 (B 9v1–3a)

אש וברד רע ודבר] [גם אלה למשפט נבֿ[ראו][41]
חית שן עקרב ופתן] [וחרב נקמות להחרים] -- [
כל <גם> אלה לצורכם נבראו <נבחרו>

Link: https://www.bensira.org/images/Manuscripts/B/B_IX_Verso.jpg

The occurrence of רַע in Sir 39:29 is disputed. The Old Greek's λιμος (famine) suggesting the reading רָעָב (famine). However, the reading of the manuscript is clear. Therefore, this is treated as a valid occurrence of רַע in Chapter 3.

---

[41] The reconstruction is highly likely based on Masıh 1:5 and the use of the verb in B 9v3. A colour photograph (which is very hard to make out) of Masıh can be found here: https://www.deadseascrolls.org.il/explore-the-archive/image/B-371464

APPENDICES

After the additional analysis, it is concluded in Chapter 4 to be highly likely to be an error of omission. This is also supported by the vast number of associations between רָעָב and דָּבָר (33 times) and the lack of other occurrences of רע standing alone in such close association with a רָעָה term.[42] Furthermore, the list is specific, but like רָעָה, רע was found used as a superordinate of these terms. Because there is no information to determine a specific referent this is semantically suspect.

The reconstruction of the verb ברא is highly likely based on Masıh 1:5 and the use of the verb in B 9v3.

Ben Sira 39:33–34 (B 9v6–7)

מעשה אל כלם <הכל> טובׄים [ ] לכל צורך <צרוך> בעתו יׄסׄפׄוק
אל <אין> לאמר זה רע מה זה <מזה> [ ] כי הכל בעתו יגׄבׄׄר <יגבר>

Link: https://www.bensira.org/images/Manuscripts/B/B_IX_Verso.jpg
טוֹבִים (good) has the two letters בי damaged. However, there is some physical evidence for the existence of the letters.

Ben Sira 40:9 (B 10r1)

דׄ[ב]ר ודם חרחר וחרב [ ] שד ושבר רעה ומות

Link: https://www.bensira.org/images/Manuscripts/B/B_X_Recto.jpg
דָּבָר is damaged with the medial ב entirely missing and the initial ד heavily damaged. Despite this, given the frequent co-occurrence and the co-associations in Sir 40:9 it seems highly likely that דבר is correct.

Ben Sira 41:17–18 (B 11r11–12, corrector)

בוש מאב ואם אל זנות <על פחׄזׄ> [ ] מנשיא יושב אל <ושׂר עַל> כחש
מאדון וגברת על שקר [ ] מעדה ועם על פשע

Link: https://www.bensira.org/images/Manuscripts/B/B_XI_Recto.jpg
The final ז in פַּחַז (reckless) is damaged, but there is physical evidence for its existence.

---

[42] "Famine and pestilence were the usual accompaniments of a prolonged siege," Skehan and Di Lella, *The Wisdom of Ben Sira*, 460–61.

310 APPENDICES

C.2 Judean Desert

The images for 1QH^a cannot be viewed online.

1QpHab X, 11–12

בעבור כבודה לוגיע רבים בעבודת שוו ולהרותם
במ[ע]שי שקר להיות עמלם לריק בעבור יבואו

Link: http://dss.collections.imj.org.il/habakkuk

מַעֲשֵׂה is missing its medial ע. However, most of the word is visible, and the clear parallel with בעבודת שוו makes this reconstruction all but certain.

1QM XIII, 1b–2a

וברכו על עומדם את אל ישראל ואת כול מעשי אמתו וזעמו
שם אֵת בֹ[ל]יּעל ואת כול רוחי גורלו

Link: http://dss.collections.imj.org.il/war

בְּלִיַּעַל is damaged here. There is plenty of evidence that this is the word (including portions of the ב and י and its common use in 1QM, cf. line 4).

1QH^a V, 20

אתה גליתה דרכֹי אֹמֹת וֹמעשי רע חוכמה ואולֹת

Much of דַּרְכֵי אֱמֶת was heavily damaged. The final ת in אִוֶּלֶת (folly) was also heavily damaged, but there is some physical evidence for the letters.

1QH^a VI, 26b–27a

וכֹול עולה
וֹרֹשע תשמיד לעד

The letters ור in וְרֶשַׁע (and wickedness) are heavily damaged, but there is some physical evidence for their existence.

1QH^a IX, 24

סוד הערוה ומקור הנדה כור העוון ומבנה החטאה רֹוח התוֹעה

The ו in תֹּועָה is badly damaged, but there is some physical evidence for its existence.

APPENDICES

1QHᵃ X, 24

והמה סוד שוא ועדת בְּלִֿיעל

The initial two letters of בְּלִיַעל (Belial) are heavily damaged. However, the word is expected here and there is some physical evidence for their existence.

1QHᵃ XIII, 9b

אריות שוברי עצם אדירים ושותי דֿמֿ גבורים

Both letters in דָּם are heavily damaged; however, this is a common association and there is some physical evidence for their existence.

1QHᵃ XIV, 8

מעדת שֿוֿא וֿמסוד חמס וֿתֿביאני בעצֿת הֿקוֿֿדֿש

The first two letters of שָׁוְא (worthlessness) are heavily damaged. All of the letters of הַקּוֹדָשׁ (the holiness) are heavily damaged. However, there is physical evidence for their existence.

1QHᵃ XV, 14

ואין פֿה לרֿוֿח הוות ולא מענה לשון לכול בֿני אשמה

The first two letters (רו) of רוּחַ (spirit) are damaged as is the initial letter of בְּנֵי (sons of). However there is physical evidence for their existence.

1QHᵃ XXIV, 23

כול שטן ומשחית

While this section of the text is highly fragmentary, the coordinate phrase is likely to demonstrate some form of semantic association and so was included in the Chapter 3 analysis.

1Q27 1i5b–6a

וגלה הרשע מפני הצדק כגלות [ח]וֿשך מפני
אור

Link: https://www.deadseascrolls.org.il/explore-the-archive/image/
B-278263

312   APPENDICES

The initial letter of חוֹשֶׁךְ is entirely missing. However, the context makes this reading certain.

1Q28ᵃ I, 10–11a

אל אשה לדעתה למשכבי זכר כיאם לפי מילואת לו עש[רי]ם שנה בדעתו[ן טוב]
ורע

Link: https://www.deadseascrolls.org.il/explore-the-archive/image/B-278249

Although טוב is missing from the text, the regularity of the expression (particularly in relation to the use of דַּעַת with the words) and the size of the gap means we can have a high degree of confidence in the reconstruction.

4Q88 IX, 6–8

להשבית רשעים
מן הארץ[ובני]עֹולה לוא
ימצאו

Link: https://www.deadseascrolls.org.il/explore-the-archive/image/B-371347

עַוְלָה likely forms part of a phrase. The first word is lost. However, the phrase is in parallelism and so the phrase can be expected to specify a group of people characterised by עַוְלָה.

4Q88 X, 11b–13a

הנֹא אואבים
יובדו ויֹתפֹרֹדו כול פֹּוֹעֹלי
און

Link: https://www.deadseascrolls.org.il/explore-the-archive/image/B-363361

פֹּוֹעֹלֵי (doers of) is heavily damaged. However, the infrared image shows some physical evidence for all letters (Accordance records the פ and ו as missing),[43] and the regularity of the phrase פֹּוֹעֲלֵי אָוֶן (doers of villainy), and the context are strong enough evidence in favour of a phrasal association with אוֹיֵב. The plural אוֹיְבִים is written אואבים with the medial י shifting to a medial א.[44]

---

[43] As of May 2021.

[44] For the existence of this type of shift in the Judean Desert manuscripts see Reymond, *Qumran Hebrew*, 119.

APPENDICES 313

4Q286 7 II, 2b–4a

וענו ואמרו ארור̇ [ב]ליעל ב̇[מ]ח̇שבת משטמתו
וזעום הוא במשרת אשמתו וארורים כול ר̇ו̇[ח]י גו̇[ר]לו במחשבת רשעמה
וזעומים המה במחשבות נדת [ט]מאתמה

Link: https://www.deadseascrolls.org.il/explore-the-archive/image/
B-513176

The phrase בְּמַחְשֶׁבֶת מַשְׂטֵמַתוֹ (because of the thoughts of his hostility)
contains a number of damaged letters. However, there is sufficient physical
evidence for its existence including the size of gaps and presence of ink.

The initial ט in טֻמְאָה (impurity) is missing.

4Q303 8

[--]ר ושכל טוב ורע ל[--]

Link: https://www.deadseascrolls.org.il/explore-the-archive/image/
B-284430 (top right)

Despite the fragmentary nature of the text, the semantic association is
clear and so was included in the analysis.

4Q368 10 I, 7b–8a

[--] מחלים
ר̇ע̇ים ו̇מ̇כֹ̇ה גד[ו]לֹה ונגעים לאין [--]

Link: https://www.deadseascrolls.org.il/explore-the-archive/image/
B-362417 (7b); https://www.deadseascrolls.org.il/explore-the-archive/image/
B-362415 (8a)

Both רָעִים (evil) and מַכָּה גְדוֹלָה (great wound) were damaged; however,
the only letter that was completely erased by damage to the scroll was the
medial ו in גְדוֹלָה. The physical evidence for the phrases in the semantic
association is sufficient.

4Q371 1a–b, 13

דברי̇[ ]ש̇קר וכול אמרי כזב

Link: https://www.deadseascrolls.org.il/explore-the-archive/image/
B-371242 (fragments 2 4, and 6 in image)

The final י in דִּבְרֵי (words of) and initial שׁ in שֶׁקֶר (lie) is damaged.
However, there is adequate physical evidence.

314 APPENDICES

4Q380 1 II, 5

עושה טוב[?] ושנאי רעים

Link: https://www.deadseascrolls.org.il/explore-the-archive/image/
B-360364

The manuscript is damaged after the ב and there is sufficient space for
the scribe to have included an additional letter. However, the space is not
so big that it would be an exceptionally large gap between words for this
scribe. Therefore, it could either have been an instance of טוב (good) or
of the feminine noun of the same word family טוֹבָה (good). The contrast
between adjective and noun occurs nowhere else in the analysed texts,
for this reason it was opted to count this as an instance of טוב.

4Q393 1 II–2, 6b–7a

ולפשעֹים דֹרֹכֹּיֹך
וחטאים השב אליך

Links: https://www.deadseascrolls.org.il/explore-the-archive/image/
B-295484 (6b); https://www.deadseascrolls.org.il/explore-the-archive/
image/B-295485 (7a)

There is some damage to the clause containing the association. However, the physical evidence for the words is sufficient.

4Q398 14–17 II, 5

והרחיק ממך מחשב{{ו}}ת רעה ועצֹת בליֹעֹל

Link: https://www.deadseascrolls.org.il/explore-the-archive/image/
B-284805 (bottom)

There is some damage to בְּלִיַּעַל (Belial), however, the physical evidence
is sufficient.

4Q410 1, 6

מה {{מ}}ᴀᴃᴀאמת טוב ומה {{מ}}ᴀᴃᴀהᵒᵒ[ ]רע

Link: https://www.deadseascrolls.org.il/explore-the-archive/image/
B-364378

There is some damage to the ר in רע here, but it is sufficiently clear. The
preceding word has been largely destroyed. However, the context is suit-
ably clear to be confident that an association exists between the highly frequent associates רָע and טוב (good).

APPENDICES

4Q416 1, 15

להבין צדק בין טוב לרֹעֹ

Link: https://www.deadseascrolls.org.il/explore-the-archive/image/
B-359117

רע is heavily damaged here, but there is sufficient evidence of its existence.
Accordance incorrectly reads this as: להכֹּון (to establish). In the hand
of this scribe, the hook at the top of the bet ‎‎בּ (as opposed to the hookless
kaph ‎כ) is clearly visible in the infrared photograph.

4Q417 1 I, 17b–18a

כי לא ידע בין
[טו]בֹ לרע כמשפט [ר]וחו

Link: https://www.deadseascrolls.org.il/explore-the-archive/image/
B-370823

The initial two letters of טוב are entirely missing. Given the regularity
of expression, the size of the gap, and the presence of part of the ‎ב, we can
be sure טוב is the damaged word.

4Q418 2+2a–c, 7

להבין צדיק בין טוב לרעֹ

Link: https://www.deadseascrolls.org.il/explore-the-archive/image/
B-364284

The final ע of רֵע is damaged, but the physical evidence makes it clear.

4Q418 81+81a, 2

ואתה הבדל מכול אשר שנא והנזר מכול תעבות נפֹשֹ

Link: https://www.deadseascrolls.org.il/explore-the-archive/image/
B-499684

The final two letters of נפש are heavily damaged, but there is some
physical evidence for their existence.

4Q423 5, 6

ה]תֹבֹונן בכל תבואתכה ובעֹבֹוֹדֹתכה השכֹ]ל בדעת ה]טֹוב עם הרע

Link: https://www.deadseascrolls.org.il/explore-the-archive/image/
B-359338 (6a); https://www.deadseascrolls.org.il/explore-the-archive/image/
B-359336 (6b)

316   APPENDICES

The context is damaged as is the initial letter of טוב. However the regularity of the association and the available text was considered sufficient
evidence that the words are in an association of opposition.

4Q434 1 I, 5a

וביד עריצים̊ לא נתנם ועם ר̊שעים לא שפטם

Link: https://www.deadseascrolls.org.il/explore-the-archive/image/
B-513122
The initial letter and two final letters of עָרִיצִים (ruthless) and the first
letter of רְשָׁעִים are heavily damaged. However, there is sufficient evidence of the letters.

4Q434 7b, 3

וישם אואביהם כדמן וכאפר ישחקם אדום ומואב

Link: https://www.deadseascrolls.org.il/explore-the-archive/image/
B-370763
The initial א of אואביהם (their enemies) is damaged. However, there
is evidence for the letter. The plural אוֹיְבִים is written אואבים with the
medial י shifting to a medial א.[45]

4Q504 1–2 III, 8

[--] חולֵיים ̗רעים̗ ור̊עב וצמא ודבר וחרב

Link: https://www.deadseascrolls.org.il/explore-the-archive/image/
B-499049 (column i in this image is column iii)
The initial ר in רָעָב (famine) is heavily damaged. However, there is
physical evidence for the letter.

4Q504 1–2 IV, 12b–13a

ואין שטן
ופג{{ר}}ע̊ רע כיאם שלום וברכה ממ̊[--]

Link: https://www.deadseascrolls.org.il/explore-the-archive/image/
B-499049 (column I in this image is column III)

---

[45] For the existence of this type of shift in the Judean Desert manuscripts see Reymond,
Qumran Hebrew, 119.

APPENDICES 317

שָׂטָן (adversary) also is cut off at the bottom, but all letters are present. There is evidence of an ע written over the top of the ר for פֶּגַע (occurrence), making this a parallel to 1 Kings 5:18.

4Q504 1–2 VI, 6b–8a

ולוא מאסנו

בנסוֹייכה ובנגיﬠיכה לוא גﬠלה נפשנו להפר

את בריתכה בכול צרת {{ת}}<<נֹ>>,פ,ישנו

Link: https://www.deadseascrolls.org.il/explore-the-archive/image/ B-499049 (column I in this image is column III)

The letters וי in נְסוּי (testing) are damaged but visible.

4Q525 13, 2

תנ]חֹל ברﬠי ﬠין תתן להֹ]ם

Link: https://www.deadseascrolls.org.il/explore-the-archive/image/ B-363145

The context is heavily damaged. However, it is clear enough that this is an example of רַע being used with עַיִן (eye) to describe a HUMAN who is רַע of עַיִן.

C.3 Other

HazGab 21b–22

שאלני ואגיד לכה מה הצמח

הרֹﬠ הזה

Photograph: Lines 21–22 can be viewed as part of a photograph covering lines 15–23.[46]

The lines are taken from Qimron and Yuditsky's transcription.[47] They demonstrate a metaphorical COMMODITY use.

---

[46] Photograph by Bruce and Kenneth Zuckerman, and Marilyn Lundberg. Matthias Henze, ed., *Hazon Gabriel: New Readings of the Gabriel Revelation*, EJL 29 (Atlanta: SBL, 2011), 190.

[47] Elisha Qimron and Alexey Yuditsky, "Notes on the So-Called Gabriel Vision Inscription," in *Hazon Gabriel: New Readings of the Gabriel Revelation*, ed. Matthias Henze, EJL 29 (Atlanta: SBL, 2011), 31.

BIBLIOGRAPHY

ABEGG, Martin G., James E. BOWLEY, and Edward M. COOK. *The Dead Sea Scrolls Concordance*. 3 vols. Leiden: Brill, 2003–2015.

AḤITUV, Shmuel. *Echoes from the Past: Hebrew and Cognate Inscriptions from the Biblical Period*. Carta Handbook. Jerusalem: Carta, 2008.

AITKEN, James K. *The Semantics of Blessing and Cursing in Ancient Hebrew*. ANESSup 23. Louvain: Peeters, 2007.

ALEXANDER, T. Desmond. *Exodus*. ApOTC 2. London: Apollos, 2017.

ALLAN, Keith, and Kate BURRIDGE. *Euphemism & Dysphemism: Language Used as Shield and Weapon*. New York: Oxford University Press, 1991.

ANDERSEN, Francis I., and A. Dean FORBES. *Biblical Hebrew Grammar Visualized*. LSAWS 6. Winona Lake, IN: Eisenbrauns, 2012.

ANDERSEN, Francis I., and David Noel FREEDMAN, eds. *Amos: A New Translation with Introduction and Commentary*. AB 24A. New York: Doubleday, 1989.

ANDERSON, A. A. *2 Samuel*. WBC 11. Waco, TX: Word, 1989.

ATKINS, Sue, Charles J. FILLMORE, and Christopher R. JOHNSON. "Lexicographic Relevance: Selecting Information from Corpus Evidence." *International Journal of Lexicography* 16 (2003): 251–80.

AUGUSTINE. *On Christian Doctrine*. Pages 513–97 in vol. 2 of *The Nicene and Post-Nicene Fathers*, Series 1. Edited by Philip Schaff. Translated by J. F. Shaw. Buffalo, NY: Christian Literature Company, 1887.

BALDWIN, Joyce G. *1 and 2 Samuel: An Introduction and Commentary*. TOTC 8. Downers Grove, IL: IVP, 2008.

BALTZER, Klaus. *Deutero-Isaiah: A Commentary on Isaiah 40–55*. Edited by Peter Machinist. Translated by Margaret Kohl. Hermeneia. Minneapolis, MN: Fortress, 2001.

BAR-ASHER, Moshe. "Mishnaic Hebrew: An Introductory Survey." *HS* 40 (1999): 115–51.

—. *Studies in Classical Hebrew*. Edited by Aaron J. Koller. SJ 71. Berlin: De Gruyter, 2014.

BARKAY, Gabriel, Marilyn J. LUNDBERG, Andrew G. VAUGHN, and Bruce ZUCKERMAN. "The Amulets from Ketef Hinnom: A New Edition and Evaluation." *BASOR* 334 (2004): 41–71.

BARR, James. *Biblical Words for Time*. 2nd ed. London: SCM, 1969.

—. "Did Isaiah Know about Hebrew 'Root Meanings'?" *ExpTim* 75 (1964): 242.

—. "The Image of God in the Book of Genesis: A Study of Terminology." *BJRL* 51 (1968): 11–26.

—. *The Semantics of Biblical Language*. Eugene, OR: Wipf & Stock, 2004.

BARSALOU, Lawrence W. "Ad Hoc Categories." *Memory & Cognition* 11 (1983): 211–27.

BARTHÉLEMY, Dominique, and O. RICKENBACHER. *Konkordanz zum Hebräischen Sirach. Mit Syrisch-Hebräischem Index*. Göttingen: Vandenhoeck und Ruprecht, 1973.

320 BIBLIOGRAPHY

BECKMAN, John C. "Concessive Clause: Biblical Hebrew." *EHLL*. dx.doi.org. ezproxy.is.ed.ac.uk/10.1163/2212-4241_ehll_EHLL_COM_00000093.

BEDNAREK, Monika. "Semantic Preference and Semantic Prosody Re-Examined." *Corpus Linguistics and Linguistic Theory* 4 (2008): 119–39.

BERLIN, Adele. *The Dynamics of Biblical Parallelism*. Rev. ed. The Biblical Resource Series. Grand Rapids, MI: Eerdmans, 2008.

BLENKINSOPP, Joseph. *Isaiah 56–66: A New Translation with Introduction and Commentary*. AB 19B. New York: Doubleday, 2003.

BLOIS, Reinier de. *Towards a New Dictionary of Biblical Hebrew Based on Semantic Domains*. New York: UBS, 2001.

BLOIS, Reinier de, and UBS. *Towards a New Dictionary of Biblical Hebrew Based on Semantic Domains*. Woerden, Netherlands: UBS, 2000.

BODA, Mark J. *The Book of Zechariah*. NICOT. Grand Rapids, MI: Eerdmans, 2016.

BOROCHOVSKY BAR ABA, Esther. "Variety in the Meaning of the Verb: General Meaning, Contextual Meaning and Polysemy" [Hebrew], *Leshonenu* 68 (2006): 105–18.

BOSMAN, Tiana. "Biblical Hebrew Lexicology and Cognitive Semantics: A Study of Lexemes of Affection." PhD diss., University of Stellenbosch, 2011.

BOTTERWECK, G. Johannes, Heinz-Josef FABRY and Helmer RINGGREN eds. *Theological Dictionary of the Old Testament*. Translated by David E. Green and Douglas W. Scott. 16 vols. Grand Rapids, MI: Eerdmans, 1975–2018.

BREZINA, Vaclav, Tony MCENERY, and Stephen WATTAM. "Collocations in Context: A New Perspective on Collocation Networks." *International Journal of Corpus Linguistics* 20 (2015): 139–73.

BROWN, Francis, S. R. DRIVER, and Charles A. BRIGGS. *The Brown-Driver-Briggs Hebrew and English Lexicon: Coded with Strong's Concordance Numbers*. Edited by E. Brown. 1906. Repr., Peabody, MA: Hendrickson, 1996.

BURTON, Marilyn E. *The Semantics of Glory: A Cognitive, Corpus-Based Approach to Hebrew Word Meaning*. SSN 68. Leiden: Brill, 2017.

—. "'You Have Bestowed Your Glory upon the Heavens': A Re-Reading of Psalm 8:2b." Paper presented at the SBL International Meeting. Helsinki, 2018.

—. "Robed in Majesty: Clothing as a Metaphor for the Classical Hebrew Semantic Domain of כבוד." Pages 289–300 in *Clothing and Nudity in the Hebrew Bible*. Edited by Christoph Berner, Manuel Schäfer, Martin Schott, Sarah Schulz, and Martina Weingärtner. London: T&T Clark, 2019.

—. "Glory in the Heights and the Deep: Some Implications of Semantic Analysis for a Biblical Theology of Glory." In *From Words to Meaning: Studies in OT Language and Theology*. Edited by Samuel Hildebrandt, Kurtis Peters and Eric Ortlund. Sheffield: Sheffield Phoenix, forthcoming.

BUTLER, Trent C. *Judges*. WBC 8. Nashville, TN: Thomas Nelson, 2009.

BYBEE, Joan L. *Language Change*. Cambridge Textbooks in Linguistics. Cambridge: Cambridge University Press, 2015.

CALVIN, John. *Jeremiah 1–9*. Geneva Series. Translated by J. O. Thrussington. Vol. 1 of *Jeremiah & Lamentations*. Edinburgh: Banner of Truth Trust, 1989.

CHRISTENSEN, Duane L. *Deuteronomy 1:1–21:9*. 2nd ed. WBC 6A. Nashville, TN: Thomas Nelson, 2001.

BIBLIOGRAPHY
321

CLINES, David J. A. "Cattle, Flocks and Other Beasts: Why Terms for Animal Groups Matter." Paper presented at the 23rd Congress of IOSOT. Aberdeen, 2019.

—, ed. *The Dictionary of Classical Hebrew*. 9 vols. Sheffield: Sheffield Academic Press, 1993–2014.

COLLINS, John J. "In the Likeness of the Holy Ones: The Creation of Humankind in a Wisdom Text from Qumran." Pages 609–18 in *The Provo International Conference on the Dead Sea Scrolls: Technological Innovations, New Texts, and Reformulated Issues*. Edited by Donald W. Parry and Eugene Ulrich. STDJ 30. Leiden: Brill, 1999.

CRUSE, Alan. *Meaning in Language: An Introduction to Semantics and Pragmatics*. 3rd ed. Oxford Textbooks in Linguistics. Oxford: Oxford University Press, 2013.

CYSOUW, Michael, Martin HASPELMATH, and Andrej MALCHUKOV. "Introduction to the Special Issue 'Semantic Maps: Methods and Applications.'" *Linguistic Discovery* 8 (2010): 1–3.

DAHOOD, Mitchell. *Psalms II: 51–100*. AB 17. Garden City, NY: Doubleday, 1968.

DAVIES, Graham I. *Ancient Hebrew Inscriptions: Corpus and Concordance*. 2 vols. Cambridge: Cambridge University Press, 1991–2004.

DEVRIES, Simon J. *1 Kings*. WBC 12. Waco, TX: Word, 1985.

DIMANT, Devorah. "Sectarian and Non-Sectarian Texts from Qumran: The Pertinence and Usage of a Taxonomy." *RevQ* 24 (2009): 7–18.

—. "The Qumran Manuscripts: Contents and Significance." Pages 23–58 in *Time to Prepare the Way in the Wilderness: Papers on the Qumran Scrolls by Fellows of the Institute for Advanced Studies of the Hebrew University, Jerusalem, 1989–1990*. Edited by Devorah Dimant and Lawrence H. Schiffman. STDJ 16. Leiden: Brill, 1995.

DUFFLEY, Patrick J. "How Words Mean: Lexical Concepts, Cognitive Models, and Meaning Construction (Review)." *Cognitive Linguistics* 23 (2012): 217–21.

DURHAM, John I. *Exodus*. WBC 3. Waco, TX: Word, 1987.

EVANS, Vyvyan. "A Unified Account of Polysemy within LCCM Theory." *Lingua* 157, Supplement C (2015): 100–23.

—. *How Words Mean: Lexical Concepts, Cognitive Models, and Meaning Construction*. Oxford: Oxford University Press, 2009.

EVEN-SHOSHAN, Abraham. *A new concordance of the Bible: for the Torah, the Prophets, and the Writings*. Rev. ed. Jerusalem: Kiryat Sefer, 1992.

FARO, Ingrid. *Evil in Genesis: A Contextual Analysis of Hebrew Lexemes for Evil in the Book of Genesis*. Studies in Scripture & Biblical Theology. Bellingham, WA: Lexham, 2021.

FILLMORE, Charles J. "Towards a Descriptive Framework for Spatial Deixis." Pages 31–59 in *Speech, Place, and Action: Studies of Deixis and Related Topics*. Edited by R. J. Jarvella and Wolfgang Klein. Chichester, UK: Wiley, 1982.

FILLMORE, Charles J., Christopher R. JOHNSON, and Miriam R. L. PETRUCK. "Background to FrameNet." *International Journal of Lexicography* 16 (2003): 235–50.

FLYNN, Shawn W. "The Teraphim in Light of Mesopotamian and Egyptian Evidence." *CBQ* 74 (2012): 694–711.

322 BIBLIOGRAPHY

FORBES, A. Dean. "On Dating Biblical Hebrew Texts: Sources of Uncertainty / Analytic Options." Pages 247–72 in *From Ancient Manuscripts to Modern Dictionaries: Select Studies in Aramaic, Hebrew and Greek*. Edited by Tarsee Li and Keith D. Dyer. Perspectives on Linguistics and Ancient Languages 9. Piscataway, NJ: Gorgias, 2017.

—. "The Diachrony Debate: Perspectives from Pattern Recognition and Meta-Analysis." *HS* 53 (2012): 7–42.

—. "The Proper Role of Valency in Biblical Hebrew Studies." Pages 95–112 in *Contemporary Examinations of Classical Languages (Hebrew, Aramaic, Syriac, and Greek): Valency, Lexicography, Grammar, and Manuscripts*. Edited by Timothy Martin Lewis, Alison Salvesen, and Beryl Turner. Perspectives on Linguistics and Ancient Languages 8. Piscataway, NJ: Gorgias, 2016.

FOSTER, Philip D. "A Delimitation of the Semantic Field of רעע in the Latter Prophets." MDiv diss., Melbourne School of Theology, 2016. https://www. academia.edu/27907405/Masters_Project_A_Delimitation_of_the_Semantic_ Field_of_רעע_in_the_Latter_Prophets.

—. "Is Everything 'Beautiful' or 'Appropriate' in Its Time? יָפֶה and Semantic Change." *JNSL* 45 (2019): 41–55.

FOX, Michael V. *Proverbs 10–31: A New Translation with Introduction and Commentary*. AB 18B. New Haven: Yale University Press, 2009.

—. *Qoheleth and His Contradictions*. BLS 18. Sheffield: Almond, 1989.

FOX, Nili S. "Kingship and the State in Ancient Israel." Pages 475–81 in *Behind the Scenes of the Old Testament: Cultural, Social, and Historical Contexts*. Edited by Jonathan S. Greer, John W. Hilber, and John H. Walton. Grand Rapids, MI: Baker, 2018.

GAFNI, Isayah M. "The Historical Background." Pages 1–34 in vol. 1 of *The Literature of the Sages*. Edited by Shemu'el Safrai. Assen, Netherlands: Van Gorcum, 1987.

GEERAERTS, Dirk. *Theories of Lexical Semantics*. Oxford: Oxford University Press, 2010.

GESENIUS, F. W. *Gesenius' Hebrew Grammar*. Edited by Emil Kautzsch. Translated by S. A. E. Cowley. 2nd ed. Oxford: Clarendon, 1910.

—. *Gesenius' Hebrew-Chaldee Lexicon to the Old Testament*. Translated by Samuel Tragelles. 1846. Repr., Bellingham, WA: Logos, 2003.

GOFF, Matthew J. "The Mystery of Creation in 4QInstruction." *DSD* 10 (2003): 163–86.

—. "The Worldly and Heavenly Wisdom of 4QInstruction." PhD diss., University of Chicago, 2002.

GOLDBERG, Abraham. "The Mishna – A Study Book of Halakha." Pages 211–62 in vol. 1 of *The Literature of the Sages*. Edited by Shemu'el Safrai. Assen, Netherlands: Van Gorcum, 1987.

GOLDINGAY, John. *Psalms 90–150*. Vol. 3 of *Psalms*. BCOTWP. Grand Rapids, MI: Baker, 2008.

HASPELMATH, Martin. "The Geometry of Grammatical Meaning: Semantic Maps and Cross-Linguistic Comparison." Pages 211–42 in vol. 2 of *The New Psychology of Language*. Edited by Michael Tomasello. Mahwah, NJ: Lawrence Erlbaum, 2003.

BIBLIOGRAPHY

HENDEL, Ronald S., and Jan JOOSTEN. *How Old Is the Hebrew Bible? A Linguistic, Textual, and Historical Study*. AYBRL. New Haven: Yale University Press, 2018.

HENZE, Matthias, ed. *Hazon Gabriel: New Readings of the Gabriel Revelation*. EJL 29. Atlanta: SBL, 2011.

HERFORD, R. Travers. *Pirkē Aboth*. 3rd ed. New York: Jewish Institute of Religion, 1945.

HOEY, Michael. *Lexical Priming: A New Theory of Words and Language*. London: Routledge, 2005.

HOFTIJZER, J. "The History of the Data-Base Project." Pages 65–85 in *Studies in Ancient Hebrew Semantics*. Edited by T. Muraoka. AbrNSup 4. Louvain: Peeters, 1995.

HOFTIJZER, J., and Graham I. DAVIES. "Semantics of Ancient Hebrew Database." http://www.sahd.div.ed.ac.uk/info:description.

HOLLADAY, William Lee. *Jeremiah 1: A Commentary on the Book of the Prophet Jeremiah, Chapters 1–25*. Edited by Paul D. Hanson. Hermeneia. Philadelphia, PA: Fortress, 1986.

HOLLMANN, Willem B. "Semantic Change." Pages 238–49 in *English Language: Description, Variation and Context*. Edited by Jonathan Culpeper, Paul Kerswill, Ruth Wodak, Tony McEnery, and Francis Katamba. 2nd ed. London: Palgrave, 2018.

HOLMSTEDT, Robert D. "Hebrew Poetry and the Appositive Style: Parallelism, *Requiescat in pace*." *VT* 69 (2019): 617–48.

HOWELL, Brian M., and Jenell Paris. *Introducing Cultural Anthropology: A Christian Perspective*. 2nd ed. Grand Rapids, MI: Baker, 2019.

HURVITZ, Avi. *A Concise Lexicon of Late Biblical Hebrew: Linguistic Innovations in the Writings of the Second Temple Period*. VTSup 160. Leiden: Brill, 2014.

ILAN, Tal. "Reading for Women in 1QSa (Serekh Ha-Edah)." Pages 61–76 in *The Dead Sea Scrolls in Context: Integrating the Dead Sea Scrolls in the Study of Ancient Texts, Languages, and Cultures*. Edited by Armin Lange, Emanuel Tov, and Matthias Weigold. Leiden: Brill, 2011.

INTERNATIONAL COMPUTER SCIENCE INSTITUTE. "Commercial_transaction." Frame Index. https://framenet2.icsi.berkeley.edu/fnReports/data/frameIndex.xml?frame=Commercial_transaction.

JENNI, Ernst, Claus WESTERMANN, and Mark E. BIDDLE eds. *Theological Lexicon of the Old Testament*. 3 vols. Peabody, MA: Hendrickson, 1997.

JOSEPHUS, Flavius. *The Works of Josephus: Complete and Unabridged*. Translated by William Whiston. Peabody, MA: Hendrickson, 1987.

KHAN, Geoffrey, ed. *EHLL*. Leiden: Brill, 2013.

KIM, Dong-Hyuk. *Early Biblical Hebrew, Late Biblical Hebrew, and Linguistic Variability: A Sociolinguistic Evaluation of the Linguistic Dating of Biblical Texts*. VTSup 156. Leiden: Brill, 2013.

KING, Philip J., and Lawrence E. STAGER. *Life in Biblical Israel*. LAI. Louisville, KY: Westminster John Knox, 2001.

KÖHLER, Ludwig, and Walter BAUMGARTNER. *The Hebrew and Aramaic Lexicon of the Old Testament*. Translated by M. E. J. Richardson, 2 vols. Leiden: Brill, 2001.

324   BIBLIOGRAPHY

KOLLER, Aaron J. *The Semantic Field of Cutting Tools in Biblical Hebrew: The Interface of Philological, Semantic, and Archaeological Evidence*. CBQMS 49. Washington, DC: The Catholic Biblical Association of America, 2012.
—. "To Come and to Enter: Synchronous and Diachronic Aspects in the Semantics of the Verb 'לבוא' in Ancient Hebrew" [Hebrew], *Leshonenu* 78 (2013): 149–164.
KRAUS, Hans-Joachim. *Psalms 60–150*. Translated by Hilton C. Oswald. CC. Minneapolis, MN: Fortress, 1993.
LAKOFF, George. *Women, Fire, and Dangerous Things: What Categories Reveal about the Mind*. Chicago: The University of Chicago Press, 1987.
LAKOFF, George, and Mark JOHNSON. *Metaphors We Live By*. Chicago: University of Chicago Press, 2003.
LANDMAN, Yael. "On Lips and Tongues in Ancient Hebrew." *VT* 66 (2016): 66–77.
LANGACKER, Ronald W. *Cognitive Grammar: A Basic Introduction*. New York: Oxford University Press, 2008.
LEAVINS, Daniel. *Verbs of Leading in the Hebrew Bible*. Piscataway, NJ: Gorgias, 2011.
LÉVI-STRAUSS, Claude. *The Savage Mind*. Translated by George Weidenfeld. Hertfordshire, UK: The Garden City, 1966.
LONGMAN, Tremper. *The Book of Ecclesiastes*. NICOT. Grand Rapids, MI: Eerdmans, 1998.
LOUW, J. P., and Eugene A. NIDA. *Greek-English Lexicon of the New Testament: Based on Semantic Domains*. New York: UBS, 1989.
MACINTOSH, A. A. *A Critical and Exegetical Commentary on Hosea*. ICC. Edinburgh: T&T Clark, 1997.
MARTONE, Corrado. "Evil or Devil? Belial Between the Bible and Qumran." *Hen* 26 (2004): 115–27.
MATTHEWS, Victor Harold. "The Unwanted Gift: Implications of Obligatory Gift Giving in Ancient Israel." *Semeia* 87 (1999): 91–104.
MATTHEWS, Victor Harold, and Don C. BENJAMIN. *Social World of Ancient Israel, 1250–587 BCE*. Peabody, MA: Hendrickson, 1993.
MCCARTER, P. Kyle. *I Samuel: A New Translation with Introduction, Notes and Commentary*. AB 8. Garden City, NY: Doubleday, 1980.
MCCARTHY, Carmel, ed. *Deuteronomy*. BHQ 5. Stuttgart: German Bible Society, 2007.
MCKANE, William. *Proverbs: A New Approach*. London: SCM, 1992.
MERRILL, Eugene H. *Deuteronomy*. NAC 4. Nashville, TN: Broadman & Holman, 1994.
MERWE, Christo H. J. van der. "Lexical Meaning in Biblical Hebrew and Cognitive Semantics: A Case Study." *Bib* 87 (2006): 85–95.
MERWE, Christo H. J. van der, Jacobus A. NAUDÉ, and Jan H. KROEZE. *A Biblical Hebrew Reference Grammar*. 2nd ed. London: Bloomsbury, 2017.
MILLER, Cynthia L., and Ziony ZEVIT, eds. *Diachrony in Biblical Hebrew*. LSAWS 8. Winona Lake, IN: Eisenbrauns, 2012.
MILLER-Naudé, Cynthia L., and Jacobus A. NAUDÉ. "A Re-Examination of Grammatical Categorization in Biblical Hebrew." Pages 273–308 in *From Ancient Manuscripts to Modern Dictionaries: Select Studies in Aramaic,*

BIBLIOGRAPHY 325

Hebrew and Greek. Edited by Tarsee Li and Keith D. Dyer. Perspectives on Linguistics and Ancient Languages 9. Piscataway, NJ: Gorgias Press, 2017.
—. "Is the Adjective Distinct from the Noun as a Grammatical Category in Biblical Hebrew?" *IDS* 50 (2016): 1–9.
MOR, Uri, "Bar Kokhba Documents." *EHLL*. dx.doi.org.ezproxy.is.ed.ac.uk/10.1163/2212-4241_ehll_EHLL_COM_00000563.
MOSHAVI, Adina. "How to Distinguish between General Words and Polysemous Words in the Hebrew of the Bible: A Study in the Verb ביקש [Hebrew]," *Leshonenu* 66 (2004): 31–48.
MURAOKA, T. "A New Dictionary of Classical Hebrew." Pages 87–101 in *Studies in Ancient Hebrew Semantics*. Edited by T. Muraoka. AbrNSup 4. Louvain: Peeters, 1995.
MURPHY, Gregory L. "How Words Mean: Lexical Concepts, Cognitive Models, and Meaning Construction (Review)." *Language* 87 (2011): 393–96.
MURPHY, Roland E. *Ecclesiastes*. WBC 23A. Waco, TX: Word, 1992.
—. *Proverbs*. WBC 22. Nashville, TN: Thomas Nelson, 2000.
MYHILL, John. "Subjective Hebrew Raʿ and Objective English Evil: A Semantic Analysis." *Humanities: Christianity and Culture* 28 (1997): 1–28.
OAKTREE Software. "Accordance – Bible Software for Mac, Windows, iPad and iPhone." https://www.accordancebible.com/.
—. "Ben Sira English." Edited by Benjamin H. Parker and Martin G. Jr. Abegg, 2008. https://www.accordancebible.com/store/details/?pid=BENSIRA-E.
—. "Qumran Non-Biblical Manuscripts: A New English Translation." Edited by Michael O. Wise, Martin G. Jr. Abegg and Edward M. Cook, 2009. https://www.accordancebible.com/store/details/?pid=QUMENG.
OFER, Yosef. *The Masora on Scripture and Its Methods*. Berlin: De Gruyter, 2018.
OSWALT, John. *The Book of Isaiah. Chapters 40–66*. NICOT. Grand Rapids, MI: Eerdmans, 1998.
PAUL, Shalom M. *Amos: A Commentary on the Book of Amos*. Edited by Frank Moore Cross. Hermeneia. Minneapolis: Fortress, 1991.
PÉREZ Fernández, Miguel. *An Introductory Grammar of Rabbinic Hebrew*. Translated by John F. Elwolde. Leiden: Brill, 1997.
PIANTADOSI, Steven T., Harry TILY, and Edward GIBSON. "Word Lengths Are Optimized for Efficient Communication." *Proceedings of the National Academy of Sciencesa* 108 (2011): 3526–29.
POLAK, Frank. "Sociolinguistics: A Key to the Typology and the Social Background of Biblical Hebrew." *HS* 47 (2006): 115–62.
PROPP, William Henry. *Exodus 1–18: A New Translation with Introduction and Commentary*. AB 2. New York: Doubleday, 1999.
—. *Exodus 19–40: A New Translation with Introduction and Commentary*. AB 2A. New York: Doubleday, 2006.
PUSTEJOVSKY, James. *The Generative Lexicon*. Cambridge, MA: MIT Press, 1995.
QIMRON, Elisha. *A Grammar of the Hebrew of the Dead Sea Scrolls*. Jerusalem: Yad Yizhak Ben-Zvi, 2018.
QIMRON, Elisha, and Alexey YUDITSKY. "Notes on the So-Called Gabriel Vision Inscription." Pages 31–38 in *Hazon Gabriel: New Readings of the Gabriel Revelation*. Edited by Matthias Henze. EJL 29. Atlanta: SBL, 2011.

RASMUSSEN, Michael D. *Conceptualizing Distress in the Psalms: A Form-Critical and Cognitive Semantic Study of the* צרר[1] *Word Group*. Gorgias Biblical Studies 66. Piscataway, NJ: Gorgias, 2018.

RENDSBURG, Gary. "A Comprehensive Guide to Israelian Hebrew: Grammar and Lexicon." *Orient* 38 (2003): 5–35.

REYMOND, Eric D. *Qumran Hebrew: An Overview of Orthography, Phonology, and Morphology*. RBS 76. Atlanta: SBL, 2013.

REZETKO, Robert, and Ian YOUNG. *Historical Linguistics and Biblical Hebrew: Steps toward an Integrated Approach*. Atlanta: SBL, 2014.

ROSEN-Zvi, Ishay. "Two Rabbinic Inclinations? Rethinking a Scholarly Dogma." *JSJ* 39 (2008): 513–39.

RUPPENHOFER, Josef, Michael ELLSWORTH, Miriam R. L. PETRUCK, Christopher R. JOHNSON, Collin F. BAKER, and Jan SCHEFFCZYK. *FrameNet II: Extended Theory and Practice*. Berkeley: International Computer Science Institute, 2016. https://framenet.icsi.berkeley.edu/fndrupal/index.php?q=the_book.

SAMET, Nili. "Qohelet's Idiolect: The Language of a Jew in a Changing World." Paper presented at the Starr Seminar. Harvard University, 2018. https://www.academia.edu/38217586/Qohelets_Idiolect_The_Language_of_a_Jew_in_a_Changing_World_by_Nili_Samet.pdf.

—. "The Validity of the Masoretic Text as a Basis for Diachronic Linguistic Analysis of Biblical Texts: Evidence from Masoretic Vocalisation." *Journal for Semitics* 25 (2016): 1064–79.

SARFATTI, Gad B. "Mishnaic Vocabulary and Mishnaic Literature as Tools for the Study of Biblical Semantics." Pages 33–48 in *Studies in Ancient Hebrew Semantics*. Edited by T. Muraoka. AbrNSup 4. Louvain: Peeters, 1995.

SAWYER, John F. A. "Root-Meanings in Hebrew." *JSS* 12 (1967): 37–50.

—. *Semantics in Biblical Research: New Methods of Defining Hebrew Words for Salvation*. SBT 2.24. Naperville, IL: A. R. Allenson, 1972.

SBL. *The SBL Handbook of Style: For Biblical Studies and Related Disciplines*. 2nd ed. Atlanta: SBL, 2014.

SCHIFFMAN, Lawrence H. *The Eschatological Community of the Dead Sea Scrolls: A Study of the Rule of the Congregation*. SBLMS 38. Atlanta: Scholars, 1989.

SCHOORS, A. *The Preacher Sought to Find Pleasing Words: A Study of the Language of Qoheleth Part II Vocabulary*. OLA 143. Leuven: Peeters, 2004.

SCHULLER, Eileen M., and Carol A. NEWSOM. *The Hodayot (Thanksgiving Psalms): a study edition of 1QHa*. EJL 36. Atlanta: SBL, 2012.

SEFARIA. "The William Davidson Talmud." https://www.sefaria.org/texts/Talmud.

SEMANTICS of Ancient Hebrew Database. "Lexeme Index." http://www.sahd.div.ed.ac.uk/info:lexeme_index.

SHEAD, Stephen L. *Radical Frame Semantics and Biblical Hebrew: Exploring Lexical Semantics*. BibInt 108. Leiden: Brill, 2011.

SINCLAIR, John McHardy. *Trust the Text: Language, Corpus and Discourse*. London: Routledge, 2004.

SKEHAN, Patrick William, and Alexander A. DI LELLA. *The Wisdom of Ben Sira: A New Translation with Notes*. AB 39. New York: Doubleday, 1987.

SMOAK, Jeremy Daniel. *The Priestly Blessing in Inscription and Scripture: The Early History of Numbers 6:24–26*. New York: Oxford University Press, 2015.

BIBLIOGRAPHY   327

STARR, John M. *Classifying the Aramaic Texts from Qumran: A Statistical Analysis of Linguistic Features*. London: T&T Clark, 2017.

STEENBERGEN, Gerrit Jan van. *Semantics, World View and Bible Translation: An Integrated Analysis of a Selection of Hebrew Lexical Items Referring to Negative Moral Behaviour in the Book of Isaiah*. Stellenbosch: Sun, 2006.

STRUGNELL, John, Daniel J. HARRINGTON, and Torleif ELGVIN. *Qumran Cave 4, Sapiential Texts, Part 2, 4Q Instruction (Mûsar Lě Měvîn): 4Q415 Ff. with a Re-Edition of 1Q26*. DJD 34. Oxford: Clarendon, 1994.

STUART, Douglas. *Hosea-Jonah*. WBC 31. Waco, TX: Word, 1987.

TATE, Marvin E. *Psalms 51–100*. WBC 20. Waco, TX: Word, 1990.

TAYLOR, Joan E., and Philip R. DAVIES. "On the Testimony of Women in 1QSa." *DSD* 3 (1996): 223–35.

TAYLOR, John B. *Ezekiel: An Introduction and Commentary*. TOTC 22. Downers Grove, IL: IVP, 1969.

THOMPSON, J. A. *Deuteronomy: An Introduction and Commentary*. TOTC 5. Downers Grove, IL: IVP, 1974.

TOORN, Karel van der. "The Nature of the Biblical Teraphim in the Light of the Cuneiform Evidence." *CBQ* 52 (1990): 203–22.

TOV, Emanuel. *Textual Criticism of the Hebrew Bible*. 3rd ed. Minneapolis, MN: Fortress, 2012.

TRAUGOTT, Elizabeth Closs. "Semantic Change." In *Oxford Research Encyclopedia of Linguistics*. Oxford: Oxford University Press, 2017. dx.doi.org/10.1093/acrefore/9780199384655.013.323.

TRAUGOTT, Elizabeth Closs, and Richard B DASHER. *Regularity in Semantic Change*. Cambridge: Cambridge University Press, 2001.

TSUMURA, David Toshio. *The First Book of Samuel*. NICOT. Grand Rapids, MI: Eerdmans, 2007.

UBS. "Semantic Dictionary of Biblical Hebrew." http://semanticdictionary.org/.

ULRICH, Eugene C., Frank Moore CROSS, Nathan JASTRAM, Judith E. SANDERSON, Emanuel TOV, and John STRUGNELL, eds. *Qumran Cave 4: Genesis to Numbers*. DJD 12. Oxford: Clarendon, 1994.

VANGEMEREN, Willem A., ed. *New International Dictionary of Old Testament Theology & Exegesis*. 5 vols. Grand Rapids, MI: Zondervan, 1997.

VERHEIJ, Arian J. C. *Bits, Bytes, and Binyanim: A Quantitative Study of Verbal Lexeme Formations in the Hebrew Bible*. OLA 93. Leuven: Peeters, 2000.

WALTKE, Bruce K. *A Commentary on Micah*. Grand Rapids, MI: Eerdmans, 2007.

—. *Genesis: A Commentary*. Grand Rapids, MI: Zondervan, 2001.

—. *The Book of Proverbs: Chapters 1–15*. NICOT. Grand Rapids, MI: Eerdmans, 2004.

—. *The Book of Proverbs: Chapters 15–31*. NICOT. Grand Rapids, MI: Eerdmans, 2005.

WALTKE, Bruce K., and Michael Patrick O'CONNOR. *An Introduction to Biblical Hebrew Syntax*. Winona Lake, IN: Eisenbrauns, 1990.

WALTON, Joshua T. "Trade in the Late Bronze and Iron Age Levant." Pages 416–22 in *Behind the Scenes of the Old Testament: Cultural, Social, and Historical Contexts*. Edited by Jonathan S. Greer, John W. Hilber, and John H. Walton. Grand Rapids, MI: Baker, 2018.

328 BIBLIOGRAPHY

WASSEN, Cecilia. "On the Education of Children in the Dead Sea Scrolls." *SR* 41 (2012): 350–63.

WATTS, John D. W. *Isaiah 34–66*. WBC 25. Waco, TX: Word, 1987.

WEBB, Barry G. *The Book of Judges*. NICOT. Grand Rapids, MI: Eerdmans, 2012.

WENHAM, Gordon J. *Genesis 1–15*. WBC 1. Waco, TX: Word, 1987.

—. *Genesis 16–50*. WBC 2. Waco, TX: Word, 1994.

WIDDER, Wendy L. *"To Teach" in Ancient Israel: A Cognitive Linguistic Study of a Biblical Hebrew Lexical Set*. BZAW 456. Boston: De Gruyter, 2014.

WITTGENSTEIN, Ludwig. *Philosophical Investigations*. Translated by G. E. M. Anscombe. Oxford: Basil Blackwell, 1958.

WOLDE, Ellen J. van. "Cognitive Grammar at Work in Sodom and Gomorrah." Pages 172–203 in *Cognitive Linguistic Explorations in Biblical Studies*. Edited by Bonnie Howe and Joel B. Green. Berlin: De Gruyter, 2014.

—. *Reframing Biblical Studies: When Language and Text Meet Culture, Cognition, and Context*. Winona Lake, IN: Eisenbrauns, 2009.

WOODS, Edward J. *Deuteronomy: An Introduction and Commentary*. TOTC 5. Downers Grove, IL: IVP, 2011.

WRAY Beal, Lissa M. *1 & 2 Kings*. ApOTC 9. Downers Grove, IL: IVP, 2014.

YOUNG, Ian, Robert REZETKO, and Martin EHRENSVÄRD. *Linguistic Dating of Biblical Texts*. 2 vols. London: Equinox, 2008.

ZANELLA, Francesco. *The Lexical Field of the Substantives of "Gift" in Ancient Hebrew*. SSN 54. Leiden: Brill, 2010.

ZATELLI, Ida. "Functional Languages and Their Importance." Pages 55–64 in *Studies in Ancient Hebrew Semantics*. Edited by T. Muraoka. AbrNSup 4. Louvain: Peeters, 1995.

—. "The Study of the Ancient Hebrew Lexicon: Application of the Concepts of Lexical Field and Functional Language." *Kleine Untersuchungen zur Sprache des Alten Testaments und seiner Umwelt* 5 (2004): 129–59.

LIST OF NAMES

Abegg, Martin G.   36, 81
Aḥituv, Shmuel   94
Aitken, James K.   3, 7-8
Alexander, T. Desmond   56
Allan, Keith   70, 245
Andersen, Francis I.   14, 104, 217, 224
Anderson, A. A.   83
Atkins, Sue   24
Augustine   1

Baldwin, Joyce G.   83, 266
Baltzer, Klaus   243-244
Bar-Asher, Moshe   12, 17
Barkay, Gabriel   94
Barr, James   2, 5, 13
Barsalou, Lawrence W.   233
Barthélemy, Dominique   36
Baumgartner, Walter   11, 239, 277
Beckman, John C.   248
Bednarek, Monika   87, 89, 99
Benjamin, Don C.   54, 253
Berlin, Adele   31
Bernhardt, Karl-Heinz   243
Blenkinsopp, Joseph   245
Blois, Reinier de   3, 4, 19-23, 37, 271, 280
Boda, Mark J.   244
Borochovsky Bar Aba, Esther   10
Bosman, Tiana   19
Bowley, James E.   36
Brezina, Vaclav   102, 216
Briggs, Charles A.   239, 250, 277
Brown, Francis   239, 250, 277
Burridge, Kate   70, 245
Burton, Marilyn E.   2, 4, 18, 32, 37, 101, 110, 212, 237-238, 252, 271
Butler, Trent C.   283
Bybee, Joan L.   27-28

Calvin, John   241
Carpenter, Eugene   243, 245
Christensen, Duane L.   77

Clines, David J. A.   4, 8, 13, 49, 52, 62, 66, 79, 81-82, 89, 91, 111, 137, 153, 227, 231, 239, 242, 244, 246, 248, 250, 255, 257, 268, 278, 283, 290, 301-302
Collins, John J.   85
Cook, Edward M.   36
Cruse, Alan   5, 20, 90, 262
Cysouw, Michael   212

Dahood, Mitchell   238
Dasher, Richard B.   27
Davies, Graham I.   3, 8
Davies, Philip R.   82
DeVries, Simon J.   83
Di Lella, Alexander A.   40, 53, 57, 75, 243-244, 252, 262, 309
Dimant, Devorah   8, 12
Dohmen, C.   5, 275-276
Driver, S. R.   239, 250, 277
Duffley, Patrick J.   26
Durham, John I.   268

Ehrensvärd, Martin   8, 12, 14-15
Elgvin, Torleif   85
Evans, Vyvyan   26
Even-Shoshan, Abraham   36, 289

Faro, Ingrid   2, 5-6, 78-79, 277
Fillmore, Charles J.   21, 24
Flynn, Shawn W.   244
Forbes, A. Dean   14-16, 217
Freedman, David Noel   104, 224
Foster, Philip D.   7, 19, 28-29, 31, 61, 65, 110, 246, 271, 277, 285, 294, 300, 306
Fox, Michael V.   125, 285
Fox, Nili S.   252

Gafni, Isayah M.   68
Geeraerts, Dirk   3, 18, 22
Gibson, Edward   14
Goff, Matthew J.   85-86

330　　LIST OF NAMES

Goldberg, Abraham　68
Goldingay, John　242-243
Grisanti, Michael A.　243, 245

Harman, Allan M.　65
Harrington, Daniel J.　85
Haspelmath, Martin　212
Hendel, Ronald S.　16
Henze, Matthias　317
Herford, R. Travers　68, 220, 292
Hoey, Michael　24
Hoftijzer, J.　3
Holladay, William Lee　240
Hollmann, Willem B.　27, 50
Holmstedt, Robert D.　31
Howell, Brian M.　54
Hurvitz, Avi　14

Ilan, Tal　82
International Computer Science Institute　38

Johnson, Christopher R.　24
Johnson, Mark　21
Joosten, Jan　16
Josephus, Flavius　1

Kim, Dong-Hyuk　16
King, Philip J.　38-39, 58, 60
Knierim, R.　243
Köhler, Ludwig　11, 239, 250, 277
Koller, Aaron J.　4, 22, 28-29, 164, 260
Kraus, Hans-Joachim　242
Kroeze, Jan H.　4, 41, 56, 241, 264, 266

Lakoff, George　21
Landman, Yael　28-29, 63
Langacker, Ronald W　18
Leavins, Daniel　4
Lévi-Strauss, Claude　20
Longman, Tremper　72
Louw, J. P.　3
Lundberg, Marilyn J.　317

Macintosh, A. A.　242
Malchukov, Andrej　212
Martone, Corrado　153
Matthews, Victor Harold　54, 84, 253

McCarter, P. Kyle　266
McCarthy, Carmel　76
McEnery, Tony　102, 216
McKane, William　125
Merrill, Eugene H.　77, 91
Merwe, Christo H. J. van der　4-5, 41, 56, 241, 264, 266
Miller, Cynthia L.　15
Miller-Naudé, Cynthia L.　4, 302
Moshavi, Adina　10
Muraoka, T.　13
Murphy, Gregory L.　26
Murphy, Roland E.　62, 72, 239
Myhill, John　6, 50, 90, 275-276, 293

Naudé, Jacobus A.　4, 41, 56, 241, 264, 266, 302
Newsom, Carol A.　36
Nida, Eugene A.　3

Oaktree Software　13, 57, 81
O'Connor, Michael Patrick　80
Ofer, Yosef　52
Oswalt, John　245
Otzen, B.　291

Paris, Jenell　54
Parker, Benjamin H.　57
Paul, Shalom M.　104, 224
Pérez Fernández, Miguel　12
Petruck, Miriam R. L.　24
Piantadosi, Steven T.　14
Polak, Frank　16
Propp, William Henry　56, 268
Pustejovsky, James　26, 38

Qimron, Elisha　12, 317

Rasmussen, Michael D.　4
Rendsburg, Gary　16
Reymond, Eric D.　10, 312, 316
Rezetko, Robert　8, 12, 14-15
Rick, D.　5, 276
Rickenbacher, O.　36
Rosen-Zvi, Ishay　290, 292-293
Ruppenhofer, Josef　24

Samet, Nili　246, 285

LIST OF NAMES

Sarfatti, Gad B.   12, 28, 75
Sawyer, John F. A.   2, 5, 216
Schiffman, Lawrence H.   82
Schoors, A.   285
Schuller, Eileen M.   36
Sefaria   74
Semantics of Ancient Hebrew Database   3
Shead, Stephen L.   4
Sinclair, John McHardy   89
Skehan, Patrick William   40, 53, 57, 75, 243-244, 252, 262, 309
Smoak, Jeremy Daniel   94
Stager, Lawrence E.   38-39, 58, 60
Starr, John M.   11
Steenbergen, Gerrit Jan van   6, 235, 237, 244, 258, 276, 281
Strugnell, John   85
Stuart, Douglas   242

Tate, Marvin E.   238, 288
Taylor, John B.   248
Taylor, Joan E.   82
Thompson, J. A.   77
Tily, Harry   14
Toorn, Karel van der   244
Tov, Emanuel   8-10
Traugott, Elizabeth Closs   27-28
Tsumura, David Toshio   266

Ulrich, Eugene C.   10
United Bible Societies   3, 23, 25, 278-280

VanGemeren, Willem A.   82, 276
Verheij, Arian J. C.   5

Waltke, Bruce K.   54-55, 62-63, 80, 125, 239, 249
Walton, Joshua T.   38
Wassen, Cecilia   81-82
Wattam, Stephen   102, 216
Watts, John D. W.   245
Webb, Barry G.   283
Wenham, Gordon J.   85
Widder, Wendy L.   4
Wise, Michael O.   81
Wittgenstein, Ludwig   20
Wolde, Ellen J. van   18, 25, 30, 38, 77-79, 255
Woods, Edward J.   78, 91
Wray Beal, Lissa M.   83
Young, Ian   8, 12, 14-15
Yuditsky, Alexey   317
Zanella, Francesco   4, 17
Zatelli, Ida   17
Zevit, Ziony   15
Zuckerman, Bruce   317
Zuckerman, Kenneth   317

LIST OF EXAMPLES

The following list indexes every ancient and Mishnaic Hebrew passage used and set as an example. It does not include references which were not set as examples (e.g. those in tables in Chapter 3).

HEBREW BIBLE

Genesis

3:5-6	84
6:5	291
8:21	291
13:13	51
19:15	254
28:8	232
28:8-9	54
31:29	47
37:20	88
38:7	232
40:6-7	63
41:19	264
47:9	250, 287

Exodus

2:13	228
5:14	267
5:19	267-268
21:7-8	43, 55, 233
21:23-24	239
32:12	266
33:3-4	69
33:27	266

Leviticus

10:17	79
26:6	88
27:14	61
27:32-33	59

Numbers

20:5	59
22:32	11
35:33-34	78

Deuteronomy

1:34-35	80
1:35	53-54
1:39	80
6:22	111
7:15	87
9:16	256
9:18	256
13:6	76
17:1	70
17:2-3	46
17:5	47
19:13	77
19:16	234
19:18-19	234
19:18-20	258
19:19-20	47
22:13-14	73
22:21	77
23:10-11	70
25:1-2	226-227
28:59	87
30:15	137

Joshua

23:15	71

Judges

3:17	25
3:22	25
9:23	283
20:12-13	78

1 Samuel

2:23	71
10:19	260
16:12	65
16:14	283
25:3	39, 284
25:28	266
29:6-7	48-49

2 Samuel

14:32	253

LIST OF NAMES

19:36	83
22:5	153

1 Kings

3:7-9	82
11:5-6	257
11:6	46
15:26	97
20:6	65

2 Kings

2:19	286
2:21-22	286
4:40-41	72
17:12-13	67
21:9	50

Ezra

9:7	253

Nehemiah

2:1-2	55
6:13	74-75
9:35	40
13:17	47

Job

4:8-9	240
5:19-20	261
5:22-23	89
21:30-31	51
22:15	238

Psalms

28:3	97
28:3-4	236
34:14-15	246
34:17	49
36:4-5	237
38:13	265
50:19-20	235
52:4-6	247
55:4	238
90:9-10	242
92:8	229
94:12-13	288
94:23	240, 265
109:20	249
119:53	227
140:2	231
140:5	231
144:10	90
145:20	228

Proverbs

4:14-16	230
6:24-25	53
12:21	248
15:15	287
20:14	38, 60
22:8	239
22:9	64
22:12	239
24:1-2	234
24:19-20	43
25:20	62
28:10	67
28:22	64

Ecclesiastes

4:3	285
8:3	72
9:12	289
12:1	288

Isaiah

5:20	98, 159
5:23	227
6:5	254
6:7	254
24:20	255
31:1-3	274
41:28-29	243
45:7	10, 31, 47, 159
55:7	237
59:2-4	258
59:3-4	235
65:12	48
66:3	245

Jeremiah

2:33	52
4:6	240
4:14-16	240
11:8	63
12:14	232
13:10	54
14:7	251
14:10	259
14:12	259
15:11	289
15:21	65
23:22	96
24:2	90
26:3	263
39:12	47
44:2-5	265

LIST OF NAMES

335

Ezekiel

5:17	88
6:10-11	260
7:3	150
11:2-3	248
13:7	235
14:13	98
14:15	98
14:17	98
14:19	98
14:21	95, 99, 221, 261
20:43-44	67
33:27	89
36:31	96, 150

Hosea

6:8	242
12:12	242

Amos

5:13	288

Jonah

3:8	247
3:10	94-95

Micah

2:1-2	235-236
6:12	249

Nahum

1:11	264

Habakkuk

1:13	247
1:16	25

Zechariah

1:4	285
10:1-2	244
10:2	234
14:18-19	255

Malachi

2:17	49

BEN SIRA

3:28	60
5:14	75
6:1	75
7:1-2	257
9:8	65

10:4-6	252
11:33	230-231
12:2-4	57
13:25	55
14:3	40
14:4-5	40
31:24	263
37:10-11	51
42:1	53
42:6	53

DEAD SEA SCROLLS

1QHª

VI, 35	228
XIX, 13-14	254

1QIsaª

XXXVIII, 13	10

1QM

VII, 6-7	70

1Q28ª

I, 4-11	81

4Q27

1 I, 5-6	160
20-22, 29	11

4Q159

2-4, 8-9	73

4Q171

1-2 II, 2-4	251

4Q169

3-4 III, 3-4	285

4Q417

1 I, 16-19	85
1 II, 12	292

4Q418

126 II, 6-7	229

4Q504

2 III, 8	261

11Q5

XVIII, 13-15	289
XIX, 15-16	291
XXIV, 6-8	256

336

LIST OF NAMES

11Q19
XLIII, 15-16   241
LVI, 10   76

INSCRIPTIONS

Ketef Hinnom
I, 9-10   94

MISHNAH

'Abot
1:11   286
2:9   68, 217
2:11   292
5:13   64

'Arakin
3:5   63

Berakot
9:5   292

Giṭṭin
4:7   74

Miqwàot
8:4   25

Nedarim
9:3   52
9:8   60-61

'Ohalot
18:6   293-294

'Orlah
1:5   293

Šabbat
2:5   284
22:4   286

Soṭah
3:5   74

Terumot
2:6   59
4:3   64

Zabim
3:1   294

Contributions to Biblical Exegesis and Theology

1. J.A. Loader, *A Tale of Two Cities, Sodom and Gomorrah in the Old Testament, early Jewish and early Christian Traditions*, Kampen, 1990
2. P.W. Van der Horst, *Ancient Jewish Epitaphs. An Introductory Survey of a Millennium of Jewish Funerary Epigraphy (300 BCB-700 CE)*, Kampen, 1991
3. E. Talstra, *Solomon's Prayer. Synchrony and Diachrony in the Composition of 1 Kings 8, 14-61*, Kampen, 1993
4. R. Stahl, *Von Weltengagement zu Weltüberwindung: Theologische Positionen im Danielbuch*, Kampen, 1994
5. J.N. Bremmer, *Sacred History and Sacred Texts in early Judaism. A Symposium in Honour of A.S. van der Woude*, Kampen, 1992
6. K. Larkin, *The Eschatology of Second Zechariah: A Study of the Formation of a Mantological Wisdom Anthology*, Kampen, 1994
7. B. Aland, *New Testament Textual Criticism, Exegesis and Church History: A Discussion of Methods*, Kampen, 1994
8. P.W. Van der Horst, *Hellenism-Judaism-Christianity: Essays on their Interaction*, Kampen, Second Enlarged Edition, 1998
9. C. Houtman, *Der Pentateuch: die Geschichte seiner Erforschung neben einer Auswertung*, Kampen, 1994
10. J. Van Seters, *The Life of Moses. The Yahwist as Historian in Exodus-Numbers*, Kampen, 1994
11. Tj. Baarda, *Essays on the Diatessaron*, Kampen, 1994
12. Gert J. Steyn, *Septuagint Quotations in the Context of the Petrine and Pauline Speeches of the Acta Apostolorum*, Kampen, 1995
13. D.V. Edelman, *The Triumph of Elohim, From Yahwisms to Judaisms*, Kampen, 1995
14. J.E. Revell, *The Designation of the Individual. Expressive Usage in Biblical Narrative*, Kampen, 1996
15. M. Menken, *Old Testament Quotations in the Fourth Gospel*, Kampen, 1996
16. V. Koperski, *The Knowledge of Christ Jesus my Lord. The High Christology of Philippians 3:7-11*, Kampen, 1996
17. M.C. De Boer, *Johannine Perspectives on the Death of Jesus*, Kampen, 1996
18. R.D. Anderson, *Ancient Rhetorical Theory and Paul*, Revised edition, Leuven, 1998
19. L.C. Jonker, *Exclusivity and Variety, Perspectives on Multi-dimensional Exegesis*, Kampen, 1996
20. L.V. Rutgers, *The Hidden Heritage of Diaspora Judaism*, Leuven, 1998
21. K. van der Toorn (ed.), *The Image and the Book*, Leuven, 1998
22. L.V. Rutgers, P.W. van der Horst (eds.), *The Use of Sacred Books in the Ancient World*, Leuven, 1998
23. E.R. Ekblad Jr., *Isaiah's Servant Poems According to the Septuagint. An Exegetical and Theological Study*, Leuven, 1999
24. R.D. Anderson Jr., *Glossary of Greek Rhetorical Terms*, Leuven, 2000
25. T. Stordalen, *Echoes of Eden*, Leuven, 2000
26. H. Lalleman-de Winkel, *Jeremiah in Prophetic Tradition*, Leuven, 2000
27. J.F.M. Smit, *About the Idol Offerings. Rhetoric, Social Context and Theology of Paul's Discourse in First Corinthians 8:1-11:1*, Leuven, 2000
28. T.J. Horner, *Listening to Trypho. Justin Martyr's Dialogue Reconsidered*, Leuven, 2001
29. D.G. Powers, *Salvation through Participation. An Examination of the Notion of the Believers' Corporate Unity with Christ in Early Christian Soteriology*, Leuven, 2001
30. J.S. Kloppenborg, P. Hoffmann, J.M. Robinson, M.C. Moreland (eds.), *The Sayings Gospel Q in Greek and English with Parallels from the Gospels of Mark and Thomas*, Leuven, 2001
31. M.K. Birge, *The Language of Belonging. A Rhetorical Analysis of Kinship Language in First Corinthians*, Leuven, 2004

32. P.W. van der Horst, *Japheth in the Tents of Shem. Studies on Jewish Hellenism in Antiquity*, Leuven, 2002
33. P.W. van der Horst, M.J.J. Menken, J.F.M. Smit, G. van Oyen (eds.), *Persuasion and Dissuasion in Early Christianity, Ancient Judaism, and Hellenism*, Leuven, 2003
34. L.J. Lietaert Peerbolte, *Paul the Missionary*, Leuven, 2003
35. L.M. Teugels, *Bible and midrash. The Story of 'The Wooing of Rebekah'* (Gen. 24), Leuven, 2004
36. H.W. Shin, *Textual Criticism and the Synoptic Problem in Historical Jesus Research. The Search for Valid Criteria*, Leuven, 2004
37. A. Volgers, C. Zamagni (eds.), *Erotapokriseis. Early Christian Question-and-Answer Literature in Context*, Leuven, 2004
38. L.E. Galloway, *Freedom in the Gospel. Paul's Exemplum in 1 Cor 9 in Conversation with the Discourses of Epictetus and Philo*, Leuven, 2004
39. C. Houtman, K. Spronk, *Ein Held des Glaubens? Rezeptionsgeschichtliche Studien zu den Simson-Erzählungen*, Leuven, 2004
40. H. Kahana, Esther. *Juxtaposition of the Septuagint Translation with the Hebrew Text*, Leuven, 2005
41. V.A. Pizzuto, *A Cosmic Leap of Faith. An Authorial, Structural, and Theological Investigation of the Cosmic Christology in Col 1:15-20*, Leuven, 2005
42. B.J. Koet, *Dreams and Scripture in Luke-Acts. Collected Essays*, Leuven, 2006
43. P.C Beentjes. *"Happy the One Who Meditates on Wisdom" (SIR. 14,20). Collected Essays on the Book of Ben Sira*, Leuven, 2006
44. R. Roukema, L.J. Lietaert Peerbolte, K. Spronk, J.W. Wesselius (eds.), *The Interpretation of Exodus. Studies in Honour of Cornelis Houtman*, Leuven, 2006
45. G. van Oyen, T. Shepherd (eds.), *The Trial and Death of Jesus. Essays on the Passion Narrative in Mark*, Leuven, 2006
46. B. Thettayil, *In Spirit and Truth. An Exegetical Study of John 4:19-26 and a Theological Investigation of the Replacement Theme in the Fourth Gospel*, Leuven, 2007
47. T.A.W. van der Louw, *Transformations in the Septuagint. Towards an Interaction of Septuagint Studies and Translation Studies*, Leuven, 2007
48. W. Hilbrands, *Heilige oder Hure? Die Rezeptionsgeschichte von Juda und Tamar (Genesis 38) von der Antike bis zur Reformationszeit*, Leuven, 2007
49. J. Joosten, P.J. Tomson (eds.), *Voces Biblicae. Septuagint Greek and its Significance for the New Testament*, Leuven, 2007
50. A. Aejmelaeus, *On the Trail of the Septuagint Translators. Collected Essays*, Leuven, 2007
51. S. Janse, *"You are My Son". The Reception History of Psalm 2 in Early Judaism and the Early Church*, Leuven, 2009
52. K. De Troyer, A. Lange, L.L. Schulte (eds.), *Prophecy after the Prophets? The Contribution of the Dead Sea Scrolls to the Understanding of Biblical and Extra-Biblical Prophecy*, Leuven, 2009
53. C.M. Tuckett (ed.), *Feasts and Festivals*, Leuven, 2009
54. M. Labahn, O. Lehtipuu (eds.), *Anthropology in the New Testament and its Ancient Context*, Leuven, 2010
55. A. van der Kooij, M. van der Meer (eds.), *The Old Greek of Isaiah: Issues and Perspectives*, Leuven, 2010
56. J. Smith, *Translated Hallelujehs. A Linguistic and Exegetical Commentary on Select Septuagint Psalms*, Leuven, 2011
57. N. Dávid, A. Lange (eds.), *Qumran and the Bible. Studying the Jewish and Christian Scriptures in Light of the Dead Sea Scrolls*, Leuven, 2010
58. J. Chanikuzhy, *Jesus, the Eschatological Temple. An Exegetical Study of Jn 2,13-22 in the Light of the Pre 70 C.E. Eschatological Temple Hopes and the Synoptic Temple Action*, Leuven, 2011

59. H. Wenzel, *Reading Zechariah with Zechariah 1:1–6 as the Introduction to the Entire Book*, Leuven, 2011
60. M. Labahn, O. Lehtipuu (eds.), *Imagery in the Booky of Revelation*, Leuven, 2011
61. K. De Troyer, A. Lange, J.S. Adcock (eds.), *The Qumran Legal Texts between the Hebrew Bible and Its Interpretation*, Leuven, 2011
62. B. Lang, *Buch der Kriege – Buch des Himmels. Kleine Schriften zur Exegese und Theologie*, Leuven, 2011
63. H.-J. Inkelaar, *Conflict over Wisdom. The Theme of 1 Corinthians 1-4 Rooted in Scripture*, Leuven, 2011
64. K.-J. Lee, *The Authority and Authorization of Torah in the Persion Period*, Leuven, 2011
65. K.M. Rochester, *Prophetic Ministry in Jeremiah and Ezekiel*, Leuven, 2012
66. T. Law, A. Salvesen (eds.), *Greek Scripture and the Rabbis*, Leuven, 2012
67. K. Finsterbusch, A. Lange (eds.), *What is Bible?*, Leuven, 2012
68. J. Cook, A. van der Kooij, *Law, Prophets, and Wisdom. On the Provenance of Translators and their Books in the Septuagint Version*, Leuven, 2012
69. P.N. De Andrado, *The Akedah Servant Complex. The Soteriological Linkage of Genesis 22 and Isaiah 53 in Ancient Jewish and Early Christian Writings*, Leuven, 2013
70. F. Shaw, *The Earliest Non-Mystical Jewish Use of Iaω*, Leuven, 2014
71. E. Blachman, *The Transformation of Tamar (Genesis 38) in the History of Jewish Interpretation*, Leuven, 2013
72. K. De Troyer, T. Law, M. Liljeström (eds.), *In the Footsteps of Sherlock Holmes. Studies in the Biblical Text in Honour of Anneli Aejmelaeus*, Leuven, 2014
73. T. Do, *Re-thinking the Death of Jesus. An Exegetical and Theological Study of Hilasmos and Agape in 1 John 2:1-2 and 4:7-10*, Leuven, 2014
74. T. Miller, *Three Versions of Esther. Their Relationship to Anti-Semitic and Feminist Critique of the Story*, Leuven, 2014
75. E.B. Tracy, *See Me! Hear Me! Divine/Human Relational Dialogue in Genesis*, Leuven, 2014
76. J.D. Findlay, *From Prophet to Priest. The Characterization of Aaron in the Pentateuch*, Leuven, forthcoming
77. M.J.J. Menken, *Studies in John's Gospel and Epistles. Collected Essays*, Leuven, 2015
78. L.L. Schulte, *My Shepherd, though You Do not Know Me. The Persian Royal Propaganda Model in the Nehemiah Memoir*, Leuven, 2016
79. S.E. Humble, *A Divine Round Trip. The Literary and Christological Function of the Descent/Ascent Leitmotif in the Gospel of John*, Leuven, 2016
80. R.D. Miller, *Between Israelite Religion and Old Testament Theology. Essays on Archaeology, History, and Hermeneutics*, Leuven, 2016
81. L. Dequeker, *Studia Hierosolymitana*, Leuven, 2016
82. K. Finsterbusch, A. Lange (eds.), *Texts and Contexts of Jeremiah. The Exegesis of Jeremiah 1 and 10 in Light of Text and Reception History*, Leuven, 2016
83. J.S. Adcock, *"Oh God of Battles! Steal My Soldiers' Hearts!" A Study of the Hebrew and Greek Text Forms of Jeremiah 10:1-18*, Leuven, 2017
84. R. Müller, J. Pakkala (eds.), *Insights into Editing in the Hebrew Bible and the Ancient Near East. What Does Documented Evidence Tell Us about the Transmission of Authoritative Texts?*, Leuven, 2017
85. R. Burnet, D. Luciani, G. van Oyen (eds.), *The Epistle to the Hebrews. Writing at the Borders*, Leuven, 2016
86. M.K. Korada, *The Rationale for Aniconism in the Old Testament. A Study of Select Texts*, Leuven, 2017
87. P.C. Beentjes, *"With All Your Soul Fear the Lord" (Sir. 7:27). Collected Essays on the Book of Ben Sira II*, Leuven, 2017
88. B.J. Koet, A.L.H.M. van Wieringen (eds.), *Multiple Teachers in Biblical Texts*, Leuven, 2017

89. T. Elgvin, *The Literary Growth of the Song of Songs during the Hasmonean and Early-Herodian Periods*, Leuven, 2018
90. D.C. Smith, *The Role of Mothers in he Genealogical Lists of Jacob's Sons*, Leuven, 2018
91. V.P. Chiraparamban, *The Manifestation of God's Merciful Justice. A Theocentric Reading of Romans 3-21-26*, Leuven, 2018
92. P. Paul, *Beyond the Breach. An Exegetical Study of John 4:1-42 as a Text of Jewish-Samaritan Reconciliation*, Leuven, 2021
93. I. Fröhlich, *David in Cultural Memory*, Leuven, 2019
94. M. Langlois, *The Samaritan Pentateuch and the Dead Sea Scrolls*, Leuven, 2019
95. A. Livneh, *Studies on Jewish and Christian Historical Summaries from the Hellenistic and Early Roman Periods*, Leuven, 2019
96. M. Rotman, *The Call of the Wilderness. The Narrative Significance of John the Baptist's Whereabouts*, Leuven, 2020
97. O. Lukács, *Sabbath in the Making. A Study of the Inner-Biblical Interpretation of the Sabbath Commandment*, Leuven, 2020
98. J.J. Spoelstra, *Life Preservation in Genesis and Exodus. An Exegetical Study of the Tebâ of Noah and Moses*, Leuven, 2020
99. T. Havukainen, *The Quest for the Memory of Jesus: a Viable Path or a Dead End?*, Leuven, 2020
100. K. De Troyer, *The Ultimate and the Penultimate Text of the Book of Joshua*, Leuven, 2018
103. Angela Kim Harkins and Barbara Schmitz (eds.), *Selected Studies on Deuterocanonical Prayers*, Leuven, 2021
104. Torben Plitt, *Wachstumsgesetz oder Kürzungstendenz? Gedächtnispsychologische Erkenntnisse zu den inhaltlichen Überhängen in den synoptischen Paralleltraditionen*, Leuven, 2021
105. Ian Wilson, *Praying to the Temple: Divine Presence in Solomon's Prayer*, Leuven, 2021